REAL ESTATE;
PRINCIPLES & PRACTICES

BY

KARL G. PEARSON

PROFESSOR OF BUSINESS ADMINISTRATION,
GRADUATE SCHOOL OF BUSINESS ADMINISTRATION,
AND DIRECTOR OF REAL ESTATE EDUCATION.

UNIVERSITY OF MICHIGAN

Fifth Printing

TABLE OF CONTENTS

PART 1

Introduction

1

The Scope and Significance of Real Estate

The Scope and Significance of Real Estate 1
Scope • Land Use • The Business of Real Estate • The Scope of Land Use Controls • The Significance of Real Estate • Real Estate As An Economic Indicator • Real Estate As A Mirror of Sociological Change • The Significance of Real Estate Markets • The Significance of the Determinants of Market Behavior • Summary • Glossary

PART II

Legal Aspects

2

License Laws and Professional Standards

License Laws and Professional Standards 21
Introduction • Legal Authority for the License Laws • Requirements for Licensure • Care and Custody of Licenses • Exemptions from Licensing • Administration of the Licensing Law • Suspension, Denial, and Revocation of Licenses • Suggested Pattern Real Estate License Law • The Code of Ethics of the Realtor • The Realtor's Obligation to the Public under the Code of Ethics • The Realtor's Obligation to his Client under the Code • The Realtor's Obligation to his Fellow Realtors • Summary • Glossary

3

Property Rights and Instruments

Property Rights and Instruments 43
The Nature of Real Property • Fixtures • Contractual Rights • The Bundle of Rights Concept • Title to Real Property • Estates in Real Property • Real Property Ownerships • Real Property Rights and the Government • Transferring Real Property Rights • Easements • Contract for the Sale of Real Property • The Deed • The Mortgage • Kinds of Mortgages • The Land Contract • Liens • Leases • Evidence of Title • The Will • Summary • Glossary

4

Planning and Zoning

Planning and Zoning 71
Introduction • Planning • The Planning Commission • Zoning • Building Codes • The Language of Zoning • Zoning Districts • Zoning Techniques • The Zoning Board • Summary • Glossary

PART III

The Business of Real Estate

5

Brokerage

Brokerage 91
The Law of Agency • The Contract of Employment • Securing Listings • The Listing Process • Prospecting • Qualifying Prospects • Closings • Summary • Glossary

6

Closings

Closings 111
What Are They? • The Closing Date • Closing Documents • Examinations • Closing Dates • Closing Statements • Sample Problem • Sample Closing Statement • Summary • Glossary

7

Appraising

Appraising 131
Its Nature • The Appraisal Problem • The Contents of the Appraisal • Background Data • Economics in Appraising • Value Approaches • Income Approach to Value • Formulae and Techniques • The Market Data Approach to Value • Special Techniques in Evaluating Investment Properties • Application of the Value Approaches • Evaluating Lease Interests • Summary • Glossary

8

Property Management 151

Its Development • Attributes Required for Property Management • Developing the Management Program • Operation of the Management Office • Compensation for Property Management • Securing Management Business • Management's Future • Summary

9

Financing 167

The Term Mortgage • Mortgages Today • Sources of Mortgage Loans • Land Contracts • Sale and Lease-backs • Farm Financing • The Mortgage Market • Governmental Financing Agencies • The Section 235 Program • The Section 236 Program • The Government National Mortgage Association • New Veterans Administration Entitlements • Housing Opportunity Allowance Program • Vacation or Second Home Financing • Variable Rate Mortgages • Ninety to One Hundred Per Cent Financing • Summary

PART IV

The Real Estate Office

10

Computerized Real Estate 191

What Does the Computer Do? • How Does the Computer Do This? • How Do You Join Up? • How is it Used in Residential Selling? • How is it Used in Investment Property Analysis? • The Consumer Effect on the Real Estate Business • Summary • Glossary

11

Sales and Office Management 207

Selecting Salespeople • Interviewing Prospective Salespeople • Training Salespeople in Sales Policies and Procedures • Training in Selling • Training Salespeople to Organize Themselves • Training Through Sales Meetings • Cultivating Sales Personalities • Compensating Salespeople • Managing Salespeople • Terminating Salespeople • Office Location • Office Interior and Furnishings • Office Procedure • Office Budgets • The Office Personality • Office Control

12

Advertising and Publicity 231

Why Advertise? • The Advertising Plan • Preparing the Newspaper Ad • What Should You Feature in the Newspaper Ad? • Classified and Display • Signs • Direct Mail Advertising • Novelties • Other Advertising • Publicity • Publicity Releases

PART V

Real Estate Investments

13

Investing in Real Estate 247

Why Invest in Real Estate • Real Estate — a Growth Investment • Real Estate — a Natural Investment • Leverage and Tax Shelter • A Place for the Small Investor • Investments in Housing • Apartment House Investments • Office Building Investments • Shopping Centers • Raw Lands and Industrial Real Estate • Resort Real Estate • Mortgages and Equity Participations • Land Contracts as Investments • Corporate Real Estate Investment • Computerized Investment Analysis • A Summing Up

14

Real Estate Investment Trusts, Limited Partnerships, Joint Ventures and Syndications 263

The Mutual Funds of Real Estate • How Are They Organized • What Is the Nature of Their Investment? • What Are Their Yields? • What Does the Money Market Think of the Trusts? • A Summing Up on the Trusts • Limited Partnership • Joint Ventures • Syndications

PART VI

Residential Real Estate

15

Housing's Wave of the Future 277

Some Definitions • The Development of Industrialized Housing • Operation Breakthrough • The Winners • Construction Workers • Materials • Assembly • Building Codes • Transportation Problems • Erection • Tests for Quality • Appearance • Financing • Marketing • Mobile Homes • The Future

16

Mobile Homes 293

What Are They? • How Did They Come About? • What Benefits Do They Provide? • Who Lives in Them? • Aren't They the Same as Trailers? • How Do You Finance Mobile Homes? • Advantages in Mobile Home Living • Disadvantages in Mobile Home Living • Mobile Home Parks • What of the Future?

17

Cooperatives and Condominiums 307

What Is a Cooperative? • "Rental" Charges • Cooperative Advantages? • What Are Condominiums? • Condominiums vs. Renting • Condominiums vs. Conventional Ownerships • Condominiums vs. Cooperatives • Resort Condominiums • Condominium Provision • The Future of Condominiums

18

Resort and Retirement Real Estate 321

Resort Real Estate • Resort Real Estate Promotions • Skiing • Snowmobiling • Boating and Fishing • Gambling and Resort Real Estate • Motor Inns • Resorts — A Summing Up • Resort Retirement Communitios • The Developers of Resort Retirement Communities • Comments

PART VII

Farm, Commercial, and Industrial Real Estate

19

Farm Real Estate 337

Nostalgia and Reality • The Dynamics of Change • Farm Listings • Farm Prospects • Farm Showings • Farm Closings • Farm Knowledge • Farm Financing • Farm Descriptions • Farm Soils • Farm Tax Factors • From Farm to Subdivision • Farms as Investments • Farming's Future • Glossary

20

Apartment Houses 351

Their Popularity • The Apartment House Boom • Apartment House Movements • Apartment House Financing • Apartment House Types • Apartment House Tenants • Apartment House Expenses • Apartment House Problems • Apartment Houses — Their Future

21

Shopping Centers 365

How They Have Grown! • The Appeal of the Shopping Center • The Economics of the Shopping Center • The Swan Song of Downtown Retail? • Financing the Shopping Centers • Kinds of Shopping Centers • Evening and Sunday Openings • Shopping Centers Abroad • Shopping Center Problems • The Wave of the Future

22

Industrial Property 379

What Is It? • What Are Its Characteristics? • What Are the Locational Factors? • Location Boosters • Industrial Property Trends • Investment Characteristics of Industrial Property • Industrial Parks

PART VIII

Real Estate and Urban Redevelopment

23

Urban Renewal and Rehabilitation 393

Urban Renewal • The Government and Urban Renewal • The Realtor and Urban Renewal • What Has Urban Renewal Accomplished? • Where Has Urban Renewal Failed? • Urban Rehabilitation • Urban Development Programs • The Federal Housing Administration and Urban Renewal • Federal Financial Assistance • Special Housing Assistance

24

Transportation and Real Estate Values 409

The Problem • How Is This Problem Related to Real Estate? • How Has Improved Transportation Enhanced Real Estate Values? • Is Building More Highways the Answer to Traffic Congestion? • Highway Construction Costs? • How Are Highway Construction Costs Financed? • Can Rail Commuter Lines Alleviate Highway Congestion? • Why Don't More Commuters Use the Rails? • Is Rail Commutation a Lost Cause? • Suppose the Commuter Trains Stopped Running? • Can Rail Commuter Service Be Maintained? • Up in the Air

25

New Towns and Model Cities 425

New Towns • New Towns in the Private Sector • New Towns and Greenbelts • Model Cities • Model Cities Problems

26

Pollution — Air, Noise and Water 439

How Bad Is the Pollution Problem? • Who Is Responsible? • What Can Be Done About It? • What Will Happen If We Do Nothing? • Glossary

PART I
INTRODUCTION

THE SCOPE AND SIGNIFICANCE OF REAL ESTATE

CHAPTER ONE

SCOPE

The scope of real estate includes the land and economic activities associated therewith, the legal rights in land acquired and legal obligations assumed. It also includes governmental land-use controls and attempts to employ real estate for the greatest social and collective good. It also embraces related areas, such as finance and investment, in as far as they affect real estate.

LAND USE

The basic land use is for production of food by means of crop cultivation and the pasturage of livestock. This takes in planting, tillage, cultivation, and harvesting of grain, fruit, and vegetables for both human and animal consumption. Soil conservation, fertilizers, irrigation, contour plowing, sod waterways, terracing, and shelter belts are factors in food production.

Underlying the land are the minerals - water, ores, and petroleum - also essential for sustenance, and land use covers their extraction. To guard against mineral depletion, proper land use limits mineral consumption in accordance with need.

Second in importance to food production is land use for shelter in the form of housing. This housing includes single-family homes, multi-family dwellings, town houses, cooperatives and condominiums, modulars and sectionals, mobile homes, motels and hotels. They range from luxury units to modest low-income housing.

Our economy could not function without land use for commerce - stores and shopping centers, warehouses and transportation terminals, office buildings, and the marts of trade. Our economy also requires land to be used for factories, steel mills, ore refineries, and industrial parks - all contributing to the production society demands.

Land is used for recreation - for the stadia for organized sports, the golf courses, the race tracks, the ski slopes and the snowmobile trails, for pitch and putt as well as for bowling on the green. Vast tracts of land are set aside for state and national parks, providing scenic vistas, fauna and flora, camping sites, hiking and exploring.

THE BUSINESS OF REAL ESTATE

The uses of land are developed, evaluated, sold, promoted, and managed by those who have found it to their interest and advantage to do so. These are the people engaged in the real estate business.

Before land development takes place, a feasibility study should be conducted which can determine whether a contemplated venture is sound and practical. The nature of the study depends on the nature of the development. A feasibility study for a shopping center would concern itself with the market clientele. A feasibility study for a new industry would concern itself with access to raw materials and markets.

Once he has determined a project to be feasible, the land developer must then concern himself with zoning and building codes, securing approvals from the many governmental agencies involved, dedication of land for appropriate public uses, financing the construction and securing permanent financing, and marketing and promoting the project. The land developer must be both an urban planner and a political economist.

The construction of development improvements includes not only the hiring of a builder-contractor, but also the employment of the construction force required, the scheduling of the work operations, the production in accordance therewith, and the ordering and financing of the building materials and the payrolls required. Over and beyond this, construction encompasses the feeder industries - lumber, steel, brick, cement, and aluminum - whose provision must dovetail into the production schedules. It also includes securing zoning ordinance variances and building code exceptions. It calls into play legal talent for drawing up the implementing legal documents and the accounting talent to take advantage of the cash flow and tax shelter available.

In order to secure financing for real estate developments, they must be evaluated to ascertain their fair market value and determine whether this will be sufficient to sustain the mortgage loan required. This evaluation requires the employment of appraisers, whose estimates should be prepared, where possible and practicable, on the basis of the cost, market, and income approaches to value. Appraisers can also help the seller determine how much he can get for his property, the buyer to determine how much he may have to pay, the renter to calculate what rental will be required, and the trader-exchangor to set a reasonable figure for this purpose.

If the property is being rented, it may be advisable to secure the services of a property manager, not only to collect the rents, but also to handle tenant complaints, get new and renew old leases, supervise building jobs, manage servicing personnel, and buy supplies to advantage.

The biggest business activity in real estate is brokerage. This accounts for the largest number of employees, and is applicable to all fields of real estate selling - residential, commercial, and industrial. Although a real estate broker serves as an intermediary between seller and buyer, his primary loyalty is to his owner client. In return for his commission, it is the broker's obligation to secure the highest price possible for the property, consistent with the current market. The broker's activities consist of listing the property, prospecting for buyers, negotiating the terms of the transaction, and closing the sale. Listings constitute the broker's stock in trade. Prospecting provides the potential customers. Negotiating channels the offers, the counter-offers, the price adjustments, the concessions and the quid pro quo's into a successful consummation of the transaction. Closing constitutes the completion of the transaction.

As most real estate transactions are financed, this requires finding a lender, arranging the terms of interest and the installment payments on principal, adapting the character of the mortgage loan to the financial situations of the parties concerned, qualifying the buyer and the property for the mortgage loan, securing title insurance for the mortgagee-creditor, getting a credit report on the buyer, and having an appraisal and survey of the property made.

As the investing public has become increasingly conscious of the importance of real estate investments, due primarily to relatively high rates of return and as a hedge against inflation, an entirely new area has opened up in the field of real estate. Real estate brokers must now be competent to advise on real estate investments. They must be able to scale the investments to their clients' financial, age, and psychological situations. They must know the inherent investment advantages of the property concerned. They must be able to project the returns from the investment over a span of time. They should be able to interpret in layman's terms the advantages of accelerated depreciation, capital gains, equity build-up, and the installment method of capital gains reporting. For the small investor, they must know real estate investment trusts - the mutual funds of the real estate field. They should be familiar with the investment advantages of limited partnership participations, joint ventures, and syndications. They should be aware of the implications of big business now immersing itself in real estate investments.

Most real estate brokers are primarily concerned with residential selling. The trade gives them the name of "house salesmen". As the purchase of a home is the major investment families make, the residential broker has a prime responsibility for finding the house best suited to his customer's personal and financial requirements. This involves not only the structure and the site on which it rests, but also the neighborhood, the availability and quality of schools and shopping centers, and the amenities and conveniences of gracious living.

Because of the ever-rising spiral in prices for homes, real estate brokers, for their less affluent customers, are suggesting mobile homes, which can provide reasonable living comfort for a price under $15,000. Brokers are also becoming conversant with the advantages of modular housing, in which individual units are constructed in a factory, with the advantage of weather-free production, quality controls, standardization of operations, assembly line techniques, lower labor costs with unskilled and semi-skilled workers, the individual modules being transported to the site, and lifted by crane into place, one on top of another, and one alongside another. This appears to be the housing wave of the future, seeming to be the only way to beat the high cost of housing construction.

Brokers are finding condominiums increasingly popular. These are structures, whose unit occupants own the space they occupy, and have a common ownership in elements, such as the land, which they use conjointly with other unit occupants. They are to be distinguished from cooperatives, in which unit occupants own stock in a corporation, which is the owner of the structure and the common elments. Because of the outside property management provided in both condominium and cooperative organizations, individual occupants are relieved of the burden of exterior household chores.

Cooperatives and condominiums are popular in town houses and multi-family structures, and save on costs by reason of common walls and land conservation. They are also used in retirement communities. As between the two forms of ownership, there now seems to be a preference for condominiums. As the condominium occupant actually owns his own unit, he gets a recordable deed to show for it, and enjoys the advantage of arranging his own financing. The cooperative occupant, on the other hand, does not himself own any real property. Rather, his ownership is confined to stock in the cooperative corporation.

As society becomes more mobile and more rootless, as the percentage of working wives increases, and as the attraction of a family homestead declines, there is a surge toward apartment house living. It suits trends of the times, eliminates the down payment required for a home, provides the flexibility desired for executive transferees, and frees the family from exterior household chores. It fits the requirements of the younger and the older segments of the population, the areas showing the largest percentage rate of increase. Apartments therefore have become increasingly popular in the market for household units and are attractive to the real estate investor for yield, the real estate broker for lease commissions, and the real estate manager for the fees secured from proper supervision.

Although the United States now has an essentially urban population, there has not been a decline in the scope of farm real estate. Rather, this area is slowly undergoing a change from the small, individualized farm operation to the large-scale corporate type. The latter enjoys the advantages of economies of scale and the opportunity to spread required farm equipment over a wide area, rather than limiting it to the small family farm. Although over-all farm prices do not in themselves provide an adequate return on farm investments, government subsidies, parity-price payments, and set-aside compensations do provide a substantial supplement, and, together with the opportunity for capital gains when farms are sold, make for an over-all substantial yield. Also, with the growing conversions of farms into urban and industrial uses, farm values tend to rise apace. Furthermore, the higher rate of commissions usually obtainable on farm sales attracts selling expertise into these fields.

With growing affluence and longer vacations, the scope of resort real estate has grown in proportion. A large proportion of American families now takes two vacations a year, instead of one. A large proportion also owns second homes which are used as vacation retreats. It is now the law of the land that in public accommodations, there may be no discrimination against black Americans, and they therefore constitute an additional potential market in resort real estate, to the extent that their financial means permit. The variety of resort real estate provides locales for the sports enthusiast, the student of wildlife, the vacationist interested solely in relaxation, and the individual bent on games and fun at the race track and in the gambling casino. Associated with resort real estate are retirement communities in the same general locale - frequently one of sun, sea, and sanctuary - providing the opportunity for consortium with one's peers, mild sports galore, relative freedom from household chores, and, occasionally, relief from school taxes.

As office space is used to handle business by phone, mail, and face-to-face confrontation, negotiations on stock and bond flotations, arrangements for financing business transactions and consummating financial undertakings, the demand for office space has grown in proportion. In fact, this growth in demand is a heartening feature in downtown real estate, where business plans and policies are formulated at central headquarters. Downtown offices are also sites for stock and commodity exchanges. There is, however, a growing trend toward office locations in suburbia, particularly in the case of branches for banks, insurance company offices, and offices for lawyers, accountants, and real estate people. This trend is especially noticeable in suburban shopping centers.

Although now an outstanding part of the American retail scene, *planned* shopping centers are relatively new, having grown from an over-all total of approximately 150 in 1951 to approximately 12,000 in 1971. But this increase in numbers does not tell the whole story of their growth, for, as time has gone on, they have grown larger, from the neighborhood to the community, to the regional, and now to the super-regional. As trade follows the customer, most shopping center growth has been in suburbia. Aside from their attractions to retail trade in the form of their department stores, supermarkets, variety stores, and specialty shops, they have often become the focal point of community life - art shows, theatre, ballet, meeting places for discussion of civic problems, offices for civic administration and the postal service, and the rallying point for political assemblies.

In industrial real estate, the significant change in scope has been from the multi-story to the one-story, requiring larger land area, and therefore a location on urban peripheries or out in the hinterland. If rail transportation is still required, this is currently often provided by belt-line railroads, encircling the city itself. Just as planned shopping centers have become popular in the retail area, so have planned industrial parks in the industrial field. They are planned for the needs of light industry, for research and development facilities, for compatible tenants, with all the needs pre-arranged for traffic artery ingress and egress, zoning variances and building code exceptions, utilities, and parking. Industrial real estate's scope has now been broadened to provide for ecological considerations, anti-pollution treatment for industrial wastes, and the circumvention of air and water pollution.

The scope of real estate has also been broadened to include urban renewal to overcome urban blight and decay, as well as urban rehabilitation to refurbish basically sound structures in need of maintenance and repair. In order to provide Americans with decent shelter and living amenities, public housing and low rentals have become part of the residential scene, as have subsidies to enable families of low and moderate income status to purchase or rent suitable housing units.

Realizing the provision of mass transit is essential to relieve clogged, bumper to bumper traffic arteries, as well as to reduce concomitant smog and air pollution, growing studies are being made of high speed mass transportation. Accessibility is a key factor in the valuation of real estate, so improved transportation brings a renewed attraction to localities otherwise removed both in time and mileage.

To relieve social and population pressures, to provide for a dispersal from cramped and crowded living and working quarters in the central city and in core and ghetto areas, new towns are being established. With grants in aid from the federal government, with outright loans to help new town promoters make their down payments and carry the financial load until the payoff period, and with the guarantee of the financial debentures provided for new town financing, the carrying charges become less of a burden. It is the intent in many of the new towns to make them integrated, with balanced proportions of ethnic, economic, and age groups, and to provide employment opportunities to make their residents self-sustaining. Inside the cities themselves, neighborhoods blighted and fallen into decay are being helped financially under Model Cities programs to make themselves viable and alive.

The National Association of Real Estate Boards is concerned about the ecology and what can be done to guard against air, water, and noise pollution, and has made this concern part of its Make America Better program. This should be a long-run concern of everyone engaged in the real estate business, dependent as it is on having an attractive environment to promote and to sell. It has become part of the subject matter of real estate courses. It is a consideration which those engaged in industrial real estate have to ponder before making recommendations on new site locations or the relocation of present ones.

THE SCOPE OF LAND USE CONTROLS

The carrying on of the real estate business is highly regulated at all tiers and in all areas of government. At the local level, the prime spheres of regulation are in the requirements of zoning ordinances and building codes, set-back and side-line restrictions, the amount of square foot space per living unit, the heights to which improvements may be erected and the safety features they must incorporate. Private land use controls are also important, and the City of Houston has depended heavily on private, restricted covenants placed in deeds. At the state level, usury statutes prescribe the maximum ceilings mortgage loans may require; state building codes in some states may now over-ride local building codes; state industrial development commissions may provide tax, financial, and land subsidies to encourage new industry to locate therein; and state highway departments and water resource commissions may stipulate that their approval must be secured before new developments may be started.

But it is at the Federal level that the greatest number of land use controls exist. The Federal Housing Administration specifies the standards that housing developments must meet before Federal Housing Administration insurance may be granted. The Department of Housing and Urban Development has a multiplicity of programs, providing grants, loans, and financial assistance to promote low and moderate income housing, industrialized housing, housing for the elderly, Model Cities, new towns, urban renewal and urban rehabilitation, public housing, experimental housing, and college and university housing. In each of its assistance programs, approval is conditional to the ventures meeting its land use controls.

The Farmers Home Administration of the Department of Agriculture provides loans and loan guarantees at relatively low rates of interest for housing in rural areas and for silos, granaries, and other buildings on the farms themselves, providing the applicants for such financial assistance comply with its land use controls.

The Department of Interior controls land use in national parks and in many areas of the public domain. The Department of Transportation correlates land use with mass transit in metropolitan areas. The Department of Commerce through its Small Business Administration makes loans, subject to its approvals, to small business for its use of real estate, when it is unable to secure financing from conventional sources.

The Army Corps of Engineers, charged with assuring the navigability of interstate waters, and the dredging required to make power and other commercial projects feasible, is a potent force in land use controls and real estate developments. Some land use controls, such as those exercised over off-shore oil well drilling and the overproduction of petroleum resources, are under the jurisdiction of more than one department of the Federal government. The operation of aircraft and the use of airports and runways are subject to land use controls of the Federal Aviation Administration, as well as those of state and local jurisdictions.

THE SIGNIFICANCE OF REAL ESTATE

The value of real estate constitutes the bulk of the national wealth of the United States. The amount of money spent for construction is a large factor in the total of the Gross National Product. Home mortgage loan financing is the chief activity of the savings and loan associations. The people employed in real estate include not only real estate brokers and sales people, but also builders and developers, financiers and mortgage bankers, appraisers and surveyors, the mortgage lending and investment personnel of the large life insurance companies, real estate lawyers and accountants, governmental personnel engaged in the regulation, management, and acquisition of real estate, construction labor, all who are employed in the care and maintenance of real estate properties, stock and bond brokers and their personnel engaged in the flotation of real estate securities, and scientific and technological organizations concentrating on the development of innovations and improvements in building construction.

Real estate also includes feeder industries channeling their products into the construction, repair, rehabilitation, and improvement of real properties. Among such industries are the steel, aluminum, zinc, copper, lumber, cement, furniture and appliance industries. Some feeder industries have set up real estate subsidiaries or engaged in joint ventures with real estate developers. Their objective has been, in part, getting their products used in buildings and improvements, and thereby providing them with a captive market and a showcase for their wares.

THE SIGNIFICANCE OF REAL ESTATE
AS AN ECONOMIC INDICATOR

The real estate cycle is part of the general business cycle, but it usually precedes the downward swing of business in general. This may come about in part because real estate constitutes a substantial outlay, and, therefore, if straws in the wind seem to show a subsidence of business in general, investment in real estate is more likely to be deferred than one in consumer goods. At the same time, once construction has been started, it is likely to be completed. Even if a recession is imminent, most builders would face the necessity of completing the structures because of legal contracts. It is also preferable to consummate construction, rather than permit the skeletal members of the structures to be exposed to the action of the elements.

Whether real estate leads a general business recovery or lags behind is controversial. The business revival that started in 1971 was preceded by a revival in real estate construction that started in the early part of the summer of 1970. This situation, of course, could have been stimulated by the introduction of federal funds on a large scale into the housing field through amendments in the National Housing Act and subsequent Congressional appropriations by way of implementation. There does seem to be general agreement that the troughs in the real estate cycle are deeper than those of the general business cycle.

The granting of mortgage loan applications and approval of building permits today will be translated into land acquisition and building construction in the future. They are therefore indicators of the economic activity residing in purchase and rental, employment of construction personnel, and the demand for building materials and supplies.

REAL ESTATE AS A MIRROR OF SOCIOLOGICAL CHANGE

Real estate mirrors changes in living habits in the preference for the three-bedroom home, the swimming pool, the attached garage, the den, the compact kitchen, the sauna baths, the patio, the picture window, and the wall-to-wall carpeting.

Real estate mirrors changes in manufacturing in the preference for the one-story industrial plant where, ideally, raw materials enter at one end and emerge as finished products at the other, machinery can rest on bedrock, there is no hauling things up and down via ramps or elevators, and high ceilings permit cranes to move about with ease and flexibility.

Real estate mirrors changes in retailing in the shift to the suburbs from downtown, in the provision of more ample parking space in shopping centers, four times as much parking space as in the stores' areas. Real estate has for a long time mirrored the preference for the planned shopping center and the magnetism of one-stop shopping it exerts.

The locational preference of the city over the farm and the small town; of suburbia and now of exurbia over the city itself; of apartment house type living and the flexibility of movement it affords to an ever more mobile population - all these are reflected in real estate choices.

The increase in the proportion of the younger segment of the population is reflected in the preferences for apartment house living and mobile homes. The increase in the proportion of the older segment of the population also shows itself in the surge toward apartment house living as well as in the increase in the development of retirement communities.

THE SIGNIFICANCE OF REAL ESTATE MARKETS

The real estate market is, on the whole, a local market. Real estate itself is fixed, and therefore cannot be moved from one place to another, as commodities can. Real estate must be used where it is. Trading in real estate has, consequently, been individualized and localized. But this may change. The use of the computer is already exposing real estate from a market in Maine to a market in Missouri, and from a market in Texas to one in Tennessee.

Real estate is unique and individual. No one parcel of real estate is exactly like another parcel. This tends also to make the real estate market a local one. Localities in themselves differ from one another. Deed and zoning restrictions in one municipality may be different from those in another. As per capita incomes may vary, not only between cities, but also between neighborhoods, these variances make for differences in buying power and consequently in what can be paid for real estate.

As real estate is heterogeneous rather than homogeneous, there are no centralized markets in real estate, as there are in stocks and bonds. The closest present approach to an organized market in real estate is in local multiple listing bureaus.

Real estate markets are also significant in the large investments they usually require. The purchase of a home may be the largest investment a family makes in the course of a lifetime. The large amount of the down payment and the length of the period of the mortgage loan are also unique with real estate markets.

Real estate markets are three dimensional - residential, commercial, and industrial. The residential market may be one in new properties or in old, in a rising subdivision and development or in homes that have withstood the passage of time, in the newly-built ranch or the pre-existing Georgian. The residential market may also be divided into homes that can be afforded only by the well-to-do, in those that fit the credit capacity of the middle income, or into homes in the price range of the poor. The residential market is further divided into prospects who wish to buy and those who wish to rent. It may also be classified by the type of residential use - the single-family conventional home, the resort home at the shore, the mountain retreat, the ski lodge, the home for the executive conferees, the rural cottage kept up for the old folks, and the home on the farm acquired as a sideline.

The residential market may also be divided on the basis of the age groups to which it caters. For the young couple starting out, unable to afford a down payment for a home of their own, the modest apartment or the inexpensive mobile home may suit best. For the older couple, the apartment may enable them to rid themselves of exterior household chores or the retirement community may provide the conveniences required along with the satisfaction of individually owned household units.

Although the residential market is primarily local, the commercial real estate market has regional and national overtones. If a chain store takes space in a local shopping center, it will require the identification known to customers not just in the local area, but also throughout the region, and perhaps in the state and the nation as well.

Just as in the case of residential markets, commercial markets may be divided into those for renters and into those for owners. The market for office space may be for downtown locations or in suburban shopping centers. These centers in turn may be classified into whether they are planned or unplanned. Some are now dominated by one merchandiser, such as Korvette, Two Guys, or the K-Mart.

Wherever commodities are traded, there is a commercial market for real estate. Wherever things are made, there is an industrial market for real estate. Some industrial real estate is in the central business district, some is located near railroads or harbor facilities, other is in industrial parks, and still other has spread out into the suburbs, the country, and the hinterland. Industrial real estate requires appropriate transportation facilities. It is usually dependent on power and industrial water. It must be done in close proximity to raw materials, markets, and labor supply, and should enjoy a favorable political climate and reasonable taxes.

THE SIGNIFICANCE OF THE DETERMINANTS OF MARKET BEHAVIOR

The economics of the area determines its income, and this in turn determines its capacity for real estate investment and, thereby, the size of the real estate market. If the area makes and distributes to markets outside itself, then such manufacture and distribution constitute its primary economic base. They enable it to derive for itself a favorable balance of trade. Detroit's primary economic base, for example, is the automobile industry.

Every area also has a secondary economic base, made up of the economic activities necessary for the support of those employed in the primary economic base. The secondary economic base therefore consists of stores, apartment houses, office buildings, and recreational facilities catering to the population as a whole.

The most important demand factor for real estate in an area is its income. Higher incomes make for higher housing demands. Higher incomes make for higher spending, and this makes for the commercial real estate markets catering to these spending needs. Higher incomes make it possible for young couples to get married earlier; and for trading-up in the home market from the present home to the higher-priced.

The bulk of the area's income comes from employment. This may be in manufacturing, in agriculture, in trade and distribution, in mining or petroleum, in government work, in tourism, or in education. Some of the income comes from dividends on securities, rentals from real estate, and interest on loans, as well as yields from pensions and annuities.

As the economic base of the area expands, so does the demand for real estate. As investors see growth and profit potential, they channel their savings into real estate projects likely to prosper as a correlative. Trade expands, resources and purchasing power grow, so real estate yields larger returns.

Stability of income is essential to sustain the demand for real estate. Stability of income makes possible keeping up the payments on the long term mortgage loan. It is a prerequisite for sustained credit capacity. Also important in making for real estate demand are the terms of acquisition. The lower the interest rate, the lower the cost of the loan. The smaller the down payment, the easier it is to finance the acquisition. The longer the mortgage loan, the lower the payments.

The determinants of real estate supply are in the profit projections anticipated. They motivate the promoter to promote, the builder to build, the owner to expand and to modernize, and the seller to sell and enjoy his capital gain. Just as supply is increased by the erection of new structures, it is reduced through depreciation and deterioration, through demolitions, and the destructive action of the elements. Supply increases not only by the erection of new buildings, but also by the conversion of old single-family homes into duplexes, and single-use factories into multi-use units.

Retarding factors in supply are advancing costs; outmoded zoning ordinances and building codes; strikes and work disruptions; and scarcity of sites, cost of access roads, inadequate water and drainage, and the absence of utilities.

SUMMARY

The scope of real estate includes the uses of land, the economic activities associated with these uses, and the land use controls imposed.

Land is used for the production of food and minerals, for manufacturing, and for distribution. The improvements made on land provide for housing and carrying on of commerce and industry.

The real estate business is composed of land development, construction, financing, appraising, property management, brokerage, and investment.

Residential brokerage includes not only conventional single-family housing units, but also industrialized housing, cooperatives, and condominiums. Commercial brokerage includes apartment houses, office buildings, shopping centers, farms, and resort facilities. Industrial real estate takes in not only the factories themselves, but also the sites on which they reside, and planned industrial parks.

The scope of real estate also encompasses urban renewal, urban rehabilitation, public housing, and subsidized housing for low and moderate income families, as well as the relationship to real estate of mass transit and improved transportation. It embraces new towns and Model Cities, and the social concerns with ecology preservation.

Land use controls are imposed by private restrictions as embodied in deed covenants, by regulations at local, state, and federal levels, and by public programs for urban re-development. All departments of the Federal government have interest spheres in real estate.

Real estate constitutes the bulk of our national wealth. Its monetary size may be measured by the monetary amounts in real estate transactions, in the financing required, in the payrolls disbursed, and in its purchases from its feeder industries.

The course of real estate constitutes an economic indicator. The activities in real estate mirror sociological changes. The markets in real estate are, for the most part, local ones, and they require relatively large investments - whether they be residential, commercial, or industrial. These markets may be classified in terms of the population groups they serve and in terms of the economic activities to which they cater.

The economic base of an area determines its income, and income is the most important demand factor in real estate, and as the economic base expands, so does the demand for real estate. Stability of income sustains real estate demand and liberal terms of acquisition can facilitate and encourage demand. The determinants of real estate supply reside in the profit projections anticipated.

GLOSSARY

BUILDING CODE - A regulation defining materials and/or performance standards for structural components, as well as heights, safety features, sanitation and health requirements, and set back and side-line restrictions.

CASH FLOW - The income generated, largely from depreciation allowances, after payments on equity and interest.

CONDOMINIUMS - Structures, whose unit occupants have fee simple ownership in the space they occupy, and ownership in common of the common elements.

COOPERATIVES - Structures, whose unit occupants have proprietary leases, based on a down payment on stock in a cooperative corporation, and subsequent periodic payments on principal, interest, taxes, special assessments, and insurance, together with maintenance, upkeep, and repair of the common elements.

JOINT VENTURES - Special partnerships for the consummation of specific projects, in which one of the partners may furnish the expertise, development, and sales promotion, and the other may furnish the capital.

LIMITED PARTNERSHIP - A partnership of two or more, in which one of the partners must be a general partner, with full personal liability, and the other partners, providing their identity is not disclosed, are immune from having their personal assets taken to pay the debts of the partnership, so long as they have paid for their participations.

LISTING - The authorization to sell, rent, or exchange.

MODULAR - A building composed of modules, joined with one another, horizontally or vertically or both, the modules themselves being self-contained sections, constructed in a factory on the assembly line.

PROSPECTING - Seeking for prospects for purchase, rent, or exchange.

SECTIONAL - Two factory-built halves erected on a foundation

SYNDICATION - Any investment combination of two or more people, including partnerships, limited partnerships, corporate alliances, joint ventures, and equity participations.

SUPER-REGIONAL - A shopping center serving a market beyond a specific region, but usually within an hour's driving time of its clientele.

TAX SHELTER - The opportunity to protect income from taxes by means of devices, such as depreciation, accelerated depreciation, "tax-free exchanges", installment method of capital gains reporting, and favorable capital gains treatment.

TOWN HOUSE - A structure whose common elements may be shared by two or more unit occupants.

TRUE AND FALSE QUESTIONS

1. The function of a property manager is limited to rent collection.　　T　F

2. A real estate broker is basically an intermediary.　　T　F

3. A real estate broker owes the same duty to his purchaser-customer that he owes to his owner-client.　　T　F

4. Mobile homes can provide reasonable living comfort for a price under $15,000.　　T　F

5. Mobile homes are the only types of homes providing reasonable living amenities in a low price range.　　T　F

6. Cooperatives are eclipsing condominiums in public favor.　　T　F

7. The rate of commissions on farm sales is usually lower on other forms of real estate.　　T　F

8. Planned shopping centers are relatively new.　　T　F

9. In industrial real estate, the significant change has been from the one-story plant to the multi-story.　　T　F

10. Urban rehabilitation refurbishes basically sound structures.　　T　F

11. It is at the Federal level that the greatest number of land use controls exist.　　T　F

12. The Farmers Home Administration is part of the Department of Housing and Urban Development.　　T　F

13. Commercial property financing is the chief activity of the Savings and Loan Associations.　　T　F

14. The real estate market is essentially a regional market.　　T　F

15. Real estate is heterogeneous.　　T　F

16. The income of an area determines its capacity for real estate investment.　　T　F

17. The secondary economic base is composed of the economic   T   F
activities necessary for the support of those engaged in the
primary economic base.

18. The basic land use is for the production of food.   T   F

19. The purpose of a feasibility study is to determine whether   T   F
a contemplated real estate venture is sound and practical.

20. Land development is not concerned with zoning ordinances   T   F
and building codes.

21. Most real estate brokers are primarily concerned with the   T   F
sale of commercial properties.

22. Modular housing and conventional housing both have   T   F
approximately the same labor costs.

23. Both cooperatives and condominiums are commonly used   T   F
in the growing retirement communities.

24. Although apartment houses suit the requirements of the   T   F
older segments of the population, they are not suitable for
the younger segments.

25. Trading in real estate has been individualized and   T   F
localized.

26. At the state level, the prime sphere of regulation is in the   T   F
form of zoning ordinances.

27. The troughs in the real estate cycle are usually deeper than   T   F
those in the general business cycle.

28. Building permits and mortgage loan applications are indi-   T   F
cators of real estate activity.

29. The use of the computer cannot change the fact that real   T   F
estate transactions must be local in character.

30. The closest approach presently to an organized market in   T   F
real estate is in local multiple listing bureaus.

31. The primary economic base consists of the commercial   T   F
activities on the local scene catering to the requirements
of the local population.

32. Land use does not concern itself with legal rights and   T   F
obligations.

33. Ideally, the land developer is an urban planner and a   T   F
political economist.

34. The fair market value of a parcel of real estate helps   T   F
determine the amount of the loan that can be secured.

35. Prospects constitute the broker's stock in trade.   T   F

36. Modular housing enjoys weather-free production   T   F

37. Large-scale corporate type farming enjoys the advantages   T   F
of economies of scale.

38. Office real estate has resisted the trend to suburbia.   T   F

39. Planned shopping centers have become a focal point of   T   F
community life and activity.

40. The scope of industrial real estate does not take in   T   F
ecological considerations.

MULTIPLE CHOICE QUESTIONS

41. The largest part of the financial burden of new towns is in their:
    ( ) Interest charges
    ( ) Taxes
    ( ) Assessments
    ( ) Carrying charges

42. The purpose of Model Cities is again to make viable real estate in:
    ( ) Cities as a whole
    ( ) Neighborhoods within cities
    ( ) Urban renewal projects
    ( ) New Towns

43. Land use in national parks is controlled by:
    ( ) The Department of Agriculture
    ( ) The Department of Commerce
    ( ) The Department of the Interior
    ( ) The Department of Health, Education, and Welfare

44. The ratio of parking space in planned shopping centers to space in the stores themselves is now on the average:
    ( ) Four to one
    ( ) Three to one
    ( ) Five to one
    ( ) Six to one

45. The bulk of an area's income comes from:
    ( ) Its population
    ( ) Its commerce
    ( ) Its employment available
    ( ) Its industry

46. The determinants of real estate supply reside in:
    ( ) Demand
    ( ) Profit projections anticipated
    ( ) Technological innovations
    ( ) Governmental subsidies

47. The instantaneous exposure of real estate listings from one part of the country to another may now be done by means of:
    ( ) Multiple listing services

( ) The computer
( ) The National Association of Real Estate Boards
( ) State real estate associations

48. The Small Business Administration is part of:
( ) The Department of Commerce
( ) The Department of Housing and Urban Development
( ) The Neighborhood Development Program
( ) The Urban Renewal Program

49. The operation of aircraft and the use of airports and runways are subject to land use controls of:
( ) The Civil Aeronautics Board
( ) The Department of Transportation
( ) The Federal Aviation Administration
( ) The Air Traffic Controllers Association

50. The form of housing construction now closest to automation is in:
( ) Pre-fabs
( ) Panel systems
( ) Modulars
( ) The stick method

ESSAY QUESTIONS

1. "Real estate is all pervasive, entering into every sphere of our economy."
   Please comment on the foregoing statement.

2. "Real estate is significant as an economic indicator".
   In what respects is this true?

3. "It has been said that real estate is subject to more regulation than any other industry, save narcotics alone."
   What evidence can you produce of such regulation?

PART II
LEGAL ASPECTS

LICENSE LAWS AND
PROFESSIONAL STANDARDS

CHAPTER TWO

INTRODUCTION

The scope and significance of real estate include broad areas of coverage and the specialized types of employment that have developed in the field. This chapter will concern itself with the character, competence, and experience requirements imposed on those engaged in real estate. These requirements come not only from the licensing laws of the various states, but also from the professional organizations established in real estate. Compliance with these requirements is necessary to practice real estate and compliance with the rules and regulations governing such practice is necessary to continue in such practice.

License laws are now in effect in all fifty states, the District of Columbia, the territories, and the five provinces in the Dominion of Canada. Over and above these license laws, there are the codes of ethics of the trade associations and professional organizations in real estate, each of which has professional standards committees empowered to suspend or revoke any membership found guilty of a violation of code provisions. The purpose of the license laws is to protect the public against exploitation, dishonest dealings, and incompetency. The purpose of the codes of ethics goes beyond this in setting forth the obligations of the membership to the general public, the client, and each other.

LEGAL AUTHORITY FOR THE LICENSE LAWS

The legal authority for the license laws resides in the police power of the state to do what is necessary to protect the health, welfare, and morals of the people of the state. Because investments in real estate are so substantial in amount, because the subject of real estate is so difficult and complex, and because a fiduciary relationship exists between principal and agent, the public interest has demanded the invocation of the police power in real estate activity.

Although the constitutionality of real estate license laws has been attacked on the grounds that they violate the Fourteenth Amendment by depriving a person of his property without due process of law, the courts have sustained their constitutionality. The basis for the attack has been that a person is deprived of his means of making a livelihood when the state restricts his entrance into a particular sphere of economic activity. The courts have decided that there has been no unreasonable restriction, as activity in real estate requires a special degree of trust and competence in order that the public interest be best served. The courts have gone on to say that the calling of real estate is invested, to a degree, with the same public interest as the practices of law and medicine. Just as the state should not permit anyone to practice law and medicine, it should not permit anyone to practice real estate. In the absence of such restrictions, the public could be misinformed in the choice of homes or real estate investments, and could be misled into making ill-conceived judgments in areas where the stakes are high in terms of health, happiness, and finance.

REQUIREMENTS FOR LICENSURE

These vary from state to state. The most common age requirement is that one be at least eighteen to be a salesman and twenty-one to be a broker. Frequently, there is no experience requirement to be a salesman. There is often a three year experience requirement as a salesman before one may become a real estate broker.

Educational requirements vary from none at all to the holding of an academic degree. If a state has minimal educational requirements, it may justify its position by pointing out that some real estate knowledge is required to pass its license examination. But the examination itself may not be demanding. It may on occasion consist of objective type true and false or multiple choice questions, preparation for which can be achieved by taking a "cram course" in real estate.

Character requirements may also be minimal. Having been convicted of a felony may bar licensure, but even this may be waived if the conviction occurred quite some time in the past. The applicant for a license may be required to provide recommendations from citizens in the community in which he resides. If he wants to get a salesman's license, the state may require that he have a sponsoring broker.

If one has his license in another state, he may still have to go through the procedures required in the new state in which he seeks a license. Some states, however, do have reciprocity in this regard, one with the other.

Applicants for licensure pay a fee for taking the examination, and another fee for the license itself. They also pay a fee for license renewal. They are commonly required to be United States citizens.

The requirements for licensure apply not only to brokers and salespeople, but usually also to real property managers and real property appraisers. They apply to both the sale and rental of real property and cover both full-time and part-time practice. Licenses are usually restricted to individual persons, and, under such restrictions, partnerships and corporations per se may not be licensed. In some states mortgage bankers and rent collectors must be licensed.

CARE AND CUSTODY OF LICENSES

The broker must display his salespersons' licenses conspicuously in his place of business. Upon severance of employment of a salesperson, the employer broker must return his license to the issuing office. If the salesperson enters the employ of another broker, a new license is then issued and sent to the new employing broker.

Each licensee is also provided with a pocket card, showing his name and address, and, in the case of a salesperson, the name and address of his employer. The pocket card certifies that the person whose name appears on it is a licensed salesperson or broker.

EXEMPTIONS FROM LICENSING

A person selling his own real estate does not have to have a license. A person buying real estate for himself need not be licensed. In fact, a person dealing strictly with real estate on his own account, not for or with anyone else, in any capacity, does not require a license. If a person acts under the authority of an executed power of attorney from a property owner, and does not receive compensation for buying, selling, or renting real estate, he does not need a license. He is also exempt if in a real estate transaction he acts as a receiver or trustee in bankruptcy, or as guardian, executor, administrator, trustee, assignee, or commissioner. A public officer performing his official duties with respect to real estate does not require a license. An attorney dealing in real estate in behalf of his client is likewise immune. An employee in a real estate office doing clerical or stenographic work in connection with real estate is also exempt.

ADMINISTRATION OF THE LICENSING LAW

The license law is administered by an appointive body, varying in nature from state to state. The members are usually compensated for their time and service. They may have a paid staff to carry out the law. In some instances, the regular staff, like a Department of Licensing and Regulation, carries out the entire administration.

If there is a separate body encharged with the over-all administration of the law, it may be called a State Real Estate Commission, it may be a branch of the Department of Banking and Insurance of the State, it may be denominated as a Real Estate Board, or it may bear the name of a Department of Real Estate.

SUSPENSION, DENIAL, AND REVOCATION OF LICENSE

If a license has been obtained by false representation or by a fraudulent act or conduct, the governing body may revoke it. It may also suspend, deny, or revoke the license of a person making a substantial misrepresentation or making false promises to enter into a real estate contract.

If a licensee pursues a course of misrepresentation or engages in misleading or untruthful advertising, he is subject also to the imposition of these penalties. If he acts for more than one party in a transaction without the knowledge and consent in writing of all parties involved, he may have his license suspended or revoked. If a salesperson accepts compensation in a transaction from anyone other than his employer broker, he is also guilty of violation of the law.

If a commission, finder's fee, or valuable consideration of any kind is paid anyone not licensed, the act has been violated. If a licensee places a "For Sale" or "For Rent" sign on any property without having secured the consent of the owner his license could be suspended or revoked. Failure to supply a complete copy of any listing, sale, lease, or other contract relevant to a real estate transaction to all signatories on it at the time of execution could result in suspension or revocation. A broker may also have his license suspended or revoked if he does not furnish each party a closing statement, showing his receipts and disbursements, at the termination of a transaction.

Brokers must account for any money coming into their possession which belongs to others. They must maintain a special or trust bank account, non-interest bearing, separate and distinct from their personal or other accounts. In this special account they must deposit all escrow funds, security deposits, and any other moneys received by them in a fiduciary capacity. They must render promptly on demand a full and complete statement of expenditures by them for advertising or promoting the sale of their clients' property.

Brokers may not pay commissions or fees to, or divide commissions or fees with, anyone not licensed as a real estate broker or salesperson. They may not accept, give, or charge any undisclosed commission, rebate, or direct profit on expenditures made for a principal. The principal is the party on whose behalf they act and by whom they are compensated.

The regulatory body may suspend or revoke the license of any licensee who has been convicted of a felony, or has failed to notify the body of such conviction. If a licensee has been adjudicated as mentally ill, his license may be suspended or revoked. But it may subsequently be reinstated on proof of the removal of this disability.

A broker may not act in the dual capacity of broker and undisclosed principal. Nor may he offer real property for sale or lease without the knowledge and consent of the owner or his authorized agent, or on any terms other than those authorized by the owner or his authorized agent. He must also affix a definite expiration date on listing contracts to which he is a party. In many states he may not in the listing contract set a "net" commission as his compensation, namely, one not included in the sales price. Nor may he insert a "blind ad," asking the reader, if interested, to write to a box number or to call a telephone number. The reader might thereby be misled into thinking the ad was inserted by the property owner.

The license law may require that the broker recommend to the purchaser that he obtain an abstract of title (a condensed history of title) or a fee title (an insurance policy confirming title validity) in the amount of the purchase price, certified or issued as of approximately the date of the closing of the transaction. The law may further stipulate that a broker recommend to the buyer that he retain an attorney to give an opinion as to whether the title is free from gaps, breaks, or defects.

The law may bar a salesman from handling the closing of his real estate transaction except under the direct supervision of his employer broker. The broker may be required to assume full responsibility for the execution of closing statements prepared by his salesmen acting under his direct supervision.

Salesmen may not advertise under their own name property for purchase, sale, rent, lease, or exchange. If, however, salesmen are themselves the owners of the property being advertised, then they have all the rights of a non-salesman owner. Salesmen may not accept a commission or any other valuable consideration from a real estate broker or any one else other than their employing broker.

Both salesmen and brokers must comply with Federal and state laws, with local ordinances, and with judgments of the courts prohibiting discrimination in the sale, rental, or exchange of real property.

SUGGESTED PATTERN REAL ESTATE LICENSE LAW

The license law committee of the National Association of Real Estate Boards has developed a suggested pattern real estate license law. It is proposed that this constitute the framework for a uniform license law for all the states and territories. The concept of a "single license to practice real estate" has been introduced in this pattern. This move follows the precedent set by the legal and medical professions in providing for a single license to engage therein.

The pattern law lists the basic activities of a broker. It recommends that the term "salesman" be dropped and the term "affiliate broker" be substituted. It says that the owner of real estate need not have a license to sell his own property and that an attorney acting on behalf of a seller or buyer does not have to have a license. It requires that the broker be licensed at the inception of the transaction. It recommends that license fees be spent for administration of the law, adequate enforcement, and real estate education.

The pattern act suggests that the requirements for broker licensure be evidence of good reputation, minimum age of twenty-one, citizenship, experience, and proof of competency. It requires that the applicant for a broker's license prove that he has engaged full time as a real estate licensee for two years prior to the date of application. However, courses in accredited institutions of higher learning may be accepted in lieu of this two-year experience requirement.

The pattern act would require that each applicant for a real estate license furnish a current credit report on himself; that a broker's office be in a room used only for the transaction of brokerage, or allied businesses; that a salesman be prohibited from advertising property belonging to others unless he includes in the ad the name of the broker with whom he is associated; and that a broker be prohibited from soliciting the sale of real estate by offering prizes, free lots, or conducting lotteries to influence a prospective purchaser to buy from him.

THE CODE OF ETHICS OF THE REALTOR

The Code of Ethics for the Realtor was developed by the National Association of Real Estate Boards as a guide for desirable standards of real estate practice. It has been adopted by state associations of real estate boards and by local real estate boards as the means of effectuating these standards as they apply to the business of the Realtor. The Code of Ethics is more extensive and more exacting than the licensing laws.

The interpretation of the Code of Ethics is the responsibility of the Committee on Professional Standards of the National Association of Real Estate Boards. It has published these interpretations, based on cases arising under the Code. The examples which follow are consistent with such interpretations and bring out the common sense concepts of ethical behavior Realtors should follow.

The Realtor's Obligation to the Public under the Code of Ethics

The Realtor has an obligation to engage in public service. In rendering such public service, he is expected to demonstrate professional competence and a thorough knowledge of public regulations affecting real estate, such as zoning and city planning. If a Realtor serves as a member of his state legislature, he renders a public service. His legislative service, therefore, should not be regarded as reducing him to the status of a part-time Realtor, but rather as a professional dedication to the public service.

If the public service rendered by a Realtor such as being head of the City Building Department, requires full-time employment, his designation should be changed to an affiliate (non-active) classification.

The Realtor must advise clients on the fair market price of their properties. If a Realtor's client overprices, the Realtor must tell him so. If a Realtor's client underprices, the Realtor must also tell him so. If a Realtor tells his client that he is not a specialist on values in a particular neighborhood, and suggests to his client that an appraiser be employed to set a value on his property prior to offering it for sale, this statement is sufficient to discharge the Realtor's professional obligations. If a Realtor overprices a property as a strategem to get a listing, he becomes liable for suspension or expulsion from his board.

It is the Realtor's duty under the Code to protect the public against unethical practices in real estate. If a Realtor, therefore, secures information about fraudulent conduct on the part of a fellow Realtor and is asked by a governmental agency to disclose this information, it is his duty to submit it to his Board's grievance committee for action.

If a Realtor acquires first hand knowledge that a broker is making commitments on sales promotions for an advance fee, and that this broker is not complying with these commitments, it is the duty of this Realtor to give public testimony to this effect. A Realtor may not offer a "free" refrigerator, television set, automobile, or "trading stamps" to those who purchase a home through him. Such offers are regarded as cheapening and degrading to the profession. But if a Realtor does not use the promise of a gift to induce the sale, he may afterward make a nominal gift to the purchaser as a goodwill gesture. A Realtor may not use the device of giving a free lot to a prospect, knowing that the prospect will find no use for the free lot, and therefore "trade it in" on a more favorable lot the Realtor will offer.

A Realtor may not make a cooperating broker out of someone who is not licensed to be one. Such an action is in violation of the Code. Such a case could arise if a barber told a Realtor that he could put him in contact with a prospect and the Realtor then told the barber, "If I make the sale to this man, there's $100.00 in it for you." If the sale were then made, and the $100.00 were paid, the Code would be violated. If a

Realtor persuades a prospect to buy a home and assume payments for it which are clearly beyond his means, this, also, is in violation of the Code.

If a Realtor finds an adverse item about the credit of a prospect in the credit report, but, rather than have the mortgage lender turn the prospect down, adds the statement, "There were extenuating circumstances," and if the mortgage lender grants the loan and the mortgagor defaults, the Realtor is in violation.

Suppose a Realtor advertises a "sure thing" investment to the first ten who put up $500 each and guarantees each of them $600 in 30 days, $800 in 90 days, and has no liquid assets in escrow to back up this guarantee. Suppose his only defense is that he was trying to develop a prospect list. He is guilty of misrepresentation and has violated the Code.

Suppose a moving van company offers to erect without charge a Realtor's "For Sale" signs, if these signs will carry the moving van company's advertisements and the Realtor accepts the offer. This is extraneous advertising, and a violation.

A Realtor may not run advertisements stating his services are available to property owners at a stated rate of commission based on sales price. His fee must be determined on the basis of negotiation with his client. The Realtor doing the former has violated the Code.

The Code requires the Realtor to ascertain all the pertinent facts on the property listed with him. If, therefore, a foreign firm solicits a Realtor's cooperation in selling land in a foreign country and sends him maps and photographs in alleged substantiation of its claims that the land will increase in value, he may not accept the solicitation, for he cannot verify the claim of value increase.

If a Realtor sells his own home and fails to disclose to the buyer that the basement drain is stopped up, that the furnace will not work properly, and that the leaking dishwasher is worn out, he is in violation. As the Realtor occupied the house as his own home, he was in a position to know these facts, and under duty to disclose them.

If a Realtor's salesman tells a buyer that any repairs to the property are unnecessary, and, shortly after the sale is made, repairs did become necessary, he is in violation of the Code. The Realtor is responsible for the statements made by his salesperson and both are therefore guilty.

A Realtor must go beyond superficial methods to ascertain pertinent facts. He professes to provide a professional service under an exacting Code and for a substantial fee. He may not therefore limit his efforts to a mere acceptance of the seller's description of the property, but is obligated to verify this description. He must also be knowledgeable of building codes and zoning ordinances affecting the building he is selling. If a prospective buyer raises a question on a pertinent point, the Realtor should not make a guess as to the proper answer, but should commit himself to get the answer based on factual data.

A Realtor may not encourage and assist a customer on procedures to get around restrictive covenants on architectural design applicable to a particular neighborhood. A Realtor must also refrain from the naming of a misleading consideration in a real estate document. This would occur where revenue stamps related to the purchase price were required on the deed, and the Realtor applied more than necessary so as to give the impression a larger than actual price were paid in order to make the property seem to be worth more than it was. He must not engage in the practice of law. He may not advise his client on the legal aspects of the transaction, but should recommend the employment of an attorney. He may not prepare a power of attorney.

It is the Realtor's obligation to see to it that financial commitments are put in writing and that copies thereof are put in the hands of the parties involved. If a prospective buyer asks whether certain equipment is to go with the sale of the property, the Realtor must find out if this is the intent of the seller, and, if so, see to it that this intent is put in writing. The Realtor must always keep other people's money in a bank account separate from his own. When offers or counter offers are made, a copy of the offer or counter offer must be left with the party making it. The Realtor may not refer to a listing contract as a contract for ninety days when, in actuality, it contains an extension provision beyond the ninety day period.

Among unethical advertising practices are the following:

1. A Realtor, to attract attention, advertised, "Local Realtor Is Convicted", and, following this headline, a story that he was convicted of having been able to secure incredible financing for his customers. This advertising is unprofessional and in bad taste.

2. A Realtor applied a qualifying modifier to the term, Realtor, like "Leading Local Realtor." This cheapened the term Realtor and was unethical.

3. A Realtor advertised a client's property, with the signature, "Call Owner WA 4-4096". This was the Realtor's own telephone number. This constituted misrepresentation.

4. A Realtor described a house as being twenty miles from a certain city. Actually, it was thirty-six miles. He characterized it as "modern". Actually, it lacked indoor plumbing. He was held in violation of the Code.

5. A Realtor described as "modern furnishings" items which were ten years old. This was a misrepresentation and a Code violation.

6. A Realtor capitalized a tax differential between two cities, as a reason for buying property in one of the two cities as against the other. As the continuation of this differential was not predictable, the Realtor was held liable.

7. Although a Realtor may put up his "Sold" sign on property after the earnest money has been paid, he is in violation of the Code if he fails to remove the sign when an agreement is reached to have the sale rescinded.

The Realtor's Obligation to His Client under the Code

The paramount obligation of the Realtor is to be faithful to the interest of his client. Neither the Realtor or his salespeople may indicate to a prospect that the owner may take less than the listed price. Even though the Realtor may have no actual knowledge that his salespeople have so indicated, he is equally liable with them.

Neither may a Realtor suggest to his client a price below what the client wants, and then persuade his brother-in-law to offer to buy at this lower price. In the case cited, the brother-in-law sold the property subsequently above the figure the client originally wanted.

Neither the Realtor nor his salespeople may suggest to a prospect that the property is overpriced. It is the obligation of the Realtor to state his opinion on the price to the client, not to the buying public. It is also the duty of the Realtor to relay on to his client any bona fide offer to buy. If, consequently, a Realtor has listed with himself a property which he is at the same time managing and receives a written offer to buy, but, fearing the loss of his management assignment, fails to communicate the offer, he is in violation of the Code.

The Realtor owes to his client the duty of engaging to the fullest extent possible in trying to sell the property. He may not, therefore, leave keys of vacant listed properties in their mail boxes and tell telephone inquirers to inspect the properties on their own and call him back if interested. This is a slipshod and degrading practice and is in violation of the Code.

The Realtor must keep himself informed with regard to legal and public policies which affect his client's interests. He must therefore be knowledgeable about proposed zoning ordinances which could influence the price to be set on his client's property. He is also under a legal obligation to deposit without delay an earnest money check for his client. If he is dilatory about so doing, and, because of his delay, the check is returned marked, "Not sufficient funds", the Realtor is in violation of the Code.

The Code of Ethics prohibits a Realtor from accepting compensation from more than one party without the knowledge and consent of all parties concerned. Suppose, therefore, a buyer agrees to pay a commission to a Realtor if a property meeting the buyer's price and other specifications is secured. Suppose the Realtor finds such a property, and collects the usual commission from the seller, without disclosing to the seller the compensation being received from the buyer. The Realtor has violated the Code.

Under the interpretations of the Code, the Realtor may not acquire an interest on behalf of himself or his family in a property listed with him unless he discloses his or his family's true position to his client and his client consents, regardless of these personal affiliations. This disclosure should be in writing. Even though the buyer is the Realtor's father-in-law, he is still regarded as a member of the family and the Realtor is still obligated to disclose this relationship to his client. Along the same line, if a salesman sells the listed property to his mother, and does not disclose this relationship to the client, the salesman violates the Code. Even though the salesman operated as an independent contractor for his Realtor, and even though the Realtor did not know the buyer was the salesman's mother, the Realtor is also in violation.

The Code of Ethics requires that the Realtor urge and accept the responsibility for exclusive right to sell listings. If a Realtor has an exclusive right to sell listings and if the property is overpriced, the Realtor must tell the client so, rather than wait for the client to find this out for himself, through lack of any interest in the property at the listed price. A Realtor may not promulgate a rule through an independent multiple listing service to prohibit open listings. Such a rule would constitute an inequitable limitation on membership.

A Realtor may not accept rebates on expenditures made for the owner whose property he is managing, unless the owner has full knowledge thereof and consents thereto. This prohibition extends to pocketing revenues from the installation of vending machines without the knowledge and consent of the owner of the managed property. This also prohibits a Realtor property manager from accepting rebates from contractors on modernization programs, unless the owner has knowledge of this and gives his consent.

A Realtor may not accept an appraisal assignment, unless he is prepared to make a thorough analysis of the property. Nor may he make an appraisal on property in which has has an interest, unless he discloses this interest to his client and his client registers no objection. Under no circumstances may a Realtor make an appraisal for a fee, contingent on the amount of the value found. A Realtor must consider all factors affecting value in connection with his appraisal. A Realtor must further disclose to his client any interest he may have in property adjoining that which he is appraising. If a Realtor is managing other property for a buyer, the Realtor must disclose this fact to a seller before appraising property for sale to such a buyer.

A Realtor may not advertise a property unless he has received authority to do so from his client. Nor may a Realtor quote any price on the property other than that agreed on by the owners as the listing price. If a Realtor gets one price in writing in the listing agreement, and another price verbally from the owner, a dual price arrangement exists, an arrangement inconsistent with a professional standard of service and therefore a violation of the Code of Ethics.

The Code requires that the Realtor present all formal written offers to the owner. If a Realtor gets one offer at the listed price and others below that price, it is still his obligation to submit all the offers to the owner. If the owner names a price and says that he will not consider anything less than this price, it is still the obligation of the Realtor to submit all bona fide offers received, even though they are below the listed price.

The Realtor's Obligation to His Fellow-Realtors

A Realtor may take no unfair advantage over his fellow-Realtors and is obligated to share with them the lessons of his experience. He may not advertise: "I'll beat your best deal." Such a slogan is regarded as unprofessional. Nor may a Realtor's salesman say in his presentations: "Our office produces sales faster than any other real estate office in town." He must try to avoid controversies with his fellow-Realtors, but, if they should arise, must arbitrate them in accordance with the regulations of his local board, rather than litigate.

If a Realtor drives a prospect around and shows him various properties, he cannot claim a percentage of the commission if a sale of one of these properties is subsequently made in an open listing through another Realtor. The Realtor's obligation to submit controversies for board arbitration cannot be superseded by submissions to a multiple listing service. A business associate of one of the parties to a controversy is not permitted to sit as a member of the arbitration committee. If the local board should decide to refer a controversy to an arbitration panel of the state association, the parties to the dispute must be governed by its findings.

Controversies between Realtors of different boards should be arbitrated by an odd-numbered panel, consisting of a Realtor from each of the boards chosen by the parties plus one other chosen by the arbitrators. This provision is mandatory, and a Realtor may not deviate therefrom on the ground that "should" is only a suggestion.

A Realtor charged with unethical conduct must place all pertinent facts before the appropriate quasi-tribunal of his local board. He cannot plead the Fifth Amendment as an excuse for failing to provide pertinent data for he is not being tried in a court of law. If a Realtor is suspended for a violation, he may not designate himself as a Realtor during the period of the suspension. If a Realtor is indicted and his board asks for facts pertinent to his indictment, he is obligated to submit them.

A Realtor may not disparage the practice of a competitor or volunteer an opinion of a competitor's transaction. If a Realtor's opinion regarding a transaction is sought, he must render this opinion with professional integrity. Under this section of the Code a Realtor becomes liable, even though the disparagement is made by a salesperson or a business associate for the Realtor assumes responsibility for them.

A Realtor is obligated to respect the exclusive agency listing of another Realtor. He may not, therefore, solicit a listing to take effect on the termination of an existing exclusive listing. If a Realtor, holding an exclusive listing, lists the property with the multiple listing service, this service may not authorize its members to transmit offers directly to the client owner. If a Realtor persuades an owner to give him an exclusive listing at the time open listings are in effect, about which the owner tells him, the Realtor is obligated to inform these other Realtors of his exclusive. If a Realtor cooperates with a listing broker, who holds an exclusive, this Realtor may not invite the cooperation of a third broker without the listing broker's consent.

A Realtor may not persistently solicit the business of an owner who repeatedly tells him that he has a continuing relationship with another Realtor and therefore does not wish to be made subject to such repeated solicitation. If a client tells his Realtor that his exclusive listing is to be handled quietly and not made public and the Realtor repeats these instructions to a cooperating Realtor, this cooperating Realtor may not discuss the listing with still other Realtors. If a Realtor has been cooperating with another Realtor during the period of the latter's exclusive listing, he is obligated to ask this Realtor whether his exclusive has expired before contacting the owner "direct" for an exclusive, prior to showing to a prospect developed during the period of cooperative status. A Realtor may not be charged with "pirating" another Realtor's listing if he solicits it after the listing has expired.

A Realtor with an exclusive listing should cooperate with other Realtors. But any negotiations concerning the property should be carried on only through the listing Realtor. A Realtor with an exclusive may not give blanket authorization to fellow Realtors to contact the owner "direct" since such action would deprive the owner of the opportunity to exercise his judgment as to with whom he would prefer to deal.

On occasion, a client owner submits to his Realtor a list of prospects under an exclusive listing and asks his Realtor to submit the property to them first. Suppose another Realtor asks to cooperate in the sale and the first Realtor replies that a prospective buyer is already considering the property, and, consequently, he prefers at this stage not to invite cooperation. Such a Realtor cannot be said to have negated his obligation to cooperate.

Realtor members of a multiple listing service cannot arbitrarily refuse to cooperate with non-member Realtors. And cooperating Realtors under the multiple listing service may not "contact" the owner "direct", but must do so through the Realtor holding the exclusive listing.

It may be that under the multiple listing service, the basis for the commission division is sixty per cent for the selling Realtor and forty per cent for the exclusive listing Realtor. It may likewise be that the customary local division outside the multiple listing service is fifty per cent for the selling broker and fifty per cent for the listing broker. It may be that in such a situation a property is listed with a Realtor and the owner asks that it be withheld from multiple listing. Under these circumstances, a cooperating broker will be compensated on the fifty-fifty basis, the customary practice outside multiple listing.

The Code of Ethics does not permit a Realtor to solicit the services of an employee or salesperson of another Realtor, without the knowledge of his employer. If, however, a salesperson for another Realtor answers an ad for a sales manager, the Realtor so advertising is not obligated to acquaint the employer. In such a case, the initiative was taken by the salesperson. On the other hand, if in a casual luncheon conversation, the salesman of another Realtor shows an interest in a position, the Realtor must discontinue the conversation until he informs the employer about his interest in this employee.

Signs should not be placed on property by more than one Realtor unless the property is listed with and authorization is given to more than one Realtor. A Realtor must remove his signs after his listing has expired. The authorization to put up a sign must come from the owner. This prerogative of the owner cannot be assumed by a Realtor on the ground that he holds a listing. Nor may a cooperating Realtor put up his sign on the property without authorization from the owner. Nor may a Realtor affix a sign which is in bad taste, such as a "Chick Sale" sign.

A Realtor is obligated to be loyal to his board and to be active in its work. He may not engage in unsubstantiated destructive criticism of his board, although constructive criticism is always welcome and cannot be construed as disloyal.

SUMMARY

The purpose of license laws is to protect the public against exploitation, dishonest dealings, and incompetency. The purpose of the Realtor's Code of Ethics embraces these same objectives, but it is in general more exacting and more demanding, going into greater detail with regard to the Realtor's duty to the public, his client, and his fellow-Realtors.

The authority for license laws comes from the police power of the state. The courts have sustained the constitutionality of license laws.

Licensure requirements vary from state to state. The most common age requirement is that one have reached eighteen to be a salesperson and twenty-one to be a broker. The license laws cover both full-time and part-time practitioners.

The broker must display the licenses of his salespersons conspicuously in his place of business. Each licensee is also provided with a pocket card, certifying that he is a licensed salesperson or broker. Immune from the licensing requirements are attorneys dealing in real estate in the performance of their duties as members of the bar; clerical or stenographic employees in a real estate office; and public officials performing official duties with regard to real estate.

License laws are administered by a public body, vested with the power to suspend or revoke licenses for misconduct and violation of the licensing rules and regulations.

The concept of a single license to practice real estate has been embodied in the suggested pattern real estate license law of the license law committee of the National Association of Real Estate Boards. This pattern act also suggests higher educational and professional standards than those now prevailing under present license laws.

Over and above the license law standards are those of the Code of Ethics of the National Association of Real Estate Boards. Under this Code, the Realtor has basic obligations to the general public. He is obligated to engage in public service. He must advise clients regarding the fair market price for their real properties. He is obligated to protect the public against unethical practices in real estate. He may not engage in cheap and degrading advertising. Nor may he make a cooperating broker out of a person not licensed to be one. His fee must be based on his negotiations with his client. He must ascertain all pertinent facts with regard to the property listed with him. He must refrain from naming a misleading consideration in a real estate document. He may not engage in the practice of law. He must see to it that all financial commitments are spelled out in writing and that copies are given to all signatories.

The Code of Ethics also spells out the Realtor's obligations to his client. His paramount obligation is to be faithful to his client's interests. He may not suggest to a prospect that a property is overpriced. He must keep himself informed regarding legal and public policies affecting his client's interests. He may not accept compensation in a real estate transaction from more than one party thereto, unless it is with the knowledge and consent of all. He may not acquire a personal interest in property listed with him unless he discloses his true position to his client and his client consents. He should urge and accept the responsibility for exclusive rights to sell listings. He must not accept rebates on expenditures made for the owner whose property he is managing, unless the owner has knowledge and consents. He must not make appraisals beyond the area of his competence. Nor may he make an appraisal on property in which he has an interest. He may not advertise a property without authorization from his client owner. He must present all formal written offers to his client owner.

The Code of Ethics also spells out the obligations of the Realtor to his fellow-Realtors. He must take no unfair advantage of them and share with them the lessons of his experience. If controversies with fellow-Realtors arise, they must be arbitrated in accordance with the regulations of the local board. If a Realtor is charged with unethical conduct, he must place all the facts pertinent to the case before the appropriate quasi-tribunal of his local board. He may not disparage the practice of a competitor or volunteer an opinion of a competitor's transaction. He is obligated to respect the exclusive agency of a fellow-Realtor. He may not arbitrarily refuse to cooperate with fellow-Realtors or with brokers not members of a multiple listing service. He may not solicit the services of a salesperson of another Realtor without the knowledge of his employer. He is obligated to be loyal to his board and active in its work.

GLOSSARY

ABSTRACT OF TITLE — A condensed history of title to property

AGENT — Someone who represents another in a business transaction

CLOSING — The settlement of a transaction

EXCLUSIVE AGENCY LISTING — One in which the broker is protected against the competition of other brokers, but not against the competition of the owner himself

EXCLUSIVE RIGHT TO SELL LISTING — One in which the broker is protected against the competition of other brokers and also against the competition of the owner himself

FEE TITLE POLICY — The title insurance policy covering the property owner.

FIFTH AMENDMENT — The amendment to the Constitution which enables a witness in a court of law to refuse to answer a question on the ground that it might incriminate him.

MULTIPLE LISTING — A service which may be set up as an adjunct to a board of Realtors or independent of them, under which the exclusive right to sell listings of members is immediately made available. to other members of the multiple listing service. Part of the commission derived from the sales goes to the listing broker, part to the selling broker, and a small part to the service for its administration expense.

NET LISTING — One in which the commission is not included in the selling price.

OPEN LISTING — One in which the listing broker is not protected from the competition of other brokers and is not protected from the competition of the owner himself.

PRINCIPAL — The seller, the buyer, the lessor, the lessee, or the trader-exchangor in a real estate transaction

POWER OF ATTORNEY — A written authorization for someone else to act for one on a business transaction.

ZONING VARIANCE — An authority secured from a zoning board to engage in a use of property not consistent with that permitted by the zoning ordinance.

TRUE AND FALSE QUESTIONS

1. License laws constitute the code of ethics in real estate.   T   F

2. The legal authority for the license laws resides in the power   T   F
of eminent domain.

3. The requirements for licensure vary from state to state.   T   F

4. The requirements for licensure usually also apply to real   T   F
property managers and to real property appraisers.

5. Upon severance of employment of a salesperson, his broker   T   F
must return his license to him.

6. Brokers may deposit money belonging to their clients in their   T   F
own account, providing that they make a strict accounting.

7. A broker may not set a "net" commission as his compen-   T   F
sation.

8. Under no circumstances may a salesperson handle the   T   F
closing.

9. If a Realtor engages in legislative service to the State, he   T   F
becomes a part-time Realtor.

10. A Realtor's fee must be determined on the basis of negoti-   T   F
ations with his client.

11. A Realtor may engage in the practice of law, so long as he   T   F
limits himself to drawing up of listing agreements, contracts
of sale, deeds, and mortgages.

12. A Realtor may capitalize a tax differential as between two   T   F
cities, as a reason for buying property in one of these cities
as against the other.

13. If a Realtor is convinced that a property listed with him is   T   F
overpriced, it is his responsibility so to tell his prospect.

14. A Realtor may not promulgate a rule through an inde-   T   F
pendent multiple listing service to prohibit open listings.

15. A Realtor may not make an appraisal on property in which   T   F
he has an interest.

16. Although a Realtor must present all reasonable offers to   T   F
his client, he is authorized to withhold unreasonable offers.

17. A Realtor charged by his board with unethical conduct   T   F
may plead the 5th amendment.

18. A Realtor may not solicit a listing to take effect on the   T   F
expiration of any existing exclusive listing.

19. A Realtor may be charged with "pirating" another Realtor's   T   F
listing, if he solicits it after this listing has expired.

20. Realtor members of a multiple listing service may not   T   F
arbitrarily refuse to cooperate with non-member Realtors.

21. A Realtor must remove his signs after his listing has expired.   T   F

22. The authorization to put up a sign must come from the   T   F
owner of the property.

23. If a Realtor buys for himself a property listed with him,   T   F
he is entitled to a commission on the sale.

24. A salesperson is prohibited from advertising real property   T   F
belonging to others unless he includes in the advertisement
the name of the broker with whom he is associated.

25. A broker must recommend to a purchaser that an attorney   T   F
be retained to pass on the marketability of the title.

26. A broker must affix a definite expiration date on all listing   T   F
contracts to which he is a party.

27. Brokers may divide their commissions with anyone helpful   T   F
in the transaction.

28. Every employee in a real estate office must be licensed.   T   F

29. An attorney dealing in real estate in the performance of his   T   F
duties must carry a real estate license.

30. Every licensee must carry a pocket card.   T   F

31. The requirements for licensure apply only to the sale of   T   F
real property.

32. All states which now have license laws also have reciprocity one with another. T F

33. There is usually an experience requirement before one may qualify to be a real estate salesperson. T F

34. The police power of the state has reference to the right of the state through its police officers to compel obedience to the law. T F

35. A broker may not act in the dual capacity of broker and undisclosed principal in a transaction. T F

36. The concept of a single license to practice real estate is applicable in the licensing laws of the various states. T F

37. It is now required that all license fees be used for administration of the license law, for adequate enforcement, and for real estate education. T F

38. A Realtor may not overprice a property as a strategem to obtain a listing. T F

39. A Realtor may advertise, saying that his services are available to the property owners at a stated rate of commission based on sales price. T F

40. A Realtor may not prepare a power of attorney. T F

MULTIPLE CHOICE QUESTIONS

41. It is the obligation of the Realtor to state what he considers as a reasonable price on the property to:
( )   The prospect
( )   The owner
( )   The multiple listing service
( )   The local real estate board

42. A Realtor may acquire an interest on behalf of himself or his family in property listed with him, only if:
( )   The price he pays is a reasonable one and entirely fair to the owner
( )   The price is based on the valuation set by an outside apprasier
( )   He discloses his true position to his client, and his client consents.
( )   Sanctioned by his local real estate board

43. If a Realtor gets one offer at the listed price, and others below the listed price, he
( )   Need submit only the offer at the listed price
( )   He may limit his submission to the best offer below the listed price, if submitted by a better credit risk than the offeror at the listed price.
( )   Must submit all offers to the owner
( )   May use his own best judgment as to which offer to submit

44. If a Realtor should be suspended by his board for a violation of the Code of Ethics, he
( )   May still designate himself as a Realtor, but he may not actively engage in real estate transactions
( )   Must surrender his broker's license to the state during the period of suspension by his board
( )   Is subject to a fine imposed by his Department of Licensing and Regulation
( )   May not designate himself as a Realtor during the period of his suspension

45. If a Realtor persuades an owner to give him an exclusive listing at the time open listings are in effect, about which the owner tells him, then the Realtor
( )   Is obligated to inform the open listers of his exclusive
( )   May completely disregard the open listers

( ) May require the open listers to remove their signs from the property

( ) Gets a "cut" of the commission if one of the open listers sells

46. If a Realtor holding an exclusive listing is authorized to enlist the services of cooperating brokers, and does so, then these cooperating brokers:

( ) May deal directly with the owner of the property

( ) May deal only through the Realtor holding the exclusive listing

( ) Are entitled to compensation for their services, even though they do not effectuate the sale

( ) Must be members of the multiple listing service

47. If controversies arise among Realtors, they should be:

( ) Litigated

( ) Arbitrated

( ) Publicized

( ) Publicly mediated

48. A Realtor may undertake an appraisal for a fee whose amount is contingent on the value found:

( ) Under no circumstances

( ) Only if the fee is reasaonable

( ) Only if the consent of the local board is obtained

( ) Only if the consent of the state real estate association is obtained

49. A broker is prohibited from using "blind ads" because:

( ) These are necessarily cheap and degrading

( ) They are necessarily limited in property description

( ) They do not state the asking price for the property

( ) They might mislead the reader into thinking they were inserted by the owner

50. If a licensee has been adjudicated incompetent because of mental illness:

( ) His license is permanently revoked

( ) His license may be revoked, but may be reinstated on proof of the removal of his disability

( ) His license may be only suspended

( ) His license must be put in escrow during the period of his disability

ESSAY QUESTIONS

1. What objectives do the license laws hope to accomplish?

2. With license laws in existence, is it necessary for professional organizations to also establish and enforce individual codes of ethics?

3. What is the value of the interpretations of the Codes of Ethics as given in the text?

PROPERTY RIGHTS AND INSTRUMENTS

CHAPTER THREE

THE NATURE OF REAL PROPERTY

Real property consists of land and whatever is annexed to the land with the intent that such annexation be permanent. It includes not only the surface of the land, but also the minerals that lie below the land, and the air rights above the land, consistent with reasonable flight of aircraft. It also includes fixtures, items which were once personal property, but have since become annexed to a building as a permanent part of the structure. Components of buildings, which, prior to assembly and fabrication into the structure, were personal property, become real property on their integration into the improvement. Intangible rights in land, such as easements, are real property. Perennials, not requiring annual cultivation or harvest, are real property.

As real property is fixed and immovable, it is essentially localized, and therefore becomes subject to the "law of the situs", meaning that the law governing real property is the law of the place where the real property is, regardless of the owner's residence. Whatever is not real property is personal property. "Realty" and "Real estate" are synonyms for real property. "Real estate", however, may be used to refer to the business itself, such as in the expression - "He's in real estate."

The physical characteristics of land are its fixed location and immobility, its heterogeneity and uniqueness, and its indestructibility and permanence. The economic characteristics of land are its relative scarcity; the fact that improvements made on it are relatively long lasting; and the value attached to it because of a particular location.

FIXTURES

If an item of personal property is incorporated into a structure with the intent that it become a permanent part thereof, it becomes a fixture and constitutes real property. If, on the other hand, a commercial tenant installs fixtures for the carrying on of his trade during the period of his lease, these trade fixtures, being subject to removal prior to the termination of the lease, are personal property. If the method of attachment of the fixtures is such as to suggest permanent annexation, as would be the case with plumbing and heating equipment, the fixtures would become real property. If the article attached is adapted to the purpose of the structure, such as fabricating machinery in a factory, it would be real property.

The criteria therefore for determining whether a fixture becomes real property are the intent of the parties, the relationship of the parties, the mode of attachment, and the adaptation of the article to the particular structure. A domestic fixture, such as a refrigerator, should be differentiated from fixtures such as counters or shelves, necessary for a merchandiser in carrying on his trade and therefore denominated as trade fixtures.

Questions concerning trade fixtures under commercial tenancies frequently arise and can usually be resolved by going back to the intent of the parties at the time of annexation. A barber, for example, leases a shop and recesses his mirrors in the wall, and anchors his chairs to the floor, seemingly making for a permanent attachment. However, his intent is, prior to lease termination, to remove his chairs and mirrors, rather than leave them as a gift, so to speak, for his lessor.

CONTRACTUAL RIGHTS

As contractual rights give rise to personal causes of action, they are personal property. A lease, for example, is a contract giving the lessee the contractual right to control and possession. A mortgage is also a contract, providing rights for both mortgagor and mortgagee, and, consequently, both leases and mortgages are personal property. Although contracts regarding personal property may in many instances be oral, those transferring title to property must be in writing to be enforceable.

THE BUNDLE OF RIGHTS CONCEPT

Real property may be regarded as consisting of a bundle of rights. The bundle includes the right of use, the right of occupancy, the right of cultivation, the right of exploration, the right to mine and to drill, the right to sell and to assign, the right to lease and to license, the right to devise and inherit, the right to dedicate and give away, the right to share, the right to mortgage and exercise a lien, and the right to trade and exchange.

Although these rights may inhere in an individual, his exercise thereof is subject to such limitations as the state may impose for the sake of the public welfare. In the case of real property publicly owned, these rights may be exercised by the state. Each of these rights may be transferred in a free economy. These rights may be individually owned, concurrently owned by two or more, or institutionally owned.

TITLE TO REAL PROPERTY

The owner of a real property right is said to have "title" to it, giving him a union of the elements necessary to provide full control and possession and providing him with a case of action against any trespass thereon.

Title to real property may be either original or derivative. Original title may vest only in the state. Original title is acquired through discovery, occupancy, conquest, or cession to the state. All other titles are derivative and vested in individuals. Derivative titles may be titles by descent or titles by purchase. In title by descent; as next of kin, one gets title from a decedent under the laws of intestacy. The decedent has failed to make a will, and, in effect, the state makes his will for him and specifies the ones, in relationship to him, to whom his property shall go. Title by purchase includes all the other ways by which individuals acquire title - by deed, by land contract, or by will. Title by will is also called title by devise.

A contract for the sale of real property gives the purchaser an equitable title. This means it is possible for him by court action to compel the seller to go through with the contract and provide him with a deed. When recourse is had to this procedure, it is had through a court decree of specific performance against the seller. With this decree, the seller must comply or be held in contempt of court. The court permits the buyer to apply for this decree, since the other remedy, money damages by breach of contract, would be inadequate, since this money would not enable him to secure another parcel of real property, exactly the same, due to the uniqueness and heterogeneity of real property.

ESTATES IN REAL PROPERTY

An estate is the degree, quantity, nature, and extent of one's interest in real property. The various kinds of estates are:

1. An estate in fee simple. This may also be called a fee simple absolute, or a fee. It is the largest estate possible for one to hold. It is a holding in perpetuity of the entire bundle of property rights, subject only to such limitations as are imposed in the instrument of conveyance.

2. A life estate. This estate constitutes a holding for the period of one's life.

3. A remainder. If the instrument setting up a life estate specifies who is to be the recipient on the death of the holder of the life estate, this recipient is said to have an estate in remainder.

4. A reversion. If control and possession of real property are to return to one on the happening of an event or after the passage of a period of time, such as when a lease expires, one is said to have an estate in reversion.

5. An estate "pur autre vie" (for the life of another). If one's holding of real property is to be measured in duration by the life of someone else, then the estate is called "pur autre vie".

6. A freehold estate. If no fixed period of time can be imposed on one's estate, as in the case of a fee simple or a life estate, the estate is called a freehold estate.

7. A less than freehold estate. If a time limit is placed on one's holding of real property, as in the case of a lease expiring on a specific date, one's estate is then called a less than freehold estate. Such a lease is also called an estate for years, the name given to a conveyance for a stated period.

8. An estate from year to year. This is a less than freehold estate. It never exists for a period beyond one year, and commonly exists only from month to month.

9. An estate at will. This is a less than freehold estate in the form of a tenancy, terminable at any time at the will of either lessor or lessee.

10. An estate of sufferance. This is a less than freehold estate - one in which a lease has expired and the tenant remains in possession, merely at the sufferance of the lessor and subject to eviction at any time.

REAL PROPERTY OWNERSHIPS

1. The fee simple ownership of real property may take the form of a "fee simple determinable". This refers to a real property ownership existing only "so long as", "while", or "during the period that" a certain use prescribed by the grant of conveyance continues. An example would be a conveyance to the University of Michigan "so long as" the real property is used for educational purposes. If, at some future time, the property was no longer so used, it would revert back to the grantor, if living, or to his heirs, if he had died. A fee simple determinable ends automatically when the purpose for which it was prescribed terminates.

2. A "fee simple on condition subsequent" comes about when property is transferred "provided that", "on the condition that" or "if" it be used for a specified purpose. If it should no longer be so used, it reverts back to the grantor, if living, or to his heirs if he has died. There are two differences between this ownership and the ownership in a fee simple determinable. In the fee simple determinable, the words employed are words of duration. In the fee simple on condition subsequent, the words employed are words of condition. In the fee simple determinable, the ownership ends automatically when the purpose specified is no longer being fulfilled. In the fee simple on condition subsequent, it is necessary for the grantor or his heirs to retake possession for the ownership to end.

3. A real estate ownership "in severalty" resides in one person only. Unfortunately, the word "severalty" seems to imply a plural ownership, but here is employed meaning the one person is severed from all others in connection with his ownership. If one individual or one corporation has exclusive ownership, the ownership is in severalty. If the ownership is that of a sole proprietorship, the ownership is in severalty.

4. The real estate ownership known as a "tenancy in common" is ownership held by two people entitling them to an undivided possession, but ownership of separate interests. Such separate interests may be in any proportion so long as the proportion applies to the entire property. For example, one may own 25 per cent, 50 per cent, or 75 per cent as his separate interest. If the instrument creating the tenancy in common fails to specify the relative interests of the separate owners, they will be presumed to be owners of equal interests. Upon the death of one tenant in common, his interest in and title to the real property descend to his heirs or devisees. During the lifetime of the tenant in common, he may sell, lease, or give away his separate interest or any proportion thereof to anyone he chooses.

5. A real estate ownership in joint tenancy is one held jointly by two or more people with equal rights to share in the enjoyment, fruits, control, and possession of the real property during their lives. The distinguishing feature of ownership by joint tenancy is the right of survivorship. On the death of any of the joint tenants, the entire ownership goes to the other joint tenant or tenants. If one of the joint tenants sells his share, the buyer becomes a tenant in common with the remaining joint tenants. Courts do not look favorably on joint tenancies and many states provide, by statute, that all grants or devises of real property to two or more shall be construed to create a tenancy in common, not a joint tenancy, unless expressly stated to be "in joint tenancy and not as tenants in common".

6. A grant or conveyance to husband and wife, in many states, creates a tenancy by the entireties. Each owns the entire title and possesses same rights as the other. On the death of one spouse, the title passes immediately to the other. Neither husband nor wife can sell or devise his or her ownership, inasmuch as the ownership is always in the two together, never in the two apart. In this respect the tenancy by the entireties differs from the joint tenancy, although with respect to the right of survivorship, it is the same. If a husband and wife become divorced they are no longer as one and cannot hold property as tenants by the entireties. In the course of divorce proceedings it is usually determined what share in the property each shall have. Not being so determined in the event of divorce, the tenants by the entireties would become tenants in common.

7. Most states provide for an interest in the real property of the decedent husband to be given to his widow. This is frequently called her dower right. In order for the dower right to apply, there must have been a valid marriage; the husband must have owned the real property during the marriage period; and the husband must have died before his wife. The wife may not be excluded from her dower right by any unilateral action on the part of her husband. If he deeds or gives away his real property, the recipient takes it subject to the dower right. If, however, she joins in the conveyance, this voluntary act on her part waives her dower right. If the husband wills his real property to someone other than his wife, the devisee takes it subject to the widow's dower right. During the husband's lifetime, the dower right is said to be inchoate, since it cannot ripen and materialize until his death. If the wife should die before her husband, her dower right dies with her. Many states provide for a counterpart right in the husband of an interest in his wife's real property, sometimes known as his curtsy right.

8. Several states, particularly in the southwest, have adopted community property laws. These provide for an interest by one spouse in any property acquired by purchase by the other spouse during the marital period. The community property right, however, does not apply to separate property. Separate property is that acquired

before marriage, or by gift, inheritance, or will. Property purchased with separate funds, belonging individually to a spouse, is also separate property.

9. Several states have enacted homestead laws which insure that the family homestead shall be immune from attachment by creditors and protect the wife in her residence against any unilateral action by her husband. Such homestead laws protect husband and wife against eviction by creditors. The wife is protected against dispossession from her husband's sale of the family residence. The widow is protected in her residence against the claims of the creditors against her husband's estate. It is possible under the homestead laws, however, for a valid deed or mortgage to be made of the homestead, provided that both husband and wife join in the conveyance.

10. Although the real estate ownerships known as cooperatives and condominiums will be discussed in detail under separate coverage, it is appropriate at this point to define their meaning. In a cooperative, the occupants buy shares of stock in a corporation that owns and manages their building and pay monthly carrying charges that cover their proportionate share of taxes, mortgages, maintenance, and insurance. Condominiums, on the other hand, are actual unit ownerships in multi-unit structures. They are undivided ownership interests in the land and parts of the structure used in common with the other occupants. They are both horizontal and vertical divisions of real estate. The buyer purchases outright the unit he occupies and gets a recordable deed to show for it. He pays taxes on his unit and his interest in the common elements. He negotiates his own financing on his own unit. On his income tax return he may deduct from his income his interest on his mortgage and his taxes on his unit as well as his proration of taxes and interest charges on the common elements.

REAL PROPERTY RIGHTS AND THE GOVERNMENT

The basis for the right of the government to tax real property is to provide the revenues to pay for the recurring costs of government and its services, such as police and fire protection for the real property concerned.

Under the state's power of eminent domain it may take an owner's real property for a public purpose on payment to him of just compensation. This power may be exercised not only by state and federal governments, but also by local governments and quasi-public bodies, such such as public utilities. The legal proceedings under which this power is exercised are called condemnation proceedings. The power of eminent domain, therefore, is employed to take private real property for the public purposes of schools, public buildings, highways, streets, parks and recreational areas, public communications systems and power lines.

Real property is also subject to the exercise of the police power of the state. This is the power of government to do whatever is necessary in the interests of the health, welfare, and morals of the general public. The exercise of the police power does not result in an actual taking of private real property, but does result in a regulation of the use of private real property. It is under the police power that zoning ordinances and building codes are set up, highway and traffic regulations established, one way streets routed, setback and sideline restrictions imposed, and minimum lot sizes marked out. If a property owner suffers monetary damage as a result of the exercise of the police power, he receives no monetary compensation. The theory is that the public good must supersede the private good.

If a decedent leaves no will and leaves no heirs, the government acquires his real property rights under what is known as "escheat". This is a lapsing or reverting of title to the state because there were no heirs and there was no will. If a real property owner is found guilty of treason or fails to pay his taxes, his real property rights may be confiscated by the state.

The state also regulates the use of real property in that it may not be employed for illegal activities; may not be used in such a way as to injure the property rights of its neighbors; and may not be sold or leased in such a manner as to bring about discrimination because of race, creed, or national origins. There is an increasing trend on the part of government to insist that the use of real property refrain from defiling the environment in the form of air, water, and noise pollution.

TRANSFERRING REAL PROPERTY RIGHTS

Real property rights are transferred by written instruments, such as deeds, mortgages, land contracts, exchange agreements, leases, and wills. Real property rights may be given to the government by dedication. The foregoing are voluntary transfers. Involuntary transfers of real property rights occur when private property is taken under eminent domain, mortgage foreclosure sales, tax sales, sales by a trustee under an involuntary bankruptcy decree, and by reason of adverse possession and prescription.

If a person occupies the real property of another for the period prescribed by law, if he does so without permission and therefore adversely to the true owner, if he does so notoriously and openly so that the true owner could see him and evict him, if he does so exclusively, his adverse possession may ripen into title and constitute a means of transferring ownership to himself. The theory behind adverse possession is that the true owners of real property should not sleep on their rights, that land should be employed for constructive advantage and that it should not lie idle.

Easements are rights in land, such as a right of way, rather than the land itself. An easement may be acquired by reason of an adverse use for the specified period of time. The name given this procedure in the case of an easement is "prescription", rather than "adverse possession".

In the cases of both adverse possession and prescription, the adverse use must be reasonably continuous. If the first adverse user dies, but his heirs continue his adverse possession, they may "tack on" their period of adverse holding to his to accumulate the required period of time for the holding.

Adverse possession or prescription may not be acquired against the government.

EASEMENTS

1. Easements are property rights, not of the property itself, but in the use of some part of the land, such as a right of way over land for certain purposes, such as for installing and maintaining sewer lines, electric lighting, telephone communications, or a right of passage, such as a driveway over someone else's property. A pipeline company exercises an easement when it is permitted to put a pipeline across someone else's land. An electric utility exercises an easement when it is permitted to put overhead or underground wires over or under someone else's land.

2. An easement may be created by selling a right in land through a conveyance in writing. An easement may be given away through an instrument in writing. The state may obtain an easement by exercising its power of eminent domain. On approval by the state public utilities commission, a private public utility may employ the power of eminent domain to secure the easement essential for the public service authorized. An easement may come about by reason of necessity inherent in a particular situation. If a tract owner sold a lot in the center of his tract, the buyer could secure egress and ingress only by crossing over other real property in the tract. The law in such a case would imply an easement by way of necessity. As has been previously indicated, an easement may be acquired by prescription.

3. If an easement is created for the benefit of another tract of land, it becomes known as an easement appurtenant and runs with the land. If there are adjoining tracts, and the owner of one grants the right of ingress to the owner of the other so that he may get to the highway beyond, he has granted an easement appurtenant. Such an easement, as previously stated, runs with the land. This means that the right thereof automatically accrues to subsequent owners of the tract benefited. The tract benefited is known as the dominant tenement and the tract serving is known as the servient tenement.

4. If an easement accrues for the benefit of an individual or corporate entity, it is known as an easement in gross. It is for his or its use and does not necessarily relate to the benefit of any parcel of land. Unlike the easement appurtenant, therefore, an easement in gross does not run with the land. If the easement in gross is to an individual, it dies with the individual.

5. Easements are different from emblements. These are the rights of a farm tenant to go on land he has farmed and garner his share of the crops he has raised.

6. Easements are also different from licenses. Licenses are merely permissions to use someone else's property for a particular purpose and create no property right in the holder. Not being real property, licenses may be created verbally. They are usually temporary in duration, and revocable at the will of the licensor.

CONTRACT FOR THE SALE OF REAL PROPERTY

This is the primary and most important document in the real estate transaction. It sets the sequential pattern and is the scenario for all that is to follow. The Statute of Frauds requires that it be in writing in order to be enforceable.

The minds of the parties must meet on the terms embodied in the contract of sale. Both parties must be of sound mind and adult age. There may be no duress imposed on either party. The objective of the contract of sale must be a legal one and consideration must be furnished by both parties thereto. The agreement of the parties to the contract of sale must be a genuine agreement, not one obtained by fraud or by misrepresentation.

The contract itself is preceded by the offer to buy. This sets forth the terms and conditions on which the buyer will buy and the seller will sell. The offer to buy includes a legal description of the property to be sold; the selling price; the instrument of conveyance, whether it be warranty deed, bargain and sale deed, or land contract; and the encumbrances, such as easements, building restrictions, mortgages, leases, mechanics' liens, and unpaid taxes, to which the title to be conveyed will be subject; the evidence of title to be furnished the buyer, whether it be in the form of an abstract or a title insurance policy; the survey of the property to be supplied the buyer; the provisions to be made for apportionments of mortgage interest, property insurance premiums, rents and other income from the property; time when possession is to be given to the buyer; and what rent is to be paid by the seller, if he retains occupancy for a period after the conveyance of title. The contract of sale also stipulates the rights of the parties in present occupancy of the property. It sets a time for the closing of the transaction as well as the place where it is to occur.

The offer to buy must be accepted by the seller in order to consummate the contract of sale. If the seller wishes to change the terms as set forth in the offer to buy, he should do so in the form of a counteroffer. After the seller accepts the offer, a copy with both the buyer's and seller's signatures should be left with him and a copy bearing both signatures should be delivered to the buyer. If the seller is married, his spouse should sign the contract in order to bar any dower or curtsy right that might otherwise exist. If the title be joint or a tenancy by the entireties, both spouses should sign as the sellers.

It is not necessary that the contract of sale be witnessed or acknowledged to establish its validity. If the seller refuses to convey title or if the buyer refuses to pay the purchase price, the aggrieved party may secure specific performance, rescission, or money damages. Rescission means calling off the whole deal.

Under an option contract, the real property owner gives another person the privilege of buying the real property at a fixed price within a specified period of time. The option contract, to be binding, must provide consideration. The option contract does not have to be consummated.

THE DEED

A deed is a written instrument conveying legal title to the property. Its grantor must be of legal age and sound mind. It must state consideration and embody words of conveyance. It must describe the property being conveyed. It must contain the signatures of the granting parties. It must be delivered to and accepted by the grantee. The marital status of the grantor should be stated. If, for example, the grantor is single and this is so stated, no doubt arises because of the failure of a spouse to be included. If the grantor is a corporation, the deed should carry the corporate seal. Some states require that the word "seal" or the letters "l. s." (place of the seal) adjoin the grantor's signature, even though he is an individual person. If tax transfer stamps are required by law they should be fixed to the deed. If title is being conveyed subject to encumbrances, these should be spelled out in the deed. It is not necessary for the grantee to sign the deed.

The contract of sale stipulates the kind of deed to be delivered to the grantee. If it is a full covenant and warranty deed, it spells out the covenants or promises that the grantor makes to the grantee. In the covenant of seizin, the grantor promises that he has, as legal owner, the right to convey. In the covenant of quiet enjoyment, the grantor promises that no one, with title paramount to his, will disturb the grantee in his control and possession. In the covenant against encumbrances, the grantor promises that there are no encumbrances against the title, except those he has specifically listed in the deed itself. In the covenant of further assurances, the grantor promises that he will execute any other documents that may be necessary to establish full title in the grantee. In the covenant of warranty forever, the grantor promises that he will defend the grantee's title, should this become necessary.

If the deed is to be a bargain and sale deed, the grantor either expresses or implies that he has an interest to convey, but nothing more. If the bargain and sale deed is with covenant, the grantor goes one step further, and says that during his control and possession of the property, he has done nothing to encumber the property nor has he permitted anyone else to encumber the property.

If the deed is to be a quitclaim deed, the grantor says that if he has any interest to convey, he quits his claim to this interest. The grantor makes no covenants or warranties. The quitclaim deed is employed to clear clouds on title and is used when the grantor has a possible interest, and it is desired to eliminate this possibility.

In order to protect himself against subsequent claims against the property, the grantee should see to it that his deed is publicly recorded. This may be in the office of register of deeds in the county where the property is located. By means of this public record, the grantor puts the public on notice that title is now vested in this grantee. This is called constructive notice, and it is just as effective as actual notice against subsequent claimants.

However, before the deed may be recorded, it must be acknowledged. This means that the grantor must appear before an official authorized to take oaths, such as a notary public, and swear that he is the person named as grantor and that he is conveying his interest of his own free will as the deed says. The notary or other public official then states on the deed that this grantor appeared before him, that he was known to him, and that he did so swear.

THE MORTGAGE

The mortgage is a pledge of real property as security for an indebtedness. The acknowledgement of the indebtedness is either in the form of a promissory note or a bond. The mortgage instrument refers to this note or bond.

There are two different theories about mortgages, the title theory and the lien theory. Under the title theory, the mortgage instrument actually conveys title to the creditor as security for the loan. This title, however, reverts to the borrower on his payment of his indebtedness. Under the lien theory of mortgages, title remains in the debtor, and the mortgage provides the creditor only with a lien, or hold, on the property as security. Some states follow the title theory. The majority follow the lien theory. Even though the debt is not paid on the due date, the borrower is permitted a period of time, called his equity of redemption, to make good his default. In order to limit the period of time during which he may exercise this equity of redemption, the creditor forecloses, or cuts off, this equity. This in turn is followed by a mortgage foreclosure sale, the proceeds of which are used to pay off the creditor. If any balance remains, it belongs to the debtor. Even after a mortgage foreclosure sale, there may be a statutory period of redemption during which the debtor can still make good his default. The mortgage may be worded to permit the mortgagee to purchase the property at foreclosure sale, enabling him to bid up to the amount of the mortgage indebtedness, without producing any cash.

The mortgage is signed by the mortgagor and acknowledged in the same manner as the deed. If the mortgagee fails to record his mortgage, he has no recourse against a subsequent purchaser who was unaware of the existence of the mortgage. Under the acceleration clause in the mortgage, the mortgagee may declare the indebtedness in the entire amount of the balance remaining, due and payable upon any default by the mortgagor. Under the property insurance clause, the mortgagor is obligated to maintain insurance on the property.

Under the prepayment clause, the mortgagor is given the privilege of prepayment if he so desires. The mortgage may contain a receiver clause, authorizing the mortgagee to secure a receiver for the property when in default. It may also contain an owner rent clause, authorizing the mortgagee to charge the mortgagor rent during the period he is in default. It may likewise contain an attorney's fee clause, empowering the mortgagee to charge the cost of his attorney's fees in the event of foreclosure against the mortgagor. The estoppel clause in the mortgage requires the mortgagor to provide a certificate of the amount of indebtedness he owes at any time on the request of the mortgagee. The mortgagee's certificate of reduction is its counterpart, inasmuch as it requires the mortgagee, on request of the mortgagor, to state at any time by how much the original principal of the mortgage has been reduced.

A subordination clause in the mortgage is an agreement by the mortgagee to subordinate his claim in favor of a new claim the debtor may put on the property. If there is a default in prior mortgage clause, this permits a second mortgagee creditor to make good a deficiency in payment of a first mortgage, add this payment to the amount of the second mortgage, and thus forestall a foreclosure of the first mortgage.

KINDS OF MORTGAGES

1. A term mortgage runs for a relatively short period of time, with interest payments being made only during this interim, and the entire amount of the principal becoming due and payable at the end of this term.

2. The usual type of mortgage today, however, is the amortizing mortgage, in which monthly payments of the same amount are made over the lifetime of the mortgage, part of each of these payments being for principal, part for interest.

3. The expression "budget mortgage" has come to be employed in cases where the monthly payments cover interest, principal, taxes, special assessments, and insurance.

4. This expression has expanded into the term "package mortgage", in which monthly payments also apply to the mechanical and electrical appliances installed in the structure.

5. "The open-end mortgage" is one which permits the debtor to open up the end of the mortgage to its original amount under certain terms, by borrowing an additional sum to make it such and thereby adding to the overall amount of his indebtedness.

6. "The blanket mortgage" is one covering two or more parcels of real property. It is accompanied by a partial release clause, which provides for the release of an individual parcel from the impact of blanket coverage upon sale of the individual parcel and earmarking the proceeds toward a reduction of the blanket mortgage.

7. A construction loan mortgage is one securing advances for construction and characterized by such disbursements being made at various stages of construction. This usually allows the borrower to pay interest only as he uses his borrowings in construction. The lender enjoys the security advantage of having more of the construction completed as he makes his advances.

8. The Federal Housing Administration insures approved lenders against losses from the failure of the borrower to make the pay-

ments required under his mortgage loan. The borrower must be capable of repaying the loan and the property must meet the standards of security as prescribed by the Federal Housing Administration. The borrower pays the premium for this insurance.

9. The Veterans Administration guarantees the payment of loans for the acquisition of homes by qualified veterans on qualified property. Under the Veterans Administration guarantee, the veteran borrower is not required to pay an insurance premium, nor is he required to pay a prepayment penalty.

10. If a mortgage is not insured by the Federal Housing Administration and not guaranteed by the Veterans Administration, it is said to be a conventional mortgage. Insurance may be secured on conventional mortgage loans from private companies, such as the Mortgage Guaranty Insurance Corporation.

If a borrower "assumes" an existing mortgage loan, he becomes personally liable for its payment. If a borrower takes property "subject to" an existing mortgage loan, he does not become liable out of his personal assets for its payment. If, for example, in a situation where the borrower has "assumed" an existing mortgage loan, and the mortgage foreclosure sale fails to bring in sufficient proceeds to make good the mortgage indebtedness, the borrower who had assumed the mortgage would be subject to a deficiency judgment for the balance, having to pay out of his personal assets. If, however, he had taken the property subject to an existing mortgage, he would not be so subject.

When the borrower has paid off his mortgage debt, he is entitled to receive from his creditor a certificate, usually known as a satisfaction of mortgage, stating that he has done so. The borrower should then get this recorded to "clear the record" of the mortgage encumbrance. A subsequent search of the record would by reason of this recording show that the mortgage had been discharged.

In some states a deed of trust is used instead of a mortgage. Under a deed of trust, a borrower conveys the real property, standing as security for the loan, to a third party in trust for the creditor. This third party trustee is empowered with the authority to foreclose the mortgage by a trustee's sale without having to resort to court proceedings.

THE LAND CONTRACT

A property owner may sell his property under a land contract. The buyer makes his payments in installments and upon payment in full receives the deed to the property. The seller retains title as security in the interim.

The land contract may be used when the buyer is unable to secure financing through a mortgage loan from an institutional lender. Or the seller may find it to his advantage to finance the sale himself, rather than have the financing go through an institutional lender. The seller could, of course, accomplish the same purpose through a purchase money mortgage, given by the buyer as security for what he owed. A purchase money mortgage is used when the seller finances the sale by loaning the borrower the difference between the down payment and the purchase price, and takes back as security a mortgage from the buyer on the property. It is called a purchase money mortgage because it constitutes part of the consideration for the property.

LIENS

Liens are the rights of a creditor to force foreclosure proceedings to sell the debtor's property upon his default. Reference has already been made to the mortgage lien, empowering a mortgagee creditor to secure a foreclosure sale of the mortgaged premises.

A mechanic's lien is a right held by anyone who has engaged in work on a property improvement or supplied materials for a property improvement to have the property sold if he has not been paid for his service or materials. The debt owed him would be satisfied out of the proceeds of such a sale. The mechanic's lien attaches from the date the first service is performed or the first materials are furnished. If, prior to that time, there was a recorded mortgage on the property, this mortgage would be superior to the mechanic's lien. The mechanic's lien is a specific lien and therefore attaches only to the specific improvement concerned.

A judgment lien, on the other hand, is a general lien and attaches to all real property within the jurisdiction where the judgment was rendered. A judgment would arise as the result of a favorable judgment in a legal action. Unless the judgment is paid, the real property may be sold to pay the amount of the judgment.

Until they are paid, real property taxes constitute a lien on the property against which they are levied and usually have priority over other liens.

LEASES

Leases are contracts in which the real property owner, called the lessor, delivers control and possession to a lessee in return for a consideration, called rent. The property interest of the lessee is called a leasehold. The property interest of the lessor is called a leased fee.

The obligations of the lessor and lessee with regard to care and maintenance of the property are spelled out in the lease itself. If no such obligations are spelled out, the lessee is under duty only to maintain the property as it was when he secured possession, reasonable wear and tear excepted.

The lease may spell out the particular use which the lessee may make of the premises. If it does not do so, the tenant lessee may make any lawful use of the property. The lessee, in the absence of a provision to the contrary, may assign his lease. His assignee then steps into his shoes, with all of the rights and liabilities of his assignor. The lessee, in the absence of a provision to the contrary, may sublet the premises. The sub-lessee then steps into his shoes, but, unlike the assignment, is under an obligation to return the premises to the lessee at a time, spelled out in the sub-lease, prior to the expiration of the lease.

1. The lease may be a "straight" or "gross" lease, in which a fixed amount of rent is payable periodically. The lessor, however, pays the taxes, the special assessments, and the insurance on the property.
2. At the other extreme is the net lease, under which a fixed amount of rent is also payable periodically, but under which the tenant assumes the responsibility for care and maintenance, and payment of taxes, special assessments, and insurance. The net lease is usually a long-term lease. To guard against the erosive effects of inflation, provision may be made in a net lease for the rent to escalate in proportion to the decline in the purchasing power of the dollar. This escalation clause may be fixed to a recognized index, such as the consumers price index, for the basis for the escalation. Or the lessor may stipulate that the property be re-appraised at designated intervals and that the rent escalate in proportion to the rise in value as indicated by the re-appraisal.
3. If real property is under lease for a merchandising operation, a percentage lease may be employed. The rent is a percentage of the lessee's gross sales, plus, usually, a guaranteed minimum rent. The percentage lease usually contains a recapture clause, authorizing the lessor to recapture the premises in the event the sales of the lessee fall below a stipulated amount. The percentage lease may also contain a clause preventing the lessee from opening up a competitive store within a certain geographical radius. The purpose of such a clause is to circumvent the possibility of a reduction in sales and, therefore, a reduction of rent due to this competition. The percentage lease may also authorize the lessor to inspect the lessee's books to make sure the lessee is reporting the true volume of sales.
4. A lease from month to month means just what it says. It is a straight or gross lease giving the lessee, on payment of the monthly rental, control and possession from month to month. If either the lessor or the lessee desires to terminate the lease, it is usually incumbent on the one so desiring to give the other party a month's notice.
5. It differs from a tenancy at will, which may be terminated by either party at any time.
6. It likewise differs from a tenancy at sufferance in which the lease has expired, but the lessee holds over, and the lessor temporarily "suffers" or permits him to continue in occupancy.
7. If the lease is for a fixed period of time and the tenant holds over, the lessor may often regard the lease as having been renewed under the same rent, terms, and conditions, but for no longer than a year's period of time.
8. If the lease is a ground lease, it is of the ground alone. This could be for the purpose of yard storage or to enable the lessee to erect a building on the ground. If the latter, the period of the lease would

usually be measured by the functional life expectancy of the building.

Regardless of the form the lease may take, it usually contains certain standard provisions. It usually specifies the use that may be made of the premises. There is commonly inserted a clause against assignment or sub-letting, except with the consent of the lessor. It may provide that the lessee put up a deposit to which resort can be had for non-payment of rent. It may also provide for the setting aside of a sum by the lessee to which the lessor can resort if the premises are damaged. This clause is appropriately called a security clause.

The lease also requires the lessee to comply with the requirements of the building department and the health department in connection with his use of the premises. If the premises should become unusable due to fire or other cause, provision is made in the lease for the cessation of rent during this period.

If the lessee is to be given an option to renew or an option to buy, the terms and conditions are set forth in the lease. If the lessor retains the option to sell or renew, but agrees to give the lessee the first opportunity, should he sell or re-lease, the right of first refusal clause exists.

If the leased property is taken by the state under its power of eminent domain, the lessor is compensated, but not the lessee. Therefore, a prudent lessee will seek to incorporate a clause providing him with a share in this compensation, based upon the value of his lease.

If the lessor permits a situation to occur in connection with the leased premises which makes it impossible for the lessee to continue in the use prescribed in the lease, it is known as constructive eviction, and the lessee may move out and be under no further obligation with regard to the lease.

With regard to liability to third parties for injuries they sustain on leased premises, the basic axiom applicable is that liability follows control. If the lessee is exclusively in control, the liability would fall on him. If the injuries are sustained on common elements - areas used in common with other tenants - the lessor would be liable. It should be noted that in many states laws have now been passed imposing on the lessor the duty to keep rented accommodations for residential purposes in repair.

EVIDENCE OF TITLE

Regardless of the property instrument employed, care should be exercised to make sure that the title being conveyed is a marketable title. If the premises are under lease, the lessee should likewise see to it that the title of his lessor is good in order to avoid the possibility of eviction by someone holding title paramount to that of the lessor. This examination of title may be either by an abstract together with a legal opinion thereon or by title insurance.

An abstract of title is a condensed history of title. It is a summary, on public record, regarding the property, together with such facts which may affect title. It contains a history of the payment of taxes imposed on the property. It is usually drawn up by an abstract company. In a sale of real property, it is usually incumbent on the seller to furnish the buyer with an abstract. Also a mortgagee creditor may require the mortgagor debtor to furnish an abstract.

In either event, the party furnished with the abstract should employ an attorney to make a thorough examination of it to determine whether the title is marketable. A marketable title is one which is free from encumbrances other than those specified in the contract of sale. The attorney's examination of the abstract should also show whether there are any defects, gaps, or breaks in the title, such as to make it unmarketable. If so, the attorney in his opinion so declares, and the buyer or mortgagee creditor either requires that they be corrected, or rescinds the transaction.

If the contract of sale specifies that the seller furnish the buyer with a title insurance policy, the title insurance company has its own searchers examine the public records with regard to the property to determine whether it is insurable. If so, an owner's policy, which continues in effect until the property is subsequently sold, is issued to the buyer. The premium for the owner's policy is payable only once. The owner's policy is not assignable. When the property is subsequently sold, it will usually be incumbent on the seller to provide the buyer with a new policy which will, of course, bring a search of the records up to date.

Over and above the owner's title insurance policy, there is a mortgagee's title insurance policy, which the mortgagor debtor furnishes the mortgagee creditor. It differs from the owner's policy in that its amount covers only the amount of the mortgage indebtedness, rather than the value of the property. It is also different from the owner's policy in that it is assignable.

In a few jurisdictions in the United States the Torrens system of title registration is employed. Under this system, the owner of an interest in real property applies to a court of competent jurisdiction to have his title registered. The court refers the application to an examiner to determine whether there are any legitimate claims outstanding against the property. The examiner reports his findings to the court and, if they are favorable in all respects, the court enters an order that a certificate of title be issued to the applicant, and that the proper notation of such certificate be entered on the public records. The applicant also pays a fee to an insurance fund, to which resort may subsequently be had in the event that an error was made in the determination of title which caused monetary damage to someone who had a legitimate claim against the property.

Once the title is registered under the Torrens system, it will not be necessary to make any examination or to draw up any abstract extending back of the date of the registration. The title registration will be conclusive evidence of its validity as of the day of its registration. The Torrens system seems such a desirable procedure that the question naturally arises as to why its adoption has been so limited. The answer is that it may cost more than title insurance, the procedure may take a substantial amount of time, and an individual who had a claim against the property may not receive notice of the Torrens procedure and thus be deprived of a hearing.

THE WILL

The will is a property instrument which designates how the property is to be transmitted at the time of the death of the owner. In the will, the real property owner is known as the devisor and the individual who is to get the real property is known as the devisee. The gift of the real property itself is known as the devise. When the property owner makes the will, he is named as the testator, if male, or the textratrix, if female. The will also names an executor to carry out and administer the terms of the will. At the time the testator makes his will, he must be of full age and of sound mind and his will must not have been made under the pressure of undue influence. If he should later make a supplement to his will, called a codicil, it must be executed in accordance with all of the requirements of the will itself.

The requirements that the will or codicil must meet are set forth in the statutes of the state where the real property is located. These usually stipulate that the testator must have had testamentary intent, which means the intent to make the will. They likewise say that he must publish his will, which means that he must in the presence of witnesses use words indicating that the document in question is his will. The requirements usually go on to stipulate two, and sometimes three witnesses, who must sign the will as witnesses, and in whose collective presence the testator expressed his testamentary intent and referred to the document as his will. The witnesses must not themselves receive anything under the will.

The will takes effect on the testator's death and is then probated, establishing to the appropriate court's satisfaction that the will is genuine, that it has been signed and witnessed as required by law, and that the testator was of sound mind.

If the real property owner makes no will, his real property passes to his heirs at law, as determined by the laws of intestacy of the state where his real property is located. An administrator is then appointed by the appropriate court to see to it that the real property is transmitted as specified by such laws of intestacy.

SUMMARY

Real property is the land and whatever is annexed to it, with the intent that such annexation be permanent. It usually includes fixtures, items which once were personal property, but have since become annexed to a building with the intent that they are to become a permanent part of the structure. Intangible rights in land, such as easements, are real property. Perennials, not requiring annual cultivation or harvest, are real property.

The physical characteristics of land are its fixed location and immobility, its heterogeneity and uniqueness, and its indestructibility and permanence. The economic characteristics of land are its relative scarcity; that its improvements are relatively long lasting; and that particular values attach to particular locations.

Anything that is not real property is personal property. Trade fixtures installed by a lessee for the period of his lease are personal property, since the lessee intends to remove them prior to lease expiration. Contractual rights, such as causes of action, are personal property, and therefore, contracts, such as leases and mortgages, are in themselves regarded as personal property, even though the subject matter to which they relate is real property. The main reason for drawing the distinction between personal property and real property is that conveyances of real property must be in writing to be enforceable and that it is governed by the law of the situs, the law applicable to the place where the real property is located. Personal property, on the other hand, may in many instances be conveyed orally and is governed by the law of the person, the law applicable to the residence of the person.

Real property may be regarded as a bundle of rights, including the right to sell, lease, use, give away, or will. The owner of the entire bundle of rights or the owner of any one or more of these rights is said to have "title" thereto. Even though a contract for the sale of real property does not in itself convey legal title thereto, it does convey equitable title to the purchaser, which enables him by court action to compel the seller to go through with the contract of sale and provide him with the deed.

An estate in real property is the degree, quantity, nature, and extent of one's interest in real property. The largest estate possible to hold is an estate in fee simple, a holding in perpetuity of the entire bundle of rights in a parcel of real property. A life estate constitutes a holding for the period of one's life. The individual who is to get the property on the death of the holder of the life estate is called a remainderman, and the estate itself is called a remainder. If the period of one's holding is indefinite in time, such as in a fee simple or a life estate, it is called a freehold estate.

The state has the power to take an owner's real property for a public purpose on the payment of just compensation. This is called the state's power of eminent domain. The state also has the power to regulate the use of real property, and this is called its police power. It is under the police power that zoning ordinances and building codes are established.

A real property ownership in severalty resides in one person only. A real property ownership in two or more, in which each has undivided possession, but an ownership of a separate percentage interest, is called a tenancy in common. A real property ownership, held jointly by two or more, under which, on the death of any of the joint owners, those remaining are automatically to succeed to his share, is called a joint tenancy with rights of survivorship. In many states, if there is a conveyance of real property to husband and wife, under which each owns the property, subject to the same rights as the other, a tenancy by the entireties has been created, and, on the death of one spouse, the title immediately passes to the survivor.

Most states provide for an interest in the real property of the decedent husband, called a dower right, to be given to his widow. Some states provide for a counterpart right in the husband in his wife's property. This is called his curtsy right. Some states have adopted community property laws, providing for an interest by one spouse in any real property acquired by purchase by the other spouse during the marital period.

Easements are real property rights, not of the real property itself, but in the use of some part of it, such as for a right of way. They are called easements appurtenant if they are to benefit, primarily, an adjacent parcel of land by making for easier ingress and egress. They are called easements in gross if they are primarily for the benefit of an individual.

The contract of sale is the most important document in a real estate transaction. It prescribes the price for the property; the terms under which this price may be paid; the kind of deed to be delivered; the time and place for the closing of the transaction. The contract of sale comes about when the offer to buy a property is accepted by the owner of the property.

The deed is the instrument which conveys title to the buyer on delivery to and acceptance by him. If it is a full covenant and warranty deed, it spells out the promises that the seller makes the buyer about the validity of the title. If it is a quitclaim deed, it merely releases whatever claim the maker may have. In order to protect himself against any subsequent claims against the property, the buyer should get his deed on public record.

The mortgage is a conveyance of real property as security for an indebtedness. If the debtor defaults, the mortgage authorizes the public sale of the property, out of which proceeds the indebtedness may be paid. The debtor is, however, permitted a period of time, known as his equity of redemption, in which he may make good his default and recover his property. The type of mortgage in most common use today is the amortizing mortgage, under which each periodic payment allocates a part for payment on principal and a part for payment on interest.

The Federal Housing Administration insures mortgage loans to qualified borrowers and by approved lenders on qualified properties. The Veterans Administration guarantees mortgage loans to qualified borrowers and by approved lenders on qualified properties. It is possible to secure comparable insurance from private lenders on qualified properties when the borrower does not have Federal Housing Administration insurance or Veterans Administration guarantees. These loans are called conventional mortgage loans.

Property may be sold under land contract by which the payment is made by the buyer in a series of installments. The seller retains title to the property until all the payments are made and only then is a deed for the property delivered to the buyer.

A mechanic's lien is a right of anyone who has provided a service in connection with a property improvement or who has supplied materials for a property improvement to have the property sold to secure payment for the debt owed him. A judgment lien is the right of a judgment creditor to have the property sold of the person against whom he secured a judgment which has not been paid. Property may likewise be sold under a tax lien if the taxes thereon are not paid.

Leases are contracts by means of which control and possession of real property are delivered to a lessee. The owner of the property is called the lessor and the rentor of the property is called the lessee. The interest which the lessee holds is termed a leasehold and the interest which the lessor holds is a leased fee.

An abstract is a condensed history of title, examined by an attorney to determine whether the title is marketable. A title insurance policy insures the holder against defects in title. The Torrens system of title registration is a means by which the conclusiveness of the validity of title can be established.

A will is the document under which the real property owner directs how his real property is to be transmitted on his death. If he does not make a will, his real property goes to his next of kin, as stipulated by the laws of intestacy where the real property is located.

GLOSSARY

ABSTRACT OF TITLE - A condensed history of title

ADMINISTRATOR - A person appointed by the court of appropriate jurisdiction to administer the estate of a decedent who left no will

ADVERSE POSSESSION - The right of an occupant of land, where his occupancy has been actual, hostile, visible, continuous, and distinct for the statutory period, to acquire title against the true owner.

CLOUD ON TITLE - An outstanding claim, which, if valid, would impair a title.

CONVEYANCE - The medium by which real property title is transferred

COVENANT - A promise

DEDICATION - A conveyance of real property for a public use and an acceptance by the appropriate public body

DEFAULT - The failure to perform an obligation

DEFICIENCY JUDGMENT - The difference between the indebtedness sued for and the amount realized at foreclosure sale

ENCUMBRANCE - A claim attaching to real property

FORECLOSURE - A court process instituted by a mortgagee to defeat the equity of redemption of the mortgagor

MARKETABLE TITLE - A title so good that a court will compel a buyer to accept it; a title free from clouds or encumbrances

PURCHASE MONEY MORTGAGE - A mortgage given by the buyer to the seller to cover part payment of the purchase price

QUIET ENJOYMENT - The right of the owner to use the property without interference by anyone having paramount title

REDEMPTION - The right of the mortgagor to redeem the property by paying the indebtedness after the due date

SPECIFIC PERFORMANCE - A decree from the court of appropriate jurisdiction compelling the defendant to carry out the terms of the contract

SUBLETTING - A leasing by a lessee of part of the period of his lease

SURVEY - The process by which a plot of land is measured

ZONING ORDINANCE - A regulation of land use by a municipality

TRUE AND FALSE QUESTIONS

1. Real property is the land and whatever is annexed to the land.   T   F

2. Real property includes perennials.   T   F

3. "Realty" and "real estate" are synonyms for real property.   T   F

4. Heterogeneity is an economic characteristic of real property.   T   F

5. Original title vests in the first holder, whether an individual or the state.   T   F

6. A title by descent comes about when one acquires real property under a will.   T   F

7. A lease is a less than freehold estate.   T   F

8. Only the state government may exercise the power of eminent domain.   T   F

9. The exercise of the police power results in the taking of real property.   T   F

10. If a property owner suffers monetary damage as the result of the exercise of the police power, he receives no monetary compensation.   T   F

11. Escheat is a lapsing of title to the state because there were no heirs and there was no will.   T   F

12. In a fee simple determinable, ownership ends automatically when the purpose specified no longer obtains.   T   F

13. Upon the death of one tenant in common, his interest automatically passes to the other tenants in common, under their rights of survivorship.   T   F

14. A tenant by the entireties may dispose of his share during his lifetime.   T   F

15. The interest in the real property of a decedent husband given to his widow is called her dower right.   T   F

16. By joining with her husband in his conveyance of real property, the wife waives her curtsy right.   T   F

17. Condominiums are unit ownerships in multi-unit structures.   T   F

18. Condominium owners negotiate their own financing on their own units.   T   F

19. Easements are rights in land.   T   F

20. An easement appurtenant runs with the land.   T   F

21. Licenses are easements of relatively short duration.   T   F

22. A contract for the sale of real property must be in writing to be enforceable.   T   F

23. Contracts of sale must be both witnessed and acknowledged in order to establish their validity.   T   F

24. A Rescission means the money damages acquired by the aggrieved party under breach of contract.   T   F

25. Both the grantor and the grantee must sign the deed in order to make it effective.   T   F

26. The only covenant made by the grantor in the quitclaim deed is the covenant of title.   T   F

27. A deed must be acknowledged before it may be recorded.   T   F

28. Foreclosure means cutting off the equity of redemption.   T   F

29. A package mortgage is one covering two or more parcels of property.   T   F

30. The veteran pays an insurance premium for the guarantee afforded by the Veterans Administration.   T   F

31. Under a deed of trust, a borrower conveys the real property, standing as security for the loan, to a third party in trust for the creditor.   T   F

32. Under a land of contract, the buyer does not receive the deed to the property until he has completed all his installment payments.   T   F

33. The mechanic's lien is a general lien.   T   F

34. The property interest of the lessee is a leased fee.   T F

35. In a straight lease, the lessor pays the taxes, the special   T F
    assessments, and the insurance on the property.

36. The net lease is usually a long term lease.   T F

37. A percentage lease usually contains a recapture clause.   T F

38. If a lease is for a fixed period, and the tenant holds over,   T F
    the lessor may regard the lease as having been renewed for
    its full original period.

39. If the lessee has the privilege of renewing the lease, this is   T F
    called his right of first refusal.

40. The buyer usually pays for the abstract of title.   T F

MULTIPLE CHOICE QUESTIONS

41. The premium for the owner's title insurance policy is payable:
    ( )   In installments
    ( )   Only once
    ( )   On execution of the contract of sale
    ( )   On the acknowledgement of the deed

42. The mortgagee's title insurance policy is:
    ( )   Not assignable
    ( )   For the amount of the mortgage indebtedness
    ( )   For the value of the property
    ( )   Required under the Torrens system

43. Under the Torrens system:
    ( )   The title is registered
    ( )   The deed is registered
    ( )   The cost is usually less than under title insurance
    ( )   There is no insurance fund

44. The will becomes effective:
    ( )   As of the date of its execution
    ( )   On probate
    ( )   On witnessing and acknowledgement
    ( )   On the death of the testator

45. The individual appointed to carry out the terms of a will is:
    ( )   The administrator
    ( )   The executor
    ( )   The receiver
    ( )   The probate director

46. The legal proceedings exercised under the power of eminent domain are:
    ( )   Police power proceedings
    ( )   Zoning proceedings
    ( )   Condemnation proceedings
    ( )   Regulatory proceedings

47. Giving real property to the government for public use is called:
    ( )   Escheat
    ( )   Prescription
    ( )   Community property giving
    ( )   Dedication

48. A conveyance of real property to husband and wife may create:
( )   A tenancy by the entireties
( )   A tenancy in common
( )   A tenancy in severalty
( )   A joint tenancy without rights of survivorship

49. The deed covenant which promises the grantee that no one, with title paramount to that of the grantor, will disturb his possession is:
( )   The covenant of seizin
( )   The covenant of quiet enjoyment
( )   The covenant against encumbrances
( )   The covenant of further assurances

50. The lease in which the lessee not only pays rent, but also assumes the responsibility for care and maintenance, taxes, special assessments, and insurance is called:
( )   The gross lease
( )   The straight lease
( )   The ground lease
( )   The net lease

ESSAY QUESTIONS

1. What should a prudent buyer require by way of title evidence?

2. Why is real property regarded as consisting of a bundle of rights?

3. What are the ways by which the government affects real property?

PLANNING
AND ZONING

CHAPTER FOUR

INTRODUCTION

Until comparatively recent times, the holding and use of real property by the individual was subject to governmental interference and control only if the individual's use was tortious to other people and amounted to a public or private nuisance. The concept of governmental restriction of real property use was regarded as a radical invasion of individual property rights. Over recent years, however, this concept has given way to a recognition that the government may regulate land use in the public interest, this use being a proper exercise by government of its police power. Restrictive regulation of what a real property owner may do with his ownership is now accepted. Planning, and its implementation by zoning, building codes, and subdivision controls, is now regarded as essential. Land use regulation has now come of age, sophisticated in form and working as a medium for the accomplishment of social, economic, and political change.

Although planning and zoning are inherently functions of the state, enabling state legislation has delegated authorization for their use at the local level, principally within the municipalities. The courts of the states usually construe this delegation liberally, and include within it not only the powers expressly given, but also those which can be fairly and reasonably implied. The courts concern themselves primarily with determining whether local ordinances are within the ground rules laid down by the state legislature.

PLANNING

The purpose of planning is to provide for orderly growth, to anticipate problems and attempt to work out solutions in advance, to formulate methods for changing the environment for the betterment of the community and its citizens, and to guide the physical manifestation of the population increase on the land.

Although the concern of this text is with planning at the local level, note should be taken of planning at the state, regional, and federal levels. Such planning may focus on a particular problem, as in the case of the planning done by water resources commissions, in which several states, like those abutting the Great Lakes, plan for their proper conservation.

The scope of planning has recently been broadened to encompass the preservation of the ecology. Such planning aims to preserve areas of open space, guard against the pollution of natural resources, make more land available for park and recreational areas, provide a milieu for attractive landscaping, utilize the natural contours of the land, and consider restraints on future population growth.

Present day planning is also concerned with balance — balancing growth on the one hand with tax ratables to sustain such growth on the other — balancing residential areas on the one hand with the economic viability of providing employment on the other — balancing aesthetic and architectural standards on the one hand with the financial limitations to pay for them on the other. Some planning concerns itself with achieving a balanced ethnic, economic, and age mix for its population.

Among the more specific planning objectives are those to facilitate mass transit, to keep through traffic out of residential areas, to revitalize downtown areas in the larger cities, to consolidate school districts, to locate high rise apartments within walking distance of employment, and to guard against urban sprawl.

THE PLANNING COMMISSION

This is the organization responsible for setting up planning objectives and suggesting the methods by which they might be attained. It may be appointed or it may be elective. It usually serves as a staff, rather than a line agency, and advises and recommends rather than ordering and directing the local body politic.

The planning commission takes physical and social inventories of the community it serves — families, age groups, their employment, income ranges, in and out migration, and present locations of homes and businesses. It meets with representative local organizations, and ascertains local needs and desires. It identifies areas of major concern to the community it serves. It reviews and evaluates research data it collects and determines the pertinence of such data to local problems.

The planning commission may require the services of a staff organization to carry out and administer its policies. This may be headed by a planning director, guiding, coordinating, and directing the work of the staff personnel and constituting the liaison with the other departments of government and the general public. He and his key personnel may be professionally trained in planning techniques.

On the basis of its studies, the planning commission recommends to the community the adoption of a master plan by which future development may be guided. The master plan outlines the areas appropriate for single-family residential, multi-family residential, and the various classifications of commercial and industrial usages. Public projects suggested in the master plan are evolved only after due consideration has been given to the ability of the locality to carry them out without the imposition of unreasonable tax burdens. The master plan outlines what utilities are needed, what recreational facilities should be provided for, and what vehicular traffic patterns are most appropriate. It suggests limitations on the density of population concentrations within specific areas. It locates major land uses separately in the areas for which they are best suited.

Subdivisions and developments must be consistent with the master plan. Zoning ordinances and building codes should be enacted with the master plan as a framework of reference. If variances in zoning ordinances and building codes are approved, they must be in harmony with the master plan. If the locality expands by reason of annexation of other areas, such expansion must not be beyond the limitations imposed by the master plan. The plan should be flexible enough to accommodate changes as events and the dynamics of growth make them necessary. Throughout, the master plan serves as a guide within which decisions on land use, whether by individuals, corporations, or the community itself, can be made.

Some master plans now incorporate planned unit developments and emphasize the preservation of the diminishing supply of open space. Some call for the acquisition of farm land and its proper development under an agricultural land trust. Some permit developers an increase in allowable densities in return for their setting aside open space. Others stipulate that facilities drawing people from wide areas - corporate office buildings, hospitals, and cultural and educational centers - be centralized in downtown areas.

The planning commission recommends to the local governing body the zoning ordinances and building codes necessary to carry out the policies and provisions of the master plan. The planning commission determines whether plats submitted for proposed subdivisions are consistent with the master plan and requires that the necessary improvements and utilities for these subdivisions be provided for before it will give its approval for the "go-ahead". The planning commission also engages in periodic reviews of the master plan and translates its current thinking into new and significant programs for incorporation into the master plan.

Many planning commissions now think that there is nothing sacred about the concept of continued growth for their communities and that the ideology of unrestricted growth is the ideology of the cancer cell. Such planning commissions are therefore recommending to their localities just how large they should be and that limitations be imposed on the amount of future population to be absorbed.

Planning commissions may recommend against the development of sites where septic tanks prove inoperable, based on soil porosity tests. They may likewise advise on proper sanitary and solid waste disposal controls and proper setbacks for dwellings in water-oriented sites. If a community is within close proximity of a navigable lake or river, the planning commission will be particularly concerned with suitable land development controls.

Suburban areas may be planned as self-contained units with their own shopping, recreational, school, church, and transportation facilities, or they may be planned as "bedroom" or "dormitory" areas for nearby urban centers. Planning commissions will advise curved street patterns for residential areas that should be kept free from the hazards of dust, noise, and heavy traffic. Where a residential area is adjacent to commercial or industrial uses, a buffer zone of parks or playgrounds may be advised by way of protection.

Planning commissions may try to guard against unattractive strip developments, decay and congestion, and making suburban land inaccessible for blue-collar jobs. They may suggest pedestrian malls, wide plazas, and vest pocket parks. They may advise the closing of downtown streets to vehicular traffic during shopping hours. Instead of emphasizing the physical shape of a city, some planning commissions are now emphasizing its social and economic developments, over both the short and long term.

The recommendations of some planning commissions are concerned with architectural continuity and the preservation of historic buildings. Others may aim to preserve the character of a small community, whose residents desire to retain the quiet country atmosphere that attracted them to settle there. It should be said, parenthetically, however, that in locality after locality, planning to achieve a desirable local environment has been superseded by planning to meet the school tax bills.

ZONING

Zoning is the tool employed to carry out the goals and objectives of planning. Zoning is to be used to accomplish these intended aims and may not be utilized to attain objectives outside of their scope. Zoning is authorized under police power and is invoked to protect the public against irresponsible uses of real property.

It is exercised by means of ordinances, adopted at the local level, which determine and regulate the use of real property. These ordinances are valid only if they promote the general welfare and are made with reasonable consideration to the character of the district to which they apply. They must be made with the intent of conserving the value of real property and encouraging the most appropriate use of real property throughout the community, taking into consideration its peculiar suitability for particular uses.

The purpose of zoning is to lessen congestion in the streets; secure safety from fire, flood and panic; to promote health, morals, or the general welfare; to provide adequate light and air; to prevent the overcrowding of land and buildings; and to avoid undue concentration of the population. The zoning adopted must be consistent with the applicable master plan.

The specified purposes and standards of zoning must be read together. They are intended to be an aid in the development of real property in planned and appropriate directions. They are not intended to be a way of unduly restricting economic and population growth. Zoning must resist pressures for favored treatment. It may not be used to control who your neighbors may be and to assure that they will be the so-called "right" people. Zoning must be kept current, for conditions in a community are constantly changing and new methods of zoning are constantly being invented. The planning commission is responsible for keeping alert and looking ahead and recommending changes in zoning ordinances as changing conditions dictate.

Zoning affects the interests of more people than any other regulation at the local level. Zoning has a lasting effect on the future of the entire community. It may likewise have an effect on adjacent communities. A zoning ordinance in one community, therefore, may not be adopted in complete disregard of a zoning ordinance in a neighboring community. It cannot, so to speak, build an impregnable municipal boundary wall around itself, and arbitrarily exclude reasonable uses from entry therein.

The zoning ordinance may include the building code and subdivision controls. It may provide for land uses, lot sizes, building set-backs and side-line restrictions, building heights, and the set-aside of open space. It may prevent the overcrowding of land and undue concentration of buildings by regulating the use and the bulk of buildings in relationship to the land surrounding them. It may protect against fire, explosion, noxious fumes and odors, heat, dust, smoke, glare, noise, vibration, and raidoactivity. It may lessen congestion on streets and public highways. It may defend against encroachments on land and air space and against unbridled population concentrations. It may use the principle of planned unit development or cluster zoning. It may provide incentives to encourage retail and residential use, and to discourage commercial uses in certain areas. It may try to create small quiet spots near metropolitan areas by banning buildings therein.

Although zoning regulations may differ from one zoning district to another, they must be uniform within the district itself. If a zoning ordinance is attacked in the courts, it is presumed to be valid, and the attacking party has the burden of proof in sustaining the contrary. The courts also take the position that it is not within their province to pass upon the wisdom of zoning legislation and substitute their judgment for that of the community.

The courts are willing to permit localities to try to adopt means which they believe will meet their problems. They have likewise sustained the principle of zoning a district exclusively for industrial or commercial use. The courts have also recognized the impact of the tax structure on the local welfare, believing that it is legitimate for a community to seek non-residential ratables and set aside land to attract them.

BUILDING CODES

Building codes usually form part of zoning ordinances and are likewise set up under police power authorizing the necessary to be done for the public health, safety, and morals. Building codes therefore guard against hazardous conditions such as inadequate means of egress in case of a fire; deteriorated or inadequate foundations; rotted, broken, or missing steps or porch members; badly cracked or bulging masonry; damaged or leaking roof gutters; inadequate waste containers; broken floor, roof, or ceiling joists; defective or rotten flooring; storage of combustible materials in basement or attic; and lack of protection against rodent infestation, within a building.

Plumbing violations include lack of required bathing or toilet facilities; inoperative flushing mechanisms in toilet tanks; gas-fired water heaters located in bath or toilet rooms; drain stoppages or leading piping; no shut-off valve on water service; and insufficient water pressure.

Among the electrical violations are excessive use of extension cords; fuse boxes and panels filled with dust and dirt; and extension cords running through doorways, under rugs stapled to wood baseboards, door casings, or through holes in partitions or floors. Other electrical violations are insufficient lighting and switches for stairways and corridors and, in multiple dwellings, no wall switches in every fixture.

Among the heating violations are combustible construction or other materials located near heating equipment; improperly vented or defective gas or oil-fired space heating equipment; chimney or smoke pipe in poor condition; fuel oil leaks and spills; and boiler defects.

THE LANGUAGE OF ZONING

"Bulk" is the term used to indicate the size and setback of a building, and its location with respect to another building or a lot line. Bulk includes the size and height of a building and the location of its exterior wall in relation to a lot line, street, or other building; the floor area; the open spaces allocated to and surrounding a building; and the amount of lot area per dwelling unit.

The "building line" describes the minimum distance which any building must be located away from a street right of way. The "floor area" of a building is the sum of the gross horizontal floor areas of the several stories of a building as measured to the exterior face of the exterior walls. The "floor area ratio" is the ratio of the floor area of a building to the area of the lot on which it is located. For example, if a floor area ratio of 80 per cent is specified, and if the lot area is 10,000 square feet, the maximum permitted floor area on that lot would be 8,000 square feet.

A "mobile home" is a detached portable single-family dwelling, prefabricated on its chassis and intended for long-term occupation. The unit contains sleeping accommodations, flush toilet, tub or shower, eating and living quarters. It is transported on its own wheels or flatbed, arriving at the site where it is to be occupied as a complete dwelling without permanent foundation, to be connected to existing utilities. A "mobile home park" is any parcel of land which is offered to the public for the purpose of accommodating more than one mobile home for living use.

A "non-conforming use" is a use which was legal at the time of its inception, but which subsequent zoning has made illegal. Inasmuch as it was in existence prior to the zoning ordinance, this non-conforming use is permitted to continue. "Spot zoning" is zoning authorizing within an area, a specific use otherwise proscribed.

"Off-street parking" consists of a land surface providing vehicular parking spaces along with adequate drives and aisles for maneuvering to provide access for entrance and exit for the parking of more than two automobiles. Shopping centers have off-street parking. "Shopping centers" are defined as groups of commercial establishments, planned, developed, owned, and managed as a unit.

ZONING DISTRICTS

Zoning districts are delineated in an official zoning map, a copy of which accompanies the zoning ordinance, and is made part of that ordinance. This map is open to public inspection, and is the final authority as to the current zoning status of any parcel of land within the jurisdiction.

The regulations in the ordinance for each zoning district are the minimum regulations and must be uniform for each class of land or building throughout the zoning district. Where there are practical difficulties or unnecessary hardships in carrying out the strict letter of the zoning ordinance, a zoning board will be authorized to modify provisions of the ordinance, so long as its basic intent is observed and the modification is consistent with the applicable master plan.

In a single family rural non-farm residential district, the intent of the zoning ordinance would be to preserve a rural character in areas fit for concentrated residential use. In a single family, suburban residential district, the intent would be to provide for single family dwellings on moderately small lots. If the zoning district was two family residential, there would be permitted two attached single family dwellings occupying a common lot. If the zoning district was moderate density multiple-family residential, it would be composed of multiple-family dwellings, abutting or adjacent to other uses which complement such a density.

If a mobile home park residential district was permitted, it would have to be an asset to the community, harmonize with the types of residential developments already in existence, and be adequately served by existing essential public services. Accessory buildings could be used only for office space, storage, laundry facilities, recreational areas, and garage facilities for park resident use. All mobile homes within the park would have to be suitably connected to sewer and water services.

In a general commercial district zone, the principal use must be general retail. In a highway commercial district, the principal use would be retail and service business activities serving the motoring public. An office zoning district would permit business, professional, executive, or administrative offices. A wholesale zoning district would permit facilities for the wholesaling and the warehousing of goods. A research and development district would permit offices related to research and development, and scientific, business, and industrial research and testing laboratories. A limited industrial district, on the other hand, would be composed of light manufacturing and other comparable limited industrial uses.

A general industrial zoning district would provide the location and space for all manner of industrial uses, and for wholesale commercial and industrial storage facilities. The zoning would protect abutting residential and commercial properties from incompatible industrial activities.

In all districts zoned for industrial, business, institutional, agricultural, recreational, residential, or other use, there must be provided at the time any building is erected, adequate off-street parking. There must also be provided off-street loading and unloading spaces for uses which customarily receive or distribute material or merchandise by vehicle.

Zoning ordinances now provide for planned unit developments. The designation of a tract for such a purpose permits variations in minimum lot areas, setbacks, and spacings among buildings. It is required that the development be adequately served by existing public facilities and services. It must be self-sufficient in size. Non-residential planned unit developments may be employed in connection with offices, commercial and warehousing, and research and development facilities.

If there is a non-conforming use, it is usually provided that this use may not be enlarged, expanded, or extended. Nor may it be moved to another site. If it ceases to be exercised for a certain period of time, the ordinance usually provides that it ceases to exist. The ordinance may also provide that if a non-conforming building is destroyed by fire to an extent of 50 per cent or more, it may not be reconstructed as a non-conforming use.

The administration and enforcement of zoning ordinances may be under the jurisdiction of a zoning inspector, who may order the discontinuance of any illegal use.

ZONING TECHNIQUES

The technique of incentive zoning is resorted to in order to persuade builders and developers to incorporate into their structures the features the community wants. For example, in order to preserve the retail character of Fifth Avenue in New York City, zoning requires that the street and the mezzanine floors of new structures be devoted to retail uses. The developer may then, if he so desires, devote the upper floors to office or to apartment units. In other jurisdictions, incentive zoning offers builders and developers so-called bonus floors in the structures they erect, in which floors they could, if they liked, incorporate office or apartment units, providing they connected their buildings with nearby subway stations.

The extent to which zoning may be used for strictly aesthetic purposes has not been definitively determined. Pressure groups in San Francisco have sought to forestall a U. S. Steel high rise project on the grounds that this would bring about a "Manhattanization" of San Francisco's skyline and constitute an aesthetic offense. They charge that the high rise would limit the view of its neighbors. On the other hand it is alleged that the right to a view does not exist in the common law and that growth inevitably brings about an elimination of old views, while, at the same time, creating new ones. Furthermore, it is alleged that building design is a subjective matter and what might be an aesthetic offense to one person, might be an aesthetic pleasure to another.

A circuit court judge in Ann Arbor, Michigan, in connection with declaring invalid the city's sign ordinance, recently ruled that aesthetics alone are not a valid basis for an ordinance. In his opinion the ordinance was an unreasonable exercise of the police power and unconstitutional violation of freedom of speech, press, and religion. He struck down as illegal the section of the ordinance requiring businesses to take down or replace non-conforming signs. In his judgment, the ordinance was a transparent attempt to exclude billboards and other forms of signs from the entire city.

California and several other states forbid the construction of low-rent housing in a community unless a majority of the voters approve its entrance under a public referendum. It has been alleged that such legislation is an attempt to fence out and exclude minority groups. It has been further alleged that such legislation prevents poor people from acquiring living space in a community and that the Constitution requires communities to permit construction of enough shelter to house the poor, despite the desires of the residents or the effect on the city's character. The California law was recently reviewed by the United States Supreme Court and found to be constitutional.

Some zoning ordinances in New Jersey stipulate that 80 per cent of the units in new apartment projects have one bedroom and 20 per cent, two bedrooms. As a one bedroom apartment is not the ideal amount of space for a family with two or more children, it is alleged that this is a form of architectural birth control and discriminatory against large families. On the other hand, the sponsors of such ordinances say they prevent parents from evading tax costs by living in apartments where the owner's tax costs per resident are lower than those of private homes. The effect of the zoning is to require families with more than one child to live in a single family home. In a case bearing some resemblance, the Pennsylvania Supreme Court recently ruled that a community cannot limit high density housing, if the only reason for doing so is to avoid the burden on municipal services.

Some zoning ordinances have stipulated a minimum construction cost for the erection or purchase of a home within their areas of jurisdiction. But a recent New Jersey case ruled such stipulations illegal on the ground that they were not related to the health, safety, or welfare of the community.

It is alleged that zoning for one-acre or half-acre plots is "economic zoning" in that it excludes workers or low income families from certain areas and is unconstitutional. The case of Black Jack, Missouri is illustrative. In Black Jack, an outside church group bought land and announced plans to put up government subsidized town houses, thereby changing the character of the community. Black Jack then incorporated itself as an independent city and zoned the vacant land for single family residences. As a suburban community, Black Jack said that it was not willing to accept an influx of low-income families with the consequent strain on schools and local services, and, subsequently, a probably tax increase. In support of this position, citizen groups in Westchester County, New York estimate the tax structure requires one house with a $50,000 market value to support one child in school and that low-income apartments do not provide that kind of a tax base.

In Lackawanna, New York, a black organization located a city-owned tract and proposed to build a low-income housing development of single family homes. The city took no action on the proposal and the black organization arranged to buy residentially zoned acreage for this development. Before its purchase was concluded, however, the city council passed an ordinance designating this as park land and halting all construction of new subdivisions until the city's sewer problem was resolved. Here, the United States Supreme Court left standing a lower court decision that the city of Lackawanna illegally interfered with blacks' efforts to build houses in a white part of the community.

In the field of ecology, Michigan has passed legislation permitting citizens to take government and industry to court to stop pollution of the air, water, and other natural resources. Citizens filing suits must substantially prove their case before any court orders are issued. The suits themselves must be filed in a circuit court in the area where pollution or other impairment of natural resources occurs.

The judge may require the complainant to post a surety bond or cash of up to $500 if he believes he cannot pay the cost of any judgment against him. A judge may dismiss a suit before it starts if he is convinced that the *prima facie* evidence presented is rebutted by the defendent. The law further provides that if an issue in one case is decided in favor of the defendant, it cannot be raised in any other circuit court in the state. Multiplicity of suits on the same issue is thereby prohibited. The act does not provide for any monetary damages to be awarded.

On the other hand, it is now possible for bounty hunters finding evidences of illegal pollution to be rewarded. Under the 1899 Rivers and Harbors Act any dumping, except that of treated sewage, is prohibited into a navigable waterway without a permit from the Army Corps of Engineers. The Act goes on to provide for a split 50-50 of the violation fines between the state and whomsoever supplies the evidence. With this incentive, bounty hunters have turned up alleged evidence of pollution on the part of four corporations on the Ohio and Monongahela rivers and one corporation on the East River in New York.

Many states have departments of natural resources which are given the authority to designate certain rivers for protection from over-development of the water-front. These departments may themselves adopt zoning regulations to implement such protection, providing local authorities fail to do so. They are also authorized to prevent the indiscriminate growth of buildings, the cutting of trees, or mining and drilling which might impair the wild, scenic, or recreational qualities of natural river areas.

A Shoreland-Flood Plain Regulation has been adopted in Wisconsin, which controls land development within 1,000 feet of a navigable lake, pond, or flowage, and within 300 feet of a navigable stream or river. The Regulation can prevent the development of sites in areas where septic tanks, based on soil porosity tests, prove to be inoperable. The regulation also sets up air pollution controls, sanitary and solid waste disposal controls, and requires that dwellings be set back at least 75 feet from the water's edge.

THE ZONING BOARD

The zoning board is a quasi-judicial body, sometimes called the zoning board of appeals and sometimes called the zoning board of adjustment, which hears and decides on applications by petitioners for variances in the zoning ordinances and building codes. It is appointed by the local governing body, such as the city council and it has its own separate counsel. It may employ the subpoena power to compel the attendance of witnesses and obtain records relevant to the cases it hears.

The variances which the board is asked to permit are minor changes of zoning district requirements where individual properties are uniquely burdened by the strict application of the zoning ordinance. Where, by reason of exceptional narrowness, shallowness, shape or topographic conditions, or by reason of the exceptional situation of a specific property, the strict application of the zoning ordinance would result in exceptional practical difficulties to, or exceptional and undue hardship upon the owner of the property, the board may authorize a variance. The petitioner, however, must prove that the property is affected by an exceptional situation, resulting in hardship, and that the combination of the zoning ordinance and the situation of the property prevents a reasonable use of the property. If a variance is granted, this grant must be in harmony with the master plan and the intent of the zoning ordinance, and must not adversely affect surrounding property or the general neighborhood.

If a property owner disagrees with local administrative officials in their interpretation of a zoning ordinance as it affects his property, he may appeal to the zoning board for its decision. If a property owner feels that he is faced with unreasonable difficulties and hardships in carrying out strict compliance with the ordinance, he will appeal to the zoning board for a variance. The burden of proof is on the petitioner.

If the applicant for a variance bought the property at the time the zoning ordinance was in effect, he was aware of the limitations it imposed and cannot subsequently complain of the hardship he suffers. If, however, in the course of time there have been such changes in the character of property usage in the area so as to make the original use requirements unreasonable, the property owner may cite this as the basis for a variance.

If the petitioner presently has a non-conforming use and requests a variance which would enlarge such use, the board would usually reject his application. If, however, his request was for permission to set up parking facilities, and would reduce congestion in the streets, the board would grant the petition, even though these parking facilities would expand the non-conforming use area.

The Board will not hear a case based solely on increased financial return to the property owner from the grant of a variance, nor one in which the hardship instanced was self-imposed and due to the fault of the petitioner. The board is not authorized to grant a variance based on the grounds that it would provide an increased tax ratable for the local ity. Nor may it heed a plea by the petitioner that he has spent large sums of money on the property to put it into condition for the violating use. Nor will it grant a variance solely on the ground that this will increase the value of the property.

As the board is a semi-court, its proceedings must be formal and its findings must be expressed in such a way that all concerned know the basis on which it reached its result. If the findings are appealed to a court of law, it must decide whether there was sufficient evidence to reasonably support the conclusion reached by the board.

It is often provided that the petitioner for a variance, at least 15 days prior to the time appointed for the hearing, give personal notice of the hearing and the nature of his appeal to all property owners within a certain distance of the property to be affected by the appeal. At the hearing itself, the petitioner may make his appeal in person, by agent, or by an attorney. If the appeal is made by a person other than the owner, a power of attorney must usually be furnished. A corporation must usually be represented by an attorney. All pertinent information must be set forth on the application for the variance.

It is considered sound practice to prepare one's case as though it may be denied, since this will assure that the grounds, the testimony, the evidence, and the records will be available for an appeal to the courts. If one's case is won, it will be because of such thorough preparation. It is of assistance to the petitioner to present maps, plans, designs, architect's sketches, and photographs about the property, so long as these documents are pertinent.

If one's case is denied, it is *res adjudicata* so far as the board is concerned and cannot be re-presented unless new evidence or materially changed conditions can be shown. In its decisions, the board should avoid stating its grounds in general terms, such as "in the public interest". These generalities will not carry weight in the court to which the case may be appealed. The board should never grant a variance merely because there is no opposition to the petition, because it feels the requested use would do no harm, or because the petitioner presents a petition containing more names than does the objectors.

The members of the zoning board are under an obligation to make a personal inspection of the property for which a variance is requested. If they have a personal interest in the outcome of a case, they are under an obligation to disqualify themselves from deciding on it.

SUMMARY

Although planning and zoning are inherently functions of the state, enabling state legislation has delegated authorization for their use at the local level, principally within the municipality. The purpose of planning is to provide for orderly growth of the area, to anticipate its problems and to attempt to work out solutions in advance, to formulate methods for changing the environment for the betterment of the community, and to guide constructively the physical manifestations of population increase. The purpose of zoning is to regulate land use and implement the policies as worked out in the planning process.

The planning commission is the organization responsible for setting up planning objectives and suggesting the methods by which these objectives might be attained. It serves in an advisory capacity. It identifies areas of major concern to the community it serves. It may recommend to its community the adoption of a master plan by which future developments may be guided. This plan delineates the areas for various classifications of land use. Subdivisions and developments must be consistent with the plan, and zoning ordinances and building codes should be enacted with the master plan as a framework of reference. The planning commission subjects the plan to periodic review, and incorporates current thinking in the form of recommendations for changes.

Zoning is the tool employed to carry out the goals and objectives of planning. Zoning, like planning, is authorized by police power and is usually exercised by means of ordinances, adopted at the local level, which determine and regulate the use of real property. The zoning ordinance may include the building code and subdivision controls. If a zoning ordinance is attacked in the courts, it is presumed to be valid and the attacking party has the burden of proof in sustaining the contrary.

Zoning districts are outlined in an official zoning map. The regulations applicable to the zoning district must be uniform for each class of land or building located therein. If there is a non-conforming use in the zoning district, it may not usually be enlarged, expanded, or extended.

Among the techniques employed in zoning are those of providing concessions to builders and developers, providing they incorporate within their structures the features deemed desirable for the community. The courts have not yet determined the extent to which zoning may be employed as a technique to bring about an aesthetic result. The effect of certain zoning techniques would be to force families with more than one child to live in a single family home.

The zoning board is a quasi-judicial body, which hears requests for variances from petitioners who allege that the strict application of zoning ordinances to their properties would result in a hardship to the property and render it unable to be put to a reasonable use. If the zoning board grants such requests for variances, the effect of the grant must be in harmony with the master plan and the intent of the zoning ordinance. Notices of the hearings on the requests for variances must be given property owners within a certain distance from the subject property so that they may have the opportunity to appear at the hearing and register their approval or opposition. The decisions of the zoning board may be appealed to the courts.

GLOSSARY

ECOLOGY — the environment

QUASI-JUDICIAL — half judicial, in that formal proceedings are required, but the decisions reached do not carry the weight of the conditions precedent of a formal court of law.

RES ADJUDICATA — this means that the issue has been decided and may not be raised again in the same tribunal unless new evidence can be presented.

TORTIOUS — like a civil wrong, for which one citizen may seek monetary redress against another citizen.

TRUE AND FALSE QUESTIONS

1. The state has delegated to municipalities authorization for planning and zoning at the local level.　　T　F

2. Planning is a tool of zoning.　　T　F

3. The scope of planning includes the preservation of the ecology.　　T　F

4. The planning commission is the organization responsible for setting up planning objectives and suggesting the methods by which these may be attained.　　T　F

5. The planning commission is the enforcement agency of the master plan.　　T　F

6. The planning commission is the legislative agency under which the master plan is enacted into law.　　T　F

7. The planning commission engages in periodic review of the master plan.　　T　F

8. The planning commission may recommend changes in zoning ordinances.　　T　F

9. The application of the zoning ordinance may be different in different parts of the zoning district.　　T　F

10. The courts take the position that it is within their province to pass on the wisdom of the zoning ordinance.　　T　F

11. Building codes are authorized under police power.　　T　F

12. Zoning districts are outlined on official zoning maps.　　T　F

13. The zoning board is authorized to grant a variance in the case of personal financial hardship to the petitioner.　　T　F

14. Incentive zoning is no longer employed.　　T　F

15. A variance does not have to be consistent with the master plan.　　T　F

16. A principal reason for the granting of variances is to provide for increased tax ratables.   T   F

17. A variance may not be granted on the ground that this will increase the value of the property.   T   F

18. The zoning board is authorized to make grants of "spot zoning".   T   F

19. The courts concern themselves primarily with determining whether local zoning ordinances are within the ground rules laid down by the state legislature.   T   F

20. Planning is carried on only at the local level.   T   F

21. The law requires that the planning commission be appointed.   T   F

22. The public projects suggested in the master plan are evolved only after due consideration has been given to the ability of the locality to carry them out without the imposition of unreasonable tax burdens.   T   F

23. It is legitimate for a community to seek non-residential tax ratables and to set aside land to attract them.   T   F

24. The "building line" describes the minimum distance which any building must be located away from a street right of way.   T   F

25. The "floor area ratio" is the ratio of the floor area of a building to the area of the lot on which it is located.   T   F

26. A "non-conforming" use is one which was illegal at the time of its inception.   T   F

27. The zoning board is a judicial body.   T   F

28. The zoning board is authorized to grant a variance, if no objections are raised to the petition.   T   F

29. Zoning board members are under an obligation to make a personal inspection of the property for which a variance is requested.   T   F

30. The petitioner for a variance must present his case through an attorney.   T   F

31. The zoning board may decide on the appropriate interpretation of an ordinance as it affects a specific property.   T   F

32. The zoning board may not employ the subpoena power.   T F

33. "Economic zoning" excludes workers or low-income   T F
families.

34. It is unconstitutional to forbid the construction of low-   T F
rent housing in a community unless a majority of the voters
therein approve its introduction under a public referendum.

35. The extent to which zoning may be used to accomplish   T F
specific aesthetic objectives has now been definitely determined.

36. The administration and enforcement of zoning ordinances   T F
is under the jurisdiction of the zoning board.

37. The planning commission determines whether plats sub-   T F
mitted for proposed subdivisions are consistent with the
master plan.

38. Present day planning is concerned with balance.   T F

39. The courts construe strictly state enabling legislation which   T F
delegates zoning authority to individual municipalities.

40. The concept of continued growth for communities is   T F
unchallenged.

MULTIPLE CHOICE QUESTIONS

41. It is now recognized that the government may regulate land use in the public interest, and that this is a proper exercise of:
    ( )   The power of eminent domain
    ( )   The police power
    ( )   The power of sovereignty
    ( )   The power of the collective good

42. The areas appropriate for single-family residential, multi-family residential, and for the various classifications of commercial and industrial usages are outlined under:
    ( )   The standards set up by the zoning board
    ( )   The state enabling legislation
    ( )   The master plan
    ( )   The plan for urban renewal

43. A detached portable single-family dwelling, prefabricated on its chassis and intended for long-term occupation is:
    ( )   Modular housing
    ( )   Sectional housing
    ( )   Mobile home housing
    ( )   Industrialized housing

44. Bounty hunters may now be rewarded for:
    ( )   Turning in dead specimens of the American bald eagle
    ( )   Finding evidences of illegal pollution
    ( )   Apprehending violators of urban renewal
    ( )   Finding evidences of misrepresnetations by land developers

45. The members of the zoning board are appointed by:
    ( )   The governor
    ( )   The state senate judiciary committee
    ( )   The state supreme court
    ( )   The local governing body

46. If a petitioner requests a variance which would enlarge an existing nonconforming use, the zoning board would usually:
    ( )   Deny the request
    ( )   Grant the request
    ( )   Refer the request to city council
    ( )   Submit the request to the planning commission for decision

47. The master plan is subject to periodic review by:
( ) The zoning board
( ) The planning commission
( ) The zoning inspector
( ) The building department

48. If a member of the zoning board has a personal interest in the outcome of a case:
( ) He must absent himself from the hearing
( ) He must publicly state his interest
( ) He must refrain from acting as a witness
( ) He must disqualify himself from deciding on the case

49. The zoning board may employ its subpoena power:
( ) To impose the collection of fines
( ) To preserve order in the courtroom
( ) To compel the attendance of witnesses
( ) To debar attorneys from practicing before it

50. The current zoning status of any parcel of land within a certain jurisdiction may be found in:
( ) The official zoning map
( ) The decisions of the zoning board
( ) The recommendations of the planning commission
( ) The master plan

ESSAY QUESTIONS

1. What is the difference between planning and zoning?

2. What is a master plan?

3. On what grounds may variances in zoning ordinances be secured?

PART III
THE BUSINESS OF
REAL ESTATE

BROKERAGE

CHAPTER FIVE

THE LAW OF AGENCY

A real estate broker is an agent, acting for a principal in a real estate transaction. The principal may be the owner of the property, an individual who is interested in buying a property, a prospective lessee, someone desiring to obtain financing, a person desiring an easement, or a developer intent on land acquisition. The principal may be an animate person or a legal entity, such as a corporation, partnership, limited partnership, joint venture, syndicate, or real estate investment trust. Likewise, the agent may be an animate individual, a partnership, or a corporation.

The agency itself may be ostensible or actual, general or special. An ostensible agency is one in which a party makes it appear to a reasonable man that he is acting as an agent, even though in reality he is not. An ostensible agency is therefore liable in damages to anyone acting in reliance thereon to his detriment. A general agency is one in which the business affairs in general of a principal are entrusted to an agent. A special agency is one set up for the accomplishment of a specific objective on which consummation, it expires. The situation wherein the owner of a property employs a real estate broker for the sale of his property is a common instance of a special agency.

As an agent, the real estate broker owes his principal the duties of loyalty and obedience to instructions, keeping his principal informed of all pertinent matters that come to his attention in connection with the agency assignment, respecting his fiduciary relationship, exercising the degree of care expectable of one in his position, and accounting for money and property coming into his hands. Having been selected by his principal because of his personal qualifications, an agent cannot delegate his authority to someone else, except for the performance of clerical and ministerial acts. If an agent should perform an act not authorized by his principal, who subsequently finds that this act is to his advantage, he may then ratify it.

If the owner of real property authorizes the real estate broker to sell it in return for a commission, the broker may not in the same transaction accept a consideration from the buyer for finding him the property. On the other hand, if the broker makes his dual position clear both to the seller and the buyer and if they are both fully cognizant that he is acting in the interests of both and receiving compensation therefore, and both consent to this arrangement, the broker may act in this dual capacity.

A real estate broker is entitled to his commission for the sale of real property when he has procured a buyer ready, able, and willing to buy on the terms as set forth by his principal or on the basis of other terms, to which his principal subsequently agrees. "Able to buy" means financially able, and "ready and willing to buy" means the buyer is going forward in good faith to consummate the transaction. Even though the broker is not the direct procuring cause of the sale, he is entitled to his commission if the facts establish that he was the indirect procuring cause of the sale. If the broker has agreed that he is entitled to his commission only if, as, and when the title passes, his commission will not be forthcoming until then. If the owner, however, is the cause for the failure of title to pass, the broker, in such an instance, is entitled to his commission.

If there is an exchange of real properties and the broker is the procuring cause of the exchange, he would be entitled, under the usual circumstance, to two commissions, representing, as he does, two "sellers" in the transaction. They must, of course, understand again the dual capacity in which he is acting and must be agreeable to the dual compensation to be received.

Under no circumstances may the broker "feather his own nest" at the expense of his principal in a real estate transaction. He may, therefore, not buy the property, should this be to his advantage, through a confederate. If he is interested in the acquisition for himself, then he must so inform the seller, so that the transaction may be conducted at "arm's length" between them. If the property under these circumstances is sold to himself, the broker is not entitled to a commission. If a relative of the broker should desire to acquire the property, the broker must inform the seller of this relationship.

Just as the broker must respect the fiduciary relationship with his principal, so must the principal show a corresponding respect for the broker. The principal may not, therefore, try to by-pass the broker by seeking to sell the property "direct" to the prospect the broker has developed and about whom the broker has advised his principal. Nor may the principal wait until the time the broker's authority has expired and then contact the prospect, thereby by-passing the broker. If the prospect whom the broker has developed should initiate the direct contact with the seller, the seller is not relieved from his obligation to pay the broker his commission.

The broker must ascertain for himself whether his principal is the actual owner of the property. If separate ownership interests are present, authority from each must be secured before the broker is authorized to act. The broker is likewise under an obligation to verify the statements the principal has made about the property - the liens and mortgage encumbrances to which it is subject, the dimensions it measures, the easements present, the setback and sideline restrictions applicable, the absence of encroachments and overlappings, and the character of sanitation facilities.

A prospect may ask the broker whether the seller will take less than the price at which the property is listed. The broker must respond that he is not authorized to indicate any price except that at which the property is listed, but that he is likewise duty bound to transmit any bona fide offer to his principal. If the broker can persuade his principal to list the property at a price range, this can be advantageous for it provides a flexibility for purposes of negotiations.

A broker is responsible for the acts and statements of his salespeople pursuant to the real estate transaction in which he has authorized them to engage. He may not disclaim such responsibility on the ground that he was unaware of what they were doing and saying. He is, of course, responsible for the statements he makes about the property in the advertisements he composes. If he words his advertisements so that the reader thinks it is the owner himself who is advertising the property, he is guilty of misleading advertising and is liable. In many states the insertion of such "blind ads" may lead to the suspension or revocation of the broker's license.

THE CONTRACT OF EMPLOYMENT

The contract of employment between the principal and the agent is the listing contract. This contract authorizes the real estate broker to sell, lease, or exchange real property at a certain price for a certain period. The name "listing" is derived from the owner listing his property with the broker.

If it is an "open listing", the owner is telling the broker that he authorizes him to sell, lease, or exchange for the time stipulated, but at the same time he may be listing the property with other brokers as well, and that likewise he is reserving to himself the right to sell the property, if he can.

When anyone of the brokers with whom the property is listed disposes of it, all the listings outstanding are terminated. There is no legal obligation on the part of the principal to notify any of the brokers that the property has been liquidated, nor is there any legal obligation on the selling broker to notify any other of the listing brokers. This could cause a situation embarrassing to a broker bringing a prospect to a listed property only to discover on contact that the property has been taken off the market.

In an open listing, there is no incentive to advertise or engage in an aggressive sales promotion on the part of a broker, since at any time he may find that the "rug has been pulled out from under him" by reason of the sale on the part of another broker. These factors do not serve to make open listing contracts popular with individual brokers, some of the more prestigious of whom will not take a listing on these terms. Most, however, will take an open listing on the theory that someone is bound to sell the property, and it might as well be they. They feel that if they do not take the listing, someone else will. Also, the property owner may feel, however mistakenly, that in an open listing he is securing the services of many brokers, rather than one.

The "exclusive listing" contract of employment seems to provide the broker with a monopoly privilege to sell the property for the period stipulated. But it is not quite what it seems. It means that the owner pledges himself not to list the property with any other broker during this period, but yet he reserves to himself the right to sell the property directly, if he can. The broker is thereby protected against the competition of other brokers, but not against the competition of the owner himself.

On the other hand, the "exclusive right to sell listing" insures the broker against the competition of other brokers, as well as the competition of the owner himself during the listing period. Under this protection, therefore, the broker feels safe in advertising and in engaging in aggressive sales promotion, for the rewards accruing from the commission will be payable only to himself. His principal is assured by reason of the incentive provided for the broker to concentrate on the sale. This contract is therefore most popular with real estate brokers and is encouraged by the boards in which they are members.

Nevertheless, a "caveat" is in order. Although the owner principal has no right to breach an exclusive right to sell contract, he still has the power to do so. If the real estate broker, after such breach should sue for damages, he could find these very limited in amount. All he could get would be for the cost of the advertisements he has run and the gasoline he has used up in showing prospects the property. He could, however, guard against this contingency by getting the owner principal to provide in the contract that in event of the owner's breach, the measure of liquidated damages is the amount or fee the broker would have received had he been able to sell the property at the price stipulated.

The listing contract may contain a clause authorizing the listing broker to relay the listing on to the multiple listing service of which he may be a member. The listing is then exposed for sale by all the other brokers members of this multiple listing service. The listing broker is protected because out of the commission derived he secures a pre-determined percentage. If he should also be the selling broker, he would enjoy the entire amount of the commission, minus a small amount necessary for the administration and operation of the multiple listing service. The property owner is "advantaged" because, theoretically, his property is exposed to the selling efforts of many brokers, rather than one.

There are occasions when a property owner will desire only one broker, with whom he has previously had pleasant and profitable relationships, to engage in the selling of the property. Most multiple listing services and real estate boards will recognize these situations and permit exceptions to be made.

Although criticisms have been levelled at multiple listing services on the ground that they make for cliques of listing brokers, with no interest in selling, most brokers like them and have found them advantageous. They do encourage cooperation among real estate brokers, and militate against "cutthroat competition". They are presently the closest approach in real estate to the selling of stocks or bonds in a stock or a bond exchange.

Just as multiple services provide for a division of commission between listing brokers and selling brokers, so does the broker's office frequently provide for a division of the portion of the commission going to the salespeople between listing salespeople and selling salespeople. This works for improvement of morale among sales personnel and for greater inner harmony in the sales organization.

A property owner may tell a broker that he must get a certain amount for his property, but that, anything over and above this amount the broker may keep for himself and regard as his commission. This is known as a "net listing", one in which the commission is not included in the sales price. Many states have passed laws declaring net listings illegal and authorizing a suspension or revocation of the license of any real estate broker engaging therein. The reason for this opposition to net listings is that some unscrupulous brokers, at least in times past, have taken advantage of the lack of knowledge by the owner of the real value of his property and let him state a minimal figure which he must get, and then have secured a much higher figure, enabling them to reap a fantastic sum as their commission.

Also, in times past, some listing contracts have contained a clause permitting the real estate broker, at his option, to extend the listing period, beyond the time stipulated as its duration. This has enabled them to sit back complacently and do nothing about promoting the sale of the property, serving only as a passive outlet for whatever offers might come in. There has been no incentive for them to exert themselves, since they do not have to do so to get a renewal of the listing. Therefore, again, many states now stipulate that every listing contract must specify a definite termination date, no extensions may be made except by a mutual agreement between both principal and agent.

As the wife of the property owner may have a dower right and the husband a "curtsy" right, the listing contract should contain the signatures of both spouses even though the property is in the legal ownership of only one. By signing the listing contract, the holders of the dower and the courtesy rights relinquish the negating effects these rights might otherwise wield.

The listing form should include the legal description of the property, the fixtures, the rooms, the furniture to be included, the times when the property may be shown, the commission applicable, and the duration of the listing. Accompanying the listing may be a letter from the heating and air conditioning company servicing the equipment, stating the condition of the units at the time. Also in order would be a present owners' termite policy and record of inspection or a letter from a bonded exterminating company as to the presence or absence of termites. Equally important would be a letter from the pool servicing company, the automatic sprinkler company, and the kitchen appliance service company stating that current inspections have been made and everything has been found to be in normal working order.

The rate of commission is strictly a matter of negotiation between the broker and his principal. It would be in violation of the Sherman

Anti-Trust Act for a real estate board to make mandatory to its members that they require a stipulated rate of commission. It would likewise be a violation for brokers to agree among themselves to be guided by such a rate. Even a recommendation by a real estate board as to the rate of commission is "suspect" because it is open to the interpretation that a member who knows on what side his bread is buttered will be amenable thereto. Currently, several real estate boards are being prosecuted on the ground that their conduct encourages price-fixing in the rates of commission their members may charge.

The listing contract should be in writing. This should be required as a matter of good business prudence and, even more so, because the laws of most states require it to be in writing to be enforceable. The contract is, of course, binding only on those of legal age and sound mind. If the contract is signed by a corporation, the signature must be of the person duly authorized by appropriate resolution of the board of directors.

SECURING LISTINGS

Wherever there is a need to relocate, there is a potential listing. The problem for the broker is to find the person who has this need and convince him of the value of his services. Many brokers say that they would trade ten good prospects for one good listing.

Satisfied customers are the single most important source of listings. From satisfied customers the broker gets his repeat business and his referrals. The individual to whom one has sold a home thinks first of his broker when he wishes to sell. The buyer of a successful investment property thinks first of his broker when considering its disposition. A satisfied customer volunteers his broker's name to his friends thinking of selling.

There is only one way to get the loyalty of one's customers and that is to earn it. It is earned in part by the customer's satisfaction with the transaction the broker has engineered. It is earned in part by the customer feeling the broker is still interested in him after the sale.

The desire to help one's customer will suggest ways to forge these links of loyalty. After the sale is over, the broker may introduce the customer to such neighbors as he may like to meet. So long as the customer is willing to have this done, the broker may circularize the neighborhood with information about him in the form of "Know Your New Neighbor" letters. The thoughtful broker will also write a letter of thanks to the customer he has served. On the occasion of the customer moving in, the broker may provide a present in the form of a plant, notebook, flag, or wastebasket. The broker may take note of the customer's birthday and send him a personally signed card. When a news item about the customer appears, the broker may clip it out, and send it to him, with the notation, "I read something about you". The broker will have on file data on the customer's interests, hobbies, and background, and may refer to these in connection with his future contacts with the customer.

Such interest in one's customers will help establish one's business reputation. A name for fair and square dealing, dependability, and integrity inspires confidence and attracts listings. A proprietor and staff who have demonstrated their sales ability and who have given unselfishly of themselves in service to their church, community, and local real estate board become known as "the real estate people with whom to deal".

Another source of listings is the owner who decides to cut out the middle-man and sell directly, but who becomes discouraged when he finds himself floundering about in a technical area in which he has no competence. He does not know the difference between a "looker" and a prospect. He does not know how to screen his prospects. He cannot tactfully frame questions to find out his prospect's financial competence. He has no professional knowledge about financing. He does not know how to appraise.

On the other hand, the broker is continuously advertising in newspapers and elsewhere, pulling prospective buyers to his attention. He keeps a list of prospects waiting for him to call them when a particular property is listed. He constantly follows through leads fed to his office by his many friends, large employers, past buyers, and others who know of new prospects. He learns of families already in the city considering a move to different property and of renters deciding to buy. Prospects will usually give the broker more details about their needs and financial information about their income, debts, and budget than they will an owner, for the broker knows how to frame the proper questions to secure this needed information.

The owner finds that when he takes on the responsibility of trying to sell his property by himself, he has taken on all the functions of the broker. And so the broker considers he is doing the owner a favor by asking for the listing. He charges nothing unless he produces a sale. Most owners who start to sell "direct" end up by selling through the broker. Because of proper pricing and experienced selling, the broker's services have cost the owner very little, if anything.

Another productive source of listings is the so-called "center-of-influence". This is a person who, by virtue of his daily activities, is in a position to know of relocations first. A routeman learns from the housewife when her family is considering a move; the diaper-service man hears about it when a home has grown too small; the barber or the beauty operator may know when a customer is thinking about getting a better-paying job elsewhere; and the security protection man can be counted on for knowledge of neighborhood gossip concerning relocations. The personnel manager of a local plant is one of the first to know when transfers in and out of the area are in the making. He is also a source of information concerning promotions which may require a new prestige home and, therefore, the sale of the old.

Other sources of listings can be found in publications, such as the local newspaper, the church weekly, the company house organ, the club news letter, which provide information on impending moves. The mention in the church bulletin of the retirement to Florida of an elderly couple can lead to a listing of their home. The death notices in the local paper may indicate that the decedent's survivors will not require their home. News of a divorce or separation will suggest smaller home requirements in the future.

The broker secures listings on commercial and industrial properties through his business friends and acquaintances. He obtains them from his business contacts in civic, service, and fraternal organizations. Attorneys and bankers who may be in charge of business properties may be responsive to his qualifications. Business firms with surplus property constitute another productive source. Civic officials and the local chamber of commerce may know of business properties available for listing. The broker secures these listings through his reputation. Satisfied customers refer friends, acquaintances, and business contacts to him. His name in the area acts as a good drawing card. His signs, newspaper advertising, publicity, and service in civic organizations call himself favorably to the attention of property owners.

THE LISTING PROCESS

"Why," the owner asks, "should I give you the listing?" A frank question deserves a frank answer. "We relieve you of cares and responsibilities." "We protect you from curiosity seekers and criminals seeking access to your property." "We save you the chore of cleaning house and preparing for showings to those unable to handle the financing." "We are Realtors. We are bound by our board and by state law to protect you." "We know mortgages, mortgage arrangements, and mortgage availabilities." "When you give us an exclusive right to sell, we pay for the advertising." "Our knowledge and experience qualify us to save you money on closing costs." "We can devise a sales program to bring out the unique features of the property sold." "We belong to the Multiple Listing Service, and the moment you list with us, your listing will be flashed to all our other members." "We cooperate with other brokers."

The broker will inspect the construction details himself: brick or brick veneer; shingles, shakes, clapboard for the sidings; cedar shingle, asphalt, or tile roof; oak, pine, or parquet flooring; plaster or plasterboard or dry walls. He will know the difference between various woods and will be conversant with the terminology of structural parts. He will find the location of sewer lines or septic tanks.

The broker may have to persuade the owner to include in the sale items considered part of the structure, such as lighting fixtures. He may also have to persuade the owner that the carpeting and furniture are better excluded since they are not desired by most buyers and only serve to add to the price and may make for a hard sale. He may have to tell the owner that buyers may assume that dishwashers, mirrors, and TV antennae are a part of the home and included in the sale and that misunderstandings regarding these can result in lost sales.

The broker will itemize information on bus routes and bus stops, where they are in relation to the home, the commuting time to the station or the shopping center, and the schedule for garbage collections. He will make sure that the owner understands all the financial aspects: purchase price, terms, financing arrangements, and down payment. He will likewise make sure that the owner does not plan to take with him part of the shrubbery or other appurtenances.

The broker will caution the owner against a short listing period. His experience in residential properties, for example, tells him that the first three months are the breaking-in period. The more expensive the property, the more unusual the property, the longer the time needed for the listing. Furthermore, most owners overprice and it may take time to bring them down to a realistic level. In the case of residential properties, many brokers find that a six months listing is best, but that a 90 day listing is acceptable.

The most difficult part of the listing process may be in pricing the listing. The owners may arrive at the price they think right by taking what they paid for the property in the first instance, adding to this their costs of maintenance, improvements, closing costs, commissions, discounts, and a "pad" with which to bargain. The broker will therefore point out to them recent sales on properties comparable to theirs. He will show that buyers buy by comparison. If the property stays long on the market because overpriced, prospects will start to think there is something wrong with it. The broker is well advised to tell the owners the truth about the value of the property at the outset, rather than to have them disgruntled six months later when the property is still unsold. The broker may use the technique of having appraisals made of the property by disinterested individuals, perhaps three selected at random from his local board, and show the owner the figures at which they independently arrived.

If the owner remains adamant on the unrealistic price he thinks he must get, many brokers will still take the listing on the thought that if they do not do so other brokers will. One of the evils of the real estate business is that some unethical brokers will give starry-eyed values to get exclusive right to sell listings. They know the price at which the property should be listed in the first place and count on their ability to push the owner down to that level to make a sale.

The broker will be helped in persuading the owner to agree to a realistic listing price if he can get close to the owner and his family, finding out who makes the decisions in the listing family. The psychology of the situation may also help bring about a realistic listing price. If the owners have to sell, many brokers will take an overpriced listing, feeling the pressure of the situation will bring about an early adjustment. If moving, the owners know they are better off taking a lower price than leaving the house vacant. If they want to sell, they will be moderately tractable. If they are merely willing to sell, they will be only slightly so. Regardless of their attitudes, the broker tries to get them to agree to a range within which their property may be sold, rather than a specific amount.

PROSPECTING

Prospects are persons, actively or passively in the market for property, who have the capital or credit enabling them to acquire the property. They may be actively searching for property or they may be mentally "set" to move on to new and better properties. The broker's objective is to find these prospects and match their needs and desires with the listings he has. Every prospect is a potential customer. Anyone needing shelter is a prospect.

Prospects are found everywhere. They are among the people to whom the broker has previously sold a property. These people may again be "on the move". The broker's customers tell him of new prospects. The broker learns about prospects through the answer to a casual question to friends or neighbors who may be thinking of a move. He hears about them through his pipelines to centers of influence, such as the local druggist, who may refer to him people he knows to be in search of properties.

Local publications provide names of prospects. The news items concerning a promotion, an engagement, a marriage, a death, or a birth can lead to prospects. The marriage of children may mean a demand by the parents for a smaller place of residence. The birth of a child may motivate apartment dwellers to search for a home of their own.

The broker finds prospects among those who answer a newspaper ad about a property, among newly-engaged couples, and those he meets at the Parent Teachers Association, the church groups, and the social organizations to which he belongs. He finds prospects among the visitors to the "Model Home" he has set up for public inspection with provisions for names and addresses in the "Guest Books" provided. He locates prospects among apartment dwellers who get fed up with the lack of privacy. He secures prospects by referrals from personnel managers responsible for finding locations for incoming executives.

The broker finds prospects among business firms whose present leases are about to expire. New arrivals in the city must find new homes. Successful men and women desire places of residence more in keeping with their increased incomes. Companies wishing to expand require more land. Companies opening up new branch offices or plant facilities need appropriate sites. Present prospects give brokers the names of other prospects. The local public schools will tell the broker about new teachers coming to town. The obituary columns may indicate a new type of home requirement for the survivors of the decedent. The broker gets prospects from among business and professional people seeking suitable properties for investment purposes.

QUALIFYING PROSPECTS

The broker qualifies prospects by getting enough information about them to determine their requirements and financial capacity to sustain the payments required. He ascertains the kind of property the prospects need and want and the price range into which they fit. If the property sought is a home, the wife usually has the major responsibility for the decision to be made and may, therefore, be the deciding factor in its selection. The broker is consequently mindful of her needs and desires. He determines the size of the family; the ages and sexes of the children; the place of work of the breadwinners and their hobbies; and the number and kinds of rooms required.

The broker gets the present address of the prospects, their names, and telephone numbers. In the case of residential prospects, he finds out all he can about their present place of abode and character of the neighborhood in which they live. He ascertains the location they would now prefer. He learns about their transportation requirements. He determines what cash they have available for deposit and how much of a down payment they can make. He develops the type of financing best suited to their requirements. He ascertains their religious preferences and whether they wish to send their children to public or private schools and, if private, whether any particular denomination is desired. He develops the reason for the family making a move. He finds out whether they have to sell their present home before they can buy. If so, he not only has a prospect; he also has a potential listing. While their home is on the market, they will have the time to look around for the kind of new home they want.

The broker must tactfully find out what the prospects can afford to pay. He may name the price of the property they like and watch their reactions. He notes whether they shrink and recoil or are still with him. He may ask the prospects how much they feel they could make by the way of monthly payments without stretching their budgets too far. If these seem acceptable, he names the down payment necessary to qualify for the type of loan they want. It is the experience of most brokers that prospects, if they like the property, will pay more than they say they can afford.

Prospects will inquire about the construction, the heating and the air conditioning systems, the sanitary facilities, the local commutation rates, the form of local government, the amount of taxes, and the kind of people in the neighborhood, and the broker must be prepared to answer these questions. He sets his pace to that of his prospects. He makes no depreciating references to other prospects, brokers, or properties. He investigates his prospects just as carefully as he investigates his listings. He does not take his prospects to properties unsuitable to their needs or which have to sell at prices beyond their ability to sustain.

In the case of residential properties, brokers report that the best place in which to qualify the prospects is in their own homes. Here they unbend, relax, provide a clear picture of the environment they seek. Their present location and the reasons they have for leaving it provide an indication of the property which will best satisfy them. Being in the prospects' home likewise provides the opportunity to get acquainted with their children and determine their requirements. What the prospects have done by way of decor and improvements in their own homes will suggest what may appeal in new surroundings.

If the broker cannot meet with the prospects in their home, the next best place in which to qualify them is in his office. Here, the broker must give the prospects his undivided attention and not permit any outside interruptions. Most brokers find it is better not to take copious notes on what their prospects say, for this makes them reticent, not wishing to be put on record. The broker tries to develop in conversation the interests he has in common with his prospects. Wherever possible, he qualifies both husband and wife at the same time.

Most brokers do not try to qualify prospects over the telephone. A telephone caller may not have a serious bona fide interest in the property. He may, in fact, be calling only get the exact address of the property so that he can contact the owner directly and thereby save the broker's commission. He may also merely be curious. In most instances, however, the telephone caller will be a "live" prospect. The broker therefore tactfully secures his name, address, telephone number, and arranges for an appointment at the earliest convenience of the caller. The caller must be made to understand that one cannot go into a detailed description of the property over the telephone and that financing terms are complicated and require a face to face confrontation for an adequate explanation. Nevertheless, the broker says just enough about the property over the telephone to whet the potential buyer's interest.

The training and the experience of the broker enable him to size up the prospects and advise them how the purchase can be financed. He is able to refer the prospects to the current fair market values of comparable properties. If the prospects detect flaws in the property, the broker is able to tell how they can be corrected, and at what cost.

CLOSINGS

The broker explains to his prospects what closing costs are and what they represent. He answers questions about lawyers' fees, taxes, title insurance, the best kind of mortgage for the prospects' situation, and the best source of funds for financing. He is fully conversant with the requirements for FHA insured and for VA guaranteed loans.

The question is often asked: "Just when should the broker try to close the transaction with the prospects?" The answer is that it is never too early to try to close. If the broker has done the necessary preparations, if he has properly qualified his prospects, if he knows the property the prospects need and want, if he knows the prospects' price range and ability to pay, and if he senses just when the prospects' interest has risen to the point of action, it is time to try to close the transaction. If the property can be bought for a small down payment, an early closing will be facilitated. If the broker knows where he can place the financing to the best advantage, the closing will be expedited.

The foregoing concerns closing the transaction and getting the prospects' signatures on the sales contract. Closing title, on the other hand, means the transfer of the money for the property bought, paying the closing costs, determining the seller's and the buyer's debits and credits, and the delivery of the deed to the grantee.

SUMMARY

A real estate broker is an agent acting for a principal in a real estate transaction. He owes his principal loyalty, obedience to instructions, keeping his principal informed, respect for the fiduciary relationship, the degree of care expectable of one in his position, and the making of an accounting of any money or property coming into his possession on behalf of his principal.

A broker is entitled to his commission for the sale of property when he has procured a buyer, ready, able, and willing to buy on the terms acceptable to his principal. He must verify the statements of his principal regarding his ownership and the property. He may not tell a prospect that his principal will take less than the price at which the property is listed. He is responsible for the conduct of his salespeople pursuant to the transaction. He may not so word his advertisements as to make the public think it is the owner who is advertising.

A listing is the authorization to the broker to act with regard to the property. An open listing is one in which the owner reserves the right to sell himself and through other brokers. An exclusive listing protects the broker against the competition of other brokers, but not against the competition of the owner himself. An exclusive right to sell listing protects the broker both against the competition of the owner and other brokers.

A multiple listing is an exclusive right to sell which also authorizes the broker to expose the property for sale by other brokers members of the multiple listing service. The listing broker gets a predetermined percentage of the commission and the selling broker, likewise, gets a predetermined percentage of the commission. A listing is one in which the commission is not included in the sales price. Many states regard it as illegal.

The listing contract should contain a terminal date and be signed by both spouses. The rate of the commission is a matter for negotiation between the broker and his principal. The listing contract should be in writing.

Wherever there is a need to relocate, there is a potential listing. Satisfied customers are the single most important source of listings. Other productive sources of listings reside in the owner who initially tries to sell the property himself but finds he is unable to do so; centers of influence; and publications providing information on impending moves.

The listing process consists of convincing the owner of the value to him of listing the property with a broker, an inspection of the property and its surroundings, the determination of the listing period, and the setting of a realistic price.

Prospects are persons actively or passively in the market for property. The broker determines their needs, their wants, and their ability to sustain the payments required for the property. The broker must be in a position to answer the prospects' questions about the property and know how its acquisition may best be financed.

Closings refer to the termination of the transaction and the passage of title to the property in the event of a sale.

GLOSSARY

GLOSSARY

CURTSY — the right which the husband has in his wife's real property
DOWER — the right which the wife has in her husband's real property
ENCROACHMENT — entry upon another person's real property
FIDUCIARY RELATIONSHIP — a relationship of trust and confidence

TRUE AND FALSE QUESTIONS

1. An ostensible agency is one in which the business affairs   T   F
   in general of a principal are entrusted to the agent.

2. A principal may ratify an unauthorized act of his agent.   T   F

3. A broker may not under any circumstances accept a com-   T   F
   mission from both seller and buyer in the same transaction.

4. "Able to buy" means financially able to buy.   T   F

5. If the broker buys the property for himself, he is still en-   T   F
   titled to the commission.

6. A "blind ad" is not a form of misleading advertising.   T   F

7. An "exclusive listing" protects the broker against the   T   F
   competition of the owner and also against the competition
   of other brokers.

8. In a multiple listing, the listing broker secures a pre-   T   F
   determined percentage of the commission.

9. A "net listing" is one in which the commission is excluded   T   F
   from the sales price.

10. If the property is held in the name of only one spouse, it is   T   F
    not necessary that the other spouse sign the listing.

11. The rate of commission is determined by the local real   T   F
    estate board.

12. A "center-of-influence" is a person who, by virtue of his   T   F
    daily activities, is in a position to know of relocations first.

13. Most brokers try to qualify prospects over the telephone.   T   F

14. A multiple listing is the same as an open listing.   T   F

15. A broker may not insert "blind ads".   T   F

16. The listing contract is a contract of employment.   T   F

17. An open listing is open to anyone, whether broker or not. T F

18. Most brokers will not take an exclusive listing. T F

19. An exclusive listing protects against the competition of other brokers. T F

20. All states now provide for a curtsy right in the husband. T F

21. The listing form should include the legal description of the property. T F

22. The commission rate is negotiated between the principal and his broker. T F

23. The listing contract should be in writing. T F

24. Wherever there is a need to relocate, there is a potential listing. T F

25. The broker may not inquire into the religious preferences of his prospects. T F

26. Buyers buy by comparison. T F

27. Most owners tend to overprice. T F

28. The owner has neither the power or the right to cancel an exclusive right to sell listing contract. T F

29. If the property under an open listing is sold, the seller has a legal obligation to notify the brokers with whom he has had it listed. T F

30. Most brokers will not take an open listing. T F

31. If a prospect makes an offer substantially below the listed price, the broker is not obligated to transmit it. T F

32. The broker is not obligated to verify the statements the principal has made about the property. T F

33. The principal may not try to sell the property "direct" to the prospect the broker has developed during the listing period and about whom the broker has told the principal. T F

34. In an exchange the broker usually gets two commissions. T F

35. Even if the broker was only the indirect procuring cause   T   F
of the sale, he is still entitled to his commission.

36. An agent cannot delegate discretionary authority.   T   F

37. A general agency is set up for the accomplishment of a   T   F
specific objective.

38. Being inanimate, a corporation cannot act as agent.   T   F

39. An ostensible agent is in reality not an agent at all.   T   F

40. An agent does not have the power to perform an act unless   T   F
it is authorized by his principal.

MULTIPLE CHOICE QUESTIONS

41. When an owner employs a broker for the sale of his property, this creates:
    ( ) An ostensible agency
    ( ) A general agency
    ( ) A special agency
    ( ) A universal agency

42. A broker is responsible for the acts and statements of his salespeople:
    ( ) Pursuant to the real estate transaction in which he has authorized them to engage
    ( ) Under no circumstances
    ( ) Only under the regulations of his real estate board
    ( ) At all times

43. If any one of the brokers with whom the property is listed under an open listing should sell the property, this:
    ( ) Requires that a share of the commission go to each of the listing brokers
    ( ) Terminates all the listings outstanding
    ( ) Requires the owner to notify the other listing brokers
    ( ) Requires the owner to pay each of the listing brokers a cancellation fee

44. Under an exclusive listing, the owner:
    ( ) Reserves the right to sell the property himself, if he can
    ( ) Promises not to compete with the broker during the listing period
    ( ) Subjects himself to a prepayment penalty, if he should sell the property
    ( ) Vests the broker with an exclusive franchise

45. Under an exclusive right to sell, the broker:
    ( ) Cannot list the property with the multiple listing service
    ( ) Cannot obtain the listing broker's fee
    ( ) Cannot collaborate with other brokers
    ( ) Is usually authorized to relay the listing on to the multiple listing service members

46. Under a multiple listing service:
    ( ) The listing broker gets a predetermined percentage of the commission
    ( ) The listing broker may not also act as the selling broker

( ) It is optional with the selling broker whether to share his commission with the listing broker

( ) The same situations prevail as under open listings

47. If the commission is not included in the selling price, then it is:
( ) A straight fee listing
( ) A contingency listing
( ) A net listing
( ) A blanket listing

48. If a real estate board required its members to be governed by the commissions it stipulated, this would be a violation of:
( ) The Robinson-Patman Act
( ) The Sherman Act
( ) The National Housing Act
( ) The National Uniform Licensing Act

49. If a listing is given by a corporation, then it should be signed by:
( ) The President
( ) The Secretary
( ) Anyone having the custodianship of the corporate seal
( ) Anyone authorized by appropriate resolution of the board of directors

50. The single most important source of listings is:
( ) From newspaper advertising
( ) From "centers-of-influence"
( ) From the civic organizations to which the broker belongs
( ) From referrals from satisfied customers

ESSAY QUESTIONS

1. What is the difference between an open listing and a multiple listing?

2. Why is it preferable to list a property within a price range, rather than at a fixed price?

3. Why should every listing contract bear a terminal date?

4. What are the objections to "net" listings?

CLOSINGS

CHAPTER SIX

WHAT ARE THEY?

Until you actually engage in a real estate transaction, you do not give much thought to the subject of "closings". About all this means to you is that the transaction is over and done with. So why all the fuss about closings? When you see ads on real estate and note some statements about low closing costs, you start thinking the subject must have some substance, because evidently money is involved. And then when you actually get involved yourself, you find out that when you have paid the purchase price you have not come to the end of your disbursements! You stop, you look, and you listen. When all of the extra items are listed for which you are going to have to pay, you may think at first that you are being exploited. Your next reaction is to take your "peeve" out on your broker. "Why didn't he tell me these things?" Most brokers try to do so. But some estimate the closing costs too low. Others are fearful that the consequences of telling the truth might force their prospect to back out of the transaction. So - let's draw aside the curtain of obscurity, lay the cards on the table, and look the facts in the face.

And, at the outset, let's avoid confusion by saying that we are not just talking about getting a buyer to assent to the terms of the purchase agreement. Here we are not limiting our consideration to the bringing together of the buyer and the seller to a meeting of the minds on the transaction. We are discussing all that is involved in the termination of the transaction - the documents that must be brought forward, the parties that must be present, the apportionment of charges that must be paid, and the imposition of various fees for services rendered to bring about a final disposition.

If the transaction is to be closed by delivery of the deed, the seller hands over this document to the buyer and the buyer, concurrently, hands the seller the purchase price. The buyer in turn may have to get the larger portion of this from his mortgage lender and, therefore, concomitantly, there may be a mortgage closing.

If the transaction is to be closed by the execution of a land contract, the buyer delivers his down payment to the seller. At the same time, the buyer and the seller enter into an executory contract. We call it executory, for so much remains to be done before the transfer of ownership becomes final.

By the terms of the land contract, the seller keeps title (ownership) until all the stipulations of the agreement have been fully carried out. Only then is a fully executed deed to the property delivered by the seller to the buyer. Only then does the buyer finally become the actual owner of the property.

Meantime, however, the buyer, under the terms of the land contract, is fully entitled to control and possession of the property and enjoys all the amenities and income it affords. If, however, the buyer defaults in any of his obligations under the land contract, then the situation changes. The seller is entitled to recover control and possession for himself by instituting legal proceedings which have come to be known as forfeiture or foreclosure.

Under the land contract, the closing may be in escrow. This means that the seller actually executes the deed, but he does not deliver it to the buyer. Rather, he puts it in the hands of a third party escrow agent. Simultaneously, he delivers to this agent the insurance policies covering the property and a copy of the land contract itself. He also hands the escrow agent a list of instructions, defining his duties and responsibilities. Since the buyer is equally concerned with the seller, both sign the instructions and, naturally, so does the escrow agent to indicate his assent to them.

The deed under the land contract bears the date of the closing and its effect therefore becomes retroactive to this time.

THE CLOSING DATE

Both buyer and seller are concerned with the closing date. The sooner it can be set, the better off both will be. The buyer will get the property that much more quickly. The seller will get his money that much more quickly.

Where is the date set? It is set out in the purchase agreement. How long a period of time must there be between the execution of the purchase agreement and the actual closing of the transaction? This depends on the time required for all the things to be done. A search must be made of the records on the property so that the buyer can be assured that he is getting a marketable title. This search results in a summary of the title history which becomes known as an abstract of title. If this is all that the seller must provide, the buyer hires an attorney to examine the abstract to make sure that there are no consequential defects, flaws, gaps, or breaks in this history of title. After the attorney has made his examination, he formalizes his conclusions in his opinion of title, which he turns over to the buyer. His opinion states whether he considers the title marketable or not.

It may be, however, that in the purchase agreement the seller agreed to provide the buyer with title insurance. In this event a title insurance company conducts the search and determines for itself whether the title is sufficiently good so that it may assume the responsibility for insurance. We should mention here, incidentally, that the buyer enjoys an advantage when title insurance is promised him. He does not have to pay the fee to an attorney for examination and rendering of an opinion on title. The title insurance company does this and is compensated by the seller.

The period elapsing before title closing is also determined in part by the time required for arranging of financing. This problem is not limited just to the securing of a mortgage loan. It may be that FHA insurance or VA guarantee is required and, if so, these organizations have to get into the act, make appraisals, examine the property, and give consideration to the credit qualifications of the borrower. Then, willy-nilly, there is some time necessary for carrying on the negotiations for the financing - rate of interest, down payment, prepayment penalty, and the length of time for the mortgage loan. If FHA insurance or VA guarantee is not applicable, the lender may desire insurance for a conventional mortgage loan, the securing of which will also take time.

It takes time also for the drafting of the various documents which must be in hand at title closing. The deed must be drawn up. The mortgage must be made out. When a property is sold, and the new owners takes out a new and possibly larger mortgage, then the old mortgage loan is paid off, and the purchase is financed by the proceeds of the mortgage loan. If a mortgage is to be assumed or taken subject to, the mortgagee-creditor must sign a reduction certificate, stating that amount that is presently due and payable. The seller may be required to furnish the buyer with a certificate of occupancy, a statement by the appropriate local official that there has been compliance with all the rules and regulations of the building and other pertinent departments. The mortgagee-creditor will demand that a survey of the property be made to make sure that the actual dimensions correspond with those stated in the mortgage document. The creditor will also have to have an appraisal made to insure that the appraised value conforms to the loan to value ratio as set for the lender.

The time of closing must also accommodate the convenience of the parties concerned. On what date can they all get together? When can they - the buyer, the seller, and their attorneys, the representatives of the lending institution and their attorneys, the insurance company, and the real estate broker - all be rounded up and answer to the roll call? The broker will be the easiest to please in this regard, for closing marks to him the consummation of the transaction which he has fathered and fostered.

Human nature being what it is and unexpected contingencies being what they are, it may be that, at the time set for closing, one of the parties may not be able to keep the date. He may be sick or have to be out of town on some more urgent mission. What happens then? This party will request that there be an adjournment of closing until another more convenient time. The lending institution may not have completed its processing of the mortgage loan or the title insurance company may not have finished with its title search. It, then, would intervene with its request for an adjournment. In these instances, there is usually no problem about getting the closing adjourned to a more convenient time.

But of this we should take note. The other party, who is ready to close at the regularly appointed time, in acceding to the adjournment request, has an option. He may specify that the prorating on the apportionments be as of the original or as of the adjourned date. He will naturally choose the one which is more to his advantage. Suppose, for example, the seller requests the adjournment. Suppose the income from the property sold is greater than its carrying charges. In this event, it will be to the buyer's advantage to specify the original date as the date for apportionments. Between the original date and the adjourned date, he will be deriving moneys coming from the property in an amount greater than those he is going to be required to pay out.

And we should carefully note that there is one closing date for which there may be no adjournment. If in the purchase agreement, the closing date is coupled with the clause, "time is of the essence", the party ready to close at the fixed date need not grant the request by the other party for an adjournment. Why should "time is of the essence" be inserted? One reason could be that the buyer has a contract on the date following for another real estate transaction whose successful consummation awaits the having in hand of the subject property.

CLOSING DOCUMENTS

The seller must of course bring the deed to the property properly executed and ready for delivery to the buyer. As it is the purchase agreement or contract of sale that specifies not only the kind of deed, but also describes the property, the consideration, and the encumbrances - everything in the deed must conform to the conditions precedent as laid out in these prior documents. The subject clause in the deed may not contain any items omitted from the purchase agreement. The two documents must correspond, just as inextricably as Siamese twins.

The deed to be delivered must be drawn up in the form to make it acceptable for recording. It should therefore show the marital status of the grantor or grantors. This, in the event the property is in the name of just one spouse, will require that the other join in the execution to release any rights in the property by virtue of marriage. The addresses of the grantor and the grantee should be shown. The grantor or grantors must sign. It is not necessary that the grantee sign. The grantor and spouse, if any, must be of legal age and sound mind.

Should consideration be recited in the deed? Yes, it should. A deed is a contract and a contract requires consideration. Does the actual amount of consideration have to be shown? This depends on the laws of the state where the property is located. In most states, it is not necessary that the actual amount be stated. Should the deed contain words of conveyance, like "bargain, sell, and release"? Yes, it should. Should a warranty deed recite the various warranties? Yes, it should.

The state where the property is located may require that revenue stamps be affixed to the deed. These are commonly in the amount of 55 cents per each $500 of value or fraction thereof. Before the deed will be accepted for recording, the recorder must see these stamps affixed. This helps the State by bringing in that much additional revenue. It is likewise of help to anyone subsequently searching the public records to find out how much was actually paid for the property. A broker or an appraiser, for example, would want to know. Would such a searcher be assured that the amount of stamps affixed was the correct amount? No. There is nothing in the law which prohibits a seller from putting on more revenue stamps than required. Why should he wish to do so? He might want to mislead subsequent searchers into thinking the property was of a higher value.

Besides the deed, the seller will also bring to the closing his latest real property tax receipts. These are issued by the city, village, township, and county treasurer. If taxes have been paid in advance, these receipts will verify the period of coverage for which the buyer is responsible, and for which, at closing, he must reimburse the seller. If taxes are to come due later on, these receipts will show the period the buyer will be paying for, and for which he is entitled to reimbursement from the seller. If the seller has been conducting a business on the premises, he should submit tax receipts for the payment of state or corporate franchise taxes required. If sewage taxes or special assessments have been imposed on the property, receipts should be submitted by the seller, verifying that these charges have been paid.

Suppose that liens - mechanic's liens, tax liens, judgment liens - have been imposed on the property. The purchase agreement will usually require that these be discharged prior to closing. The seller should therefore also bring to the closing what are called "satisfaction pieces" verifying the liquidation of these encumbrances.

Suppose that there has been a mortgage on the property. Suppose, furthermore, that the buyer has not agreed to assume it or take subject to it. Then the seller is obligated to bring to the closing a satisfaction piece that this mortgage has been discharged. This will be entered on the public record to erase the encumbrance.

Suppose that the seller has paid insurance premiums for coverage on the property for a period extending into the buyer's control and possession. The seller is then entitled to reimbursement for this protection to the buyer. This in turn will require the seller to bring the policies to the closing for purposes of verification. If the insurance carrier and the buyer are willing, the buyer may take over these policies in full. At closing, the seller will make the assignment and the insurance company will register its assent.

If income property is being sold and tenants are occupying the premises, the leases under which they hold control and possession should be brought to the closing and assigned by the seller to the buyer. The seller should, in this instance, concurrently write a letter to each of the tenants, telling about the sale, and naming the buyer as their new lessor, to whom subsequently the rent checks should be mailed. As a corollary to this, the seller should bring to the closing the rent roll, describing the unit occupied and the amount of rent appertaining. If the seller has in hand any deposit or security rentals from present tenants, these now no longer belong in his custody. He should consequently at closing deliver them to the buyer and obtain a receipt for so doing. To make assurance doubly sure, he should likewise obtain from these tenants their permission that the buyer should now hold these amounts.

If, as often happens, personal property, like furniture, is included in the sale, the seller should bring to the closing the bills of sale together with a warranty that title to them is good and marketable, and assign them to the buyer.

If a survey of the property is not required by the purchase agreement, it will be called for under the terms of the mortgage loan and therefore should have been prepared and brought to the closing and delivered to the buyer and/or the mortgage lender.

In many localities the seller may have to bring to the closing and deliver to the buyer a certificate of occupancy, signed by the appropriate local official, certifying that all local plumbing and electrical standards have been met. If there should presently be anything about the premises that constitutes a violation of any local codes, the seller, at closing, must either produce proof that this dereliction has been corrected or put in escrow funds sufficient to cure the defect.

EXAMINATIONS

If examination of the title has disclosed defects, quitclaim deeds from those concerned should be obtained, clearing such clouds. These deeds should be officially recorded.

If the property is in a jurisdiction where the Torrens system of title registration prevails, there will be public advertising that anyone having a claim should make it heard at a public hearing on a subsequent date. At this public hearing, these alleged claims will be adjudicated. Also a sum will be set aside and put into an insurance pool to compensate any subsequent successful litigant who did not have an opportunity previously to be heard. As a result of these proceedings, the title itself will be registered, and stand as irrefutable.

The examination of the survey will disclose not only whether the buyer is actually getting what he bargained for by way of property dimensions, but also whether the improvements that have been made are within the property lines. It will likewise indicate whether the buildings extend beyond the setback restrictions imposed by local building codes. It will further show whether eaves and bay windows extend over adjoining properties. By the same token, it will apprehend any encroachments by these neighbors.

CLOSING COSTS

Closing costs are many and varied, and practice and custom in a particular area, rather than law, dictate their allocation.

The seller is usually chargeable for the expense of drawing up the deed. If the law of the particular state requires the affixation of revenue stamps, it is customary for the seller to pay for these. These may be in the amount of 55 cents for each $500.00 of the purchase price over $99.00. If there is a mortgage on the property which is to be discharged, the seller pays for drawing up the discharge as well as for getting the discharge recorded. If an abstract of title is to be furnished, it is chargeable to the seller. If title insurance is to be furnished the buyer instead of the abstract, it is also the seller's responsibility. If a prepayment penalty is assessed for paying off the mortgage loan before the due date, the seller also pays.

The buyer pays for the cost of recording the deed, the drawing up and recording of the new mortgage on the property, the attorney's opinion on the title in the event an abstract is furnished in lieu of title insurance, and the survey made on the property. The buyer usually pays for the credit report run on him. The mortgagee-creditor may also require the buyer to pay the fee for its attorney.

If the property is being leased rather than sold, the lessor pays for the cost of drawing up the lease. If the buyer is being given an option to buy the property, the optionor usually pays for the cost of drawing this up. If personal property is being sold along with the real property, the seller is generally responsible for drawing up the bill of sale therefor.

Before the mortgagee-creditor will make a loan on the property, he will require that an appraisal be made to determine its fair market value. He will frequently charge the debtor-mortgagor with the cost of this appraisal.

Apportionments are also made at the time of closing of title. If, for example, title is closed on July 1, and taxes have been paid in advance for the year by the seller, the buyer must reimburse him for the taxes for the second half of the year. If mortgage interest has been paid by the seller for a period when the buyer will be enjoying control and possession of the property, the buyer must reimburse the seller for the interest applicable to this period. If a property insurance policy on the property is being assigned by the seller to the buyer and is agreeable to the insurance company for the assignment to take place, and if the premium paid by the seller covers a portion of the time when the buyer will have title, the buyer must reimburse the seller for this period.

If income property is being sold and rents have been paid in advance, the seller must reimburse the buyer for the rent due after he acquired title. If utility bills come due after title has been transferred and cover a portion of the period when the seller had title, the seller must reimburse the buyer for this period. This particular problem, however, does not usually arise, for the utility companies are asked to read the meters as of the day title closes.

The broker is concerned with these apportionments as well as with closing costs, for he may be asked to draw up the closing statements. Both buyer and seller also look to the broker for an explanation of the closing costs. The broker likewise draws up a statement at closing showing what money has come into his hands and how he has disbursed these funds.

But why is it necessary to make these apportionments? Why cannot the buyer and seller be billed for the fractional periods when interest charges, insurance premiums, utility bills, tax levies, and rents accrued? In most instances this would be found to be impracticable. It is, furthermore, reassuring to start out with a clean slate at the exact time that ownership changes hands.

How are these apportionments set forth? In closing statements in the form of credits and charges of the seller and credits and charges of the buyer. The credits and charges balance each other off. The apportionments making these up are usually calculated as of the day on which ownership changed hands. Anything prior to that day was the seller's. Anything on that day and after is the buyer's. For simplicity's sake, these apportionments are frequently calculated on the basis of a 30-day month. Each month in turn represents one twelfth of the annual charge, and each day represents one-thirtieth of the monthly charge.

Among the apportionments in favor of the seller are fire insurance premiums he has paid for the period the buyer will be the owner; taxes he may have paid in advance; and rent in arrears. Among the apportionments for the buyer are interest he may pay on the mortgage loan for the period the seller was the owner; insurance premiums in arrears, which may cover in part the seller's ownership; rent paid in advance; taxes in arrears; and wages accrued and unpaid.

And now we get to the "nitty gritty" of actual closing costs. In times of tight money, it may be necessary for the buyer to pay a loan application fee. He may also be chargeable for "points" - in effect a bonus for making him the loan. Although the seller may be obligated to furnish him with an owner's title insurance policy, the buyer will have to pay the premium for the mortgagee's policy for the benefit of his creditor. The buyer will usually have to pay for the survey on the property. A credit report will be made on the buyer as a condition precedent to making the mortgage loan and for this the borrower will have to pay. He will likewise be chargeable with the appraisal fee for evaluating the property as security for the loan. He will pay the recording fees for both deed and mortgage to the attorney he has employed and he may have to pay the fee for the attorney for the mortgage lending institution.

The impact of closing costs is not quite as heavy on the seller. It is customary and traditional for the seller to pay the revenue stamps, if these are required, to be affixed to the deed; release fees and recording charges for satisfactions of liens and mortgages and quit claim deeds to clear clouds on title; the broker's commission; the fee for his attorney; and, if escrow is employed, the escrow fee.

CLOSING STATEMENTS

These are reports, so to speak, on pertinent matters occurring at title closing. They incorporate the apportionments, the charges, and the disbursements. One closing statement is prepared for the buyer. Another is prepared for the seller. In some states the broker prepares the closing statements. In others, the attorneys for the respective parties prepare them.

The closing statement for the buyer describes the property, names the parties, and gives the time and place of closing. It may also name those present at the closing and indicate the capacities in which they acted. It sets forth the charges against the buyer - the sales price he must pay, the apportionment of property insurance premiums, attorney's fees, prepaid interest, and tax defrayments, if any. It likewise sets forth the credits due the buyer - the earnest money he paid; the mortgage loan he assumed; the rents due him; the taxes he paid for the period covering the seller's occupancy; and wages accrued, but unpaid.

The closing statement for the seller naturally differs in that it shows the charges against him - the mortgage assumption by the buyer, the cost of abstract or title insurance, real estate tax transfer stamps, if required, the commission owed the real estate broker, and the fee for the seller's attorney. On the other side, it shows the credits due the seller - the sales price, the insurance premium paid for the period of the buyer's ownership, and prepaid taxes.

For his own records, the broker may prepare a closing statement consisting of an accounting of the moneys that passed through his hands. These will be the earnest money he received from the buyer, and the amount delivered by the buyer as a condition precedent to closing. It will further show the amounts he disbursed - what was due the seller at closing, the premium for title insurance, the revenue stamps if required the attorney's fees, and his own commissions. It will incorporate both buyer's and seller's closing statement.

If the closing is in escrow, the deed and purchase price are delivered to a disinterested third party to arrange for title examination; if the title proves clear to the buyer, to pay the purchase price to the seller; and record the deed. If a land contract is employed and an escrow agent used, the period will be long term and the escrow holder will retain deed and other documents until all terms of the land contract have been performed. Thereupon, the escrow agent delivers the deed to the buyer, and ownership passes to him.

The mortgage loan closing statement shows the service charge to the borrower for obtaining the loan, the attorney's fees, the title examination and title mortgage insurance costs, brokerage fee for getting the mortgage loan, credit report charge, and the mortgage recording fee.

As mortgagor-debtor, you are required to take out title insurance and name the mortgagee-creditor as beneficiary. Title insurance premium is a one-time disbursement and the policy is written for the amount and life of the mortgage loan. As borrower, you also take out property insurance and make the mortgagee-creditor the beneficiary for the amount of the loan.

SAMPLE CLOSING STATEMENT

A real estate closing is to take place on April 11, 1971.

The selling price is $18,900.00, with cash to a new Federal Housing Administration mortgage in the amount of $17,500.00.

The buyer has deposited earnest money in the amount of $1,000.00. The seller's present mortgage has a balance on April 1, 1971 of

$10,525.00, with the five per cent interest paid to that date. The broker's commission is six per cent. Recording tax stamps are required and are to be calculated.

The broker has paid out the following costs:

Fee title insurance policy provided by the seller	$85.00
Recording charges for - mortgage discharge	2.00
- new mortgage	2.50
- deed	2.00
Attorney for preparation of the deed	15.00
Appraisal fee	50.00
Credit report on the buyer	3.00
Legal fees of the mortgagee	75.00

City and school taxes have been prepaid for the period, July 1, 1970 to July 1, 1971 .... 180.00

County taxes have been prepaid for the period, December 1, 1970 to December 1, 1971 .... 108.00

The insurance prepaid premium for three years, January 1, 1970 January 1, 1973 .... 225.00

(the policy will be assigned to the buyer)

The Closing Statement

Selling price	$18,900.00
Deposit	1,000.00
Abstract extension fee	
Abstract legal opinion fee	
Title insurance policy fee	85.00
Existing mortgage	10,525.00
Existing mortgage assumed	
Interest on existing mortgage	
5 per cent paid to April 1, 1971	
Record mortgage discharge	2.00
Preparation deed	15.00
Revenue stamps, calculate	
Commission - 6 per cent	
Appraisal fees	50.00
Credit report	3.00
Legal fees, lender	75.00
Record mortgage	2.50
Record deed	2.00
City and school taxes, July 1, 1970 to July 1, 1971	180.00
County taxes, December 1, 1970 to December 1, 1971	108.00
Insurance, 3 years, Jan. 1, 1970 to January 1, 1973	225.00

Date of Closing Sale, April 11, 1971

Seller's Closing Statement   Charge   Credit

	Charge	Credit
Selling price		$18,900.00
Mortgage paid	$10,525.00	
Title Insurance	85.00	
Mortgage Interest, pro-rated	14.62	
Mortgage discharge, recorded	2.00	
Deed preparation	15.00	
Recording tax stamps	20.90	
Commission	1,134.00	
City and school taxes		40.00
County taxes		69.00
Insurance		129.16
Sub-total	11,796.52	
Amount due seller to close	7,341.64	
Totals	$19,138.16	$19,138.16

Buyer's Closing Statement   Charge   Credit

	Charge	Credit
Purchase price	$18,900.00	
Deposit		$1,000.00
New mortgage		17,500.00
Appraisal fee	50.00	
Credit report	3.00	
Legal fees - lender	75.00	
Record new mortgage	2.50	
Record deed	2.00	
City and school taxes	40.00	
County taxes	69.00	
Insurance	129.16	
Sub-total		$18,500.00
Amount due from buyer to close		770.66
Totals	$19,270.66	$19,270.66

Interest on old mortgage

$10,525.00 × 5 per cent	=	$526.25
$526.25 ÷ 12 months	=	$43.854/month
$43.854 ÷ 30 days	=	$1.462/day
10 days @ $1.462	=	$14.62

Insurance

$225.00 ÷ 3 years	=	$75.00 per year
$75.00 ÷ 12 months	=	$6.25/month
$6.25 ÷ 30 days	=	.208/day
1 year @ $75.00	=	$75.00
8 months @ $6.25	=	50.00
20 days @ $.208	=	4.16
		$129.16

Recording tax stamps

$18,900.00: 18 @ $1.10	=	$19.80
2 @ .55	=	1.10
		$20.90

Commission

$18,900.00 × .06	=	$1,134.00

City and School Taxes

$180.00 ÷ 12 months	=	$15.00/month
$15.00 ÷ 30 days	=	.50/day
2 months @ $15.00	=	30.00
20 days @ .50	=	10.00
		$40.00

County Taxes

$108.00 ÷ 12 months	=	$9.00/month
$9.00 ÷ 30 days	=	.30/day
7 months @ $9.00	=	$63.00
20 days @ .30	=	6.00
		$69.00

SUMMARY

Closings constitute the terminations of the transactions. If the closing is by delivery of the deed, the seller hands over this document to the buyer, and the buyer, concurrently, hands the seller the purchase price. If the closing is to be by land contract, the buyer and the seller enter into this contract.

The closing date is determined by estimating how long a period of time will be required for title search, arrangement for financing, and the drawing up and executing of the documents that must be available at closing. If the closing date is accompanied by the clause, "time is of the essence", then the closing must be on that date, or the transaction can be rescinded.

Among the documents to be brought to the closing are the deed, the mortgage, tax receipts on the property, satisfaction pieces for the discharge of encumbrances that have to be liquidated, insurance policies, leases and rent rolls, survey, and appraisal.

Closing costs are many and varied, and whether they are to be assessed against the buyer or the seller will be determined by practice and tradition. Apportionments are also made at closing. These are determinations of the appropriate share for the buyer and the seller of taxes, insurance premiums, and mortgage payments.

Closing statements are reports on pertinent matters occurring at closing. They incorporate the apportionments, the charges, and the disbursements. One statement is prepared for the seller and one for the buyer. The broker prepares a statement, accounting for the money that has passed through his hands.

Over and above the closing statement for the purchase, there will be a closing statement regarding the mortgage transaction from which the financing is obtained.

GLOSSARY

ASSUMING A MORTGAGE: This means taking over someone else's mortgage obligation, and making oneself fully responsible out of one's personal assets for paying the mortgage obligation

JUDGMENT LIEN: A legal hold extending to all the property of a judgment debtor, and enabling the judgment creditor to get the property sold to pay the amount of the judgment

MECHANIC'S LIEN: The hold given to the party who has supplied services or materials in connection with a structure, and enabling him to get the structure sold if necessary to pay the bill outstanding

ESCROW AGENT: This is a third party in connection with a real estate transaction who, acting under instructions, holds a document like a deed, or a sum of money, like a deposit, until the terms governing the subject matter have been complied with

TAKING SUBJECT TO A MORTGAGE: This means that one is taking over a property on which presently a mortgage is outstanding. One recognizes the mortgage obligation, and that it may be foreclosed, if the debt for which it stands as security is not paid. However, one does not agree to be responsible out of one's personal assets for the amount of the obligation.

TORRENS SYSTEM: This is a procedure, first evolved in Australia, under which the title is registered and is subsequently unchallengeable.

TRUE AND FALSE QUESTIONS

1. Apportionments are part of closing costs.   T F

2. If revenue stamps are required to be affixed to the deed,   T F
   the seller usually pays for them.

3. Title insurance is usually chargeable to the seller.   T F

4. The buyer usually bears the cost of abstract of title.   T F

5. The seller pays for drawing up the mortgage discharge, but   T F
   the buyer pays for having it recorded.

6. The lessor pays for drawing up the lease.   T F

7. The mortgagee creditor usually pays for the appraisal.   T F

8. The seller must secure from the tenants authorization to   T F
   turn over to the buyer their rental and security deposits.

9. Utility companies usually read the meters as of the date title   T F
   closes.

10. The seller usually pays for drawing up the bill of sale.   T F

11. The seller generally pays the prepayment penalty on the   T F
    mortgage being discharged.

12. The buyer pays for the expense of drawing up the deed.   T F

13. The buyer pays for having the deed recorded.   T F

14. Under a land contract closing in escrow, the seller does   T F
    not execute the deed.

15. If a mortgage is to be assumed or taken subject to, it is not   T F
    necessary for the mortgagee creditor to sign a reduction
    certificate.

16. If "time is of the essence", it is still customary to grant a   T F
    reasonable period of adjournment, on the request of one
    of the parties.

17. The deed must be consistent with the purchase agreement.   T F

18. It is essential for validity that the grantee sign the deed.   T F

19. Consideration need not be stated in the deed.   T F

20. If personal property is being included in the sale, the seller should bring its bills of sale to the closing.   T F

21. Quitclaim deeds are used to clear clouds on title.   T F

22. State law dictates the allocation of closing costs.   T F

23. The buyer pays the cost of drawing up a new mortgage on the property.   T F

24. The mortgagee-creditor usually pays for the credit report on the buyer who is securing a new mortgage.   T F

25. Apportionments arc usually calculated as of the day on which ownership changed hands.   T F

26. The impact of closing costs is usually heavier on the seller than on the buyer.   T F

27. The real estate broker is not permitted to prepare the closing statements.   T F

28. The broker's closing statement consists of an accounting for the moneys that passed through his hands.   T F

29. Title insurance premium is a one-time disbursement.   T F

30. Mortgage title insurance is written for the amount and life of the mortgage loan.   T F

31. The attorneys for the parties are required by law to prepare their closing statements.   T F

32. The mortgagee-creditor is not permitted, under the law, to charge the borrower the fee for the attorney of the mortgagee-creditor.   T F

33. If the buyer is given an option to buy, the seller usually pays for the cost of drawing up this option.   T F

34. Under the Torrens system, the title is registered.   T F

35. The certificate of occupancy is the authorization given by   T   F
the seller to the buyer to occupy the property.

36. The purchase agreement will usually require that liens be   T   F
discharged prior to closing.

37. A deed is a contract.   T   F

38. The deed need not show the marital status of the grantor.   T   F

39. If an abstract is furnished, the buyer hires an attorney to   T   F
give him an opinion on the title.

40. Under the land contract, title is transferred at the time the   T   F
contract is signed.

MULTIPLE CHOICE QUESTIONS

41. The statement by the appropriate local official that the structure being sold complies with all the rules and regulations of the building and other pertinent departments is called:
( ) A certificate of compliance
( ) A certificate of occupancy
( ) A certificate of authority
( ) A certificate of code compliance

42. The party acceding to the request for an adjournment of closing:
( ) May recover liquidated damages
( ) May specify that the apportionments be either as of the original or the adjourned date
( ) May declare that "time is of the essence".
( ) May resort to the "save harmless" clause

43. If liens on the property are to be discharged prior to closing, the verification of their discharge is affirmed by:
( ) Satisfaction pieces
( ) Cancellations
( ) Expungements from the record
( ) The seal and signature of a notary public

44. Apportionments are set forth in the closing statements in the form of:
( ) Graphs and tables
( ) Profit and loss
( ) Credits and charges
( ) Income and expenses

45. Whether the improvements made on the property are within property lines can best be disclosed by:
( ) The deed
( ) The appraisal
( ) The property plat
( ) The survey

46. If the seller has been conducting a business on the premises, then he should bring to the closing verification:
( ) That franchise taxes have been paid
( ) That his use of the premises has been consistent with local ordinances

( )   That his outstanding bills have been paid
( )   That no accrued wages are outstanding

47. With regard to the statement of consideration in the deed:
( )   The exact amount in most states must be shown
( )   In most states it is not necessary that the actual amount be shown
( )   It is not necessary to state any consideration in the deed
( )   This must be sworn and attested to before a notary public

48. If there is default under a land contract, the seller regains control and possession:
( )   By mortgage foreclosure
( )   By foreclosure under power of sale
( )   By summary and forfeiture proceedings
( )   By deficiency judgment

49. The deed under the land contract:
( )   Bears the date of closing of the land contract
( )   Bears the date the last installment payment is made
( )   Bears the date of the purchase agreement
( )   Bears the date of the first installment payment

50. Setback restrictions are imposed by:
( )   Building codes
( )   The police department
( )   The traffic engineer
( )   The highway department

ESSAY QUESTIONS

1. What will the survey disclose?

2. How are apportionments set forth?

3. What will the broker's closing statement include?

4. Where and how is the date for closing set?

APPRAISING

CHAPTER SEVEN

ITS NATURE

An appraisal is a written estimate of value based on a logical analysis of relevant information concerning a particular property.

It is made as of a certain date. Most appraisals are made as of the date inspected. Some, however, are made as of a date in the past. In a few instances, an attempt is made to ascertain the value of a property as of some date in the future. Admittedly, this last can turn out to be just crystal ball gazing. Value is a mental judgment - not a mathematical concept.

Some states specify that fee appraisers be specially licensed. Others require only that a person have a license as a "salesman" to collect a fee for acting as an appraiser. No licenses are required for appraisers working for governmental agencies as salaried employees, for salaried employees of financial institutions, or for appraisers appointed by the courts.

Professional appraisers are frequently members of professional organizations and many clients demand that their appraisers be members of such professional organizations. Outstanding among these are the American Institute of Real Estate Appraisers, an affiliate of the National Association of Real Estate Boards; the Society of Real Estate Appraisers; and the American Society of Appraisers.

Every appraisal is made to solve a client's valuation problem, which may be to determine the market value of a property to ascertain whether it will sustain a mortgage loan, to determine a basis for a realistic buying or selling price, to determine the proper basis for tax assessments, or to determine just compensation in connection with a taking of a private property for a public purpose under the exercise of the power of eminent domain.

THE APPRAISAL PROBLEM

Every appraisal should have a purpose, the purpose of providing some type of value estimate. The purpose of most appraisals is to obtain market value. Other values commonly ascertained are condemnation value or just compensation, which constitutes the basis for the acquisition of property under the public power of eminent domain; assessed value, which is the basis for the power of taxation; leasehold value, which is the value of a lease, and which can be broken down into a leasehold estate (the tenant's interest) and leased fee (the landlord's interest); reversion value, which is the discounted worth of an estimated value at the time possession of real property reverts to the owner; and remainder value, which is the value estimate for property remaining or left over after a condemnation acquisition.

The American Institute of Real Estate Appraisers defines market value as the highest price in terms of dollars which a property will bring if exposed for sale in the open market, allowing a reasonable time to find a purchaser who buys with knowledge of all the uses to which the property is adapted and is capable of being used. It is also required that the transaction be an arm's length transaction and that there be a willing buyer and a willing seller in the situation.

The function of an appraisal is the reason a value estimate is required. The function may be for purposes of taxation, either *ad valorem* or Federal Internal Revenue; for a mortgage to provide security for financing; for use, to determine the marketability or feasibility of the property; for sale, to assist in the transfer of ownerships; for insurance, to provide the value required for coverage; and for condemnation, to establish the basis for just compensation under the taking resulting from the exercise of the power of eminent domain.

THE CONTENTS OF THE APPRAISAL

Every property to be appraised must be appropriately identified. This should be by lot and block number of city property, for example, lot 3 in block 72 in the map of the city engineer filed at City Hall, City of Ann Arbor, Michigan, January 29, 1972. If it is farm property, the legal description may be of such and such a quarter, of such and such a section, in such a township, in such a county. Or it may be by metes and bounds description, metes standing for measures, and bounds for directions, such as starting from a known point, extending 100 feet to the north, 100 feet to the east, 100 feet to the south, and 100 feet to the west, back to point of origin. These legal descriptions may be supplemented by reference, in the case of urban property, to street address. The improvements and buildings must also be appropriately described.

The property rights appraised are usually those of a fee simple interest, the largest possible interest it is possible to acquire in a parcel of real property, comprising the entire bundle of rights inherent in the complete ownership of the parcel. Some appraisals, however, are made of parts of these bundles of rights, such as appraisals of leaseholds, easements, and mineral rights.

The appraisal states its purpose and the function this purpose is to perform. It includes the definition of the value that is being sought. The definition of value will, of course, determine the pattern of the appraisal. Insurable value, for example, will encompass a valuation only of the improvements, since land does not constitute an insurable interest.

The appraisal engages in an analysis of the data found and usually comes up with three estimates of value - one based on a cost approach to value, one based on an income approach to value, and one based on a market data approach to value. The values, thus indicated, are then correlated into one final value estimate.

BACKGROUND DATA

The appraiser collects all the data possible on the property, forming the subject matter of the appraisal. These data are called specific data.

The appraiser also collects data concerning the area surrounding the property, called general data. These general data enable the appraiser to analyze the economic climate within which the values are set. The major general data which affect values are the effects of social movements on the property; the effects of the economy on the property; and the effects of governmental activity on the property.

ECONOMICS IN APPRAISING

The primary factors affecting value are utility - the property must have a useful purpose; scarcity - land, for example, is relatively scarce, and is in limited supply; and desirability - someone must want to control and possess the property.

These factors find their reflection in economic principles. Among these is the principle of the highest and best use. This is the use of the property which will produce the greatest net return to the land over a period of time. The use must be a reasonably probable use. The period of time is usually the economic life of the improvements. This is also defined as the most profitable likely use. Although properties used for the residence of the owner may not have a net return in monetary terms, they do provide a net return in amenities. These amenities are measured in the agreeableness and pleasantness inherent in residence on the subject property.

Valuation is subject to constant change. It is determined by the interaction of the demand for and the supply of real property. The value of an individual component of the property depends upon how much it contributes to the value of the whole. Maximum values in properties are usually found where there is a reasonable degree of similarity between and among other properties. This, however, does not mean "barracks-like" duplication.

The value of a property may also be measured by how much it would cost to acquire an equally desirable substitute property. Value may likewise be estimated by anticipation of future benefits to be derived from the property. Courts, in fact, say that value is the present worth of future benefits. Value, also, is based on the utility of the property. It is affected by whether the property is now being developed to its highest degree of usefulness, whether it is in a static position, or in a state of decline or decay. Value is determined likewise by the principle of balance - whether there is a proper proportion of the various parts in the whole.

VALUE APPROACHES

There are three basic approaches to value, all based on application of the foregoing economic principles. These approaches are the appraiser's tools, which he employs in order to develop value indicators.

The cost approach is based on the estimated reproduction cost of the improvements, plus the value of the land. The income approach is based on an estimate of the economic income to be derived from the property, less expenses. This net income in turn is capitalized into value. The income approach is used only where the property has an income potential. The market data approach is based on an analysis of sales or offerings for similar properties. It is used when there is market activity in the property type being appraised.

These value indicators are correlated so as to derive a final estimate of value. Correlation is the process of relating the value indicators to the appraisal problem. The final estimate of value is not to be considered as an average of the value indicators. One of these value indicators, due to the circumstances of the appraisal, may be stressed more than the others. All three approaches, in fact, have the market place as their source of data.

The Cost Approach

The first step in the cost approach is to make an estimate of the reproduction cost of the improvements new. This reproduction cost is derived from current local building costs as determined by the local market place. These costs may be based on a detailed engineering analysis called the quantity survey method, which produces an accurate result, but is extremely expensive and time consuming. Or these costs may be derived by breaking down the components of the building and determining the cost of each. This method is called unit-in-place and is moderately accurate, but quite expensive. Or they may come from information services, which supply costs per square or cubic foot on the basis of current construction estimates. These costs are reasonably accurate, but should be checked against those actually prevailing on the local scene.

The next step in the cost approach to value is to determine the amount of depreciation the improvements have suffered and to deduct this from the reproduction cost new. This depreciation may be in the form of physical deterioration, caused by loss from wear and tear, action of the elements, structural decrepitude, and distintegration through use. It is usually the least damaging form of depreciation in terms of dollar or value loss and applies to the buildings only. Depreciation may also take the form of functional obsolescence, which is a loss due to old-fashionedness, lack of modern design, or lack of modern facilities. This is a moderately damaging form of loss, but can, in many cases, be corrected, and applies only to the improvements. Depreciation may also take the form of economic obsolescence, a loss due to economic decay, the infiltration of inharmonious elements or lower income levels, or the presence of nuisances. This is the major cause of loss in value and usually cannot be overcome. Economic obsolescence applies both to the land and to the building. The value of the land, under the cost approach, is usually developed by the application of the market data approach.

To determine the loss in value, appraisers may use the quantity survey method, which is an analysis of building losses observed. Or they may use the effective age method, which relates value loss to the typical economic life of the building in relation to its present effective age.

The usual way in which appraisers estimate depreciation is by the breakdown method. This breaks depreciation down into each of its categories - physical, functional, and economic - and tries to estimate the loss in value due to each. With regard to the physical deterioration inherent in the building, the appraiser analyzes the losses on the basis of either a cost to cure, if the depreciation is curable, or a percentage loss of the value of the building for those items which cannot be cured.

For functional obsolescence, which is inherent in the building, the appraiser determines the deficiencies or excesses which can be corrected and estimates the cost to cure. For those deficiencies or excesses which cannot be economically corrected, the appraiser makes an estimate of the loss in net income they cause.

As economic obsolescence is extrinsic to the property, it is usually considered to be rarely curable. The loss economic obsolescence causes to the value of the building is determined by capitalizing the income loss because of this external condition. The loss economic obsolescence causes the land has already been taken into consideration by computing the value of the land by the market data approach. Obviously, people will pay less on the market for land which has been subjected to the erosive effects of economic decay.

Income Approach to Value

The income approach to value is based on the rent-producing capacity of the property. The appraiser gives consideration to the relationship between the income capacity of the property and its value by employing what is called the capitalization process. The key factor in this process is the determination of the capitalization rate. This rate is the return a prudent investor requires for putting his money into the property.

The formula for determining value under the income approach is I ÷ R = V, in which I means net income; R means capitalization rate; and V means value.

In the income approach the appraiser first estimates gross income from the property. This is an annual income estimate, based on rentals derived from the market place. Market rentals are called economic rentals. The actual rentals for a property are those called for by the contract of lease. They may be less than the economic rentals, for the lease may have been taken out some time ago when rentals in the market place were lower. Or they may be higher than economic rentals, for the economic circumstances applying at the time of the lease inception required higher rentals. Gross annual income from economic rentals is considered as potential or collectible income.

From this gross annual income there must be deducted the loss in rentals due to vacancies. Properties are not usually rented 100 per cent of the time. There must also be deducted losses from failure to collect rents. Not all tenants pay their rent. The amount of vacancy and collection losses will vary from time to time, from place to place. If income is received from the property over and above that required to satisfy a prudent investor, it is called surplus or excess income and is added to the economic rentals. The effective gross income from the property becomes total gross income after adding surplus and deducting vacancy and collection losses. This effective gross income can be considered to be collected income and will often approximate the actual income being derived from the property. The expenses on the property may be fixed expenses, operating expenses, or reserves for replacements, and are deducted from effective gross income to arrive at net income. This net income is the appraiser's estimate of the amount that can be imputed to the property and is used as the basis for capitalization.

The operating statements the appraiser uses to arrive at net income will be different from the operating statements of the owner of the property. The owner can legally include among his expenses the interest he pays on his mortgage and his debt service costs as deductible items for income tax purposes. The appraiser does not include these items, inasmuch as most properties are appraised on a free and clear basis. The owner's operating statements will include depreciation as a deductible expense for income tax purposes. But depreciation in such a context is merely a "bookkeeping" type. The appraiser, on the other hand, treats depreciation as "recapture" in his capitalization process.

The appraiser's operating statement includes as fixed expenses *ad valorem* taxes and insurance property coverages, such as fire and casualty. For operating expenses, the appraiser includes the appropriate charge for management. He assumes professional management. Individual charges for management will of course vary by property type and amount of services rendered by the manager. The utility charges to be deducted under operating expenses are those for gas, electricity, and water. Other operating expenses are those for maintenance and repairs, both inside and outside, day to day expenses for upkeep, and other expenses for operating the property.

The reserves for replacement the appraiser deducts are not necessarily cash reserves. Rather, they are set up as an account to recognize the need for replacement of items of relatively short life. The appraiser makes an estimate of the pro-rata replacement cost of such short life items as roof, furnace, air conditioning equipment, stoves, and furnishings. Reserves for replacements are proper to deduct in arriving at net income.

Formulae and Techniques
1. The net income can now be converted into a value by use of the formula: $I \div R = V$. For example, suppose the net income is $10,000 and the capitalization rate is 10 per cent. Using the formula we have $\dfrac{\$10,000}{10\%} = \$100,000$.

2. The net income and a selling price can be used to find a capitalization rate in the market place by use of the opposite formula: $I \div V = R$. For example, suppose the net income is $10,000 and a selling price is $100,000. Using the formula we have $\dfrac{\$10,000}{\$100,000} = 10\%$. If the net income were $10,000, and the selling

price were \$200,000, we would have $\dfrac{\$10,000}{\$200,000}$ = 5%. If the net in-

come were \$10,000 and the selling price was \$50,000 we would have $\dfrac{\$10,000}{\$50,000}$ = 20%. These examples in turn teach that the higher the rate, the lower the value, and the lower the rate, the higher the value.

3. So far, our examples have concerned themselves solely with the return *on* the investment, or the interest rate. The capitalization rate, however, should include also the recapture rate, or the return *of* the investment.

   The capitalization rate can be found in the market place by the direct comparison method. This considers the property to be a single investment unit with no split between land and buildings. It develops an over-all capitalization rate, inclusive of both the interest rate and the recapture rate. It is most applicable in cases in which an accurate split between land and buildings cannot be found in the market place.

   The recapture rate is based on the remaining economic life of the improvements. If they have a 50 year life, the recapture rate would be 2 per cent. If they have a 20 year life, then the recapture rate would be 5 per cent.

4. The summation process, or, as it is sometimes called, the built up rate theory, is occasionally resorted to in order to develop the interest rate, or the rate of return on the investment. It is a form of analysis, which is not generally used, since its conclusions in general are based on subjective judgment, and not on fact. This technique builds up an interest rate by giving consideration to the following factors:

   1. The government bond rate . . . . Factual
   2. Rate to compensate for the illiquidity of real estate . . . . Conjectural
   3. Rate to compensate for the management required in a real estate investment . . . . Conjectural
   4. Rate to compensate for the risk inherent in a real estate investment . . . . Conjectural

   The conclusion is the sum of these four parts, but it cannot be supported in fact or in the market place.

5. The band of investment process is sometimes employed to develop the interest rate, or the rate of return on the investment. It recognizes that the typical real estate investment is made up both of equity and mortgage financing. It assumes that the relative risk of each type of investment is reflected in the return required for its portion. Data for the use of this process can be obtained from the market price. The method is factual and realistic. An illustration of this process is given below.

Type of Money	Portion of Value	Return Required	Composite Rate
First Mortgage	60%	6%	3.6%
Equity	40%	10%	4.0%
	100%		7.6%

The mortgage rate is contained in the instrument financing the investment. The equity rate can be obtained by interviewing representative investors or by the application of the direct comparison method to the equity position.

6. The gross rent or income multiplier may also be used to try to develop the appropriate rate of return. It finds comparable properties and what they have been selling for. It ascertains what the gross annual income from these properties has been. So, if the consensus disclosed that the gross annual income has been one-tenth of the sales prices, the gross multiplier would be ten. If the gross annual income of the subject property is $10,000, then the application of the multiplier of ten would give a value of $100,000. The multiplier is a good tool if utilized properly, with proper analysis by the appraiser.

The Market Data Approach to Value

This approach tabulates and analyzes sales and listings of comparable properties in comparable neighborhoods. It compares the physical aspects of these comparables and makes adjustments for differentials. It compares the social and amenity aspects of these comparables and makes adjustments for differentials. It selects comparables of reasonably current status. It picks these comparables on the basis of comparable amenities and comparable utilities.

This method uses a number of comparables so that the market data may be sifted. Any situations that do not conform to normal may thereby be eliminated. This eliminates "distress" sales and distorted prices from consideration. This safeguards against being misled by isolated transactions reflecting abnormalities.

This process recognizes that "prices" do not in themselves reflect value. These "prices" may result from situations having nothing to do with value. The seller may have been forced to sell and the buyer to buy. Trading at "arm's length" may have been absent. There may have been personal or filial relationships between buyer and seller. The buyer or the seller may have been ill-informed and acted imprudently.

This market data approach to value is sometimes referred to as the "comparative" or "comparison" approach. It is a direct reflection of the actions and reactions of buyers and sellers in the market place and is based on the principle of substitution. It realizes that asking prices do not represent value and must be adjusted for the typical difference between asking and selling prices. Offerings will typically represent the value ceiling in a rising market and the bottom in a falling market.

Special Techniques in Evaluating Investment Properties

The land residual technique is usually employed when the building is new and its cost reflects present day values; when the land value cannot be ascertained from the sales of comparables; and when the building represents the highest and best use of the land.

The land residual technique assumes that you can establish the value of the building at, for example, $100,000. It also assumes that you have arrived at a capitalization rate for the building, say, 10 percent, made up of 8 percent rate of return and 2 percent, recapture rate. It assumes further that you have arrived at a net income for the entire property, both land and building, of say, $12,400. Given the foregoing factors, the problem is to find the value of the land.

The value of the building is $100,000, and the capitalization rate on the building is 10 percent, and this makes the income from the building $10,000. The rate of return for the land is 8 percent. The recapture rate does not apply to the land, since the land is not subject to recapture. As $10,000 income out of the $12,400 is attributable to the building, $2,400 must, then, be attributable to the land. The land value, therefore, must be $2,400/.08, or $30,000. This land value of $30,000 added to the building value of $100,000 makes for a total value of $130,000.

The land residual technique may also be used when the building itself is not in existence. In such a situation, a hypothetical new building which represents the highest and best use of the land is conceived, and its cost calculated.

****

The building residual technique may be used when land value can be estimated from the application of the market data approach.

The building residual technique assumes that you have arrived at a land value, for example, of $30,000. It also assumes that you have arrived at a rate of return of, for example, 8 percent. It assumes, further, that you have arrived at a total net return from the property, both land and building, of $12,400. As the value of the land is $30,000, and as the rate of return is 8 percent, this makes the income attributable to the land — $30,000 + .08, or $2,400. Subtracting the $2,400 from the total net income of $12,400 leaves a net attributable to the building of $10,000.

With a rate of return of 8 percent and a recapture rate of 2 percent or a total capitalization rate of 10 percent applicable to the net of $10,000 on the building, this leads to a building value of $10,000/.10, or $100,000. Adding the land value of $30,000 to this building value of $100,000 leads to a total value of the property of $130,000.

****

The property residual technique regards the property as one investment unit. It assumes that the investor does not think of a return partially from the land and partially from the building, but as a return on the property as a whole. It is used where land value cannot be accurately estimated.

Application of the Value Approaches

Certain valuation problems require the use of all three approaches to value. But some valuation problems lend themselves to only one or two of the approaches.

The cost approach is particularly applicable to new or nearly new buildings. It is also employed for special use or special purpose buildings, such as those for a non-profit objective.

The income approach is particularly applicable to properties which produce an income stream.

The market data approach is applicable to any property of a type which has an active market.

EVALUATING LEASE INTERESTS

Today's real estate market reflects increasing interest in long-term leaseholds on investment properties. The long-term lease provides the property owner with a steady income on his real estate investment with only nominal additional risk above typical security investments and gives him a shelter from Federal income taxes and a greater amount of cash flow. The tenant also benefits in being able to write off rental payments as business expense and being able to free his capital for business use.

The terms in lease investments should be understood. The leased fee is the value of the lessor's interest in the property. The leasehold is the value of the lessee's interest in the property. Economic rent is the amount which should be paid for the use of the property by the lessee. Contract rent is the amount actually paid by the lessee for the property.

Although income approach procedures are usually followed in the evaluation of lease interests, a major difference occurs in their application. Normally, the income approach is based on economic rent or the market rent from similar properties. But in the evaluation of a lease, we are not concerned with what should be paid as rent (economic income), but rather with what is actually being paid, or the contract rent.

The owner, who leases, relinquishes, or transfers one of his rights in the "bundle of rights" still possesses all the remaining rights, plus an income as compensation for this temporary transfer of one of the rights. Thus, the owner has two factors to consider: (1) the lease and the income to be derived from it, and (2) title to the property subject to the lease, including the return or recovery of the whole property at the end of the lease or a reversionary interest.

When considering whether a lease is long term or not, it is generally accepted appraisal practice that a lease in excess of ten years to a good tenant is long term and anything else is short term. The rental income from a long-term lease is a measurable commodity which represents a value increment to the present owner or to any potential purchaser from him.

In order to develop a proper analysis of the lease for purposes of valuation, the appraiser must consider several factors. He must pay attention to the parties and their relationship to one another; the length of the lease and any options included therein; the rental and how it is to be paid; the duties and the responsibilities of the parties and the treatment of tenant-installed improvements, fixtures, or betterments.   Any one of these factors which is not typical or standard procedure can have either a plus or minus effect on lease values.

Although the value of the leased fee, together with the leasehold, tend to equal the value of the property free and clear of the lease, there are circumstances in which the value of the entire property may be more or less than the value of these separate parts.   This comes about because of a variation between contract and economic rentals.   A contract rent less than economic rent will be an advantage to the lessee and will represent a leasehold value; conversely, an excess rental when capitalized will provide an intangible additional value to the lessor.   This concept is known and referred to as the "two property concept".

A corollary may be drawn between the lessor under a lease and the mortgagee under a purchase transaction, and likewise between the lessee and the holder of the equity position in a purchase transaction.   The lessee and the equity positions represent a higher degree of risk than do the lessor and the mortgagee positions.   Recognition of this variation in degrees of risk is essential for the selection of proper capitalization rates.

The long-term lease resembles an annuity, which is the right to receive money at given periods of time.   We assume that the long-term lessor has an annuity type of investment and will receive monthly or annual rent payments just as he would receive payments from a life insurance company if he had an annuity contract with it.   The annuity capitalization process is based on this concept and a variety of mathematical tables have been published to assist the appraiser in computing values.   As the discussion of annuity capitalization is a complex subject, our considerations will be confined to the underlying formula:

Value = Income × Factor

The evaluation of a lease is made by application of this formula to the income stream, using the so-called "Inwood" or present worth of one per period tables.   These tables provide factors for various interest rates and periods of time.   They tell us what one dollar payable periodically is worth today.   The factor so developed is a form of capitalization rate, including, as it does, both interest or return on, and recapture or return of the investment.

Applying these data to a simple example, assume a 7 percent interest rate or rate of return on the investment, and a term of ten for the annuity.   Referral to the "Inwood" or table indicates a factor of 7.024.   Thus, it is obvious that the receipt of $1.00 each year for ten years is worth $7.024 today.

A similar process applies to evaluation of the reversionary interest, or the value of the property at a later date, such as at lease termination, today.   In this instance, a different table is used: present worth of one or what one dollar due in the future is worth today.   Assuming the same facts as to rate and term, a factor of .5083 is given.   Applying this factor to a dollar, it is obvious it would be worth only about one-half of this amount today.

The valuation of a typical lease situation takes on a combination of values for the income stream and the reversion, plus a valuation of any differential between economic and contract rents. For example, a property was recently sold, subject to a lease for $128,000. This property's lease was a ten-year net contract to a good tenant. The annual contract rental was $10,000. Investigation in the market place indicated a 7 percent interest rate as proper. The estimated reversion was for land only, and in the amount of $100,000. The economic rental, based on comparable properties, would be $11,000 per year.

Applying the proper annuity capitalization process to the real property, we develop, by the income approach, a value indicator of $128,000.

Net income before recapture: $11,000
Less land requirement: $100,000 × 7% 7,000
Net income imputed to building $4,000

Capitalization Process:
$4,000 × 7.024 .... $28,096
Add land value 100,000
                                                             128,096
          Rounded off 128,000
Now, analyzing the lease and its value:
Leased Fee:
    Value of income stream:
    (Contract rental) $10,000 × 7.024 .... $70,240.
    Value of reversion:
       $100,000 × .5083 .... 50,830.
    Value of leased fee .... $121,070.

****

The second portion of the valuation is that of the leasehold. This is illustrated below, using the same facts, plus the estimate of economic rent of $11,000 per year and an interest rate of 10% to reflect the additional risk present in the lessee's position. This gives an Inwood factor of 6.145.

    Leasehold:
       Computation of the differential:
          Economic rent $11,000
          Contract rent 10,000
          Differential $1,000
The differential represents a plus of $1,000 per year to the lessee, which, when valued, produces a value increment of $6,150.
       Value of differential:
          $1,000 × 6.145 $6,145 or rounded off to $6,150.
Combining the two separate sets of computations, the distribution of interests becomes:
       Value of leased fee (lessor's interest) $121,070
       Value of leasehold (lessee's interest) 6,150
          Total Value $127,220
          Rounded off to $127,200

SUMMARY

An appraisal is a written estimate of value based on a logical analysis of relevant information concerning a particular property. Every appraisal is made to solve a client's valuation problem. The purpose of most appraisals is to obtain market value. This is defined as the highest price in terms of dollars that a property will bring if exposed for sale in the open market, allowing a reasonable time to find a purchaser who buys with knowledge of all the uses to which the property is adapted, and for which it is capable of being used. The transaction should be at arm's length and there should be both a willing buyer and a willing seller. The function of an appraisal is the reason a value estimate is required.

Every property to be appraised must be properly identified. The appraisal must be made as of a certain date. Specific data are collected on the property itself and general data collected by way of background. The appraiser gives consideration to the principle of the highest and best use. This is the use of the property which will produce the greatest net return to the land over a period of time. The value derived will be the present worth of future benefits from the property.

Three approaches are employed to determine value. The cost approach is based on the estimated reproduction cost of the improvements, plus the value of the land, and minus the physical deterioration, the functional obsolescence, and the economic obsolescence the property has suffered. The income approach is based on an estimate of the net economic income from the property, duly capitalized into value. The market data approach is based on an analysis of sales and offerings of comparable properties. These value indicators are then correlated so as to derive a final estimate of value.

The appraiser also evaluates lease interest - the value of the leased fee of the owner of the property and the value of the leasehold of the lessee of the property. The value of the leased fee consists in discounting the value of the income stream from rentals over the period of the lease and in determining the value today of the reversionary interest of the owner-lessor at the time of termination of the lease. The value of the leasehold consists in the discounted value today of the differential between the contract rent and the economic rent over the period of the lease.

GLOSSARY

AD VALOREM - According to value

CAPITALIZATION - determination of the value of an income stream

FEE APPRAISER - one not in continuous employment of a client, but hired for a fee to conduct a specific appraisal

TAX ASSESSMENT - the valuation of real property by a tax assessor.

TRUE AND FALSE QUESTIONS

1. A relatively high capitalization rate makes for a relatively high valuation. T F

2. The land residual technique is usually employed when the building is old. T F

3. The land residual technique may be used only if the property is presently in existence. T F

4. The building residual technique may be used when land value can be estimated by the use of the market data approach. T F

5. The property residual technique does not consider a return partially from the land and partially from the building, but as a return from the property as a whole. T F

6. The capitalization rate selected must reflect the risk of the investment. T F

7. The lessor's interest is called the leasehold. T F

8. The band of investment technique takes into account that in investments there is usually a mixture of equity and lending. T F

9. The safe rate in the built-up rate theory or technique is usually the current interest rate on government bonds. T F

10. The rate for recapture enables the investor to get a return of his investment. T F

11. Under the cost approach the value indicator is developed by adding the depreciated cost of the improvements to the value of the land. T F

12. The land residual technique assumes that an estimate has been made of the net income for the entire property. T F

13. The built-up rate technique is based on one interest rate for equity investment and another rate for mortgage investment. T F

14. The building residual technique is a part of the cost approach.   T   F

15. In investment property appraising, the capitalization rate is applied to the net income from the property.   T   F

16. Under the market data approach, land is separated from the building.   T   F

17. Land is depreciable for taxation purposes.   T   F

18. In the cost approach the appraiser estimates the reproduction cost of the improvements.   T   F

19. Appraisals are made to determine just compensation for a property taken under the exercise of the power of eminent domain.   T   F

20. The final estimate of value is arrived at by averaging the value indicators under the market, cost, and income approaches.   T   F

21. Economic obsolescence is a result of wear and tear.   T   F

22. The value of a property for insurance coverage is different from market value.   T   F

23. The cost approach uses the market approach in connection with its valuation of land.   T   F

24. The appraiser usually makes his estimate of reproduction costs by the quantity survey method.   T   F

25. In defining value, courts say it should be determined only with respect to the situation at the present time.   T   F

26. A difference of 1 per cent in the capitalization rate would make for only a small differential in overall evaluation.   T   F

27. The lessee's interest is called the leased fee.   T   F

28. The reversionary interest is what the lessor gets back at the termination of the lease.   T   F

29. Income taxes are included in operating charges.   T   F

30. Capital improvements are part of operating expenses.   T   F

31. The unit in place method estimates the cost of the major   T   F
    components.

32. From the lessor's standpoint, the evaluation of lease   T   F
    interests consists in the evaluation of the rentals and the
    reversion.

33. Mortgage lenders are concerned with the market value of   T   F
    the property serving as security for the mortgage loan.

34. The quantity survey method of cost estimation is a short   T   F
    method.

35. The rates in the built-up theory are realistic rates.   T   F

36. The recapture rate provides a return of the investment.   T   F

37. Net income is determined by deducting depreciation from   T   F
    gross.

38. The gross income multiplier is seldom used.   T   F

39. Depreciation is recaptured in the capitalization rate.   T   F

40. The appraiser does not regard rent as subject to recapture.   T   F

MULTIPLE CHOICE QUESTIONS

41. Comparing the physical aspects of comparables and making adjustments for differentials is part of:
    ( ) The definition of the appraisal problem
    ( ) The assembly of appraisal data
    ( ) The correlation of value conclusions
    ( ) The market data approach

42. Most appraisals are made to determine:
    ( ) Market value
    ( ) Sales value
    ( ) Rental value
    ( ) Assessed value

43. The principal factor in investment property appraisal is determining the:
    ( ) Rate for risk
    ( ) Interest rate
    ( ) Capitalization rate
    ( ) Recapture rate

44. The building residual technique assumes you can establish beforehand:
    ( ) The band of investment rate
    ( ) The equity investment rate
    ( ) The net income from the property as a whole
    ( ) The net return from the building only

45. The method which estimates the cost of the major components is:
    ( ) The quantity survey method
    ( ) The subcontract method
    ( ) The unit in place method
    ( ) The comparative method

46. The built up rate theory gives consideration to all the following factors, except one. Which is that one?
    ( ) The safe rate
    ( ) The rate for inflation
    ( ) The rate for illiquidity
    ( ) The rate for management

47. The formula employed in developing leasehold values is:
( )   I/R = V
( )   V = I x R
( )   V = I x F
( )   R/I = V

48. The percentage to be deducted for rental losses from vacancies:
( )   Will be 5 per cent
( )   Will range between 5 per cent and 10 per cent
( )   Will range between 0 and 5 per cent
( )   Will vary with the property

49. The courts say that value is:
( )   The future worth of the benefits to be derived from the property
( )   The present worth of future benefits
( )   The price paid for the property
( )   The replacement cost of the property

50. Usually, the least damaging form of depreciation in terms of value loss is:
( )   Functional obsolescence
( )   Economic obsolescence
( )   Physical deterioration
( )   Economic decay

ESSAY QUESTIONS

1. What is the usual way by which appraisers try to estimate depreciation?

2. What criticism is made of the summation method, or built up rate theory, of trying to develop the appropriate rate of return on an investment?

3. Why is the market data approach called the "comparative" or "comparison" method?

PROPERTY MANAGEMENT

CHAPTER EIGHT

ITS DEVELOPMENT

The origins of property management are lost in antiquity. It arose the first time a property owner realized he would be better off by having someone else look after his property for him. In our country we first saw it on a substantial scale after the Civil War, when building construction zoomed and each of the structures required management. Prior to 1900 most property management was in downtown office buildings and commercial hotels.

From 1900 to 1920 there was a shift in rental housing to the apartment building and a concurrent awareness of the need for its efficient management. The high rental boom in apartment houses between 1920 and 1929 further underscored the importance of good property management.

During these periods there was no training of managerial personnel. There were no courses being taught. There were no professional organizations in management with high performance standards. Junior employees of brokerage firms collected rents and supervised repairs on properties managed. The broker's bookkeeper furnished the property owner with the monthly report of what rents came in and what operational expenses were paid. But as brokers began to realize that management could be a profitable activity in and of itself, they engaged in a process of self-education in management, for themselves and their employees.

And then came the depression and in its wake rising vacancy ratios, defaulting tenants, negotiations for rent reductions, and defaults on the mortgage loans with income property as security. The lending institutions had to foreclose on their mortgage loans, and thereby became the involuntary owners of apartment houses, office buildings, hotels, farms, and residential properties. These properties had to have tenants and many of them had to be repaired and rehabilitated.

The financial institutions taking over these properties threw up their hands and confessed their incompetence. Property management was not their line. They did not know how to service and care for these properties. They lacked the "savvy" for sales promotion, prospecting techniques, merchandising showmanship, and the give and take of lease negotiation. They found themselves in a new world of handling tenants and tenant complaints, of collecting rents and collecting them on time.

These financial institutions therefore turned to real estate brokers for the professional competence and knowhow in these new areas. After all, it was the brokers' business to merchandise real properties. The brokers' experience should provide the knowledge for efficient and economical operation. And the real estate brokers, finding selling a lean and hungry business in the early 1930's, were delighted to secure the extra income that management provided.

Unfortunately for property management, many of the new broker entrants did not have the administrative ability and the staying qualities and tenacity that success in management required. They were motivated solely by the commissions to be earned. The true professionals in management therefore decided to form an organization whose members would stand for integrity and a code of ethics, high standards of performance, and a reputation for getting the job done to the satisfaction of both the owner client and the tenant customer.

In 1933, a society of individual professional property managers, founded the Institute of Real Estate Management, affiliated with the National Association of Real Estate Boards. It certifies the character and ability of its members, to whom it awards the coveted designation, CPM, Certified Property Manager, and AMO, Accredited Management Organization, to qualified management firms. It thereby identifies the individuals and the firms qualified to manage real property. It likewise makes available specialized services in property management and publishes *Property Management,* which informs its readers of what is new and advantageous, to them in this field.

ATTRIBUTES REQUIRED FOR PROPERTY MANAGEMENT

The property manager must have a thorough knowledge of real estate. He must know current values, the current market, the economic and secondary base of his area, local business conditions, personal income levels, local industries, and the supply and demand of rental space. This knowledge enables him to sense management opportunities, recommend appropriate land use, set rental levels, suggest profitable conversions for present properties, and set up effective merchandising campaigns for capturing the tenant market.

The property manager finds sales and brokerage experience helpful in carrying out his management assignments. This has given him a wide array of contacts from whom he may secure management business and present and future tenants. They may likewise serve as listening posts and refer to him what they hear regarding needs for property management and rental space. Furthermore, the manager's selling experience has taught him the kinds of merchandising appeals that are most effective in marketing land use. The give and take employed in negotiating real estate transactions are equally applicable in negotiating new leases and lease renewals.

The appraisal knowhow of the property manager is pervasive in everything he does. He employs the income approach to value in appraising in setting up a proper capitalization. He employs the income approach in management in determining what net revenues must be enjoyed from the property to make it a going concern. He employs the market approach in appraising in setting values on the basis of what comparables are selling for. He employs the market approach in management in setting rentals on the basis of what comparable properties are bringing in.

If the property manager has been charged with superintending salespeople in a brokerage firm, he gains experience in handling personnel useful in property management. If he has acted in the role of office manager in a brokerage firm, he will find the knowledge thus gained of office procedures and systems, together with the most effective ways of working with clerical personnel, of value in his new role. As property manager he has the responsibility of securing the greatest amount of productive effort from building superintendents, custodial personnel, porters, doormen, security people, and cleaning crews.

It is said that a property manager must have the patience of Job and the wisdom of Solomon. Tenants may be the type that try managers' souls. But the manager, on the surface, remains unruffled and serene. Tenants may operate on the principle that the wheel that squeaks the loudest gets the most juice. But the manager pours on the oil only when the lubrication is essential. Tenants may be "deadbeats", resourceful enough to devise the most ingenious expedients to avoid their obligations, but the manager's stratagems must be effective in circumvention. The property owner himself may be unreasonable, penny wise and pound foolish, grasping and greedy, short-sighted and stupid. But the manager must be able to tactfully show him the error of his ways and teach him to look on his disbursements not as outright expenditures, but as investments for a greater future return.

The property manager is a salesman when he merchandises space. He is a purchasing agent when he buys supplies and equipment for his property. He buys in bulk and gets the bulk discounts. He shops around and gets the best "buys". He buys fuel oil and other fuels for heat generation. He buys the services of scavengers and charwomen. He buys paint and varnish, hammer and nails, bricks and lumber. He must know where he can get the quickest and most convenient deliveries and who are the most dependable and reliable sources.

The property manager is an analyst. He weighs the pros and cons of investment projects.   He determines what the payout will be.   He analyzes his market potential and develops the most effective approach to win it over. He is a realist and does not permit himself to be carried away.

DEVELOPING THE MANAGEMENT PROGRAM

The manager first finds out everything he can about the property he is to manage. He informs himself of its past history, its present status, and its future prospects. He makes an analysis not only of its present tenancies, but also of what can be done to expand its rental potential. His survey takes in an analysis of the local rental market, particularly of the neighborhood where the property is located. He also makes a study of the competition with which he must cope and develops the features unique to his property and advantageous to his tenant prospects.

The manager gives consideration to other uses to which his property might be put and in what respects they are preferrable to the present. He tries also to determine whether the present type of tenant is best for his property or whether another type should be solicited. He makes a physical analysis of the property to ascertain whether it should be modernized by the employment of a new style, whether it should be rehabilitated under a renewal program, or whether it should be remodeled by means of a change in the structure.

The data the manager collects enable him to develop a rental program. This involves merchandising the rental space and setting forth the advantages the property has to offer. This likewise means being aware of the disadvantages from which the property suffers and how they may be offset or eliminated.

The rental program also involves setting the rental rates. The manager knows he must be competitive, and therefore finds out what competition is charging for comparable space. He may take a typical rental unit, price it, and then value the other units up or down from the typical one, depending on their superiority or their inferiority. In considering what rates to charge, he keeps in mind the rent paying capacity of his tenant market. His rents will also be based on the physical characteristics of his space. Corner office space will usually carry an increment of value. Upper floor space may rent for more than lower floor space in an apartment. If offices have windows unobstructed to light and view, they will carry higher rentals than others not so advantaged.

The manager also develops an advertising program for the property. For his classified ads, he will state the location, rental, amount of space, and specific advantages. For his display ads, he will use illustrations and go into greater detail in his description. For his brochures, he will see to it that his illustrations and layout are works of attractive art. In his direct mail, he will call attention to special features of interest to his selected list of potential tenants. His signs will tell the viewing public about the unique advantages of the property.

In developing his management program, the manager will evolve the policies by which he will be guided. Among these will be the periods of the leases, the kinds of leases, the escalation clauses - if any - to be incorporated, and the deposit and security rentals to be required. His policy on rent collections will include what leeway, if any, to give delinquents, whether to send out rental statements to tenants in advance of the due date or to consider they will pay automatically without such reminders. His policy on re-decorating will indicate how often this may be done and whether the tenant should be required to share in the cost. He may likewise have a policy on whether to grant rental remissions for the first month or two, as an incentive to get in new tenants.

The manager also develops the tactics he will employ in qualifying and handling tenants. He will make clear when the lease is signed that the rents are due on time. He will follow up arrears quickly and firmly. He will notify tenants in arrears of the serious consequence of further delay. He will pay the tenant in arrears a personal visit prior to the institution of legal action. He will employ eviction only as a final resort. In handling tenant complaints, he will provide a respectful audience and try to get the grievances in proper perspective. He will remain calm and collected throughout the grievance interview and give the tenant plenty of time to air his problem. If he has to turn down a tenant's request, he will do so tactfully and diplomatically. Above all, he will treat all tenants alike and play no favorites.

A most important item on the manager's program is conducting himself well in his relationships with his owner client. He will, of course, make out a monthly report showing what has come in, been paid out, and left for the owner. He will naturally keep his client's funds in a bank account separate from his own. He must have permission from the owner to make disbursements of reasonable amounts for the property without each time having to get his consent. In his management contract, he will have spelled out his authority to hire and fire, to draw up and sign leases, to negotiate on leases, to arrange for insurance, and to pay the bills as they come due. The contract will contain a "save harmless" clause under which the owner will take over any law suits concerning the property leveled at the manager.

OPERATION OF THE MANAGEMENT PROGRAM

Policies are one thing. Operation is another.

Your policy is never to let the tenant get behind in the payment of his rent. What do you do to forestall this unhappy event? An ounce of prevention is worth a pound of cure. You check the tenant's reputation for prompt payment of his bills before you take him on. You develop a tactful reminder letter to be sent the tenant whose check for the rent has not been received a few days after due date. You have a plan of action of subsequent phone calls and personal visits if the rent check still fails to arrive.

Your policy is to keep the property well maintained. You operate this policy by making periodic inspections and finding out what needs attention. On every visit you check the cleanliness of the public spaces and the boiler tubes. You check the condition of the screens when they are taken down in the fall. You inspect the screens in the spring as they are painted and repaired.

Your policy is to keep the premises "ship-shape". You execute this policy by having your apartment tenants deposit their waste in the incinerator and their garbage in garbage bags. You provide ash and rubbish containers for your office tenants. You enforce standards of cleanliness and make them conditions precedent for continued use of the property.

Your policy is to maintain the structural integrity of your building. You put this policy into effect when you shore up the building to compensate for settling and movement. You use water proofing to stop leakage. You restore mortar joints through tuck-pointing. You check to make sure that your electrical system is not overloaded. You arrange for elevator maintenance under an outside contact, rather than try to do so with your own staff.

Your policy is to have an efficient office building. You therefore arrange for automatic elevators, both for dispatching and interval control. Most managers find it advisable to contract out the office cleaning. The bulk of this is done at night. A day cleaning crew may, however, be employed to clean lobby floors, elevator cabs, front walks and entrances, and outside areas and windows. How about alterations in the office building that may have to be made from time to time? These may be carried out by appropriate specialists in your building crew.

Who are the key people on your office building staff? One is your chief engineer. He is responsible for the heating plant, the plumbing system, the electrical system, and the maintenance. The other is your building superintendent. He is responsible for cleaning, alterations, decorating, and rendering tenant services. Your security staff may report either to you or to your building superintendent.

If you are acting as manager of a store property, your lessee will usually assume the responsibility for fuel and heating plant operation, for his store front, for decorating and interior alterations, for water and utilities, for electrical and mechanical equipment, and for janitor service. In the case of a shopping center, tenant associations will usually take the responsibility for or contribute to surfacing, cleaning, marking, and illuminating the parking lots, as well as for cleaning, illuminating, landscaping, and maintaining the public spaces.

Your management of a medical building will reflect its unique character. You will assure the right amount of wiring for the special types of electrical therapy required. You will comply with special requirements for air conditioning and ventilation. Cleanliness is a must. The interior and the surroundings must be kept immaculate. There will be heavy all-day traffic and elevator service must be available to accommodate it. You may find it necessary to have one manually operated elevator to provide for the special services needed for those in wheelchairs or otherwise disabled as well as for individuals so disturbed as to be fearful of automatic elevators.

OPERATION OF THE MANAGEMENT OFFICE

You will have drawn up the job specifications for each position and you will see to it that your personnel meet these criteria. You will make a thorough investigation of each prospective employee to determine his past record and reputation. You will have developed an "employment manual", which will inform your personnel what is expected of them and what, in turn, they may expect from you. Where possible, you will find it to your advantage to "promote from within". You will be friendly to all, but chummy with none. Knowing the desire on the part of everyone to receive recognition, you will give credit where credit is due.

As your office records provide the data required for rental billings, income statements, and condition of the property, you will keep them meticulously and accurately. You will develop labor and material costs for each job to be done on the property to provide a comparison of what the costs would be via alternate methods. Your payroll summaries will post entries to the appropriate classifications. Your records on heating costs will enable you to determine the relative economy of methods available - whether, for example, electricity is more economical than gas. Your rental records will also show the rentals per room or per square foot of rentable area.

You will prepare realistic budgets for future operations and, where possible, always stay within these estimates. Your income projections should assure that payrolls will be met and bills paid. You will also make sure that insurance premiums are paid, social security records kept, income tax withholdings made, and painting and decorating schedules kept.

In all these areas, you will be helped by computer hookup. This will save on time and effort. This will find its place in billing, record keeping, cost comparisons, and cost analyses. This robot slave will become your indispensable servant.

COMPENSATION FOR PROPERTY MANAGEMENT

The usual arrangement is for the property manager to receive a percentage of the rents he collects. This percentage will be negotiated with the owner at the time of agreement on the management contract. Real estate boards also make studies as to the appropriate percentage. It may be possible for the property manager to supplement this by securing a percentage of the expenditures for the making of property improvements which are supervised. As property manager, you may also secure a commission on new leases obtained and old leases renewed.

Your compensation will not be limited to what you enjoy in your management role. You will also be securing brokerage, insurance, and appraisal business from friendly tenants and suppliers.

SECURING MANAGEMENT BUSINESS

Any owner of income property who does not wish to assume the burden of management or who is not in a position to do so is a prospect. He may be an individual owner, a trustee, a corporation, an investment syndicate or a real estate investment trust, a mortgagee in possession, an involuntary property owner through foreclosure, an absentee landlord, or a charitable or educational institution.

The most effective way to secure management business is to become known as a better manager than your competitors. You can build this reputation by actually being an effective manager, through favorable publicity you receive on properties you manage, through the persuasive presentations you make before prospective owner clients, through the earnings records you are known to have made for the properties you have managed, and through the esteem in which you are held in your community.

You will constantly cultivate real estate investors. You will convince them of your ability to do more for them than your competitors or they could do for themselves. You will show them the purchasing power you command through the number of properties you manage. You will point out to them that the scope of your operations enables you to employ carpenters, painters, and plumbers on a full time basis with resultant cost savings.

You will also secure additional management business through referrals. Your fuel oil and other suppliers will reciprocate your business by referring to you building owners they contact who are considering a change in management. Your concessionaires for vending and washing machines presently in your buildings can act as listening posts for management business.

But most of your management business will come to you because of your reputation. This, you achieve by adherence to your Realtor's Code of Ethics. This you earmark by the attainment of the Certified Property Manager designation. This you get by having salvaged income properties given up as lost. This you make by your money-making ideas in cutting down on cost without cutting down on service. This you earn by your impeccable honesty, never accepting a rebate from suppliers and never feathering your own nest at the expense of your principal.

MANAGEMENT'S FUTURE

Your future is part and parcel of economic growth, encompassing the increasing number of structures serving this growth. The growth of high rise office buildings and apartment houses, the growth in shopping centers, the growth in recreational type properties, the development of new towns and satellite cities, and the growth in urban renewal projects — all these make for a corresponding growth in the demand for property management.

SUMMARY

Prior to 1900, most property management was in downtown office buildings and commercial hotels. From 1900 to 1920 there was a shift in management to the apartment building. The high rental boom of the 1920's further underscored the importance of property management. But during these periods there was no training of management personnel.

During the early 1930's, by virtue of their foreclosures on mortgage loans, financial institutions became the involuntary owners of apartment houses, office buildings, hotels, farms, and residential properties. They turned to real estate brokers for the management. The professionals in management formed in 1933 the Institute of Real Estate Management, and awarded the designation, CPM, Certified Property Manager, to qualified individuals and the designation, AMO, Accredited Management Organization, to qualified firms.

The property manager is a salesman, a purchasing agent, an analyst, a personnel manager, an appraiser, and a diplomat. He develops a rental program for the property with which he is charged. He sets the rental rates. He develops the advertising techniques. He evolves the policies. He tries to keep his tenants placated and his owner-client satisfied with his return.

He never lets the tenant get behind in the payment of his rent. He keeps the property well maintained. The structural integrity of the building is his primary concern. He sees to it that the office building is efficiently operated. In a large management project, his key aides are his chief engineer and his building superintendent. He sees to it that his personnel meet the criteria for the specifications of the positions they hold. He prepares realistic budgets for future operations.

As his compensation, he derives a percentage of the rents he collects, and a commission on new leases secured, and old leases, renewed. He secures new business by reason of his reputation: He constantly cultivates potential real estate investors.

TRUE AND FALSE QUESTIONS

1. The origins of property management are found in the 1920's. T F

2. During the period, 1920-1930, courses were set up for the T F
training of property management personnel.

3. During the early 1930's, financial institutions looked to T F
real estate brokers for professional competence in management.

4. The Institute of Real Estate Management is an affiliate of T F
the National Institute of Real Estate Boards.

5. The designation, CPM, is awarded to management firms. T F

6. The property manager employs the income approach to T F
determine what net revenues must be secured from the
property.

7. The property manager is a salesman. T F

8. The property manager is a purchasing agent. T F

9. The rental program does not include merchandising the T F
rental space.

10. Corner office space does not carry an increment of value. T F

11. The "save harmless" clause in the management contract T F
is for the protection of the client owner.

12. The effective property manager does not let the tenant get T F
behind in his rental payments.

13. The bulk of the cleaning in an office building is done at T F
night.

14. The chief engineer is responsible for the heating and T F
plumbing.

15. Individual store tenants in a shopping center take over the T F
responsibility for cleaning and maintaining public spaces.

16. The management of a medical building is similar to the   T   F
management of an office building.

17. Real estate boards prescribe the managers' compensation.   T   F

18. The property manager usually receives as his compensation   T   F
a straight salary.

19. The property manager may secure commissions on new   T   F
leases obtained and old leases, renewed.

20. The property manager's income potential is limited to what   T   F
he can secure in his role as property manager.

21. Any owner of income property is a prospective client for a   T   F
property manager.

22. The Realtor's Code of Ethics is applicable to any holder   T   F
of the designation, CPM.

23. Property managers do not operate on the principle of   T   F
reciprocity in dealing with suppliers.

24. It is proper for a property manager to take a rebate from a   T   F
supplier, if the price obtained for the supplies is the lowest
available.

25. From 1920 to 1930 there was a shift in rental housing to   T   F
the apartment building.

26. Prior to 1900 most property management was in downtown   T   F
office buildings and in commercial hotels.

27. CPM's in the 1920's limited themselves to rent collection.   T   F

28. The Institute of Real Estate Managers certifies the character   T   F
and the ability of its members.

29. Modernizing a property means a change in the structure.   T   F

30. Remodeling a property means the employment of a new   T   F
style.

31. In a high-rise apartment upper floor space may rent for   T   F
more than lower-floor space.

32. Property managers never engage in a policy of rent   T   F
remissions.

33. The property manager must keep his owner client's funds in a bank account separate from his own.　T　F

34. Property managers have the office cleaning done by their own employees.　T　F

35. The computer is not used in property management operations.　T　F

36. The property manager is prohibited from securing from his owner client a percentage of the funds disbursed for additions and improvements to the structure, which he supervises.　T　F

37. The property manager usually receives a percentage of the rents he collects.　T　F

38. If the manager is also a broker, he may supplement his income by securing brokerage business from friendly tenants.　T　F

39. The property manager may secure additional clientele by showing the purchasing power he commands through the number of properties he manages.　T　F

40. Most of the new property management secured comes to the manager because of the reputation he has achieved.　T　F

MULTIPLE CHOICE QUESTIONS

41. The Institute of Real Estate Management:
    ( ) Serves as a multiple listing service for properties to be managed
    ( ) Identifies individuals and firms qualified to manage real property
    ( ) Is open to all qualified brokers who manage real property
    ( ) Sets the rates of commissions its members may charge

42. Most property managers employ eviction:
    ( ) Only as a final resort
    ( ) Only after a thirty day waiting period
    ( ) Only after the tenant's statutory period of redemption has expired
    ( ) Only after a judgment in summary and forfeiture proceedings has been secured

43. The clause in the management contract under which the owner agrees to take over any law suits concerning the property leveled at the manager is:
    ( ) The subrogation clause
    ( ) The substitution clause
    ( ) The save harmless clause
    ( ) The assumption of risk clause

44. In a large office building management staff, the person responsible for the electrical system is:
    ( ) The building superintendent
    ( ) The electrical contracting service
    ( ) The technical man in the building division
    ( ) The chief engineer

45. In a large office building, the person responsible for rendering tenant services is:
    ( ) The building superintendent
    ( ) The chief engineer
    ( ) The service man
    ( ) The porter

46. The type of building in which it may be necessary to have one manually operated elevator is:
    ( ) The loft type building

( ) The merchandise mart
( ) The medical building
( ) The self-service building

47. The manager's compensation is determined by:
( ) The schedules drawn up by the Institute of Real Estate Management
( ) The recommendations of the local real estate board
( ) Negotiations with the owner of the building
( ) Schedules prescribed by the state real estate commission

48. The most effective way to secure management business is:
( ) To advertise for it
( ) To solicit the business of owners who present management contracts are soon to expire
( ) To engage in competitive bidding
( ) To become known as a better manager than your competition

49. The Realtor's Code of Ethics applies to:
( ) All property managers
( ) Property managers, members of the National Association of Real Estate Boards
( ) Property managers, members of an independent multiple listing service
( ) Property managers, licensed by the state real estate commission

50. Real property management in the United States came about on a substantial scale for the first time:
( ) With the industrial revolution
( ) With the Civil War
( ) At the beginning of the 20th Century
( ) In the 1920's

ESSAY QUESTIONS

1. What factors occasioned the large rise in the demand for property managers in the early days of the depression?

2. What specific fields of real estate knowledge must the property manager have?

3. How does the property manager develop a management program?

FINANCING CHAPTER NINE

THE TERM MORTGAGE

The term mortgage is a mortgage loan granted for a term, generally from three to five years. It is usually renewed or refinanced, if payment is demanded, at the end of this period. Interest on the mortgage loan is made payable quarterly or semi-annually. This was the usual type of mortgage until the days of the depression.

When the depression struck, it became most difficult to pay off term mortgages. The banks which had loaned out their money on the security of such mortgages were confronted by a heavy rate of default. On foreclosure, the banks became the involuntary owners of frozen assets in real estate. This further impaired their liquid position in these difficult times.

It was at this juncture, in the year 1933 - the year of the national bank holiday - that the Home Owners Loan Corporation, a temporary financial relief agency, was formed in the Federal government. Its obligation was to refinance outstanding term mortgages under an amortizing basis by which interest and principal payments could be spread evenly for periods as long as 15 years. At the time of its creation, home mortgages were being foreclosed at the rate of 1,000 a day. By refinancing over a million mortgages, it acted as a salvage agency. It demonstrated the feasibility of amortizing mortgage loans as against the use of term mortgages with their so-called "balloon payments" at maturity.

MORTGAGES TODAY

Mortgages today are based on the amortizing principle in the great majority of cases. The mortgage agreement provides that periodic payments - usually monthly - be made, which, over the length of the loan extinguish the amount of the principal indebtedness. In fact, that is how they get their name, "amortizing". With the making of each one of the payments, part of the debt is liquidated. The periodic payments are usually for a fixed amount, covering payment on principal, interest, taxes, special assessment, and insurance. This is why the term, "budget mortgage", is often used to describe the arrangement. It is as if the mortgagor-debtor budgeted his income every single month to allocate a portion for these purposes.

As homes are usually sold with mechanical appliances, like oven, range, refrigerator, garbage disposer, and dishwasher, the so-called "package" mortgage was developed. The monthly payments under the package mortgage include charges for these items. This package mortgage loan enables the home buyer to confine his dealings to just one lender. It distributes the payments for this home equipment over a longer period than ordinarily possible. Such a loan is beneficial to the buyer, for the interest on it is usually less than the carrying charges under an installment sale separately made of these mechanical appliances.

As time goes on under the mortgage loan, the mortgagor-debtor may wish to secure additional advances to cover new home improvements, remodeling, rehabilitation, or renovation. If he has what is called an "open-end" mortgage loan, he may obtain these additional borrowings, usually up to the amount of his original indebtedness. The mortgagee-creditor feels perfectly safe under this arrangement. The mortgagor-debtor has usually increased his credit capacity with the passage of time and the additional improvements enhance the overall security. The mortgagee-creditor has strengthened the security of his investment portfolio. If interest rates have risen at the time the open-end provision is used, the mortgages-creditor may look to the provision in the agreement permitting him to apply the new rate equated with the current money market. The open-end mortgage is to be distinguished from the "open" mortgage, one that has come due, but has not been paid. In other words, it is open for payment.

The construction loan mortgage is unique in that payments are made on an installment basis in the course of progress on construction. One payment may be made to enable the builder to begin work. A second payment may be made when the building is under roof; a third, when the structure is plastered; and the final, when the building has been completed and is ready for occupancy. In some areas, interest is paid on the loan throughout on the theory that the mortgagee-creditor has set aside the entire amount for the project. In other areas, interest is paid only at the times the amounts are advanced and the builder is actually using the money.

This is advantageous to the borrower, for he becomes indebted for interest only when the amounts advanced are productive for his purpose. The construction loan mortgage is advantageous to the lender, for he disburses the principal amount at the times for the most part when the security has been improved and more value added to the property. The construction loan agreement provides for the advances to be made only when inspection verifies that the progress has been in accord with the plans and specifications. The mortgagee-creditor may also hold back a part of the amount at structure completion for a short period to guard against the interposition of mechanics' liens.

A blanket mortgage loan is one which covers two or more parcels of real property. It is quite common in subdivisions and developments which may cover an entire tract. It usually contains a partial release clause. This states that an individual parcel may be released from the impact of the blanket mortgage if the proceeds from its sale are allocated to a partial reduction of the blanket mortgage. Were it not for this partial release clause, a prospect for a particular parcel would be unwilling to buy, for his individual purchase would be subject to foreclosure should the overall blanket mortgagor-debtor default.

In a participation mortgage loan, the over-all amount is so large that it becomes necessary for several creditors to participate, each with his own share. A number of lenders are pooling their resources to make the loan possible. The terms of the mortgage agreement set forth what share of the return each of the participants is entitled to and what portion of the principal amount each has contributed.

In a purchase money mortgage, the seller is actually doing the financing himself. The borrower is usually making a down payment, and the balance due becomes owed to the seller, secured by a mortgage on the property. It is called a purchase money mortgage, because the amount due equals what is owed as purchase money. This type of mortgage is commonly employed when the borrower cannot secure financing from the usual institutional sources and the seller is so desirous to sell, that, rather than lose the sale, he agrees to engage in the financing himself. The situation could also be one in which the seller considers it to be to his financial advantage to put his money out at what seems to him an attractive return. In order to persuade the seller to do the financing, it is also possible that the buyer may pay a premium price for the property.

If the mortgagee-creditor holds a first mortgage, he can resort to the property for satisfaction of the indebtedness before anyone else. If he holds a second mortgage, he is entitled to his "take" only after the first mortgagee-creditor has been paid. He is then also called a junior mortgagee, for he is junior to the first. There could also be a third and a fourth mortgagee-creditor, each of whom would be junior to those preceding.

An FHA mortgage loan is one insured by the Federal Housing Administration. It is made for the most part on one-through-four-family dwellings. It may also be made to finance the alteration, repair, improvement, or conversion of existing structures. It may be used for the insurance of loans on rental housing projects.

A VA mortgage represents a mortgage loan guaranteed by the Veterans Administration. This VA guarantee does not constitute insurance. It therefore does not require the payment of an insurance premium, as is essential under an FHA loan. The guarantee usually covers only a portion of the loan, applicable to principal, interest, taxes, assessments and insurance premiums, repairs, and foreclosure costs. A VA loan must provide for the prepayment privilege without penalty. It can be issued without a down payment being required.

If a mortgage loan is not FHA-insured and not VA-guaranteed, it is known as a conventional mortgage loan. So popular, however, has the insurance feature become that a private organization, the Mortgage Guaranty Insurance Corporation, entered the conventional field to provide insurance for qualified borrowers on qualified properties. Other organizations have similarly entered these lists, and these loans are now called MGIC, after the initials of the progenitor in this area.

SOURCES OF MORTGAGE LOANS

About 60 per cent of home mortgage loans in terms of dollar amounts emanate from savings and loan associations. These associations get savings from the public and put this money to work earning interest on loans secured by real estate mortgages. They not only encourage thrift in their depositors, but also encourage home ownership by making funds available on liberal terms for financing such acquisitions. They have popularized the pay as you go, or amortizing plan, of home purchase more than any other institutions.

Savings and loans may be organized either under Federal or under state law. If under Federal, they automatically become members of the Federal Home Loan Bank System and the Federal Savings and Loan Insurance Corporation. Such membership makes it possible for them to borrow from a district Federal Home Loan Bank and provide assurance to their depositors of the safety of their savings.

If savings and loans are organized under state law, they may still secure the foregoing advantages by applying and qualifying for membership therein. They find it particularly worthwhile to secure the emblem FSLIC (Federal Savings and Loan Insurance Corporation) to use in connection with their advertising.

Savings and loans are usually locally owned and privately managed. By virtue of their local character, they keep their finger on the local credit pulse. They know property values and property trends in their local area. They know their own local people and how well these people comply with the requirements of credit capital, capacity, and character.

Savings and loans are not limited to making loans for the purchase of a home. They also re-finance and make loans for repairs, construction, and home improvements. They may also buy any mortgage loan they could have made themselves. Where the law permits, they may set up branch offices in suburban areas, shopping centers, and elsewhere. As a matter of conservative lending practice, many savings and loans limit the monthly payments to 20 per cent of the take-home pay of the borrower. They are now permitted to make loans on mobile homes.

In deciding whether or not to grant a mortgage loan, savings and loans are particularly concerned about the neighborhood in which the property is located. They look for signs of appreciating or depreciating influences on value. Some of them actually classify neighborhoods in their locale as most desirable, desirable, declining, or risky. They particularly esteem neighborhoods of economic stability.

Savings and loans adjust the payments and the period of loan amortization to the financial capacity of the borrower. They may impose an extra charge for the privilege of prepayment. They will have to charge enough for the loan to cover their costs and make a reasonable profit. The determining factor in the amount of interest they charge is the cost of the money to them, the expenses of their operation, and what their competition is doing.

Whether the savings and loan will grant the loan is determined by the character, the earning capacity, and the other loan commitments of the applicant. It is also determined by the value of the real property the would-be borrower will put up as security. Particular attention will be paid the total obligations outstanding against the borrower, for the savings and loan cannot assume that he will give his mortgage loan with them any preference over the others. And of course in a period of tight money, it may be quite difficult for savings and loans to accommodate as many borrowers as it would like.

Their primary assets are amortizing first mortgages secured by residential real estate. They also keep balances with commercial banks. They likewise hold vault cash and government securities.

They have promoted thrift by establishing a variety of accounts to suit the financial situations of their customers. They have promoted customer goodwill by liberal, considerate, and understanding treatment. They have worked in close cooperation with real estate practitioners.

Commercial banks have also rendered a remarkably fine financing service. Although they concentrate on business loans to finance inventories, payrolls, and working-capital, they have, nevertheless, been a potent factor in long-term mortgage financing. They usually adhere to a lower loan to value ratio than do savings and loans. They ordinarily take a conservative approach to the qualifications of the borrower and security of the property. So large has mortgage lending become in the operations of many commercial banks that they have set up separate mortgage loan departments. In small towns, where savings and loans may not exist, commercial banks may be the only source of institutional lending. They quite commonly engage in construction loans, if an advance commitment for the long term loan has been obtained.

Although life insurance companies will be interested in taking over a package of home mortgage loans developed for them by their correspondents, their direct lending will be on larger multi-unit and commercial and industrial properties. They are also unique among lending institutions in that they may make their mortgage loans in any part of the country. In order to secure a hedge against inflation, some life insurance companies have recently been insisting on equity participations as a condition precedent to granting the loan. This may consist, for example, of two to three per cent of the gross income derived from a particular income property.

Although mortgage bankers serve primarily to act as intermediaries between borrowers and lenders, they may on occasion make interim loans, pending a subsequent assumption by an institutional lender. Their prime objective, however, is to originate and service mortgage loans for mortgage investors.

They serve as loan correspondents for life insurance companies, since the majority of the loans they acquire find their way into the portfolios of these institutions. They are more active in arranging financing for new properties than for old and, in this connection, frequently arrange short-term credit for builders for new construction. They may secure the assignment of servicing the mortgage loan from their institutional clients. This means that they collect the payments when due, inspect the property serving as security, and take appropriate action in the event of delinquencies.

LAND CONTRACTS

The seller may finance the sale himself by taking back a purchase money mortgage, or he may employ the land contract. This is an agreement under which the buyer makes his payments under the install-ment plan. He does not receive title to the property until he has fully liquidated his indebtedness.

Suppose you sell your property to me for $66,000 under land con-tract and I make a down payment of $6,000. I agree to make equal monthly payments of $600.00, which will include six per cent interest on the declining land contract balance.

If you find it to your advantage, you may sell your land contract to someone else, who will try to buy it from you at a discount. If your buyer purchases at a ten per cent discount, he will pay $54,000 for the land contract, but will be receiving $60,000 in principal payments plus six per cent on the declining balance. He will, because of the discount, of course, secure a rate of return in excess of six per cent.

As the holder of the land contract retains title to the property, he may try to secure a mortgage loan on this ownership. Whatever amount he secures decreases his own dollar investment, and frees this sum for advantageous investment elsewhere. If, for example, he were able to borrow at five per cent, and put this out at six per cent, he would be employing to advantage the principle of leverage - O. P. M., other people's money - to enhance his own.

In the land contract itself, it may be stipulated that a higher penalty rate of interest is to apply during the period that a payment may be in default. For the protection of the holder, a clause is inserted giving him first claim on the insurance proceeds in the event of damage to the property. It is also specified, that in the event of a taking under eminent domain, not only would the holder be compensated by means of the proceeds, he would also be made whole from any other damage he might sustain. The obligation to pay taxes under the land contract is imposed on the buyer. The contract further provides that the vendee may not assign his rights under it without the consent of the vendor and that the vendor may declare the entire amount due and payable at the time of any default.

Surveys show that the parties use land contracts when it is not possible for them to resort to FHA, VA, or conventional loans. The buyer may not have sufficient funds to qualify for the down payment required under these arrangements. Sometimes the land contract will be used by a building contractor to sell to a vendee for a short term, just long enough to enable him to build up an equity sufficient to qualify for the down payment under an FHA-insured loan. The parties may also use a land contract when the financing called for is beyond the limits presently authorized under FHA. Also, shell houses (foundations, walls, and roofs, but not electricity, plumbing, plastering, and interior) do not qualify for FHA, VA, or conventional loans, but may do so under land contracts. Most land contracts, however, arise in the case of the sale of one-through-four-family dwellings, farms, and vacant lots.

Among the factors determining the amount of discount at which an investor may purchase a land contract are: the credit character and capacity of the vendee; the stability in value of the property; the ratio between the value of the property sold and the balance due under the land contract; and the risks from physical deterioration, functional obsolescence, and economic obsolescence in the property itself. The yield under the land contract investment will arise from the discount at which it was purchased, the interest payments on the declining loan balance, and the degree to which the principle of leverage may be exercised.

SALE AND LEASEBACKS

These commonly come about in the case of merchandising establishments, such as supermarkets and department stores. They buy land and put up the building. They then sell the land and the building to an institutional investor, like a life insurance company, on condition that the property be leased back to them for a period measured by the functional life expectancy of the structure.

Everybody benefits. If things work out as planned, the buyer-lessor gets rental payments high enough to recover his investment over the period of the lease, plus a satisfactory rate of return on his investment. He also comes into full control and possession of the property at lease expiration. If the structure still enjoys a functional life expectancy, he may again lease it out. Whatever return it then provides constitutes an extra surplus. He may deduct depreciation on the building against his income tax liability. Hopefully, he has a gilt-edge tenant, sure to pay the rent and pay it on time. As the lease is a net lease, he is not burdened with the chores of management and has no disbursements to make for taxes, insurance, special assessments, maintenance, and repairs. To guard against the erosive effects of inflation, he may have been able to negotiate an equity participation over and above the fixed rental.

The seller-lessee too, is in a happy position. He has been able to keep his capital in his merchandise, rather than invest it in real estate. It is therefore constantly at work for him in his trade, turning over with each turnover of merchandise and, concurrently, bringing in its increment of profit. He, too, is in a fortunate tax position, for he may deduct the rent he pays against his own income tax liability. When the security analysts examine his financial statements, they are pleased to note that he shows a liquid and healthy working capital position. He is not "locked in" with fixed assets. As the buyer-lessor at lease termination will have recovered his investment, he may be agreeable to a lease renewal at substantially lower rentals.

FARM FINANCING

As farm operations become increasingly mechanized, more financing is required for farm machinery. As farms, like most other forms of real estate, enhance in value, more financing is necessary for their acquisition. Although much of the expense for farm soil conservation is paid for by the Department of Agriculture, the balance remaining will have to be financed by the individual farmer.

Just as the institutional lender concerns himself with the property productivity of commercial and industrial real estate on which loans are requested, so does this same lender concern himself with farm productivity. This in turn leads to an inquiry into the nature of the soil, the degree to which crop rotation has been practiced, the extent to which soil enriching legumes have been planted, and the amount of soil conservation undertaken.

This same institutional lender likewise concerns himself with the credit capacity and character of the individual farmer. In this connection, he finds out whether the return from the farm is such as to provide a decent living for the farmer and his family and still leave them with enough to make their payments.

What do these farmers use these loans for? Some buy other farms. Others acquire mechanical equipment. Still others refinance present loans. They may use the money for seed and fertilizer, hiring additional help, and investment in livestock.

Do these farm mortgage loans carry the prepayment privilege? Many do just as a matter of course. Others do, providing a penalty is paid for the privilege of its exercise.

When we look around and identify the sources of farm loans, we see a somewhat different picture from other kinds. Commercial banks in many rural communities may constitute the only source. Life insurance companies also participate. Individuals, such as neighboring farmers, play important lending roles. And farmers themselves form loan associations which may, on proper qualifications, secure loans for their members from Federal Land Banks. There is also the Farmers Home Administration, created by Congress to supply special financing help. It will make loans to farmers of good credit repute who have tried to no avail to secure financing elsewhere.

The loans can be for an amount as high as the appraised value of the farm serving as mortgage security. The proceeds may be used for building or repairing farm homes and farm buildings. Nor is their coverage restricted to the farms themselves. People living in rural areas may secure such loans for the financing of their homes. And this is not the whole story. The Farmers Home Administration will also insure loans made by private lenders for these purposes, providing the farmers themselves qualify as credit risks and the security supplied supports the loan.

THE MORTGAGE MARKET

We are accustomed to think of markets in terms of commodities, stocks, and bonds. It may therefore be a new departure in our thinking to conceive of such a thing as the mortgage market. Actually, however, it is like the bond market, for it is made up of evidences of indebtedness, such as bonds and promissory notes, secured by mortgages.

If a borrower and lender are getting together and initiating a mortgage loan, then, since this loan has not been in existence before, we say that we are in a primary mortgage market. If, however, the mortgage loan is already in existence, and the holder is selling it to someone else, we say that we are in the secondary mortgage market.

Another new concept to some of us is that of mortgage warehousing. It is hard to think of mortgages in terms of goods on the shelf or stacked in the warehouse. Nevertheless, the term is quite apropos. It is applied to the mortgage portfolio of someone, such as a mortgage banker who has accumulated these rights, but has no intention of holding on to them until their maturity. Rather, he is trying to dispose of them to his advantage, just as a department store would try to sell off goods in its warehouse. In the interim, however, they are "warehoused" with him.

GOVERNMENTAL FINANCING AGENCIES

The techniques we exercise in getting and arranging for financing are, of course, under governmental supervision. As we have already learned, we might not even have been able to secure financing, had it not been for the assurance provided for our application by reason of the Federal Housing Administration and the Veterans Administration. We would not enjoy the degree of stability in the value of our FHA and VA loans, were it not for the support given the secondary market in these obligations by the Federal National Mortgage Association. The fruits of special assistance programs, such as those for new towns, would not be for us to have and hold were it not for the guarantee of debentures for these purposes given by the Government National Mortgage Administration.

The Section 235 Program

Section 235 of the National Housing Act provides home ownership assistance in the form of a monthly payment to the mortgagee, reducing his interest cost as low as one per cent if the homeowner cannot afford the mortgage payments with 20 per cent of his adjusted gross income.

Assistance is provided for the acquisition of new or substantially rehabilitated single-family dwellings approved prior to the beginning of construction or substantial rehabilitation. Also eligible is a substantially rehabilitated two-family dwelling, providing one unit is occupied by the owner. A one-family unit in a condominium project also qualifies. Thirty per cent of the assistance allocation is available for existing construction.

The mortgage on a single family property may be as high as $18,000 and can escalate to $24,000 in high cost areas. Up to $3,000 may be added for property consisting of four bedrooms bought by a family of five or more persons. The mortgage may include the mortgage insurance premium. It may be for a 30 year term and, under special circumstances, be extended to 35 or 40 years. The home-buying family must make a minimum investment of $200.

The mortgagor must be a family of two or more, related by blood, marriage, or operation of law; a handicapped person; or a single person of age 62 or over. The family must have an adjusted family income not over 135 per cent of the income a same size family eligible to move into local public housing units has. Adjusted family income means the income from all sources during the preceding twelve months, before taxes or withholding, of all adult members of the family living in the unit, excluding unusual and temporary income, and deducting $300 for each minor under 21 as well as their earnings. Twenty per cent of the assistance payments is authorized for families with higher incomes, but not higher than 90 per cent of the income limits for 221 (d) (3) housing. This section provides special terms for housing located in approved urban renewal areas sponsored by public agencies and sets a maximum interest rate of three per cent. Income recertification under Section 235 is required every two years. The family assets cannot exceed $2,000, excluding $300 added for each dependent. The assets may be as high as $5,000 for someone over 62.

The Mortgage Insurance Certificate is the contract between the Federal Housing Administration and the mortgagee. The issuance of this certificate obligates the Department of Housing and Urban Development to pay mortgage assistance payments for the mortgagor and requires the mortgagees to get biennial recertification of income. The assistance payment will be the difference between the total monthly payment as it is and what would be required at an interest rate of one per cent, excluding the mortgage insurance premium.

The Department of Housing and Urban Development is now authorized to compensate the owner of a Section 235 home for structural or other defects which seriously affect the use and livability of the dwelling and impose the basic responsibility for the repairs on the seller of the property. Accordingly, any individual who sells an existing house under the Section 235 program will be required to reimburse the Department for any payments made by it to correct or compensate the buyer for structural or other defects of the home. In the case of a non-occupant seller, the new regulations require him to escrow cash or post a bond for a 14 month period in an amount equal to five per cent of the sales price of the property. But the seller's liability is not limited to the five percent escrowed. It extends to the full amount expended to repair the premises.

The Section 236 Program

This is the program for rental and cooperative housing for low- and moderate-income families. It provides assistance in the form of monthly Federal payments to the mortgagee, thereby reducing the cost to the occupant by paying part of the interest at the market rate.

In order to be eligible, the project must consist of five or more units. They may be detached, semi-detached, row, or elevator. It may consist of either a new or rehabilitated structure. It may include non-dwelling commercial, but must be predominantly residential.

The mortgagors may be non-profit, limited distribution, or cooperative entities. They must have a management program. The tenants and cooperative occupants must meet the specified income requirements and one of the following: be a family (two persons related by blood, marriage, or operation of law), single (at least 62 years of age), or handicapped. Ten per cent of the dwelling units may be for single people under 62. Priorities will be given to those displaced by urban renewal, government action, or national disaster.

The adjusted income of the occupants cannot exceed 135 per cent of the limits applicable to local public housing. The adjusted income is the current income of all members of the family occupying the unit, from all sources before taxes, excluding a five per cent deduction for unusual or temporary income, less $300 for each minor and less earnings of each minor. The income must be recertified every two years and the needed adjustments in rental charges made.

The eligible tenant pays the basic rental - the over-income tenant pays the fair market rental. The basic monthly rental charge is set by an operation at one per cent interest rate mortgage. The eligible tenant pays the greater of this basic rental charge or 25 per cent of adjusted income. The fair market rental for over-income tenants is based on operation at the market interest rate. The monthly rental includes utilities, except telephone. The financing may be by private lenders, through loans, by state or local governments, or under a state or local program of loan insurance or tax abatement.

The Government National Mortgage Association

This Association's mortgage-backed securities provide a way by which private financing can be tapped to provide funding for low-income housing under Sections 235 and 236 and other programs. Pools of Federal Housing Administration, Veterans Administration, and Farmers Home Administration mortgages at a common rate of interest are assembled and submitted to the Association for its guarantee. The issuer then issues securities against the face value of the pool at an interest rate less than the interest rate of the pool.

The Government National Mortgage Association (GNMA) commits itself also to buy Government under-written mortgages on lower income housing at prices favorable to the project sponsors and then sells them to the Federal National Mortgage Association at market prices, with GNMA absorbing the difference.

GNMA is also authorized to guarantee the payment of principal and interest on any securities issued by the Federal National Mortgage Association (FNMA), which are backed by earmarked pools of mortgage portfolios. GNMA is likewise authorized to guarantee securities issued by private parties approved for this purpose when the securities are backed by Federally underwritten mortgages.

New Veterans Administration Entitlements

A recent legislative change and policy decision expanded the opportunity to sell and finance properties using Veterans Administration no down payment loans. Public Law 91-506 makes all loan guarantee and entitlement available until used, whether the entitlement is derived from World War II, the Korean conflict, or post Korean conflict service.

The Federal National Mortgage Association has stated "effective immediately, the maximum amount of any VA guaranteed mortgage that will be considered for purchase by FNMA is increased to $50,000, subject to the limitation that the original mortgage amount may not exceed four times the guaranteed portion of the loan." Because of this, it is now possible for a lending institution to make 100 per cent loans up to $50,000.

This new policy of easier financing for more expensive homes permits the sale of a home to the veteran who prefers using his money for investments, rather than as a down payment on a home. The veteran who is able to have his money earn more than the current VA interest rate will be better served, using these moneys to acquire an income producing investment in other real estate, rather than as a down payment on a home. Veterans who are doctors may wish to use this money to start or enlarge their practice, business veterans to invest in their business, and real estate investors to buy income property.

Entitlement is a guarantee available to a veteran that he can use to secure a mortgage loan. The VA will guarantee the lender, who grants the loan, that in the event of default, it will pay him 60 per cent of the balance in default or the maximum entitlement available at the time the loan was granted, whichever is less. The maximum entitlement available to veterans is now $12,500. The entitlement was increased on July 12, 1950, from $4,000 to $7,500; on May 7, 1968, from $7,500 to $12,500. A veteran who bought a home prior to July 12, 1950 with a VA guarantee will have a remaining entitlement of $8,500. A veteran who bought a home between July 12, 1950 and May 7, 1968 will have a remaining entitlement of $5,000.

The recent changes permit many veterans who previously used a portion of their entitlement to purchase a home to purchase another home. A veteran who used $7,500 of his entitlement to buy a previous home with a GI loan has $5,000 of entitlement remaining. Applying the limitation that the original mortgage amount may not exceed four times the guaranteed portion of the loan, this veteran could purchase another home that he intends to occupy for $20,000, with no down payment. Also, a veteran who had used $4,000 of his entitlement would have $8,500 remaining, which he could employ to buy a home of four times that, or $34,000, with no down payment. In both cases, should the veteran wish to purchase a more expensive home than the maximum mortgage above, the difference could be made up in cash. Also, a veteran occupant can buy a home from one to four living units and still take advantage of these opportunities. In the case of such a multi-family dwelling, however, the veteran must live in one of the dwelling units.

A veteran may now pay more for a home than the VA-appraised reasonable value. But the amount of the loan obtained by the veteran cannot exceed the VA appraisal. The veteran must then pay in cash the difference between the VA "reasonable value" appraisal and the actual sales price of the home.

Housing Opportunity Allowance Program

Moderate-income families who earn too much to get federal sub-sidies, but not enough to qualify for conventional home loans are now eligible for $1,200 in aid on their mortgage payments. A home owner who qualifies will receive $20 a month toward his mortgage payments for the first five years. The loan itself, to which these payments apply, can be for as long as 30 years and for as much as $25,000. The interest rate will vary by area. The purchase may be without a down payment, if the lender is willing, or may require one as large as 30 per cent.

To get this subsidy payment, a family's income must not be more than $7,000 to $12,000, depending on the size of the family and the section of the country. The mortgage must be for the purchase of the buyer's principal residence and not for a second home or a home to be rented out. The residence could be a condominium.

Mortgages carrying this subsidy will be made by savings and loan associations, members of the Federal Home Loan Bank System. The loans will be conventional loans. Whether it will participate is up to each savings and loan. This program will be particularly helpful to young families with prospects enabling them to get out of dependence on subsidies after five years.

Vacation or Second Home Financing

Federal Housing Administration insurance is now available on housing intended for seasonal occupancy. The mortgage must not be over $18,000 and may not be in excess of 75 per cent of the appraised value of the property. Buyers must make an investment of at least 25 per cent of the appraised value. The mortgages may cover single family homes only. The home must be occupied for part of the year by the mortgagor. The dwelling must be on property that is being developed in a manner consistent with the conservation of the natural resources of the area in which the property is located.

VARIABLE RATE MORTGAGES

The variable interest rate mortgage loan permits the interest rate to rise and fall in accordance with the credit market and thereby keeps the investment by the lender in tune with the market. Although the variable interest rate favors the lender by assuring that his return will rise if the price of borrowing money goes up, the borrower would benefit if the market should fall.

The monthly payments may remain fixed, despite the varying yields to the lender. This is done by using more of the monthly payment for interest, when rates rise, and less, if they fall. If rates rise without falling, the payments would remain the same, but the term of the mortgage would be increased because less of each payment would go for principal and more for interest. Higher rates in times of tight money would enable the lenders to increase their earnings. This, in turn, would permit them to pay out more interest to their depositors, and thereby attract still more lendable funds. Laws would be needed to let variable rates apply to new loans insured by FHA or guaranteed by VA.

Suppose a family takes out a 30-year loan of $25,000, with a variable interest rate that starts at eight per cent. Suppose it is agreed that this rate can be changed only by a formula based on rises or declines in specific market rates. The formula might be based, for example, on changes in yields on three- to five-year Treasury securities. Suppose that at the end of the first five-year period, increases in the market rates called for a boost in the mortgage rate to 8.5 per cent. The home buyer's monthly payment would rise from the initial $183 a month to $191 a month and hold there for the next five years. If interest rates continued to climb, the home buyer would find his monthly payments going up accordingly. But if the country entered on a period of falling rates of interest, the home buyer would find his monthly payments declining.

Another family might choose to hold its monthly payments constant and accept the burden of making payments for an increased number of years. Or, if interest rates declined, the family would pay off the mortgage more quickly. If interest rates rose, more of the constant monthly payment of $183 would go to pay the higher interest, and less would go to pay off principal on the home loan.

NINETY TO ONE HUNDRED PER CENT FINANCING

One hundred per cent financing has been obtained by developers from landowners through land contracts and purchase money mortgages. In neither situation has the developer been required to make a down payment. In both situations, payments were deferred until such time as the developer had derived proceeds from the sales in his development.

One hundred per cent financing has also been available under the sale and lease-back. Here the developer sells the land to the investor on the condition that it be leased back concurrently with the sale and that "rentals" be paid from the proceeds of the sales of the developed units. The lessor agrees to deed the individual units to the buyers.

One hundred per cent financing has also been available under the sale and buy back, under which the developer sells the land to the investor and buys it back on the installment basis, the payments coming from the proceeds he secures from the purchasers of the developed units.

One hundred per cent financing may also be secured for construction. The developer may secure such a loan from a commercial bank, persuaded to make the advance by an advance commitment or take-out letter from an institutional investor, such as a life insurance company. This document certifies that on completion of the development, the life insurance company will provide a mortgage loan on the entire development, the proceeds from which loan will be used in part to pay off the bank's construction loan.

One hundred per cent financing may also be secured in a joint venture "front money" transaction. The investor puts up 100 per cent of the cost. The developer contributes his expertise, experience and time. The division of ownership and profits between the developer and the investor is negotiated. If the investor puts up all the cash, he will try to get his money out first with a return on the investment, before any split on the net income occurs.

Organizations, like Building Resources Corporation, consisting of building materials suppliers, have been formed to provide 90 per cent mortgage loans to builders and developers. They do so because they recognize that builders and developers may be unable, on their own, to provide a substantial percentage of equity funds.

Federal savings and loan associations are now authorized to make 100 per cent loans on single-family homes to borrowers with a gross income up to 150 per cent of Section 235 limits (for example if the Section 235 limit were $8,000, the family could qualify even though its gross income were $12,000). The maximum price of the home may not be over $25,000, and the period of the loan may range between 25 and 30 years, depending on the section of the country.

An organization called Home Capital Funds, Inc., operates a joint loan program with a clutch of institutional investors to provide a 90 per cent mortgage for homebuyers. The institutions supply a 75 per cent mortgage loan and home capital funds tacks a 15 per cent piggyback loan on top. This 90 per cent package is treated as one loan with one payment. This organization is backed by 16 large companies, all of which have sizable positions in the homebuilding market.

Some homebuilders have come up with a 100 per cent guarantee to the homeowner that he will not lose any part of his equity for a three-year period. Under this plan, the homeowner can move for any reason during the period and is guaranteed the return of his entire equity, including down payment and the equity added through monthly payments. The only cost to the home buyer is the interest paid during ownership. These homebuilders will also arrange to resell the home, with the profit from the sale, less their commission, going to the owner over and above the return of his equity. This guarantee is called "three for free" and is designed for persons unsure of their economic situation or subject to job transfer.

One hundred per cent mortgage deficiency insurance is now available. It takes care of the case of a transferred executive whose loan is assumed by another home buyer, but who will be relieved of personal liability if a lender forecloses on the mortgage and obtains a deficiency judgment. The insurance can be issued to the transferred executive, employer, or his agent, and a single premium is paid, covering the ten year period. The insured parties are covered during this period, no matter how many times the property is sold. This insurance can be used for conventional, FHA or VA, or on mortgage loans insured by private carriers. One hundred per cent of the deficiency will be paid, up to a maximum of 20 per cent of the amount of the loan at the time it is assumed.

SUMMARY

The term mortgage is for a relatively short period, three to five years. The amortizing mortgage, on the other hand, is for a relatively long period of time, with periodic payments extinguishing the amount of the principal. The budget mortgage is one in which the periodic payments provide for interest, principal, taxes, special assessments, and insurance. The package mortgage includes all these, and, likewise, payments on mechanical appliances installed in the home.

An open-end mortgage authorizes additional borrowing up to the amount of the original indebtedness. Under the construction loan mortgage payments are made on an installment basis in the course of progress on construction. A blanket mortgage covers two or more parcels of property, and is usually accompanied by a partial release clause. In a participation mortgage, a number of lenders pool their resources to make the loan possible. In a purchase money mortgage, the seller finances the transaction himself. He may also finance the transaction by means of a land contract.

A first mortgage has claim to the property prior to any mortgage junior to it. An FHA mortgage is one insured by the Federal Housing Administration; a VA mortgage, one guaranteed by the Veterans Administration; and a MGIC mortgage, one insured by a private agency.

Most mortgage loans on residential properties in terms of dollar amounts come from savings and loan associations. Commercial banks make loans on homes, as well as on income properties, and likewise engage in construction loans. Mortgage bankers serve as intermediaries between borrowers and lenders.

Among the many financing techniques are sale and leasebacks in which an institutional financier buys the land and building, and leases it to a merchandising organization for a period based on the functional life expectancy of the building.

The mortgage market may be a primary one or a secondary one. The Federal National Mortgage Association and the Government National Mortgage Association are in the secondary mortgage market.

GLOSSARY

ADVANCE COMMITMENT - the agreement by an institutional investor, such as a life insurance company, to provide long-term financing for a project on construction completion

FARMERS HOME ADMINISTRATION - an adjunct of the Department of Agriculture, to provide financial assistance for farmers and others living in rural areas, where this is not available on reasonable terms from private sources

FRONT MONEY - the money necessary to launch a real estate project

INTERIM LOAN - the loan made for a short period until other financing becomes available

REFINANCING - paying off a present obligation, and assuming a new obligation instead, usually on a more favorable financing basis

SERVICING MORTGAGE LOANS - collecting the periodic payments, inspecting the property, and taking appropriate measures on the obligor's default

TAKE-HOME PAY - what remains in wages and salary after deducting withholding of federal and state income taxes, health insurance, social security, pension plan payments, and contributions

TRUE AND FALSE QUESTIONS

1. An open mortgage is synonymous with an open-end mortgage. T F

2. The land contract is a form of mortgage. T F

3. In a purchase money mortgage, the seller takes back a mortgage as part of the purchase price. T F

4. The outstanding characteristic of a package mortgage is the privilege of prepayment. T F

5. A mortgage that permits additional borrowing up to its original amount is an open end mortgage. T F

6. A partial release clause is usually employed with a blanket mortgage. T F

7. In a sale and leaseback, the seller may deduct depreciation on the building sold. T F

8. In a sale and leaseback, the vendee comes into full control and possession of the property at lease expiration. T F

9. Open end mortgages permit borrowing for future additions to the property up to the original amount of the mortgage loan. T F

10. A package mortgage is synonymous with a blanket mortgage. T F

11. A conventional mortgage is synonymous with an FHA mortgage. T F

12. Life insurance companies may not loan on real property as security. T F

13. The Home Owners Loan Corporation is now active in the mortgage lending field. T F

14. Most mortgages today are based on the amortizing principle. T F

15. Savings and loan associations may be organized either under   T F
state or Federal law.

16. Life insurance companies may make mortgage loans in   T F
any part of the country.

17. The Farmers Home Administration may finance homes   T F
only on farms.

18. Section 235 loans are made by the Department of Housing   T F
and Urban Development to low- and moderate-income
families.

19. Condominiums do not qualify under the Section 235 pro-   T F
gram.

20. Section 236 provides for payments to the mortgagee.   T F

21. GNMA may guarantee securities issued by FNMA.   T F

22. A veteran may not pay for a home more than VA appraised   T F
value.

23. The purchaser under the HOAP program must make a   T F
down payment.

24. The HOAP program applies to conventional and to FHA   T F
and VA loans.

25. Vacation or second homes may not enjoy FHA insurance.   T F

26. Monthly payments under the variable rate mortgage may   T F
remain fixed.

27. 100 per cent financing may be obtained under land contracts.   T F

28. 100 per cent financing for the developer may be enjoyed in   T F
joint ventures.

29. Federal Savings and Loan associations under no circum-   T F
stances may make 100 per cent loans.

30. Under the "three for free" guarantee, the only cost to the   T F
homeowner is the interest paid during ownership.

31. 100 per cent mortgage deficiency insurance is now available.   T F

32. To get FHA insurance on second homes, the mortgagors   T F
must occupy them part of the year.

33. FHA insured second homes may now be multi-family.   T   F

34. A mortgagor under Section 236 may be a cooperative.   T   F

35. The adjusted income of occupants under Section 236   T   F
programs cannot exceed 135 per cent of the limits applicable
to local public housing.

36. To be eligible for Section 235 assistance, family assets   T   F
can be as high as $10,000.

37. The mortgage banker usually holds the mortgage loans he   T   F
makes until they mature.

38. The mortgage banker engages in mortgage warehousing.   T   F

MULTIPLE CHOICE QUESTIONS

39. Under the sale and leaseback, the buyer lessor:
    ( ) Deducts rent as against his income tax liability
    ( ) Deducts depreciation on the building as against his income tax liability
    ( ) Assumes the expense of maintenance and repairs
    ( ) Operates under a gross lease

40. Under the land contract, the seller is secured by:
    ( ) A purchase money mortgage
    ( ) A first mortgage
    ( ) Title retention
    ( ) A subordination agreement

41. As a hedge against inflation, life insurance companies in making long-term mortgage loans may now require:
    ( ) A prepayment penalty
    ( ) A defeasance clause
    ( ) An equity participation
    ( ) Divestiture proceedings

42. State savings and loan associations:
    ( ) May not secure membership in the Federal Savings and Loan Insurance Corporation
    ( ) May secure membership in the Federal Deposit Insurance Corporation
    ( ) May apply for membership in the Federal Savings and Loan Insurance Corporation
    ( ) May not apply for membership in the Federal Home Loan Bank System

43. The Mortgage Guaranty Insurance Corporation insures:
    ( ) FHA loans
    ( ) VA loans
    ( ) GNMA loans
    ( ) Conventional mortgage loans

44. In a purchase money mortgage, the seller:
    ( ) Is employing a land contract
    ( ) Loses the benefit of a first mortgage position
    ( ) Is financing the transaction
    ( ) Is not permitted to require a down payment

45. In a construction loan mortgage:
( ) The loan is advanced at the beginning of construction
( ) The loan is not advanced until construction is complete
( ) The loan is advanced in installments at stages of construction
( ) Interest on the entire loan starts running at the beginning of construction

46. The mortgage under which additional borrowings may be made up to the original amount of the indebtedness is:
( ) The open-end mortgage
( ) The open mortgage
( ) The blanket mortgage
( ) The package mortgage

47. The mortgage which covers mechanical appliances, over and above interest, principal, taxes, and insurance is called:
( ) The over-all mortgage
( ) The package mortgage
( ) The blanket mortgage
( ) The amortizing mortgage

48. The term mortgage:
( ) Operates on the amortizing principle
( ) Runs usually for a period of three to five years
( ) Runs usually for a period of thirty to forty years
( ) Is usually a variable rate mortgage

ESSAY QUESTIONS

1. What did the Home Owners Corporation do?

2. Aside from home financing, what other lending areas may savings and loan associations pursue?

3. What are the main functions in which mortgage bankers engage?

PART IV
THE REAL ESTATE OFFICE

COMPUTERIZED
REAL ESTATE

CHAPTER TEN

WHAT DOES THE COMPUTER DO?

The computer matches listings with prospects and prospects with listings. It persuades the seller to agree to a realistic selling price and the buyer a realistic buying price by showing what comparables have recently sold for. It enables the customer instantaneously to find the properties, within a specified area, which meet his requirements on price, style, and features. It tells the present status of listings, whether they have been sold or if there has been any change in price or terms.

The computer speeds up and simplifies the evaluation of real estate for mortgage loans. It provides immediate data on comparables to facilitate the work of the appraiser in setting up a value based on the market approach. It calculates the over-all cost factors by the square or cubic foot for the appraiser as the basis for his valuation by cost approach. It will provide complete income data for the determination of value by the income approach.

The computer can now be programmed to show the investor the taxable income, the gross spendable income, the net spendable income, and the net equity income for any income property. It can also show the effect on the rate of return of a two, a five, or a ten per cent growth rate in the area of the property. It can make such investment analyses for a period of months or years. In so doing, it takes into account the individual investor's financial position, whether he is in the 30 per cent, the 50 per cent, or the 70 per cent income tax bracket. It likewise shows the effect on the rate of return of the particular type of depreciation taken.

The computer can produce "profiles" of any community to enable a potential transferee, whether individual or corporate, to determine if it conforms to the standards prescribed.

The computer develops cost control and accounting data for the property manager; market research data for the subdivider and developer; and data on selling aptitudes, the relative effectiveness of selling techniques, and the sales returns from the use of various advertising appeals for the real estate broker.

The computer can pool property data of an entire city to help in the re-evaluation of tax ratables and the determination of problem areas, such as those with a high incidence of crime and urban blight.

HOW DOES THE COMPUTER DO THIS?

The real estate broker or salesperson finds out what information his client wants. He translates this information into numbered codes and taps out these codes on the buttons of a Touch Tone phone. He can do this from his own phone, a pay phone, or a small portable terminal he may carry with him into his client's home or office. The computer comes back with the answer in seconds. It can do so orally, on a TV-screen, or on a teletype print-out.

All this comes about because of the relatively new ability of computers to communicate by telephone. The signals used by computers are coded in the form of audio tones and transmitted over conventional telephone lines. One computer can handle simultaneous inputs from many remote sources. Although the computer may be processing many other programs at the same time, it does so with such speed that the user has the impression that the machine belongs exclusively to him.

The information for the computer memory bank is collected from the Multiple Listing Service in a particular area and continuously updated to include new offerings, deletions of sold properties, and price changes. The regional and national computer service therefore becomes a cooperative organization of local Multiple Listing Services.

The computer's prime attribute is its ability to do arithmetic at incredible speed. The computer calculates in nanoseconds or billionths of a second. The cost of making one million calculations has declined from $30,000 in pre-computer days to about 30 cents today.

All the parts making up the computer are interconnected by wires through which pulse information flows as directed by instructions given to the computer. These instructions are called programs. The programmer must know the kind of statements he can use in communicating with the computer. He must know how to write these statements sequentially to get the computer to answer the problem he wants solved. The language he uses is called a source language. A computer program, stored in the machine's memory, converts this into machine-language instructions which the computer carries out.

Suppose, for example, a real estate broker or salesperson wants to assure a seller that he is getting a fair price for his house or a buyer that he will be paying the going market price. He taps out his request in code for a numbers list of all the comparable pieces of real estate sold during the previous year. The computer searches its memory and instantaneously reports a numbers list of the pieces of real estate that answer the request.

Or suppose a prospect wants to buy a home. He specifies what he wants: a $30,000 three-bedroom colonial with fire place, two car garage, two baths, and swimming pool. The broker or salesperson picks up his phone, dials a security code, then another code of numbers, and within seconds knows what houses with the customer's criteria are available. The broker or salesperson then goes to his files, pulls out matching photos and a card of information. The next step is the actual showing of the properties in which the prospect has the greatest interest.

It usually takes 60 days for a local real estate board to adapt itself to the computer system. A map must be developed with coded location numbers pinpointing specific areas and the listings put on computer punch cards.

HOW DO YOU JOIN UP?

There are many computer services available. The best known and the largest in the real estate field is the Realtron Corporation. The National Association of Real Estate Boards has contracted with Realtron to utilize its computerized property information system. The National Association also organized Realtors Computer Service to act as liaison between Realtron and the customer. Realtors Computer Service bills the local real estate boards for the Realtron Service. The local board in turn bills its members.

The local boards which elect the Realtors Computer Service sign a one year contract. Their individual members do not, however, have to take the service. Those who do, sign up for 90 day periods and are permitted to cancel out on 30 days notice.

Just as a doctor is identified by his little black bag, a real estate salesperson is coming to be identified by his little black box, the portable terminal which he carries with him into his customer's home or office. The portable terminal provides communication with the computer. Smaller than a portable typewriter, this 11½ x 13 inch, eight-pound unit is easy to operate. It has selector switches enabling the salesperson to select the exact specifications of the property. The salesperson then puts the telephone headset into the special cradle provided by the terminal and the response comes back, by voice, through a built-in amplifier. If a real estate office wants a print-out machine or to arrange for the computer's answers to appear on a TV-screen, these facilities will be provided for an extra charge.

There are several competitors to Realtron, each working hard to persuade local boards and individual brokers of their advantages. Some emphasize time sharing, under which the computer moves swiftly from user to user, processing programs both sequentially and independently.

The Society of Real Estate Appraisers has set up a subsidiary, SREA Market Data Center, Inc., to provide computerized appraisal service. It handles a nationwide accumulation and distribution of comparable sales data. Inputs are provided by lending institutions, such as savings and loans, banks, insurance companies, and mortgage bankers.

HOW IS IT USED IN RESIDENTIAL SELLING?

The prospects tell the broker or salesperson just what they want and where they want it; one story or more; their price range; the number of bedrooms; the down payment they can make; and the special features they require, such as dining room, fireplace, den and library, attached two or three car garage, swimming pool; and whether they desire brick, frame, or stucco. Each one of these specifications has a code number.

The broker or salesperson taps out on the code button the number of the centralized computer office. He gets a "beep", indicating it is ready to respond. He taps out the security code - this is changed for each board once a week to prevent unauthorized entries. He taps out the other numbers corresponding to the various requirements. The computer responds within five seconds. The salesperson jots down the answer in the appropriate spaces on the pad which he brings with him. Or the answer may appear, if the facilities have been so arranged, on TV-screen or on print-out.

The computer is given the liberty to explore prices $3,000 above and $2,000 below the figure the prospects have given. By tapping out another code button the computer is also given the liberty to search for the property most nearly meeting the prospects' requirements. If the computer is still unable to find a property, it comes back with the answer: "None meets request".

The computer's answer on properties available comes back in the form of the numbers under which these properties are listed by the Multiple Listing Service. The Service's code book in turn contains a card with photo and complete description of each of these properties. The sales advantage lies in the fact that the properties shown are exactly those the prospects have asked for. It is they who have made the decision, not the real estate agent.

The request can be coded to supply information in one specific area, such as a city or section of a city, within a one square mile area, within a nine square mile area, within a state or within the entire country.

If the prospects are interested in the current status of a particular property - its present terms and its present price - the request for this information will be transmitted by code button corresponding to the multi-list property in the Multiple Listing Service and the answer will likewise be immediately forthcoming.

If it is desired to secure the sales price of comparable properties, the requests for this information are likewise coded, together with those from a period back, such as nine months or a year. This request can be so coded as to confine the comparables to a specific area, a one square mile area, or a nine square mile area.

Real estate agents find it helpful to let the prospects themselves tap in the code buttons. The prospects thereby get the feeling of participating. The awesome answer in terms of the robot's voice becomes even more compelling. The portable terminal box becomes a fascinating toy, but with a practical, down-to-earth use. As the answers given are completely impersonal and objective, the prospects accept them, without disbelief, such as they might display to a salesperson's replies. There is no argument. This is no sales talk. A question is asked and the answer is given.

The real estate agent can establish price trends for a particular neighborhood by securing the responses from the computer as to what prices have been paid for real estate over successive periods of time. This information is particularly helpful in guiding prospects to the selection of the proper neighborhood.

HOW IS IT USED IN INVESTMENT PROPERTY ANALYSIS?

Everyone is now aware of the tremendous opportunities in investment real estate - a hedge against inflation, a relatively high rate of return, the opportunity for leverage, the tax shelter afforded, and the increased cash flow available.

But it is hard to understand and explain terms like gross spendable income, taxable income, equity income, net spendable income, growth rate, and equity income rate, together with cost basis and adjusted cost basis.

It is even harder to make the calculations to show the prospective investor what his income position will be if he makes a particular investment. And when the prospective investor asks what his position will be three or five years hence, most real estate practitioners have to throw up their hands in despair. They are all searching for some way by which they can demonstrate the investment potential - quickly, accurately and persuasively. Now there is such a way - through the use of the computer.

But the computer has to be properly programmed to supply the answers. It first has to know what the market value of the property is - $30,000 or $50,000, $80,000 or $100,000. It has to know what the net operating income is. Since leverage is to be a factor, it has to know the amount of the loan on the property. It likewise has to be told the interest rate on this loan and the amount that is to be paid each year on principal. It must also know the income tax bracket of the client, the particular month or year the investment return is to be projected, what percentage of value the improvement constitutes, the type of depreciation to be employed, and the estimated growth rate for the area.

All these factors are represented by individual code numbers, tapped accordingly, together with the security code.

So, assume we start with a property with a market value of $50,000, on which we secure a loan of $40,000 and an interest rate of 8 per cent. We tap in the market value at 050, the loan amount at 040 and the interest rate at 80. As the investor, we know that we shall get the yield on the $50,000 property, deduct our interest and principal payments, and take what is left as our return on the equity of $10,000 we actually put up in cash.

Our investment property will show us a certain over-all return from our rents and other income, say $10,000. From this, we have to deduct our expenses of operation, such as our payrolls, supplies, our property taxes, and insurance, amounting to say, $4,000, leaving us with a net operating income of $6,000, which we tap as 060.

Just as in all mortgage loans, part of the payments we make go to pay off the principal of the loan and part to pay interest. The more we pay off on principal, the more we build up our equity.

From our net operating income of $6,000, we deduct the interest we pay on our mortgage loan and the depreciation on the building to arrive at the income we have left, which is subject to income tax. Of the

$50,000 market value of the property, let us say that the value of the building is $40,000, or 80 per cent - a reasonably normal percentage. We then tap into the code the improvement per cent as 80.

Say the building has a functional life expectancy of 20 years. We tap the code button 20. If we used straight line depreciation, then we could deduct 5 per cent of the $40,000 or $2,000 for depreciation for each of these 20 years. But if the building were a new residential rental, the present tax law would permit us to use 200 per cent of this, or $4,000, for depreciation the first year. We could also use the sum of the year's digits, which would allow us almost as much. This can be explained as follows: Assume an income property has a functional life expectancy of five years adding up the digits comprising five - 1 & 2 & 3 & 4 & 5 - equals 15 the first year. 5/15 depreciation could be deducted the second year, 4/15, and so on. If the building was any new commercial or industrial property, the present tax law would permit us to use 150 per cent depreciation the first year, or $3,000. Suppose we decide to use 150 per cent. We than tap one in the code button. Two would stand for the 200 per cent method, three for the sum of the years digits, and four for the straight line method.

So, from our net operating income of $6,000, we could deduct the $3,200 interest paid on our mortgage loan and assuming 150 per cent depreciation, the $3,000 depreciation, leaving us with a taxable income of minus $200. Aside from the fact that we have no income from this property subject to tax, we can regard this minus $200 as a tax credit to deduct from our regular income, as from salary.

After paying $3,200 interest on our mortgage loan and paying, say $1,000 on the principal of the loan, we actually have left $1,800 free and clear, and this we call our gross spendable income. If we had any income tax to pay, we would deduct the amount of this from our gross spendable, leaving us with our net spendable income. In this case, we actually have a minus of $200 in our net spendable, which we can use to deduct from other income.

To determine just what over-all tax benefit would accrue, we have to know our income tax bracket, whether it is 30 per cent, 40 per cent, 50 per cent, or 70 per cent. Say, in our case, it is 30 per cent. We then tap in 30 at this particular spot.

Over and above our gross spendable of $1,800, we should add the $1,000 we have paid on our principal, leaving us with a total of $2,800. Since this belongs to us and is the same thing, therefore, as ownership, we call it our equity income. As we put $10,000 of our own into the property, this $2,800 is a 28 per cent return.

One other thing we should know is our adjusted cost basis. Cost basis refers to what we paid for the property, like our $50,000. Adjusted cost basis means this amount plus the value of any improvements we have made to the property. In our case, there were none. Adjusted cost basis also includes our deductions from cost due to depreciation. Here we had $3,000 depreciation, which makes our adjusted cost basis at the end of the year, $47,000 - $50,000 minus the $3,000 depreciation.

We have to know this adjusted cost basis because when we sell, the capital gains tax we pay is on the difference between our adjusted cost basis and selling price.

There is still something else we might want to add to our equity income and our equity income rate, and that is the percentage rise in real estate values that may have occurred in the area where the property is located. A 5 per cent rise in many areas is common. But let us say, to be conservative, a 2 per cent rise in the $50,000 value we had when we started. This would mean at the end of the year we would add another $1,000 to our equity income, making it $3,800, or 38 per cent on the $10,000 we put up. We also have a code for this growth rate which we would tap in to give this amount.

We can likewise show our investor where he will be income-wise three, five, or ten years hence by tapping in the appropriate codes. If these projections show that his return is falling instead of rising at the end of any of these periods, we make a note at that time to reconsider and perhaps switch into a more lucrative investment.

It took a long time to write the foregoing and it takes time to say it, but the computer will give us the answers right away in the twinkling of an eye, or, should we say, with the speed of sound.

THE COMPUTER'S EFFECT ON THE REAL ESTATE BUSINESS

The operations of the computer can show the effects in investment property analysis of tax-free exchanges, the installment method of capital gains reporting, depreciation recapture under the tax laws, multiple exchanges, and estate planning.

The computer will put no salespeople out of work. Rather, it will free salespeople from the chores and drudgery of looking up data on listings and comparables in files and records. It is estimated that the computer will give salespeople 30 per cent more selling time. The computer will transform the real estate business from a local business to a regional, national, and international one by the instantaneous communication of listing, prospecting, comparables, and investment analysis data. The computer will speed up and simplify real estate transactions, cut down on operating costs, eliminate guesswork and substitute facts. It will constitute the major fact gathering tool not only in brokerage, but also in investing and mortgage lending, appraising, market research, subdividing and developing, tax assessments and re-evaluations, and urban and regional planning.

SUMMARY

The computer matches listings with prospects and prospects, with listings. It speeds up and simplifies the evaluation of real estate as security for mortgage loans. It can be programmed for investment analysis.

The computer's prime attribute is its ability to do arithmetic at incredible speeds. There are many computer services available. The best known and the largest in the real estate field is the Realtron Corporation. The National Association of Real Estate Boards has contracted with Realtron to utilize its computerized property information service.

Over and above making information available instantaneously on the properties in which the prospect is interested, the computer can advise on the current status of a particular property - its present terms and its present price - on the sales prices of comparable properties or on price trends for a particular neighborhood.

In investment property analysis, the computer will show the return on equity, the net operating income, the taxable income, the amount deductible for depreciation, the gross spendable income, the net spendable income, the equity growth rate, and forward projections on investment returns.

The computer can show the effects in investment property analysis of tax-free exchanges, the installment method of capital gains reporting, the depreciation recapture, multiple exchanges, and estate planning.

The computer will give real estate salespeople 30 per cent more selling time, by means of relieving them from the chores and drudgery of looking up data on listings and comparables. It can transform the real estate business from an essentially local economic activity into a regional and a national one. It can constitute the major fact gathering tool, not only in brokerage, but also in investing and mortgage lending, appraising, market research, subdividing and developing, tax assessments and re-evaluations, and in urban and regional planning.

GLOSSARY

AUDIO TONES - sounds

INPUT - what is fed into the computer

MEMORY BANK - the data collected by the computer

"PROFILES" OF A COMMUNITY - data showing the characteristics of the community

SUM OF THE YEARS DIGITS - an accelerated depreciation method, best illustrated by the example of an improvement with a five year functional life expectancy; adding the digits making up the five, one plus two plus three plus four plus five, making a total of fifteen; meaning that five-fifteenths of the building's cost may be deducted the first year; four-fifteenths, the second; three-fifteenths, the third; two-fifteenths, the fourth; and one-fifteenth, the fifth.

TAX RATABLES - property subject to taxation

TELETYPE PRINT-OUT - the answer of the computer, printed out on paper.

TRUE AND FALSE QUESTIONS

1. The computer matches listings with prospects and prospects with listings.   T   F

2. The computer tells the present status of listings.   T   F

3. The computer provides immediate data on comparables to assist the appraiser in his market data approach.   T   F

4. The computer's capacity to make investment analyses is limited to investment returns as of the present time.   T   F

5. The computer cannot show the effect on the rate of return made by the particular kind of depreciation employed.   T   F

6. The computer can produce "profiles" of a community.   T   F

7. The computer's answers to questions asked are limited to voice answers.   T   F

8. One computer can handle simultaneous inputs from many remote sources.   T   F

9. The instructions given the computer are called inputs.   T   F

10. It usually takes a local real estate board six months to adapt itself to the computer system.   T   F

11. Real estate salespeople can carry portable terminals which provide communication with the computer.   T   F

12. By reason of the responses from the computer, price trends for a particular neighborhood can be established.   T   F

13. Adjusted cost basis means what is paid for the property.   T   F

14. The capital gains tax is paid on the difference between the adjusted cost basis and the selling price.   T   F

15. The unfortunate effect of the computer is to put salespeople out of work.   T   F

16. It is estimated that the computer will reduce by 30 per cent   T   F
the need for salespeople.

17. The computer can provide instantaneous communication   T   F
of real estate data on both a regional and a national scale.

18. The computer's assistance to the appraiser is limited to the   T   F
presentation of data for the market data approach.

19. The computer can pool property data to assist in the re-   T   F
evaluation of tax ratables.

20. The computer's signals are coded in audio tones.   T   F

21. The computer can persuade the seller to agree on a realistic   T   F
price.

22. In investment analysis, the computer fails to take into   T   F
account the individual investor's financial position.

23. The computer is not pertinent to the work of the property   T   F
manager.

24. A time lapse of approximately ten minutes occurs before the   T   F
computer comes up with its answer to the question asked.

25. The language the programmer uses is called a source   T   F
language.

26. The only computer service available is that of Realtron.   T   F

27. Under time sharing, the computer moves swiftly from user   T   F
to user, processing programs, both sequentially and
independently.

28. The purpose of a security code is to prevent unauthorized   T   F
entries.

29. If the computer is unable to find the kind of property re-   T   F
quired, it indicates its failure by going off the circuit.

30. Leverage is a factor in real estate investment analysis.   T   F

31. For investment analysis, it is unnecessary to know the   T   F
functional life expectancy of the building.

32. The equity income rate is the rate of return on the overall   T   F
amount of the investment.

33. The computer can be used to persuade the buyer to agree to   T   F
a realistic buying price.

34. Net spendable and net equity income are synonymous.   T   F

35. The computer can provide market research data for the   T   F
developer.

36. The portable terminal is slightly larger than a portable   T   F
typewriter.

37. The SREA Market Data Center handles a nationwide   T   F
accumulation and distribution of comparable . sales data.

38. The "beep" from the computer indicates it is ready to   T   F
respond.

39. The computer is not given the liberty to explore prices   T   F
above and below the price stipulated by the prospect.

40. When prospects tap in the code buttons, this gives them the   T   F
satisfying experience of participating.

MULTIPLE CHOICE QUESTIONS

41. To determine the specific overall tax benefit to the investor, it is necessary for the computer to know the investor's:
    ( ) Net worth
    ( ) Balance sheet
    ( ) Tax bracket
    ( ) Dollar averaging

42. The 200 per cent double declining method of depreciation may be used only with:
    ( ) New commercial or industrial property
    ( ) New residential rental property
    ( ) Residential property with a life expectancy of twenty years or more
    ( ) Existing income property

43. The 150 per cent method of taking depreciation may be used with:
    ( ) New commercial or industrial property
    ( ) Existing residential income property
    ( ) Loft type buildings
    ( ) Improvements in industrial parks

44. The sum of the years digits method of depreciation may be used with:
    ( ) Income properties with a life expectancy of twenty years or more
    ( ) New residential rental property
    ( ) Any new commercial or industrial property
    ( ) Existing residential rental properties with a life expectancy of 20 years or more

45. The cost basis means:
    ( ) Net cost after depreciation deductions have been taken
    ( ) What was paid for the property
    ( ) What was paid for the property plus additions made
    ( ) Gross minus operating expenses

46. The answers given by the computer to the questions asked are:
    ( ) Automatically accepted by the Internal Revenue Service
    ( ) Biased in favor of the seller
    ( ) Based entirely on data supplied by the Multiple Listing Service
    ( ) Impersonal and objective

47. Boards, members of the National Association of Real Estate Boards:
( ) Are now required to take the computer service
( ) Are required to sign up with Realtron
( ) May take out the computer service at their option
( ) Must engage in computer time sharing

48. The parts making up the computer are connected by wires through which:
( ) Pulse information flows as directed by instructions given to the computer
( ) Recommendations are made on commission rates to be charged
( ) Courses are conducted in the computer language to be employed
( ) Examinations are given on programming

49. The information for the computer memory bank is commonly collected from:
( ) The files of local boards
( ) The multiple listing service in a particular area
( ) The National Association of Real Estate Boards
( ) The state real estate association

50. The computer can be programmed to show the investor:
( ) Taxable income
( ) Gross spendable income
( ) Net equity income
( ) All of the above

ESSAY QUESTIONS

1. How does the computer operate?

2. How is the computer used in residential selling?

3. How will the computer affect the real estate business?

SALES AND
OFFICE MANAGEMENT

CHAPTER ELEVEN

SELECTING SALESPEOPLE

The personality traits sought are those that inspire confidence, such as: a prepossessing personality, one to which people naturally respond; a seasoned personality, one which seems mature, competent, and experienced; an "honest" personality, one which represents a person whose word is his bond; an articulate personality, one using words that can be understood, telling what needs to be told; and a persistent personality, one persevering in sales objectives, despite difficulties and discouragements.

Salespeople who have real estate experience can be found among those working elsewhere. It is unethical, however, to proselyte. If these individuals apply for sales positions with a real estate broker, and do so on their own volition, well and good. Then, he may consider them for his own sales organization. He is, however, wary of those who come to him from other brokers. They may be chronic "job-hoppers". They may be "lone wolves", incapable of teamwork. They may be driven by personality conflicts. They may turn out to be professional malcontents.

Sales people may be found among those wishing to change their present callings. But their desire to change must be because of a preference for real estate, not because of the expectation of a "fast buck". They may have heard how easy it is to make big money in real estate. All such stories are exaggerated in the telling and re-telling. The lure is false, but nevertheless beguiling. They must be made to realize that the price of success in real estate comes high. It must be paid for in long and irregular hours and the sacrifice of evenings and weekends. There may be long droughts between sales. The competition is keen. Real estate selling does not tolerate the weak-kneed and faint-hearted. It requires the patience of Job, the diplomacy of a statesman, and the tenacity of a bulldog.

Salespeople may be found among retirees. They may have a ready-made clientele of friends and acquaintances. They may have built up a solid reputation in the community. They usually have a financial backlog to tide them over their period of sales training. It is important, however, to make sure that these retirees have the motivation necessary for success in selling. It may be that they are looking only for employment in terms of something interesting to do, which, at the same time, will supplement their retirement income. It is essential to make sure that they are willing to expend the time, the physical and mental effort, and subject themselves to the personal inconveniences required for success in real estate selling. One must also try to make sure that their physical and mental health is such as to give them the stamina for success in sales.

Salespeople may be found among real estate brokers who want to return to selling full time. But the reasons they give for wishing to revert to selling full time should be analyzed to make sure there is nothing in their character, temperament, or personality that will constitute an unstable or negative factor. In their cases the answers must be secured to these questions: Did they as brokers get the cooperation and loyalty of their salespeople? Did they as brokers properly budget their time and expenses? Did they as brokers enjoy a reputation for honesty, fair-dealing, and dedication to their Code of Ethics? Can they bring with them the prospect clientele they have enjoyed as brokers? It is understandable, of course, that 'a sales personality may wish to concentrate on selling alone and leave the details of administration and the responsibility of office work to others.

Salespeople may be found among housewives whose families are now grown and who desire constructive and interesting employment as well as supplemental income. But it is one thing to like homes, which these ladies do, and another thing to be able to sell them. It is important, therefore, to make sure that these ladies can "take" the personal rebuffs, the cutting competition, the slights and the personal affronts that come their way. Their feminine sensitivity is advantageous in enabling them to feel the needs and desires of others, but it is disadvantageous if it makes them worried, upset, and ill at ease. Most sales ladies are tactful, diplomatic, and discreetly aggressive. Unfortunately, a small minority are loud and brash and addicted to high pressure tactics. These prospective sales ladies must be in reasonably good health and be able to withstand the physical rigors associated with real estate selling.

Among candidates for sales positions will be business women, presently engaged in fields of opportunity narrower than those to be realized in real estate. They can bring with them the advantages of business experience, working with others, and the discipline of business practice. But their reasons for changing to real estate require analysis. Have they reached a "dead end" in their present calling? Does this fault lie in themselves or in their present business environment? Does their dislike for being "tied down to an office job" mean a lack of self-discipline? Does their expectation of "more money" in real estate mean that the monetary lure is their be-all and end-all? Does their dislike for present associates indicate an inability to work in harmony with others? Can they adapt themselves to the real estate environment? Will they take courses in real estate selling? Will they be happy with the commission basis of compensation? Will they be able to take constructive criticism?

Some brokers will hire part-timers. They feel these part-timers may have relatives, friends, or acquaintances who have property to buy or list. They feel there is nothing to lose, for part-timers are paid nothing unless they make the sale or get the listing. They think that part-timers may be useful in carrying out such chores as house to house canvassing.

Other brokers will not hire part-timers. They believe that real estate requires full-time people, since it is a day to day, during the week, and weekend business. They believe that salespeople should make themselves available, not at times convenient to them, but at times convenient to their customers. They feel that part-timers may not be able to give the empathy, the enthusiasm, and the services required. It may be that part-timers will create morale problems. Full-timers may begrudge them the listings they get and commissions they make. Some part-timers may not reflect favorably on the firm. They may be inexperienced and lack knowledge. Some real estate boards frown on their members employing part-timers.

One's own salespeople may recommend suitable candidates from among their own friends and acquaintances. One's own salespeople know the firm's policies and procedures, the present personnel and their characteristics, and, other things being equal, they should recommend only those who will fit into this scheme of things. The risk run in accepting their recommendations is the possible development of self-perpetuating cliques and factions, a clannishness disruptive of morale. Politics in the sales organization may thereby rear its ugly head. Therefore, the actual reasons for their recommendations should be analyzed. Do the salespeople merely wish to do a good turn for a friend or relative now out of work? Is the recommendation merely the return of a favor?

Salespeople may be found among graduating students in colleges and universities who have majored in real estate. If their parents or relatives are real estate brokers, it is natural for such graduates to go with them. But unless such family ties are present, it is difficult to persuade such graduates to go into real estate selling. These graduates are being offered relatively high salaries in commerce and industry. They are, therefore, not prone to accept the commission basis of compensation in real estate. Many are recently married and feel they must have the security that an assured salary provides.

And, strange as it may seem, there has been a "downgrading" of selling in colleges and universities. The overtones of the market place are not always regarded as consistent with social and cultural aspirations. Some graduates regard selling as demeaning and relegate it to the echelon of the circus barker. College and university graduates occasionally go into real estate indirectly - in employment, for example, with real estate trade associations, with real estate departments of industrial organizations and chain store organizations.

INTERVIEWING PROSPECTIVE SALESPEOPLE

It is important to find out what sales applicants have done that gives promise of a successful selling career. This means finding out their sales records in previous employment; their development of successful sales presentations; their building up of sales campaigns and subsequent follow-through of these to successful completion; their writing of ads with "pulling power" and sales effectiveness; their successful promotion of new products or of new approaches in the sale of old products; their success in putting on demonstrations resulting in increased sales of products demonstrated; and their successful conduct of sales conferences and seminars.

It is essential also to ascertain for whom these sales applicants have worked to check out their performance with these previous employers. It is important to watch what the applicant says. Does he go out of his way to criticize those for whom and with whom he has worked? Does he feel that he has been ill-treated? Does he complain of "personality conflicts"? Does he run down those with whom he has been in competition?

One should find out how often he has changed jobs and whether each change he made resulted in the promotion to a better job. Was he dismissed from prior employment? If so, why? Is he by nature a "rover boy"? Above all, what do his previous employers say about his honesty, his character, and his working habits? Did he give previous employers adequate notice of his intent to terminate his work with them?

In the interview with sales applicants, one can determine their education, the amount and kind of sales training they have had, and their attitude toward continuing education. It is not essential to be a college graduate to be a success in real estate selling. But it is essential to use good English, to have a speaking acquaintance with construction and architecture, to know the community in which one's selling efforts will take place, and to be conversant with the real estate market.

Continuing education in real estate is a "must". Real estate is always changing. It is responsive to changes in finance, technology, communications, business conditions, the tax structure - in fact, in all habits of life. Real estate is a "people business" and people are constantly changing. The need for continuing education is self-evident.

The interview can bring out facts about the applicant's family - the attitude of the other spouse toward real estate selling and the number of dependent children the applicant has. It is essential to determine whether the spouse will be happy in the applicant's selection of a real estate selling career. Will the spouse be reconciled to the absences from home during the evenings and over weekends so necessary to pursue sales prospects? Does the spouse regard real estate selling as a respectable and worthwhile calling? If the spouse is influenced by what friends and neighbors say about real estate, then — "what do they say"?

The more dependent children the applicant has, the more he should be motivated to succeed in real estate selling. But the critical question is whether the applicant can sustain his family during his initial period of lean commissions. Also, a fine balance must be maintained between the demands of one's family and selling job on his time. The family must not be neglected and the demands of the selling job

must not result in a nerve-wracked, unpleasant disposition to make
for unhappiness in family life.

The interview should ascertain the applicant's basic goals and
objectives. There is nothing to be ashamed of in making just as much
money as one can. But money alone is not enough. The satisfaction
that comes from the sale, the glow of achievement, the self-fulfillment
through sales accomplishment - these are the goals worth-while.

If the applicant wishes ultimately to have his own real estate business,
well and good. This is only natural and shows that he is ambitious.
The foundations for this objective will be laid in the sales achievements
he wins under the firm's leadership. But if the applicant wants to get
into real estate only to make enough money to "get out", he should not
be considered. If, on the other hand, the applicant wants to make all
kinds of real estate experience and real estate education his province,
he has the desired objectives.

It should be determined whether the applicant has a constructive
attitude toward real estate and real estate people, if he thinks this is
the best possible business with the best possible people. This means
further that he puts service above self, wishes to participate for
mutual betterment in the activities of his real estate board, and is
willing to accept responsibilities in real estate organizations. It means
also that he will take the time to participate in real estate seminars,
conferences, conventions, and educational institutes. It means likewise
that he will try to get his firm and board to adopt the policies in which
he believes. But, if other policies are adopted, he will work for these
with might and main, bowing his head to majority rule. The applicant
must be one who will not publicly criticize others in the real estate
business, but will keep controversies within the privacy of his real
estate business family.

The interview can determine the applicant's reactions to and attitude
toward the sales policies as set forth in the policy manual. It can
ascertain whether the applicant has sufficient financial resources to tide
him over his development period. The interview can also be so staged
as to see how the applicant will handle typical customer reactions.
The interviewer can therefore ask the applicant:

"Why should I list with you?"

"Why should I buy from you?"

"How would you handle the prospect who says, 'I'll think it over.'"

"The price is too high. I can't afford it."

The applicant deserves the interviewer's undivided attention. The
interviewer should not permit the interview to be interrupted by telephone calls or other people coming in. The interviewer should always
bear in mind that a man well hired is seldom fired.

TRAINING SALESPEOPLE
IN SALES POLICIES AND PROCEDURES

This can be done in part through the firm's policy manual. This
tells the salesperson his hours, his floor time, his splits on commissions,

his vacation time, his use of advertising, the telephone and secretarial service available to him, and his desk facilities. It also spells out the salesperson's duties - to meet his listing and sales quotas; to maintain up to date files on properties under his control; to keep in contact with the office; to have a sales kit with necessary data and equipment; and to attend sales conferences.

The policy manual may suggest ways for the sales person to organize his work, such as to plan his day's work in advance, set up an itinerary for his day, and do his paper work on floor days. The policy manual may suggest techniques for improving sales effectiveness on the telephone: identify yourself; ask questions of the caller - bedrooms needed, price range preferred, how many adults and how many children, their ages and sexes, locational preferences, down payment available, when possession is needed, and whether the caller has property to trade; talk with a smile; avoid high pressure; get the caller's name, address, and telephone number, and set up an appointment; talk with animation; articulate slowly and distinctly; and use proper grammar.

With regard to listings, the policy manual may suggest getting all the details on the property; learning why the owner wants to sell; trying to list close to market value; preparing a folder on each property listed; and servicing the listing. On prospecting, the policy manual may suggest preparing a prospect file; learning the prospect's motive for buying; following up prospects expeditiously; and matching the prospect with the property that fits his needs. On offers, the salesperson should present all bona fide offers to the owner and turn over earnest money and deposits to his employer broker.

The salesperson should be instructed to cooperate with competitors and speak well of them, if he can. If he cannot, he should refrain from comment. If the salesperson's office belongs to or is affiliated with a multiple listing service, the salesperson should learn its rules and regulations and abide by them, using its services to the fullest advantage. Membership in the local real estate board is desirable and support of it a must.

The salesperson should know why the community is a good place in which to live and to work, the advantages it has to offer, its schools and cultural attractions, its taxes and government, the reasons why it will progress, and its present and future economic promise.

The salesperson must comply with the Realtor's Code of Ethics. This is not a set of pious platitudes. This is a call to action binding on all Realtors and made meaningful by the many illustrations of its application.

TRAINING IN SELLING

The new salesperson should go out with the broker or experienced salespeople and observe their methods of securing listings and prospects, negotiating, and closing.

The broker or an experienced salesperson should go out with the new salesperson on his first selling assignments, see how he performs, and, subsequently, tell him his good points and his bad. He should also be educated in the instruments used in selling - purchase agreements, deeds, mortgages, financing documents, listing agreements, deposit receipts, and exchange agreements. He should be asked to fill out these forms. This makes him apply his knowledge and helps it sink in.

The salesperson should be encouraged at all times to be courteous, drive carefully, show the prospects only as many properties in one day as they can digest, be an interested listener, have the answers ready for the questions to be asked, discreetly insist on a decision, qualify the buyer, and understand all the types of financing available.

Training involves bringing up the arguments the owner will make against listing the property and the arguments the buyer will make against buying the property and showing the most effective ways of handling these arguments. The salesperson should be shown that selling is servicing and that success in selling depends on the empathy the salesperson has with the buyer.

Each salesperson should be given a check-up from time to time, just as a doctor would do, to show him what he did, what he did not do, what was good and what was bad about his performance. Suggestions should be made for further improvement. This check-up is sometimes called a "How am I doing?" session.

TRAINING SALESPEOPLE TO ORGANIZE THEMSELVES

Salespeople should be trained to plan their work and work their plan. They should be given forms to fill out showing just what they will do the following day. When they have time between appointments, they should use it for inspecting properties or servicing listings. They should check their work plans at the end of the week and find out for themselves just how many of their objectives they accomplished.

Salespeople should be trained to establish priorities for themselves in what they do. They should determine who is most likely to list and likely to buy and concentrate their time accordingly. They should limit the amount of time they spend with just chance acquaintances. When they go someplace, they should ask themselves, "Is this trip necessary?" They should also ask themselves, "What else can I do while I am out?" They should write down everything they did in the course of a day and go over this to find out for themselves how they could have used their time to better advantage.

TRAINING THROUGH SALES MEETINGS

Sales meetings provide, through post mortems, the opportunity to find out how sales were won and lost. Selling experiences are shared and selling ideas exchanged. Teamwork and cooperation are developed.

Sales meetings can be made successful by requiring prompt attendance and by starting them on time. The leader should stick to the agenda. The leader should get participation. He can do so by asking questions. Participation can also be secured through role playing. This means acting out in hypothetical selling situations the role of the owner, the sales person, and the prospect. Everyone should be encouraged to speak up, and, in doing so, to confine himself to the subject. Questions asked should be repeated so that all can hear, comment, and respond.

CULTIVATING SALES PERSONALITIES

In telephone selling, this can be done by developing an empathy for the person at the other end of the telephone line. While the other party is finding out about the property, you are trading information and finding out about him. You are asking questions about the caller's needs and desires, thereby demonstrating your interest in serving him.

You cultivate a sales personality by using the smile, not the grin. You do so by thinking positively and constructively. You do so by striving to handle the biggest sales assignment, but still not considering yourself above the humblest job. You develop a "nose for deals" and see all properties as possible "deals". You develop an emotional identity with your listers and prospects.

COMPENSATING SALESPEOPLE

There is no uniform practice on the percentage paid the selling salesman. Some offices pay 50 per cent, some 60 per cent, some more, some less. There is no requirement by local boards on the way their members must split their commissions.

Some offices provide periodic statements for each salesperson, showing how much in commissions he has earned. Some give the salesman his portion of the commission as soon as the transaction is closed.

The listing salesman's portion of the commission in some firms is 10 per cent, in some firms more, in some firms less. If the listing salesman is also the selling salesman, he usually gets both the listing commission and the selling commission.

Some offices favor advances and draw accounts. They believe they are necessary to sustain the promising beginner during his unproductive training period as well as the good salesman in a temporary selling slump. Other offices are against them, believing that they weaken incentive and encourage bad financial habits on the part of the salesperson.

Regarding the giving of bonuses on the attainment of certain sales levels, some bonus plans establish a sales goal and pay bonuses when this is reached. Other plans set up a minimum sales level and pay bonuses in varying percentages at levels beyond. These may take the form of a sliding scale incentive. The commission percentage is increased, as each new and higher level of sales or listing volume is reached.

Prizes for winning sales contests take many forms. Some offices pay for trips to real estate conventions for those salespersons who reach certain sales goals. Others give such salespersons short vacation trips or money awards. The more salespeople who have a reasonable chance of being among the winners, the better.

The theory of profit sharing with salespeople is sound. Brokers reward each salesperson with a percentage of the firm's profits, based on his contributions to the profit. To qualify for profit sharing, some offices require the salesperson to be working for the firm at the end of the year and to have earned a certain minimum for that year, like $10,000. At this minimum level, he would get, say, three per cent of the profits. From here, he would advance in his percentage, and get, say, four per cent when his own earnings reached $12,000, then going on to still higher percentages as he went on to higher earnings.

Other benefits given by some firms are group insurance and medical plans and retirement programs.

MANAGING SALESPEOPLE

Their faults should be pointed out in private, and in a tactful, diplomatic, and impersonal manner. If the person's individual faults are pointed out in public, this may damage his ego and incur his personal resentment. The faults may be personal ones - lack of neatness in dress and appearance, bad breath, loud mouth, improper grammar, being argumentative, brash, discourteous, drinking on the job. Or the faults may be in the way the salespeople carry on their business - high pressure, talking too much and listening too little, taking advantage of others, misrepresenting and exaggerating, lack of teamwork with associates, failing to keep appointments on time, tardiness and absenteeism, spending too much time in the office, failing to call in when out in the field, and lack of follow through.

When salespeople become despondent, their spirits may be bolstered by giving them a "pep" talk - showing you believe in them. They may be given a "pat on the back", reminding them of their good attributes and past success. They may be told about comparable problems you faced, how you overcame them, and how they can do the same.

The broker should wean his salespeople from dependence on him. He should get them to go out and produce results on their own. When his help is not needed he should leave them alone. He should give them latitude, telling them it is up to them to determine how to do their sales job.

Brokers may set their production goals for each salesman in terms of the minimum income he should earn. For example, some firms set this at $1,200 a month. Some brokers require that each salesperson secure, on the average, one sale and six listings per week.

Production goals may be set in terms of the gross sales each salesperson should average per month. Some brokers have set this at $60,000. Production goals have also been set on the basis of the net commission the office should realize per month from the salesperson's efforts. However determined, the production goals established should be reasonable ones and possible of attainment.

Managing salespeople means seeing to it that they accord themselves with standards of good behavior - no drinking while working, no profanity, telling the truth at all times, never running competitors down, and complying with the Realtor's Code of Ethics. Good management always means creating a climate for and reflecting enthusiasm and optimism, giving individual interest and encouragement to each salesperson.

There is no "sure fire" way of retaining sales people. But good management should see to it that only sales people will be engaged who will fit into the organization. Salespeople will be inclined to stay with your organization, if they feel they are advancing and getting somewhere. This they feel if they reach their production goal. They appreciate your giving them appropriate recognition. They like to participate in decision making on sales approaches and sales promotions. They like to be put into the kinds of real estate selling best suited to their talents. Some may thereby go from residential to commercial or industrial. If there is team spirit in your organization, a spirit of success, morale will be high and there will be less inclination to leave.

TERMINATING SALESPEOPLE

When it becomes clearly evident that salespeople do not have it in themselves to produce, you do them and yourself a favor by suggesting they employ their time and talents elsewhere. The occasion for termination may be repeated failure to meet sales quotas; lack of cooperation; lack of compliance with policy; and display of unethical and dishonest practices.

OFFICE LOCATION

The real estate office should be readily accessible to clients and customers. In a small community, the office should be on or near the main street. In suburban communities, the office may to advantage be located in a shopping center where ample parking is provided. If the office specializes in the sale or rental of commercial and industrial properties, it will find desirable a location in a downtown professional building. If it engages in property management or land development, a location in a regional shopping center might be most convenient. Whatever the type of office, its location should accommodate the convenience of the travel patterns of its particular market.

The office design should be in good taste and reflect attractive architecture. The office windows should be large enough to provide adequate display for the pictures of the homes and commercial properties available. The decor should invite the passer-by to walk in. The office exterior, in fact, is the outer dress of the organization and its style is expressive of the personality of the organization.

A ground floor office is always preferable. It may, however, not be practical in the case of a downtown location. The office sign should be easy to read and easy to identify. It should be visible both day and night. It is desirable for the office to be illuminated both day and night. The small extra charge for the electricity will prove to be a profitable investment. The sign itself should not be garnish and flamboyant, but rather, neat and conservative.

OFFICE INTERIOR AND FURNISHINGS

The furnishings should be attractive and in good taste. The equipment should be functional. The chairs should be comfortable. The salespeople's desks should be large enough to enable them to spread out maps and other bulky material. There should be adequate space between the salespeople's desks. If too crowded, it could resemble a boiler factory. The name plate of every salesperson should be on his desk. The desks should be kept meticulously clean and in good order.

There should be a conference room where interviews can be conducted in absolute privacy, where closings can be transacted, and where meetings can be held. In small offices the broker's own room may have to suffice for these purposes. If the office concentrates on residential selling, it may to advantage provide a home decor with wall-to-wall carpeting, the type of furniture you would expect to find in a well-kept home, and with curtains and wallpaper the counterparts of what would be in a nice residence.

It is desirable to install a listing control board, showing the listings by expiration date, type of property, and price. Partitions and dividers may be employed to afford greater privacy. If the office can afford it, it should have a reception room and a receptionist. They can give a pleasant introduction, and make the caller feel welcome and at home.

Records must be kept - sales records, commission records, appraisal records, client and prospect records. One must be able, quickly and conveniently, to pull these out when the need arises. A good filing system makes these readily available.

Set up these files in the way that best suits the needs of your office. The advice and consent of your secretaries, bookkeepers, and other clerical workers will be essential. You will have many prospect files, providing the data necessary to determine their needs, desires, and financial capabilities. You will have files on listings, describing the properties, the sales prices and the terms of sale, the rentals and the stipulations concerning control and possession in the cases of lease, and the bases for trade and exchange properties.

Your files on your customers can be your real treasure trove. These will tell you their birthdays, anniversaries, hobbies and special interests, and enable you to remind them of pleasant circumstances connected with their transactions. All this information will provide pleasant opportunities for continuing liaison.

Your files on your listing contracts, present and past, will verify for you the legal relationships between you and your clients. These are the springboard for your sales campaigns.

Once a transaction is over and done with it should not be forgotten. Therefore, so-called "morgue files" on transaction histories will be kept, to which reference will be made in time to come for comparables in appraising, tried and true procedures to be employed in current transactions, and tax and financial data.

One will want to have files which will remind him of the dates on which he should be taking certain action. These are appropriately called "tickler" files, for they tickle your memory as to these times. They will remind you not only of personal items, such as birthdays, but also business items, such as expiration dates for leases and listings.

As your files contain confidential information, you will permit access to them only to authorized and trustworthy personnel. As a situation may arise at any time making it necessary to refer to them, you will not permit their removal except by the person responsible for them. This person you will have picked for the exercise of good judgment and discretion.

You will find it advantageous for your files on properties to be cross-indexed with other files containing inter-related data. You then have a convenient reference medium.

You may have created your own mailing list. You may have classified prospects for residential, commercial, or industrial properties. You may have further refined it by income levels and vocational classifications. Such divisions will have pre-arranged screening for your direct mail advertising, sending it only where there is a reasonable likelihood of response. You will be sure to review your names and addresses from time to time to keep them up to date. People move, die, get married, retire, and change jobs. Your mailing list should reflect their present status.

Every real estate office should be furnished with a library. This means much more than just having textbooks on real estate principles, finance, law, and appraising. It means also having periodical literature on these and other related subjects. It means likewise having street and farm maps of the area, with the names and addresses of the residents. Every office should also have the publications put out by the state real estate association for these provide the names and addresses of all the Realtors in the state and are classified by local real estate boards. Over and above this would be the publication by the National Association of Real Estate Boards which would give the same type of information, but on a national scale with breakdowns by individual states. This national publication also gives the names and addresses of the principal officers of the affiliates of the national association. The recommended commissions for the various types of real estate transactions usually appear under the local real estate board classifications of the state directories.

The library should likewise contain bound volumes of the publications, from past years, of the institutes of real estate and farm and land brokers. These publications contain highly pertinent sources of reference for the solution of current problems. They are usually indexed both by subject matter and author.

In as much as mathematical problems and computations are constantly recurring, the library should also contain tables for computation of monthly payments on mortgage loans, ascertainment of depth values, discounted values of reversionary interests, and determination of leasehold evaluations.

From time to time bulletins and guidelines will be published on subjects such as the truth in lending bill, open housing legislation, and the effects on investment real estate of new tax bills. All these deserve a place in the Realtor's library.

Most of the other furnishings for the real estate office are obvious - typewriters, adding machines, bookkeeping machines, calculators, and photo-copying machines. Naturally, there should be a copious supply of stationery, letterheads, carbon paper, scratch pads, inter-office memos, pens, pencils, paper clips, and pins. The office should have a stapler, a stamp meter, outgoing and incoming mail baskets, and a safe.

Although the importance of being equipped with a computer tie-in belongs more appropriately under the heading of sales management, its pertinence to office management cannot be dismissed. The larger offices will be using computers to perform their bookkeeping operations, get out their billings and statements, and find out the ratio of office and overhead costs to the total volume of sales.

OFFICE PROCEDURE

Every member of the sales force will take his turn in the assignment of floor duty. He will then be taking care of the sales inquiries that come in over the telephone. He will also attend to the people who walk in from the street to ask questions about properties they may have read about in ads or been attracted to by reason of the pictures in the office window. Naturally, the sales person assigned to floor duty will have thoroughly familiarized himself with regard to all current listings so as to be able to answer questions and supply information. He will also be keeping a record of these inquiries and where they have been made in response to advertisements. This record will assist in evaluating the pulling power of the ads. If such activity should slow down, the floor duty salesperson can constructively use his time by engaging in telephone solicitation, writing advertisements, or going over the listing and prospect files and bringing them up to date.

Unless the salesperson has been assigned floor duty, he will be spending his time away from the office, making outside contacts, running down leads, seeing his prospects and his clients. But he will make sure that he can always be reached by his office, where possible, leaving the telephone number of the place where he is likely to be at such and such hours. He will also call into the office every two hours or so to find out whether there have been any inquiries which he should be answering.

Since it is so important that salespeople always have access to listed properties for purposes of inspection and showing, most offices will set up a keyboard where the keys to the various properties will be hung. When a salesperson takes one of these down, he leaves word with the office that he has done so. Upon leaving the particular property, he likewise makes sure that all doors and windows are locked and checks the property to insure that nothing has been disturbed.

The lifeblood of selling is enriched by the exchange of helpful information and learning from one another. Consequently, the office will have salesmeetings at which the problems that have been met with will be discussed and solutions suggested. Postmortems will be conducted on sales lost and recitations will be presented on the techniques by which sales were won. Participation at these sales meetings will be mandatory for the sales force.

The only way by which the office can determine whether it is progressing is by reference to its record against the standards it has set. Every office wants to know just how much it cost to make the sale. How does this line up against the commission derived? What was the advertising expense, the car mileage expense, and the entertainment expense? By ascertaining these costs, as incurred by individual salespeople, and comparing them with the revenue brought in, the office can find out which ones are responsible for the greatest profits to the office.

Bearing in mind that it costs money to train · the salespeople; to provide them with desks, office space, stenographic and clerical assistance, and telephones, some offices figure out what salespeople must have achieved by reason of net earnings to themselves to make their operations profitable to the office. Some say that salespeople must make for themselves at least $10,000.00 per year to make them profitable to the office. Other offices try to achieve this same objective by means of break-even charts which show how much revenue the office must bring in just to meet its expenses. And, as a constant reminder to the salespeople themselves, other offices set up gross sales charts, which demonstrate to salespeople how much they must produce in gross sales to justify such and such expenditures for mail, telephone, advertising, and clerical expense.

When an office advertises "open house", it must be sure that someone is in charge there at all the advertised times. This logically and naturally falls to the lot of the salesman responsible for the open house listing. He is highly conscious that he must not absent himself from the property during advertised hours unless he has arranged for competent coverage.

OFFICE BUDGETS

Every real estate office must set up a budget as a guide for its future operations. This budget serves as its standard for performance. It tries to anticipate the expenses that will be incurred and revenue that will be brought in. It breaks down these basic categories into meaningful divisions and sub-divisions. It does so for a month ahead, a quarter ahead, a half year ahead, and a year ahead. The longer in time the projection is made, the greater the chance of situations occurring which could not be foreseen and which make changes and adjustments necessary.

The income the office derives emanates from the commissions enjoyed. These in turn must be broken down by what percentage is to go to the salesperson and what percentage is to go to the office. If there are both a listing and selling salesperson involved, this category must be further broken down. If a cooperating broker is to receive a share of the commission, the budget must so indicate. What residue the office itself derives, will, in turn, under the budget, be disbursed among the cost categories established. Sometimes the commission will be split 50 per cent for the salespeople and 50 per cent for the office. Other offices may give the salespeople 60 per cent and the office 40 per cent.

What is left for the office must be disbursed for the various operations engaged in. A larger office may have a combination receptionist-telephone operator. A smaller office may have just a combination secretary, telephone operator, and bookkeeper. During seasons of peak operations, it may be necessary to hire part-time people. Although individual offices will vary in what percentage of their revenues they will disburse for these salaried personnel, ten per cent is not uncommon.

Although it might be thought that selling expenses would be limited to the portion of the commission the salesperson gets, this is by no means the case. A larger office may have a sales manager who superintends the individual salespeople. The traveling expenses of salespeople to sales conferences and sales conventions must be paid for. Likewise, the disbursements necessary for sales training and other educational courses. There are the dues for membership in professional organizations, such as the state association, the local real estate boards, and national organizations, such as the National Institute of Real Estate Brokers. There are also the expenses incurred for the entertainment of clients and prospects. If the office is connected with the Realtors Computer Service, there is the selling expense for the sales facility this provides. What percentage of the office dollar should be set up for all of these? Past experience as to their costs can serve as a guide. So can the experience of other offices similarly constituted. So can individual studies prepared by professional organizations. Whatever the source of these data, they are likely to indicate 15 per cent, and perhaps even higher.

Although advertising paves the way for the sale and could logically fall under the heading of selling expense, it is so important that it is entitled to a separate category. It takes in not only newspaper advertising but also that carried on in other media as well. It includes signs and direct mail. It encompasses the ball point pens and the many other give-aways in which the office engages. It is the institutional advertising and public relations expense in which the office engages to enhance its public image. It takes in the anniversary cards sent out to one's customers and all the other reminders that you are still interested in them. Whatever percentage we budget for advertising is likely to be wrong in the light of retrospect. Hindsight is much easier than foresight. Based on the experience of many offices, however, 13 per cent of the office revenues would not seem to be too wide of the mark.

Then there are the mundane items of rent, utilities, janitorial and cleaning service, and heat and electricity. Sometimes we call them occupancy costs. We know in advance what our rent is going to be. Even if we own our office, rent is still a charge. We must then pay this amount to ourselves. Although our utility charges will depend on the season of the year, as will our costs for heat, we will not find it too hard to derive a rough figure from month to month. As custodial charges usually go just one way, and that is up, we must budget liberally for them. The net of all this is that we may have to put our occupancy costs at a fifteen per cent basis.

We should never stint on telephone expense. We must have sufficient extensions so that our lines do not get tied up. We must be accessible at all times. Even though we may not actually sell over the phone, we find out things about our clients and prospects. We answer inquiries by telephone. We conduct telephone solicitation. We keep in touch by phone. Therefore, in line with the experience of many successful offices, we put down seven per cent for our telephone expense.

Over and above our selling and advertising expenses is our expense for sales management. If we have a sales manager, he is paid out of this. If we, as a broker, do the sales managing, we should be compensated accordingly. Sales management is not alone the superintendence and direction of our sales personnel, but also the interviewing of prospects for our sales force. It is preparing the agenda for and conducting sales meetings. The amount to be set aside for sales management will be geared to the amount of sales production. It will usually be ten per cent of our office revenues.

What percentage of our budget should be allocated to administration and overhead? Out of this amount we shall provide for our legal and accounting fees, our stationery and supplies, for the depreciation on our equipment, and our pension and profit sharing schemes (if we have them). Some offices budget as low as five per cent; others as high as 13 per cent. We are inclined to take a mid-way figure such as eight per cent.

The most perplexing category of all is that for miscellaneous items and contingencies. This is a catch-all to take care of things that do come up, but for which we forgot to itemize. This is the cushion to which we can return if we underestimated our other expenses. Our experience shows, that in planning a budget, we should do so on the high side here. So we put this down at five per cent.

This leaves 17 per cent as the profit for the particular office. Out of this profit will come the income tax it will have to pay. Out of this profit will be set aside an amount for future growth and expansion. This profit is the over-all compensation for the risks of proprietorship and the burden of general management and supervision.

Reviewing the budget of the revenues that go to the office:

Salaries	10%
Selling expenses	15%
Advertising	13%
Occupancy costs	15%
Telephone expense	7%
Sales management	10%
Administration	8%
Miscellaneous	5%
Profit	17%
	100%

THE OFFICE PERSONALITY

The office should always express its personality in a way to make its clients and prospects feel it is interested in them, it is trying to be helpful at every stage, and its attitude is warm and friendly toward them. On the telephone therefore, the office employee identifies himself or herself, asks questions to determine the caller's requirements, and gets the caller's name, address, and telephone number. The voice with the smile never goes out of style. Everyone connected with the office is pleasant and friendly, builds goodwill through a winning personality, and makes everyone coming to the office feel a real welcome. In the written communications sent out from the office, brevity is always the soul of wit, the short sentence suffices, the words make clear the meaning intended, and get attention, maintain interest, and convey conviction.

Although a small office may have the sales and office activities concentrated in one individual, it may be penny wise and pound foolish to have the sole proprietor take up his valuable time with clerical activities. The role of better judgment may therefore dictate at least part-time stenographic and secretarial assistance. In a large office, the activities may be organized into departments - sales, management, appraisals, and mortgage banking. Each may have its own personnel.

Reasonable rules and regulations apply to the office as well as the sales force. Office hours, the time for the coffee breaks, the luncheon periods, the rest periods, and the usual holidays are specified. Employees who have been with the firm one year are normally given two weeks vacation. Employees with the firm for longer periods are given additional vacation time. Although offices try to accommodate vacation time preferences, the requirements of the organization are paramount, and individual desires may have to be rescheduled. Most real estate firms try to be generous about sick leave, particularly if the employee has been with the organization a reasonable period of time. Many firms now have health insurance plans. Salespeople are required to carry public liability and property damage insurance on their cars in amounts deemed appropriate to cover any claims that might arise.

OFFICE CONTROLS

Each listing is given a number, and the signed copy of the listing is carried in a permanent folder. This must never be permitted to leave the office. If it is necessary to get information from this, these data can be copied down. The listing will, of course, show the expiration date. A service record on the listing will be kept, indicating the signs on the property, the name of the salesperson who is servicing the listing, the ads run, the times the property was shown and the offers received.

The sales file will document the fact that the offer was accepted, will contain a progress check sheet on the closing, and will have duplicate closing statements. It will, in effect, constitute a complete history of the sales transaction, how it developed, the steps in between, and the happy consummation of the sale itself.

The forms the office uses are there for just one purpose - to make for office efficiency. And so there will be a phone message form, interoffice memo forms, salesperson's production records, daily work plans, employment applications, employee selection and evaluation, job description, monthly summary of sales activities, and appraisal summary sheets.

The office accounting system provides the basis for analyzing and recording the transactions. It provides a measurement for sales productivity versus sales costs, for tax liability considerations, and how actual performance compares with that anticipated.

The accounting system will consist of journals in which transactions are entered for subsequent transfer to specialized accounts; of ledgers, in which entries are summarized and posted to proper accounts; of profit and loss statements and balance sheets. It will also include a sales ledger, showing expected and actual dollar volumes of sales.

Transactions affecting ledger accounts are entered in the general journal. The accounting system will also show net worth, which consists of the capital invested and the earnings retained.

TRUE AND FALSE QUESTIONS

1. A sales manager's job is to produce sales, not to control selling costs.   T   F

2. The computer can be used as an effective sales tool only in the larger sales office.   T   F

3. Most college graduates are highly desirous of going into real estate selling.   T   F

4. Retired people are too old to become effective in real estate selling.   T   F

5. There is no "sure fire" way of retaining sales people.   T   F

6. If a salesperson's faults are pointed out by his sales manager in public, this may hurt his ego and incur his resentment.   T   F

7. Prospects should be shown in the course of a day as many properties as they have time to view.   T   F

8. A prepossessing sales personality is one to which others respond.   T   F

9. College graduates tend to feel they must have the security of a salaried job.   T   F

10. The computer is making for new methods in real estate selling.   T   F

11. The firm's policy manual confines itself to sales matters.   T   F

12. Local boards stipulate how their members should split their commissions with their salespeople.   T   F

13. In the sliding scale incentive bonus plan, the commission percentage is increased as higher levels of sales of listings are attained.   T   F

14. It is desirable to arrange sales contests so that all who make a substantial try may be among the winners.   T   F

15. Local boards set up sales dollar production goals, whose attainment is required as a condition of membership.　　T　F

16. The computer relieves salespeople of clerical work.　　T　F

17. "Morgue files" relating to out-of-date transactions can be eliminated.　　T　F

18. The easiest category to budget for is Miscellaneous.　　T　F

19. The salesperson who procured the listing is usually responsible for "open house".　　T　F

20. Each salesperson should be given a desk.　　T　F

21. The ledgers serve the same purpose that the journals do.　　T　F

22. Financial budgets are also called sales ledgers.　　T　F

23. Electronic data processing equipment increases the storage space required for the data collected.　　T　F

24. There is general agreement that advertising expense should be reduced in line with sales declines.　　T　F

25. If a sales manager is not employed, then it is unnecessary to budget for sales management.　　T　F

26. Any salesperson may at any time remove any file containing data pertinent to his listing.　　T　F

27. Breakeven charts show how much revenue the office must bring in to meet its expenses.　　T　F

28. The salesperson responsible for "open house" may not leave it during the hours it is advertised as open, unless he secures coverage.　　T　F

29. The uncertainties of real estate make it impossible to forecast expenditures for periods longer than one month.　　T　F

30. Advertising expense is usually so large that a separate budget classification is usually set up to account for it.　　T　F

31. One sentence may be all that a letter requires, if the sentence conveys the message, and does so in a friendly way.　　T　F

32. The computer's response is limited to an oral response.　　T　F

33. The computer enables the prospect by himself to screen out   T   F
the properties in which he is not interested.

34. Accounting records are confined to the balance sheet and to   T   F
the profit and loss statement.

35. Office requirements are the determining factor in whether to   T   F
grant employees the preferences they request for vacation
periods.

36. Salespeople are required to carry liability and property   T   F
damage insurance on their cars.

37. The salesperson should present all bona fide offers to the   T   F
owner.

38. Retirees may be limited to their sales incentives by how   T   F
much Social Security may permit them to make.

39. The sales manager's objective is not to win a popularity   T   F
contest among his salespeople.

40. The net result of the computer will be to eliminate selling   T   F
jobs.

41. If at a sales meeting, the salespeople are called upon to act out the roles of owner, prospect, and sales person, this is called:
    ( ) Play acting
    ( ) Role playing
    ( ) Sales rehearsal
    ( ) Personality identity

41. In contacts with prospects, it is important for salespeople to be:
    ( ) Fast talkers
    ( ) Interested listeners
    ( ) Effective in argument
    ( ) Impressive in the use of big words

43. The Realtor's Code of Ethics is:
    ( ) Advisory only
    ( ) Binding on all Realtors
    ( ) Enforceable by courts of law
    ( ) Binding on all real estate licensees

44. If a salesperson receives earnest money or deposits, he should:
    ( ) Put these in a separate bank account
    ( ) Earmark the deposit slips with the name of the person giving the money
    ( ) Turn these over to the owner of the property
    ( ) Turn these over to his employer broker

45. The publication setting forth the salesperson's duties is:
    ( ) The policy manual
    ( ) The Realtor's Code of Ethics
    ( ) The salesman's license law
    ( ) Realtor's headlines

46. Net worth consists of:
    ( ) The aggregate of fixed and current assets
    ( ) Capital invested and earnings retained
    ( ) Cash on hand and accounts receivable
    ( ) Accounts receivable and reserves for depreciation

47. Transactions affecting ledger accounts are entered in:
    ( ) The cash receipts and disbursements journal

( )   The general journal
( )   The financial journal
( )   The profit and loss journal

48. The prime benefit the budget provides is:
( )   To establish a standard for performance and cost control
( )   To provide the data for the profit and loss statement
( )   To give a sales forecast for ensuing periods
( )   To analyze the sources from which sales are derived

49. Of the budget allocations suggested, the highest percentage was for:
( )   Administration
( )   Profit
( )   Selling
( )   Salaries

50. If a broker wishes to return to selling only under you full time:
( )   He should be hired at once
( )   The consent of your local board must be obtained
( )   The reasons he gives for this desire should be checked and
       analyzed
( )   This means he has been unsuccessful as an administrator

ESSAY QUESTIONS

1. Why is it important to determine in the case of a sales applicant the attitude of the spouse toward real estate selling?

2. In what ways should salespeople be trained to organize themselves?

3. What are the faults encountered in salespeople, and how should they be pointed out?

4. What does floor duty involve?

ADVERTISING AND PUBLICITY

CHAPTER TWELVE

WHY ADVERTISE?

You advertise to pave the way for the sale. You advertise to get listings. You tell property owners how and why you can get their properties sold. Your advertisements introduce the listings to their prospective markets. They point out the advantages of the listings in such a way as to attract qualified prospects. In times of "tight" money they show how you are still able to tap the fountains of finance.

You advertise to build good will. You tell the public about your reputation for effective service. You indicate that you are an old and established firm. You refer to the professional designations you carry - "Realtor", GRI (Graduate Realtors Institute), and MAI (Member of the American Institute of Real Estate Appraisers.)

You advertise to tell the public that you can handle their needs, not only in brokerage, but also in finance, appraising, investments, management, and land planning and development. You are a complete and integrated real estate office.

THE ADVERTISING PLAN

Should your advertising budget go up or down, depending on how much business you are doing? Should you advertise heavily when sales are high and nominally when sales are low? You may find this plan penny wise and pound foolish. The success of advertising is based on its continuity. Your name and repute are not self-perpetuating. You will find that a greater advertising effort is required when business is slack than is necessary to keep up the momentum when business is soaring.

Your advertising plan requires you to check the effectiveness of your advertising. You therefore keep a record of calls received in response to advertising used. You ask your customers whether they saw the ad. You get your salespeople to report whether their prospects commented on the ad. You keep a record of the number of persons inspecting "open houses" that have been advertised. Your advertising plan also fixes the responsibility for ad preparation and measurement of results. You maintain a record of inquiries about the property advertised and what comments were made about the advertisement itself. You require each of your salespeople to become familiar with each property being advertised.

Your advertising plan determines what appeals are to be used. Pride of ownership constitutes a strong appeal in advertising a home. There is a social prestige that comes about with the ownership of a fine home. There is a lovely living room in which to receive your guests. There is privacy and sanctuary for you and your family. Your advertising plan also describes the homes advertised as abodes for children.

There is a yard for them to play in. Here they may fraternize with their playmates under the watchful eyes of their parents. Here they may develop their individual skills and exercise their individual hobbies.

Your ads reveal the ease and comfort that accompany home ownership. There are the mechanical appliances installed in the home that make for easy living. There is the convenience of the compact kitchen. There are the heating and the air conditioning systems adjustable to individual tastes and preferences. There are the lawn and patio made for outdoor living.

You appeal with the view that the home provides - the home on the hill and the view of the countryside below; the view of the lake, the river, and the woods beyond.

Your ad appeals with the accessibility to the shopping center, the schools, the religious and cultural facilities, and the closeness of public transportation.

In advertising investment property, your ad appeals with the earnings opportunities it presents, the appreciation and the capital gain to be enjoyed, and the tax shelter and the cash flow to be provided.

PREPARING THE NEWSPAPER AD

You write the ad mentally as you go through the property. You measure the dimensions, note the rooms and other space and the purposes they serve, the physical condition of the premises, and the heating and electrical systems. You jot down the unique and distinctive features of the property and, in the case of a residence, give special attention to the amenities it provides.

You start out with your ad with a provocative lead - ask a question, give the neighborhood, state the price, the mortgage assumption available, the proximity to the nearby country club. You evolve your headline after you have written your copy for the body of your ad. Your headline requires extra special attention. It determines how effective your ad will be in evoking appropriate response. It is the magnetizing force attracting attention.

You think of your homes as a woman's life and think of all the accessories she would like to make for better living. Then you try to describe them the way she likes to have them appear in your ad. But you do not write too long or detailed classified ads on homes, for this will not only be costly, but it will also discourage readership.

You ask the present owners what they like about their home and why they bought it in the first place. The answers they give may provide good copy for you. As your prospects comment on your ads, you keep a record of what appealed to them. These features you re-use in subsequent presentations. You make your format interesting, attractive, and distinctive by using headlines, subheadlines, and white space.

WHAT SHOULD YOU FEATURE IN THE NEWSPAPER AD?

In the case of residential properties, your prospects want to know the price, location, taxes, down payment required, number of rooms -

particularly the number of bedrooms, unique characteristics of the property and what these will do for the prospect, and whether an existing mortgage may be assumed. They wish also to know the accessibility to schools, shopping centers, and public transportation.

In the case of business properties, your prospects want to know the yield and price, the financing available, the location, the uses to which the properties may be put, the space, dimensions, and setbacks, the parking area and the transportation facilities, the applicable zoning and building codes, the conveniences provided, and the character of the neighborhood. They wish also to know about the tax shelter and cash flow available, the tax concessions the municipality or county may make, the skills and tractability of the labor supply, and the power and utilities afforded.

CLASSIFIED AND DISPLAY

Advertising rates are based on the newspaper's circulation - the higher the circulation, the higher the rates. The open rate is the one applicable to the "once in a while" advertiser. It is the highest priced rate. Contract rates may be in the form of space contracts. A certain rate is given you, based on your agreement to use so much space over a period of time. This is called a quantity discount rate. Your contract rate may also be based on your agreement to run so many ads over a period of time. This is called a time frequency discount rate.

If you are unable to live up to your contract commitment, you are billed for the differential between your contract rate and the rate applicable to the lineage you actually used or the frequency for which you were actually responsible. This is called "short rating".

Classified ads, for the space used, are usually less expensive than display ads. Classifieds are aimed at the reader going through the classified section with his mind intent on finding out what real estate is offered that may suit his requirements. This eliminates the "waste readership" to which you are subject in display. Classified readership is "screened" in advance by the mental set of the particular reader.

Classifieds' primary competition is from other classified ads. Classifieds meet with no competition for the reader's attention from news items, illustrations, cartoons, editorials, and letters to the editor, as does display advertising.

Newspapers may provide "classified display". This permits ads with borders, illustrations, and boldface types on the classified pages. Some newspapers may permit the use of trademarks and logotypes in the classified.

How can you achieve visual domination in the classified pages? You can do so by using larger ads than others in the same classification. You can use large type for the headline and/or the name of the Realtor. You can practice "scatteration," using ads of consistent style, but in various parts of the classified section.

Your ad is officially inserted by means of an insertion order with the newspaper. You try to avoid telephoning in the ad, for there is too much of a chance of a garbled communication.

It is helpful to analyze classified ads in order to determine what appeals are used. One hundred eighty randomly selected home advertisements from 12 editions of the *Wall Street Journal* (the Real Estate corner in its Friday edition) and from 12 editions of the *Detroit News* were analyzed. The purpose was to compare so called "high-class" appeals to high income readers in the *Journal* with everyday appeals to middle income readers in the *News*. The thought was that this might act as a guide in determining appeals to be employed, depending on the kind of news medium used.

Appeal	*Wall Street Journal* Times Used	*Detroit News* Times Used
Privacy	24	
Lakeside	48	
Number of acres	62	
Wooded area	26	14
Stone construction	23	
Landscaping	37	
Patio	35	4
Fireplace	78	60
Second kitchen	48	
Air conditioning	71	
Paneling	24	
Recreation facilities	63	
Garage	72	114
Number of baths	83	66
Pool	26	2
Stables	27	
Time to city	23	
Beach	53	
Executive home	35	3
Location	74	118
Bar	25	
Family room	30	48
Resort facilities	24	
Carpeting	31	37
Heating systems	24	18
Furnishings	39	
Price	56	84
Kitchen facilities		42
Bathroom facilities	16	66
Colonial style	6	24
Brick construction	19	66
Basement	18	55
FHA financing		37
Abbreviations	36	70

This survey shows that advertising the location is important both for high and for medium price homes; that advertising the price is more important for middle-income appeal; that garage facilities are important both for high and medium income classes; that bathroom facilities should be accentuated in appeals to middle income, the upper income presumably taking them for granted; and that brick construction and basement have a high appeal for middle income.

As a classified advertiser, you should know the language the newspaper uses in connection with your ads. The space you use may be measured by agate lines, each of which is 1/14 of an inch in height. Or it may be measured by column inches, a column inch being one column, 14 agate lines long. The words you use in your ad are called "copy". The expression "layout" refers to the form of the ad. The width of your copy is called the "copy block". The space between the lines in your ad is referred to as "leading".

If you use display advertising, it will of course appear on the pages which contain news and/or editorial matter. Display ads are usually larger than classifieds and are commonly illustrated, carrying a generous amount of white space. If you wish to put your display ads on special favored pages or in special favored positions on a particular page the newspaper may charge extra.

Display ads may be economically justified for new subdivisions and developments, in which case their cost may be spread over many individual parcels. Or they may have their rationale in business properties, whose higher price warrants the extra expenditure and importance justifies the better position. You may also find it worthwhile to use display for high-priced residential properties.

Whether you use classified or display, most newspapers will lean over backwards to accommodate you - honoring your position and edition preferences and even your late insertions.

SIGNS

The controversy over signs rages loud and long. Some consider them demeaning and cheapening. Some local ordinances and real estate boards prohibit them. Some think of them as defacing the landscape.

But signs do have their proponents as well as their opponents. "For Sale" signs do help make sales. They do tell property owners in the neighborhood that the subject property is available. These owners in turn may tell their friends and acquaintances who may be interested in purchasing at this location. They do stimulate the production of "prospect leads". They do attract the interest of prospects who may be "scouting" the neighborhood for properties. They do "alert" other property owners to the opportunities for negotiating advantageous sales. Some brokers find them the most economical form of advertising, producing far more response than other forms. Many say that an inquiry from a sign is worth ten inquiries from a newspaper ad. People have seen the property if they have seen the sign.

Signs of course may be put up *only* when permission has been secured from the property owner. If you are a member of a real estate board, you must comply with its rules and regulations on sign installation. If a property owner objects to putting up a sign, you may wish to remind him that the lack of a sign leads to the loss of the most likely prospects, those who have seen the property and have "taken" to it. You should of course not install a sign, unless you have an "exclusive" on the property. Otherwise, the property could become "weedy" with competitive signs.

You, as the listing salesman or broker, may put up the signs yourself or hire a specialist to do so for you. You will of course see to it that your signs are so "positioned" that they can be easily read. They should naturally be put in place as soon as possible after the listing agreement is signed. And, coincidentally, with the erection of the sign, a photograph of the property and sign should be taken and made available for advertising display.

Your signs reflect you. You will therefore see to it that they are neat, clean, and up-to-date, and that their shape and wording are such as to be readily identifiable with your office. The lettering on your signs should be so large that it will be readily readable from across the street. Your name and phone number should also stand out.

How about "Sold" signs? Should they be used? Indeed they should, assuming your local board is willing, that the property owner has no objection, and that no zoning ordinance bars the way. "Sold" signs show you to be an effective sales organization and thereby commend you to prospects and property owners alike. They help also in demonstrating that real estate in a particular area must be in demand. And they can be used with an overlay: "Sold by _____ , let us sell yours."

If you are promoting new developments, you will put up signs showing the way. The signs should be large as should the lettering, so that the directions may be read some distance away, indicating the route to take. These signs should be supplemented by smaller signs at each turn or road junction.

Your signs on the walls of buildings make you known and your name recognized. Your billboard advertising likewise identifies you to the driving public. Your procedure here will be to lease space from an outdoor advertising company, which will paste your advertisements over the billboard.

Your office may be illuminated by attractive electric signs. The entrance to your parking area may be lit up by inviting signs. Your window displays may be kept alight and you may wish to use interior lighting at night. You will find this quite inexpensive.

DIRECT MAIL ADVERTISING

Where individual properties warrant the expense of direct mail, you may employ it to circularize selected prospects. How do you get their names and addresses? You may get them from the visitors to your

"Model Homes", from your local real estate board, from persons who have made inquiries on properties to your Chamber of Commerce or local personnel managers, and from your former clients and customers. Over and above creating your direct mail lists yourself, you may rent or buy lists from direct mail companies. If your direct mail piece is to go to a limited number of prospects, you will want to "personalize" it by your own signature.

For business properties, your direct mail pieces should show the income to be derived, tax shelter afforded, leverage possible, and safety assurance of the principal. It should, of course, indicate the business uses to which the property can be put, utilities available, location and its advantages, the tax concessions, if any, possible.

Your direct mail may also take the form of institutional advertising. Here you will be calling attention to yourself and your willingness to serve in the sale or purchase of properties. You will send such direct mail not only to people whom you have served, but also to people you can serve.

Institutional direct mail advertising takes many forms. It may consist of a report to your clientele on properties you have recently sold. Or it may set forth a portfolio of your current listings. It could be your organization's magazine or newsletter. It might consist of bulletins on the new developments you are promoting. Perhaps it will be composed of brochures, providing detailed data on larger residential or business properties. Sometimes it will be in the form of postcards with short descriptions of new listings. If the person to whom you have just sold is willing, you might send out mailings to property owners in the neighborhood, telling them about their new neighbor.

NOVELTIES

Real estate people, by way of goodwill advertising to their public, make use of hundreds of different kinds of novelties. They try to evolve devices that will serve a useful purpose and be durable so that they will serve for a long time to come to remind the recipient of the donor. Naturally they will have inscribed on them the name, address, and phone number of the practitioner.

The list is long and varied. Here are just a few examples: key rings, rain bonnets, pot holders, paper weights, telephone book covers, playing cards, pocket combs, clips to hold sheaves of documents together, handkerchiefs, packages of matches, wastebaskets, pen and pencils, calendars, desk blotters, "novelty of the month" (a new and different device received the first of every month), date and reminder pads, maps, calculation tables, and notebooks.

OTHER ADVERTISING

Your radio advertising may consist of tapes you work up on real estate techniques or short programs describing your present listings and soliciting new ones. You may sponsor local programs on the news, weather, and home town events. You may also buy time in the form of spot announcements, ranging from a few seconds to one minute, setting forth your advertising message and placed before, in between, or after popular programs.

Some brokers sponsor telecasts conducted by a dynamic personality, describing listings so that the audience is thereby convinced that the advertising broker can answer any and all questions connected with real estate. Other telecasts will dramatize short stories on selling situations in real estate. You may on television also use drawings, visualizing the values to be enjoyed in specific properties. Perhaps you will sponsor news or sport telecasts. Promotion of your developments can likewise be effectively merchandised on television.

You may wish to solicit the cooperation of other brokers in your trade journal advertising. This can also call attention to the types of brokerage business you can handle and the specialized services you are able to provide - financing, managing, appraising, and insurance. Trade journal advertising may be used to keep your name and repute favorably in the public eye.

PUBLICITY

Some say publicity is advertising you do not pay for. Indeed, some publicity stories resemble advertising. They tell how you and your firm have participated in civic growth and progress. They quote testimonials from your clients and customers. They provide space for you to expand on the significance of the Realtor in the life of the community. In some cases the amount of publicity you get may in part be due to the amount of advertising you do. You may actually buy advertising space in order to create a favorable public image for yourself. You may take out cooperative advertising during Realtor Week. You may advertise your salespeople, showing their pictures and qualifications. You may advertise the worthwhileness of civic causes, such as those for expanded school programs.

You may likewise participate in civic service, creating a favorable public image, which is duly publicized. Your service on planning and zoning boards is of such a character. So is your leadership in United Fund and Red Cross drives. You will get publicity for your sponsorship of the Little League, Boy Scouts and Girl Scouts, Junior Achievement, and Future Farmers of America. As a member of a service club, you will help get out the vote on election day and will lead in fund raising drives for scholarships. These contributions may be noted in the public press. If in your community you help formulate a workable plan for urban renewal or urban rehabilitation, it will likewise be written up. In the present times of stress and strain, your help in training the jobless in core and ghetto areas will receive a partial reward in favorable publicity.

Other kinds of civic service that may result in favorable publicity are active and constructive membership in your Parent Teacher Association, Neighborhood Civic Association, and service on your local board of education. Your enthusiastic participation in the activities of your local Board of Realtors will be publicized when these contribute to the welfare of your community. Likewise, service on the budget advisory commission to your mayor and acceptance of welfare responsibilities in the church of your choice will receive public appreciation.

Perhaps the best publicity of all is word of mouth, confirming your observance of your obligations to your client, general public, and fellow Realtors, making yourself known as the epitome of honesty and fair dealing.

PUBLICITY RELEASES

You will get your releases published by doing the things that make for news and maintaining a close and friendly relationship with the individual on your local newspaper who is responsible for real estate news.

Your news items can be many and varied. You may have just sold an outstanding and well known property in your area. You are making predictions on whether real estate prices are going up or down and whether money will remain tight and expensive or whether credit will ease. You promote people in your organization. This has news interest for your friends and acquaintances and the people they know in the real estate field. Or you add new personnel. You open up a new branch office. Your public service is rewarded by an appointment to public office. You are elected to office in your local real estate board. You make speeches on live topics before civic, religious and/or educational organizations.

You should prepare your news release in the way the newspaper wants it. This means it should be neatly typed on 8½ x 11 inch paper, triple spaced, and with wide margins. This in turn will provide space for the editor to make additions, corrections, or deletions. It should have a release date in the upper right hand corner. You should omit the headline. The editor considers this as his prerogative. It should be submitted only in the original. If a carbon copy were sent, the recipient would feel you regarded him as inferior to someone else. It should be accompanied, where appropriate, by glossy prints with clear pictures in which each person is identified by name and by title.

If your publicity release is published, the individual on the paper to whom you sent it should receive a thank-you letter. If it is not published, this same individual should be thanked for giving it consideration. This will stamp you in his eyes as a reasonable person - not a grouch and guilty of "sour grapes" - and ingratiate you with him for your next publicity release.

You will sense your competitors' reaction to the publicity you get. You will watch this and avoid antagonism. Some hostility on their part could come about if they thought you were trying to "hog" the spotlight, taking the lion's share of the credit in civic projects, or thinking of publicizing yourself first and your civic cause second.

Your newspaper is not bent on providing you with free advertising under the name of publicity. Nevertheless, when you do or say something that makes for news, you are entitled to special consideration when you are also a valued customer of the paper.

TRUE AND FALSE QUESTIONS

1. The advertising budget should go up, if sales go up; down,   T   F
   if sales go down.

2. An advertising plan should fix the responsibility for ad   T   F
   preparation and for measurement of results.

3. Advertising plans should describe the homes in terms of   T   F
   their being abodes for children.

4. In general, the approach in advertising investment properties   T   F
   is the same as the approach in advertising residential.

5. One should write the ad mentally as he goes through the   T   F
   property.

6. The headline should be written first.   T   F

7. The advertiser should regard the home as a woman's life.   T   F

8. The quantity discount rate is the rate available for agree-   T   F
   ment to use a certain amount of space over a period of time.

9. The highest rate is the open rate.   T   F

10. Classified readership is "screened" in advance.   T   F

11. Classified's primary competition is from display ads.   T   F

12. Newspapers may provide "classified display".   T   F

13. "Scatteration" is using ads of consistent style, but in   T   F
    various parts of the classified section.

14. The most prevalent appeal from the survey of ads in the   T   F
    Wall Street Journal and in the *Detroit News* ads was
    location.

15. An agate line is 1/12 of an inch.   T   F

16. A column inch is one column, 12 agate lines long.   T   F

17. "Copy" means the words used in the ad.   T   F

18. The length of the copy is called "copy block".   T   F

19. Layout is the form in which the ad appears.   T   F

20. The space between the lines in the ad is called "margins".   T   F

21. "For Sale" signs stimulate the production of "prospect   T   F
    leads".

22. An inquiry resulting from seeing a sign usually has more   T   F
    sales potential than an inquiry resulting from reading an ad.

23. Signs may be put up only when permission is given by the   T   F
    owner.

24. Signs should be installed, regardless of the type of listing.   T   F

25. "Sold" signs indicate the advertiser is an effective seller.   T   F

26. Billboard space is leased from an outdoor advertiser.   T   F

27. Radio spot announcements are usually five minutes long.   T   F

28. The news release should be single spaced.   T   F

29. The news release should have a release date in the upper   T   F
    left hand corner.

30. The news release should have a "catchy" headline.   T   F

31. Radio advertising may consist of tapes.   T   F

32. Institutional advertising calls attention to oneself and one's   T   F
    willingness to serve in the sale or purchase of properties.

33. In composing your ad, you should start with the headline.   T   F

34. The listing agreement automatically provides authority for   T   F
    putting up a "For Sale" sign on the owner's property.

35. If the direct mail piece is to go to a limited number of   T   F
    prospects, it should be personalized by the signature of the
    sending broker.

36. The pride of ownership appeal can be mirrored in the social   T   F
    prestige that comes with ownership of a fine home.

37. The law prohibits a listing salesman from himself erecting   T   F
    a "For Sale" sign.

38. "Sold" signs may not be used with an overlay.   T   F

39. News releases are usually on 8½ x 11 paper.   T   F

40. For a Realtor to paint his sign on a building wall is cheap   T   F
    and degrading, making the Realtor guilty of Code violation.

41. Display ads are subject to the competition for readership   T   F
    attention by news and editorial matter.

MULTIPLE CHOICE QUESTIONS

42. The purpose of the ad's headline is:
    ( ) To excite the reader
    ( ) To make the reader read the ad
    ( ) To make the reader buy
    ( ) To make the reader go see the property

43. Classified ads with borders, illustrations, and bold face type are called:
    ( ) Classified white space
    ( ) Classified "mix"
    ( ) Classified display
    ( ) Classified logotype

44. In times of "tight money", the ad could most appropriately stress:
    ( ) The low cost of the finder's fee for getting the mortgage loan
    ( ) That points are likely to go higher than they are at present
    ( ) That usury ceilings will be raised
    ( ) That a mortgage carrying a rate of interest lower than the rate presently applicable may be assumed.

45. "Scatteration" means:
    ( ) Using ads of inconsistent style in various parts of the classified
    ( ) Using ads of consistent style in various part of the classified
    ( ) Using both classified and display in various parts of the newspaper
    ( ) Using ads scattering the advertising message among residential, commercial, and industrial properties

46. "For Sale" signs may be put up, but only with the consent of:
    ( ) The building inspector
    ( ) The civic neighborhood association
    ( ) The property owner
    ( ) The local zoning board

47. The rate quoted the occasional advertiser is:
    ( ) The open rate
    ( ) The regular rate
    ( ) The standard rate
    ( ) The uniform rate

48. The rate for the advertiser is usually set forth in:
( ) The insertion order
( ) The space contract
( ) The space schedule
( ) The purchase agreement

49. The quantity discount is based on:
( ) The number of times an ad is inserted over a given period
( ) The amount of space used over a given period
( ) The dollar volume payable for the ads over a given period
( ) The number of editions of the newspaper in which the ad appears over a given period

50. The time discount refers to:
( ) The discount available for prompt payment
( ) The discount for advertising at stated times, like Christmas and Easter
( ) The discount available for frequency of appearance
( ) The discount available for the time of the edition - morning or evening

51. The actual insertion of the ad is carried out under the:
( ) Space contract
( ) Release schedule
( ) Notice to print
( ) Insertion order

ESSAY QUESTIONS

1. What should the direct mail pieces on business properties show?

2. How should news releases be prepared?

3. What are the reasons for advertising?

4. How should the ad be prepared?

PART V
REAL ESTATE
INVESTMENTS

INVESTING IN REAL ESTATE

CHAPTER THIRTEEN

WHY INVEST IN REAL ESTATE?

If you invest in real estate, do you not have three strikes against you? Your investment will be non-liquid in character. Your investment will burden you with the problems of management. Your investment will entail a degree of risk.

During the depression of the 1930's, real estate was in many areas a frozen asset. It lacked a market. It fell into a slough of despond and failed to rise. It was difficult to secure a loan on it. It became a mill-stone saddling the property owner with taxes and maintenance.

Such conditions encumbered real estate with non-liquidity then. They may do so again. Real estate is part and parcel of the business cycle. When the cycle contracts and recedes, so does real estate. In fact, the troughs of the real estate cycle are usually deeper than the troughs of the general business cycle.

There is as yet no stock market in real estate, as there is in stocks and bonds. There is no organization geared to quickly dispose of real estate as there is in the case of the stock exchange. True, multiple listing systems do make data on listings available to all members of the system and thus bear a semblance to a local "offering" market. Computerized real estate will in time transform real estate from an essentially local market to a regional and a national one. But, at the present time, compared with stocks and bonds, real estate is less liquid. An offsetting factor, however, is the 70 per cent, 80 per cent, or 90 per cent loan in liquid funds that may be secured on real estate.

In the case of stocks and bonds, the individual investor suffers no burdens of management. He may fill out a proxy form for a stock-holders' meeting, but this is nominal. He may have to clip coupons or deposit dividend checks, but this is a pleasure.

In the case of a real estate investment, on the other hand, there is a burden of management. Even though the property owner hires a manager, he has to scrutinize the manager's operations to make sure he is doing a satisfactory job. And, of course, he has to pay the manager a fee.

If he does not hire a manager, the property owner has to take care of maintenance and repairs, mowing the lawn, shoveling the snow, doing the landscaping, seeing to the painting, attending to the leaking roof and cellar, handling termite infestation, chasing off trespassers, guarding against vandalism and malicious mischief, and so on and so on "ad nauseam".

If he rents out the property himself, he has to select the tenants, collect the rents, handle "gripes" and complaints, settle arguments between and among the tenants, handle requests for rent reductions, cope with tenants' strikes and withholdings, see to it that leases are renewed on satisfactory terms, and keep the books and records. If the tenant becomes a "bad actor", he will give the rental unit a bad name. If the tenant does not pay the rent, the landlord may have a difficult time getting him evicted. If the tenant goes in for illegal activities, the landlord may be "smudged". Certainly burdens of management exist.

True, real estate investment means risk. But so does every investment. Some say government bonds are virtually riskless. This is not so. Think of the bonds you bought when the purchasing power of the dollar was higher. Think of these bonds today when they mature in terms of the lower purchasing power they now command. Inflation has made deep inroads on their value.

Real estate dropped in value during depression years. So did blue chip common stocks. Some ceased payment of dividends entirely and their market value "hit the skids".

There is no such thing as a riskless investment. So, to the charge that real estate investment is risky, we demur. To the charge that real estate is non-liquid and requires management, we say, "True, but we still want to invest in real estate".

Real Estate — a Growth Investment

A high pressure demand is moving against a fixed supply of land. A growing population requires more housing and real estate for the commercial and industrial facilities which sustain it. A more affluent population with more vacation time wants second homes, resort real estate, and land for the expressways to reach its destination. A more mobile population necessitates more real estate transactions incident to its moves from one place to another.

Business expansion and increased service and professional personnel require ever growing amounts of office space. Proliferating governmental organizations intensify office building demand. Computer centers and research and development agencies cry out for "lebensraum".

Shopping centers are growing to mammoth proportions and providing not only merchandise, but also the facilities for community life, along with tremendous parking areas, pedestrian malls, and landscaped plazas.

The popular one-story industrial plants now being built stretch out over more and more land and industrial parks, multiplying fast, are expanding over ever broader acreage.

Real Estate — a Natural Investment

An investment in good real estate, well located, provides the best possible hedge against inflation. For the last 25 years, such real estate has shown remarkable increases in value, its dramatic rise outdistancing the inflationary spiral.

Stocks may skyrocket for a while, and then crash with a calamitous thud. Companies may prosper and fall by the wayside. But real estate is always there. The land is indestructible. The improvements are long lasting. There is an enduring quality about real estate.

Real estate in general produces more percentage points of income than do other investments. It enjoys a margin over after-tax yields on stocks. It provides a return for some concerns, such as railroads with real estate investments, higher than that of their principal operation.

Good real estate constitutes excellent borrowing power, and loans of 70 percent and higher of its value can be secured.

Leverage and Tax Shelter

Good real estate can be acquired with a smaller percentage of equity than most other investments. Even though you obtain a large percentage of the purchase price in the form of a loan, whatever appreciation in value the property enjoys and whatever income it affords belong to you.

Suppose you buy a $50,000 income property and put up yourself cash of $15,000 and pay for the balance with a loan of $35,000 - 70 percent of the price. Suppose five years elapse and you then sell the property for $100,000. Out of the proceeds you pay off your loan of $35,000 and are left with $65,000. Deducting from this your original cash outlay of $15,000, you are left with a net of $50,000, or a gain of 333 1/3 percent on your original investment. This, of course, will not be all yours, for you will have had to pay interest on your loan - which, incidentally, is income tax deductible - and a capital gain tax on the profit from you sale.

Suppose the net income from this property comes to $5,000 a year. This will be a 33 1/3 percent annual return on your $15,000 equity. On this you will, of course, have to pay income taxes, but their impact will be lessened by the deductibility of the interest on your loan.

It is also true things might not turn out as well as anticipated. The value of the property might go down, rather than up, and the income might not materialize.

Investment real estate also provides tax shelter. Mortgage loan interest and real property taxes are income tax deductible. So is depreciation and if it exceeds amortization, it constitutes tax free cash flow. If a book loss is shown, it may be deducted from other income, such as salary. If your income property is sold under the installment or deferred payment plan, you may spread your capital gain over a period of years, rather than suffering the full tax impact in the year of the sale. You may also devise a "tax-free exchange", carrying over the cost basis of the property surrendered to the property acquired.

A PLACE FOR THE SMALL INVESTOR?

Should the small investor shy away from real estate, feeling it is too big for him to handle? If he has as much as $30,000, his chances are good for securing a loan to finance the acquisition of a $100,000 income property. It is not unusual, in fact, to acquire a $100,000 property with an equity of as little as $20,000 or even $10,000.

Or the small investor may put his money in group participations, such as joint ventures, syndications, and limited partnerships.

Or he may make his investment in the mutual funds of real estate, namely, the real estate investment trusts. If they pay out 90 percent or more of their earnings to their investors, they themselves are immune from the Federal corporate income tax. They therefore do not suffer the impact of double taxation, as corporate stockholders do. They provide ready liquidity, for their investment certificates are transferable, some being traded in on organized stock exchanges, and others, over-the-counter. The better trusts yield a relatively high rate of return.

INVESTMENTS IN HOUSING

Housing investments are not limited to the land and buildings. They extend also to construction materials and equipment, to the mortgage loans with housing as security, to the "new towns" in some instances enjoying the blessing of government subsidies and guarantees, and to the rehabilitation of old, but essentially sound housing. They may be made by you as an individual, through group participations, through real estate investment trusts, developers, housing corporations, pension funds, and insurance companies.

Housing is the biggest underdeveloped market in our country. From 1972 to 1999 our population will grow substantially from its present 208 million. To provide housing for this growth and replace demolitions will require about 2.5 million new homes per year. But we have, on the whole, fallen far short of this rate of production. Yet new household formations have been steadily climbing. Young couples are getting married earlier, placing an additional strain on existing housing. The marriage rate has been rising since 1965.

One of the strongest segments of the housing market is mobile homes. Their sales in 1971 totaled approximately 500,000, as against approximately 400,000 in 1970. But there is a decided shortage of mobile home parks. The demand for parks is now such that they are in many cases yielding a net of 25 percent on the investment. Some park loans are currently being made on 90 percent to value ratios with Federal Housing Administration insurance provided and are being amortized over ten years.

Pre-fabs and manufactured housing are coming strong, propelled against the housing shortage by Operation Breakthrough. Building practices and codes, some as antiquated as the Pyramids, are at long last beginning to reform.

Apartment House Investments

This pace-setter in the housing market has everything coming its way. Apartments are "on line" with the transient psychology of our times. They are adapted to the flexibility of movement so necessary in a country like ours where one family out of every five moves every year.

Apartments fit the financial limitations of young couples unable to afford the down payment for a single family home. They are ideal for older couples, relieving them from the physical exertions of exterior household chores. The increasing number of working wives look with favor on apartments. They are adapted to the limited space needs of widows, widowers, and other individual householders, such as the young unmarried, the divorced, and the separated.

Apartment house investments profit from inherent economic advantages. They conserve on land use in an ascending scale from the "walk-up" to the high-rise. They enjoy a relatively high ratio of building to land, enabling the investor to derive more depreciation from his income tax liability. Financing for apartment houses is easier to get than for single family homes. The mortgage lender likes the higher yield and the opportunity for equity participations.

Condominium apartment investments become ever more popular as the condominium market grows. Condominiums satisfy both the desire for home ownership and the desire for freedom from exterior household chores and responsibilities.

Office Building Investments

Many investors prefer office buildings to apartments. Office tenancies are more stable. Businesses do not move as people do. They usually limit themselves to daytime occupancy, and thus impose less wear and tear. They may require less parking proportionate to the number of tenants. Office tenants do not pose the problems of pets and antics of children.

The demand for office space has been exceptionally high. Business now necessitates more book work, more overhead, more administration, more negotiation, and more face to face confrontation, all of which cry out for more office space. The surge in new office construction has been taking place both in central business districts and in new suburban areas. Although many people cry that downtown is doomed, in some cities there is a soaring demand for office space downtown. The concentration of administrative, professional, and financial activities in the central core is well established. But there is also an increasing influx of branch offices in suburbia, both legal and medical, of banks and insurance companies, of accountants and real estate brokers. Suburban locations in new shopping centers are capitalizing on their freedom from parking and traffic congestion and their convenience of access from the growing communities which surround them.

Shopping Centers

These are exciting, growing and rewarding investments. Their proportions of the retail market are at an all-time high. More and more new shopping centers are being built and the future demand seems insatiable. Never in history have so many stores been pushing so hard to expand their operations. Major department stores alone, for example, anticipate in the next five years a 75 percent increase in their shopping center branches.

The magnetizing power of the shopping center is the convenience of one-stop shopping. The shopping center caters to the shopper's wants in merchandise and provides plenty of parking. The larger ones may offer central pedestrian malls, satellite plazas, and the beauty of sculptured gardens, trees, fountains, and pools. With their art exhibits, fashion shows, plays and concerts, civic events, postoffices and police departments, and even houses of worship, they are becoming the focal point in the lives of many communities.

Their future pattern is fascinating to behold. The new centers will be even larger than the old. The trend is toward the super-regionals large enough to dominate a complete trading area. Almost all will locate in suburbia. They will provide for an increasing proportion of office buildings. Some will wrap their parking around their stores, with two parking levels per floor. Others will lay out their parking in zones, tributary to dominant merchandisers. All will provide convenient accessibility to main traffic arteries.

RAW LAND AND INDUSTRIAL REAL ESTATE

Omnipresent is the demand for raw land - for urban growth, express-ways, parking areas, mobile home sites, the length and the breadth of the one-story plant, the space-hungry town house development, airport expansions, ever enlarging suburbia, and the fast-growing industrial parks.

As industry moves farther and farther out into the hinterland, its demand for raw land moves on apace. It requires land for access roads, employee parking, and landscaping areas for its new far-reaching one-story plants.

The reasons for the growth of industrial parks loom up for all to see. They provide a controlled environment. They plan for a compatibility of tenancies. They cater to light industry, research and development, warehousing, and collateral office use. Although most space is leased, some is owned. Industrial parks enjoy a relatively high ratio of building improvements to over-all value with a resultant tax shelter. They provide access roads, storage areas, and utilities for the clients they serve.

RESORT REAL ESTATE

Investments in raw land are also being converted into resort real estate, now enjoying an amazing and animated growth. The affluence of America now puts resort pleasures within the economic reach of the average family. Increasing disposable incomes now open up an entirely new resort market among the 70 percent of our population who have never flown, the 50 percent of our people who have never stopped in a hotel, motel, or motor inn, and the 55 percent who have never taken yearly vacations. Over and above these new markets are those of the black population who in times past may have been deterred from vaca-tioning.

The market for resort real estate is also expanding with the increase in life expectancies and the desire of older people for a resort locale in their retirement years. The increase in vacation time from two weeks to three and four also brings about a corresponding increase in the demand for resort facilities. Many people now take both a winter and summer vacation and the Southern California Research Council predicts that by 1985 Americans will be taking annual vacations of 25 weeks. Interstate highways now make it easier and quicker for Americans to get to the resorts of their desire. As Americans now think in terms of driving time to resorts rather than distance in miles, they seem even closer. Father and son combinations on happy hunting grounds, executive retreats at the mountain lodge for surcease from care and the rapport of hearty camaraderie - sun, sea, and sanctuary - stir the adventure in our soul and the wanderlust in our blood and promote the demand for resort real estate.

Nor is the outdoor life the only lure. Resort real estate is also required for the racetracks, gambling casinos, bars and nightclubs, and restaurants and shops that service those in attendance.

For resort purposes more and more Americans are acquiring a second home; at the beach, on the lake, or in the mountains. Such seasonal homes now enjoy the financial advantage of Federal Housing Administration mortgage loan insurance. Condominiums and town houses are numerous there. There are also A-frames and pre-fabs. Of the new mobile homes, ten per cent are second homes. Nor are they all lodged far afield. Three out of five second homes are within 100 miles of the family's principal residence.

Many retirement communities are located in resort areas. They are growing in popularity, gratifying the desire for independence in the later years and the consort with one's peers, providing all the amenities, plus relief from all exterior and some interior household chores, plus hobby facilities and milder sports galore. Some retirement communities are set up as legal entities devoid of school age children and the tax burdens of school districts. Earlier retirements and increased life expectancies are swelling the market not only in the south, but also up north.

MORTGAGES AND EQUITY PARTICIPATIONS

Investors in first mortgages on real estate have long been attracted by the relatively good interest rate and the soundness and solidity of the security. Where a high cushion of value remained after the first mortgage, there has been no want of investors in second mortgages providing still higher yields, but with shorter maturities. A recent entrant into the second mortgage field in real estate has been the credit subsidiary of a leading automobile manufacturer. It now makes second mortgage loans on apartments, office buildings, shopping centers, and single-tenant properties, under long-term lease, at 10-11 percent plus 2 percent commitment fee.

But inflation has now reared its ugly head. The five per cent interest on first mortgage loans of yester-year fades into lack-luster in the light of prime loans of eight and nine per cent in the here and now. Unrealistic usury statutes and interest ceilings on Federal Housing and Veterans Administration loans have dampened investment ardor. Even where these artificial barriers do not apply, no one knows how high interest rates may go in time to come. The omnipresent problem is how to escalate the mortgage rate of return to at least keep pace with inflation.

The mortgage lenders have come up with their answer: Tie the mortgage loan in with a participation in the equity. Get an "equity kicker" and a "piece of the action." Use this as your inflation hedge. Secure a share in the profits of the real estate enterprise you finance, over and above the interest you derive on your mortgage loan. Require this equity participation as a condition to making the loan.

And so developers, hard pressed for mortgage credit, are now providing their lenders with shares in their anticipated profits as a partial return for the financing furnished. This share may consist of a participation in land ownership, gross rentals, or rental increases. It may be a share in the gross after the first year of the property's operation or a share in the "overage" rents, which means part of the "take" after rents hit a certain level. It may also be "rights" to buy stock at favorable prices in the company being financed.

LAND CONTRACTS AS INVESTMENTS

When you sell your real estate under a land contract, you keep title until all the installment payments have been made. You are in a strategic bargaining position as seller, for your buyer is usually someone whose credit capacity or lack of sufficient down payment may disqualify him from the usual first mortgage loan. You, as seller, may therefore be able to charge a premium over and above the ordinary selling price. This premium constitutes part of your return on a land contract sale. If the law permits, your superior bargaining position may also enable you to charge him a premium interest rate on his declining balance.

As you, the seller, continue to hold title, it may be possible for you to get a mortgage loan on your property and thereby reduce your equity, by virtue of leverage increasing your rate of return on what you have outstanding. If your buyer should default, you may repossess and keep his payments as rent.

If a third party should buy your land contract from you, you would liquidate your position and he would succeed to the investment benefits you enjoyed, plus the discount at which he may have purchased.

CORPORATE REAL ESTATE INVESTMENTS

If confirmation were required of the foregoing advantages in real estate investments, it could be found in the examples of the growing investments of oil, paper, lumber, automobile, steel, aluminum, and electrical appliance companies, as well as the railroads. Some regard their real estate investments as ancillary to their principal operations. An oil company may desire to pre-empt the marketing sites in the new town in which it invests. A steel, aluminum, or electrical appliance company may incorporate its products as show cases for its wares and captive markets in the structure it builds. A railroad may look on its real estate investments as traffic builders for its freight. But all profess to have been attracted by the long-range yields inherent in their real estate investments than from the freight they carry.

These corporations are in an ideal investment position. They generate investment funds internally through earnings retentions, cash flow, and depreciation. Their high credit standing enables them to secure mortgage loans and concomitant leverage. Their financial resources give them the staying power for the early unproductive period of their real estate development.

COMPUTERIZED INVESTMENT ANALYSIS

The computer may now be programmed to instantaneously provide an analysis of any real estate investment. Given basic data, the computer will immediately tell you your gross spendable income, your net spendable income, your taxable income, your net equity income, and your net equity rate, as well as your adjusted cost basis. It will do so for the period or periods ahead for which you wish to forecast. It will indicate when it may be desirable to switch into another investment. It will do all this conveniently with any telephone hook-up, whether this be at your home, your office, or at a pay station. It will do all this at a relatively small cost.

A SUMMING UP

The opportunities in real estate investments are bounded only by the limitations of your insight and reach of your imagination. The rewards can be great. But they do not come to the "fast buck" addict, the believer in the "hot tip", or the "get rich quick" enthusiast. They come only to the investors who have made careful studies and analyses, weighed the disadvantages against the advantages, and have taken into account the risks entailed against the profits to be earned.

TRUE AND FALSE QUESTIONS

1. The troughs of the real estate cycle are usually deeper than the troughs of the general business cycle.   T   F

2. Real estate is less liquid as an investment than stocks and bonds traded in on an organized securities exchange.   T   F

3. Since the real estate investor can hire a property manager, this relieves him entirely of the burden of management.   T   F

4. The rise in real estate values has not kept pace with the inflationary spiral.   T   F

5. Good real estate can constitute excellent borrowing power.   T   F

6. Investment real estate can be acquired with a relatively small percentage of equity.   T   F

7. Investment real estate can provide tax shelter and cash flow.   T   F

8. Real estate investment trusts suffer from double taxation.   T   F

9. The demand for mobile home parks is, relatively, less than the demand for mobile homes themselves.   T   F

10. Apartment houses are adapted to the mobility of our population.   T   F

11. High rise apartments conserve on land use as against single family detached housing units.   T   F

12. Condominiums do not satisfy the desire for home ownership.   T   F

13. Office tenants usually limit themselves to day time occupancy.   T   F

14. The magnetizing power of the shopping center is the convenience of one-stop shopping.   T   F

15. The trend is now toward smaller shopping centers.   T   F

16. Industrial parks cater both to light and to heavy industry.   T   F

17. Second homes are not eligible for FHA insurance.   T   F

18. About ten per cent of mobile homes are second homes.   T   F

19. "Equity kickers" are participations in the equity.   T   F

20. Corporate real estate investments may be ancillary to regular   T   F
    corporate operations.

21. There is now a stock market in real estate.   T   F

22. Multiple listing services operate as securities exchanges do.   T   F

23. The demand for mobile homes has been subsiding.   T   F

24. A high rise apartment house enjoys a relatively high ratio   T   F
    of building to land.

25. Office tenancies are in general more stable than apartment   T   F
    house tenancies.

26. Shopping centers in many areas have become the focal point   T   F
    of community life.

27. The new shopping centers will provide for a lesser pro-   T   F
    portion of office buildings.

28. Most of the new shopping centers will be in suburbia.   T   F

29. Most of the space in industrial parks is owned, not leased.   T   F

30. Some retirement communities are being set up as legal   T   F
    entities, devoid of school age children.

31. Land contract sales provide for a first mortgage in the seller.   T   F

32. In a sale and leaseback, the seller-lessee deducts de-   T   F
    preciation on the buildings.

33. There is no such thing as a riskless investment.   T   F

34. If a book loss on investment real estate is suffered, this   T   F
    may be deducted from other income, such as salary.

35. It is possible to spread capital gain over a period of years.   T   F

36. In a "tax-free exchange", the investor may acquire the full   T   F
    cost basis of the structure being acquired for depreciation.

37. Real estate investment trusts provide ready liquidity.   T   F

38. Housing investments are limited to the land and buildings.   T   F

39. Apartments fit the financial limitations of young couples.   T   F

40. Super-regional shopping centers dominate a trading area.   T   F

MULTIPLE CHOICE QUESTIONS

41. Industrial parks provide:
    ( ) Freedom from zoning
    ( ) A controlled environment
    ( ) A lower tax rate
    ( ) Facilities for heavy industry

42. The seller in a land contract:
    ( ) Requires a first mortgage as security
    ( ) Requires a power of sale of mortgage foreclosure by advertisement
    ( ) Retains title until all the installment payments have been made
    ( ) Must grant the pre-payment privilege to the mortgagor-debtor

43. In a sale and leaseback, the seller-lessee:
    ( ) Takes depreciation on the structure
    ( ) Gets control and possession of the structure at lease termination
    ( ) Retains title as security
    ( ) Deducts rent as against income tax liability

44. In a sale and leaseback, the buyer-lessor:
    ( ) Reduces his fixed assets position
    ( ) Reduces his net worth
    ( ) Is relieved of management obligations
    ( ) Increases his working capital position

45. Corporate real estate investments:
    ( ) Are contrary to the Sherman Anti-Trust law
    ( ) Are in violation of the Clayton Act
    ( ) Can provide a captive market for the corporation's products
    ( ) Cannot enjoy accelerated depreciation

46. The real estate cycle:
    ( ) Is part of the general business cycle
    ( ) Constitutes a cycle, separate and apart from the business cycle
    ( ) Does not expand and recede
    ( ) Is not affected by the interest rate

47. If depreciation taken exceeds amortization, this constitutes:
    ( ) An extra income tax imposition

( )   Tax free cash flow
( )   A reduction in interest rate
( )   A tax concession

48. The small investor in real estate may use:
( )   Real estate investment trusts
( )   Limited partnership participations
( )   Syndications
( )   All of the above

49. Industrial parks cater to:
( )   Office buildings
( )   Heavy industry
( )   Shopping centers
( )   Light industry

50. A railroad may look on its real estate investment as:
( )   Potential tax losses
( )   Providing the base for rate increases
( )   Traffic builders for its freight business
( )   Increasing its passenger traffic business

ESSAY QUESTIONS

1. Why are large corporations in an ideal position for real estate investment?

2. What accounts for the popularity of retirement communities?

3. Why is real estate a growth investment?

4. Why is real estate an investment natural?

5. In what ways does a real estate investor suffer the burden of management?

REAL ESTATE INVESTMENT TRUSTS, LIMITED PARTNERSHIPS, JOINT VENTURES AND SYNDICATIONS

CHAPTER FOURTEEN

THE MUTUAL FUNDS OF REAL ESTATE

Providing a vehicle whereby the small investor can put his money to work in real estate, real estate investment trusts serve the same purpose in this field as mutual funds do in the fields of stocks and bonds. They sell shares to the public and invest the proceeds in income-producing property or in mortgages. Shareholders participate in the gains in proportion to their respective interests. They are like the closed-end mutual funds.

Through these investment media, growing numbers of small investors across the country are acquiring interests in office buildings, apartment houses, and shopping centers. They let the trust worry about managing these income properties, while they collect an eight per cent or higher return on their small investments. The interests acquired may be in mortgage loans on such properties, or in the return on equity investments.

Just as conventional mutual funds are traded in on organized stock exchanges and on the over the counter markets, so are real estate investment trusts. In the instance of both conventional mutual funds and real estate investment trusts, investment and management expertise are furnished the small investor.

If real estate investment trusts distribute at least 90 per cent of their income to their shareholders, they are immune from the 48 per cent corporate income tax. In this particular, they enjoy a special tax advantage as against conventional mutual funds.

If a 48 per cent corporate income tax were applicable to the earnings of a corporation in any given tax period in which profits amounted to $100,000 a corporation would first have to pay out $48,000 in taxes, leaving only $52,000 available for distribution to its shareholders. The real estate investment trust, on the other hand, could distribute the entire $100,000 to its shareholders.

Like conventional mutual funds, real estate investment trusts certificates are transferable at will, thus providing easy liquidity.

HOW ARE THEY ORGANIZED?

Their organization must conform to the specifications of the Congressional enactment of January 1, 1961 which gave legal status to their tax immunity.

It was not the desire of Congress to make this tax privilege available to a small clique in the form of a personal holding company. Congress therefore decreed that there must be at least 100 beneficial owners.

Nor was it the desire of Congress that out of these beneficial owners, a small aggregate could arrogate to itself most of the earnings available. Therefore, no fewer than five can own as much as 50 per cent of the shares.

The trust must be an investment medium. It is therefore forbidden to act as a dealer in real estate, constantly buying and constantly selling. It may of course sell from time to time and achieve a capital gain. It may of course buy in order to have the fruits of a productive property.

They may not show a tax loss or give their investors a loss carryover. Gains on the sale of real estate held less than four years may not constitute more than 30 per cent of their gross income. At least 75 per cent of their income must be attributable to real property.

They must be constituted as an unincorporated association managed by one or more trustees. They have, however, the characteristics of a corporation in the limited liability imposed on their shareholders, and in the enjoyment of continuity of life.

These characteristics hark back to the time of their original formation about the middle of the nineteenth century. They suffered a severe setback under a Supreme Court decision rendered in 1936 which said they were to be taxed as a corporation. This, however, was reversed by the tax immunity grant by Congress effective in 1961.

They may be organized with the objective of investing primarily in mortgages and construction loans. Or they may be constituted as equity trusts, having as their prime objective investments in office buildings, apartments, shopping centers, and other income property.

Some equity trusts have been called "one shot trusts" where their purpose was to invest in a specific income property; others, "exchange trusts" where they took advantage of the tax-free exchange privilege; and still others, "blank check trusts", where no restriction was imposed on the type of investments, but it was left entirely up to the discretion of the management trustees.

WHAT IS THE NATURE OF THEIR INVESTMENT?

Some mortgage trusts are engaged primarily in construction and development loans, leaving permanent financing to be supplied by others, such as large insurance companies. Tight money market conditions have contributed to a favorable operating environment for real estate investment trusts specializing in construction lending. They have moved into the tight money vacuum left by banks and other construction lenders. They derive their income from interest earned and discounts received during their amortization.

Most mortgages held are short term, one or two years. The largest percentage of the mortgage loans are for apartment buildings, shopping centers, and other commercial developments. A smaller percentage is for loans on land and single-family housing projects. Such long-term mortgage loans as are made are usually insured by the Federal Housing Administration or guaranteed by the Veterans Administration.

Mortgage trusts do not enjoy cash flow from depreciation, and dividends paid are taxable as ordinary income. Nevertheless, many investors prefer the liquid character of such operations. And high interest rates and a shortage of conventional mortgage money have created unprecedented investment opportunities.

Equity trusts have invested primarily in office buildings, apartment houses, and shopping centers. The more aggressive have borrowed as much capital as possible, some putting up as little as ten per cent of their own capital at the time of purchase. The more conservative have limited their borrowings to two-thirds or less of the property's cost. By reason of such borrowings, the trusts profit from the spread between what they must pay for money and the rate of return from the property in which it is invested.

Some equity trusts are investing in motor inns and hotels. Others are engaged in land development, acquisition of unimproved land, and subsequent construction and operation of income-producing properties. Still others are considering investing in natural resources, such as oil and natural gas. One diversified trust has acquired two racetracks.

Equity trusts regard undeveloped land as offering the largest profit potential; apartment houses, as sound investments, and providing fast depreciation; new office buildings, good; and regional shopping centers, excellent.

The trend is for equity trusts to also take on mortgage lending. Here they can derive a return of 14 per cent or more based on sound security. Here they find their overall rate of return somewhat higher than on strictly equity ownership.

WHAT ARE THEIR YIELDS?

Returns on equities in income property are commonly between 12 and 15 per cent. On development and construction loans, they may run even higher. From these yields expenses of operations must be deducted. But as trusts are cheap to run, these are relatively small, ranging from 1½ per cent to 2 per cent.

There is a relatively constant spread of around five per cent between the prime lending rate of commercial banks and blue chip construction loans.

The stock market may assign a price-earnings multiple to the trust's shares when they begin trading, thus producing capital gains.

As time goes on, additional shares may be offered to new investors at levels higher than those paid by existing holders, and this may bring to the trust additional amounts of low-cost money, and thereby benefit existing holders.

In order to attract additional investment capital, a trust may "sweeten" a debenture offering with the sale of warrants and with a provision for subsequent conversion of debentures into shares at desirable levels.

For their lines of credit, trusts may pay ¼ of one per cent above the prime rate, plus compensating balances at the banks from which loans are obtained. They will quite commonly be able to loan out these borrowed funds at five per cent over the prime rate.

Most of the newer trusts have been popular in the "new issues" market, sometimes rising 20 to 100 per cent above their offering prices.

Many trusts have been able to exchange their stock for properties acquired, and this has resulted in a signigicant improvement in their earnings on a per-share basis. By leveraging shareholder equities with bank loans, they have been able to derive a yield above 15 per cent. Some have done even better than this, employing only a small amount of equity to generate a large return through borrowing. For example, if a trust acquired a $10 million property by putting up $1 million of its own money and borrowing the remaining $9 million at six per cent interest, and the gross after operating expenses and depreciation but before interest was $800,000, then, after paying interest, the trust would have $260,000, or 26 per cent on its investment. If the trust had purchased the property outright, then its $800,000 return would have been eight per cent on its investment.

By reason of depreciation available on income properties, trusts have generated substantial cash flows, which in many instances they have passed on, at least in part, to their shareholders income tax free. As this is regarded as a return on capital, it does have the adverse effect of reducing the basis of the shares.

WHAT DOES THE MONEY MARKET THINK OF THE TRUSTS?

Many in the money market are not competent to express an intelligent opinion, for they know so little about the trusts. Talk to your own stock broker, and only too often he will register a blank when you ask him about them. This is unfortunate for the average small investor, for he naturally turns first to his own broker for information. Too many stock brokers are conditioned only to stocks and bonds, and tend therefore to divert their inquirers to what they consider the tried and true, and pass over the trusts. Many small investors, therefore, have been dissuaded from pursuing their original interest in the trusts, for they have been left high and dry without any place to resort to for an investment agent. Only too often also when they seek out data on trusts in their local library, they find no literature available. There are, of course, exceptions, and occasionally on the financial pages you will see an ad of a broker claiming to specialize in real estate investment trusts.

You will find some analysts in the money market who will assert that you can more safely take advantage of the real estate investment boom by buying stock in a conglomerate or another type of diversified company with a real estate subsidiary.

Some analysts look with favor on the trusts, for they note that larger investors, such as pension funds are increasingly looking to trusts as an investment outlet. Others view the trusts' popularity as a danger signal, for it means that increasing numbers of trusts are being created, thus sharpening the competition for the lush investments available. Still others blandly dismiss the trusts as being too risky for the small investor, without bothering to explain why. They may end up by giving trusts the kiss of death by saying that they are selling at high-price earnings ratios.

A SUMMING UP ON THE TRUSTS

The trusts have met and overcome the objections a small investor might raise against real estate investments.   By the investment of relatively modest amounts, he is enabled to participate in large-scale real estate projects.   By investing in different kinds of trusts, different in geographical area covered and different in some being mortgage trusts and others being equity trusts, the small investor is able to diversify.   As trusts are traded in on the organized stock exchanges as well as on the over the counter market, the small investor achieves liquidity.   He likewise achieves expertise in management in trusts where investment selection is left to competent specialists.

Not only do the trusts provide the investor with diversification, they also endow him with limited liability.   He likewise has the assurance of continuity of life in the trust organization.   He enjoys all the attributes of a corporate investment, but without the burden of the corporate income tax.

LIMITED PARTNERSHIPS

They are increasingly popular as investment media in real estate. They must be organized with one or more as general partners, fully and personally liable for all the debts of the project undertaken.   The limited partners, however, are immune from the debts of the partnership so long as their identity is not made known, their names do not appear on the masthead or the decal of the investment project, and they "keep under wraps" so that no creditor could say that he advanced credit because of the credit stature of a limited partner.

Limited partnerships pool the investments of individual limited partners.   The general partners then invest these funds as they think best in real estate mortgage loans, construction or long-term loans, and real estate equities.   They "pass through" to the limited partners the earnings thereby derived and earmark those that constitute ordinary income and capital gains.   The individual limited partners pay income tax on the shares of the earnings attributable to them.   The limited partnership per se is not subject to the Federal corporate income tax. The limited partnership is not subject, as are real estate investment trusts, to the requirement that 90 per cent or more of its earnings must be disbursed.

Limited partnership participations may be sold in both low or high amounts, per individual share.   They are freely transferable.   They are more advantageous than the Sub Chapter S corporation, for it is limited to 20 per cent of its overall returns being derived from real estate. Limited partnership participations tend to be sold for higher prices than do individual holdings in real estate investment trusts.

JOINT VENTURES

As real estate investment trusts and limited partnerships engage in joint ventures, these likewise should engage our investment attention. A joint venture has in mind the consummation of a real estate project - an apartment complex, a series of office buildings, or new shopping centers. In such a situation, the real estate investment trust might supply the capital and a land developer might supply the expertise and the promotion.

Suppose a materials supplier, on the other hand, is desirous of having its product incorporated in the real estate improvements to be constructed. It might provide its materials on an attractive price basis with a long credit period to the developer in return for his using them in his development. This would, so to speak, give it a captive market. It would likewise enjoy an advertising value through public awareness that its products were now integrated in the over-all project. The developer would benefit, for he would be obtaining 100 per cent financing in the purchase of these materials. And so joint ventures have been engaged in with developers and steel companies, electrical appliance manufacturers, lumber dealers, aluminum fabricators, and plumbing and insulation suppliers.

Realizing that developers may be hard put to find funds for even the down payment for land acquisition, builders' resource organizations have sprung up, agreeing to supply part or all of this in return for a share in the profits of the development, and having the products of their organization used in construction.

The diversification into real estate has likewise prompted other companies to league up with developers in joint ventures for the consummation of large-scale real estate projects. Railroads, for example, in several instances, have so diversified and affiliated with real estate developers in such undertakings.

SYNDICATIONS

Syndicates constitute substantial investment media. They pool the financial resources of individual investors to make real estate investments requiring large amounts of capital. The syndicator is the general partner who organizes the property investing group. The investors are the limited partners.

As the syndicate is a limited partnership, it avoids the double tax, the tax on corporate profits and the tax on stockholders' dividends, to which a corporation would be subject. The syndicate itself pays no tax. The members pay a tax only on their shares of the profits received. Each member of the syndicate may deduct on his tax return his share of depreciation in the income property acquired.

The more spectatular syndications have had their day. Some of these have scattered their shots and gone their way. Some have found competition for choice real estate investments too intense and have therefore given up the search. Some have used high pressure artists and bucket shop dealers to sell their participations, reaped a harvest of commissions, and moved on, for fairer fields to conquer. Some have made most of their pay-outs in the form of cash flow generated by accelerated depreciation, and, when this dried up, as did the source of returns, the investments turned sour.

Some syndicates have sinned in bad investment judgment, the payment of excessive fees and salaries to their promoters, and gross under-estimation of construction and operating costs. Some have gone in for payouts so high that nothing was left in the till for repairs, maintenance, supplies, and the carrying of vacancies in rental units.

Some have invested in marginal real estate with uncertain and fluctuating income and the promised milk for their investors turned sour. Others sank to a point of no return and engaged in a frantic search for buyers of their properties at distress prices. Some invested in apartment houses at prices demanding top rentals in the areas of their location, only to be confronted with a subsequent declining rental market. Others have assumed that inflation would never end, only to find, in specific instances, such assumptions were unwarranted.

There have been syndicators who have failed to provide their investors with reports on their operations. There have also been syndicators who have invested in real estate with equity margins so thin that a tumbling market soon wiped them out. They have failed to realize that what goes up may come down and that leverage can work both ways, on the downside as well as the upside. When rentals fell and overhead rose, they paid out more than they generated from operations and the day of reckoning came to hand.

Some would form one syndicate. Then this syndicate would buy real estate from another syndicate under their control at an unreasonably high figure and thereby milk their assets to the advantage of the syndicators and the loss of the investors.

There is nothing wrong with the syndicate form as an investment medium. As a syndicate, you may take advantage of favorable financing techniques, such as the operation of the leverage principle, accelerated depreciation, and return to investors tax free of depreciation cash flow. The form itself offers the small investor an opportunity to develop a modest equity in a substantial real estate investment, and to take advantage of the tax advantages inherent therein.

The wrong has been in the abuse of the syndicate form, and in the employment of unsound management. In such situations, as new sources of equity dried up, the real estate empires of some syndications have been smashed, and the organizations they have established have gone into bankruptcy. It is from situations such as these that the expression "sins of syndications" came into being.

TRUE AND FALSE QUESTIONS

1. Real estate investment trusts serve the same purpose as mutual funds.   T   F

2. Real estate investment trusts are like open-end mutual funds.   T   F

3. The interests acquired by real estate investment trusts must be equity.   T   F

4. Some real estate investment trusts are traded in over the counter.   T   F

5. If real estate investment trusts distribute 90% of their income to their shareholders, they are immune from the Federal income tax   T   F

6. Real estate investment trusts certificates are non-transferable.   T   F

7. There must be at least 100 beneficial owners in a real estate investment trust.   T   F

8. The real estate investment trust may act as a dealer in real estate.   T   F

9. Real estate investment trusts may pass through to their shareholders their tax losses and loss carryovers.   T   F

10. Real estate investment trusts are incorporated.   T   F

11. Mortgage trusts enjoy cash flow from depreciation.   T   F

12. Real estate investment trusts leverage shareholder equities with bank loans.   T   F

13. Real estate investment trusts can pass through cash flow to their shareholders.   T   F

14. Limited partnerships must have at least one general partner.   T   F

15. The limited partners themselves must not be known to the general public.   T   F

16. The limited partnership is subject to the Federal corporate   T   F
    income tax.

17. Limited partnership participations are freely transferable.   T   F

18. In a joint venture, one may supply the capital, and the other,   T   F
    the expertise and the experience.

19. The syndicate is usually a limited partnership.   T   F

20. The syndicate advantages are available only to the large   T   F
    investor.

21. The syndicate is a limited partner.   T   F

22. The syndicate itself pays income tax.   T   F

23. Limited partnerships must disburse at least 90 per cent of   T   F
    their earnings.

24. Sub chapter S corporations are usually employed in real   T   F
    estate.

25. The real estate investment trust provides a continuity of   T   F
    life.

26. The investor in a real estate investment trust has limited   T   F
    liability.

27. Real estate investment trusts may have to carry a com-   T   F
    pensating balance with the banks from which they obtain their
    loans.

28. Equity real estate investment trusts may not take on   T   F
    mortgage lending.

29. Real estate investment trusts are unincorporated associ-   T   F
    ations.

30. No fewer than five in a real estate investment trust can own   T   F
    as much as 50 per cent of the shares.

31. One hundred per cent of the income from a real estate   T   F
    investment trust must be from real property.

32. Real estate investment trusts may not derive gains on the   T   F
    sale of real estate held for less than four years.

33. Real estate investment trusts are relatively inexpensive to   T   F
    operate.

34. The stock market may assign a price-earnings multiple to a   T   F
    trust's shares when they begin trading.

35. Real estate investment trusts are not permitted to exchange   T   F
    their stock for property they acquire.

36. Real estate investment trusts provide diversification.   T   F

37. The general partner in a limited partnership enjoys limited   T   F
    liability.

38. A joint venture usually has in mind the consummation of   T   F
    specific real estate project.

39. The investors in a syndicate are general partners.   T   F

40. The criticisms of syndicates have been directed toward the   T   F
    abuse of this investment form, rather than against syndicates
    per se.

MULTIPLE CHOICE QUESTIONS

41. Cash flow is regarded as:
    ( ) Net profit
    ( ) A return of capital
    ( ) Gross profit
    ( ) Marginal earnings

42. Mortgage trusts derive their income from:
    ( ) Returns on equity
    ( ) Interest earned and discounts received
    ( ) Net profits
    ( ) Return of capital

43. Real estate investment trusts under a 1936 Supreme Court decision:
    ( ) Were to be regarded as a Sub Chapter S corporation
    ( ) Were to be treated as a limited partnership
    ( ) Were to be denied the benefits of depreciation
    ( ) Were to be taxed as a corporation

44. If no restrictions are imposed on the kind of investment a real estate investment trust may make, it is then called:
    ( ) A blank check trust
    ( ) A diversified trust
    ( ) A mixed trust
    ( ) A discretionary trust

45. If a real estate investment trust is to invest in one specific property, it is:
    ( ) A one shot trust
    ( ) A specific trust
    ( ) A limited trust
    ( ) A limited venture trust

46. Construction loan mortgages are usually:
    ( ) Five years or less
    ( ) From one to two years
    ( ) Combined with permanent financing in the same mortgage
    ( ) Held by mortgage bankers

47. If a real estate investment trust offering provides the privilege of subsequent conversion into other shares at advantageous levels, this is:
   ( ) An equity participation
   ( ) A "sweetner"
   ( ) A put and a call
   ( ) A terminable option

48. Shares in limited partnerships are sold as:
   ( ) Certificates of beneficial interest
   ( ) Preferred stock
   ( ) Participations
   ( ) Class A stock

49. A joint venture consists of:
   ( ) Only two
   ( ) Two or more
   ( ) A Sub Chapter S corporation
   ( ) Any corporation engaged in real estate

50. The real estate investment trust investor enjoys liquidity if:
   ( ) His shares are traded in an organized securities exchange
   ( ) He holds his shares under an irrevocable trust
   ( ) He holds his shares under a living trust
   ( ) He holds his share in a joint tenancy

ESSAY QUESTIONS

1. Please evaluate real estate investment trusts from the standpoint of the small investor.

2. How are real estate investment trusts organized?

3. What have been the principal investments of equity trusts?

4. What gave rise to the expression, "sins of syndications"?

PART VI
RESIDENTIAL
REAL ESTATE

PART VI
RESIDENTIAL
REAL ESTATE

HOUSING'S WAVE
OF THE FUTURE

Factory-assembled housing is the wave of the future—three-dimensional modules, complying with building codes, assembled in the factory, transported to and bolted together on a prepared foundation. The modules are pre-finished, pre-wired, and pre-plumbed. They travel down the assembly line through stations for painting, flooring, carpeting, plumbing and electrical wiring, and placement of walls, doors, windows, appliances, interior trim, and roof.

SOME DEFINITIONS

The modular is the completed structure, composed of the individual modules. Two or more modules may be stacked, placed side by side, or otherwise joined to form the structure.

The sectional is a modular formed by joining two modules at the home site. Panels are two-dimensional units — like walls, floors, and ceilings — assembled on site. Shell housing is composed of sufficient panels to form the shell of the house. Pre-fabs are structural parts, fabricated in advance, and assembled on site. Mobile homes are three-dimensional single-family units, built to be towed on their own chassis, and not required to satisfy local building codes. They are usually regarded as personal property, rather than real. Mobile modulars are modulars resting on transport wheels.

THE DEVELOPMENT OF INDUSTRIALIZED HOUSING

The traditional housing industry is the one that the Industrial Revolution overlooked. Construction practices date back to Biblical times and the days of the Pyramids — stick on stick and brick on brick — incapable of responding to mass market. In order to survive, the housing industry is going to have to make the transition to industrialized housing.

Spurred on by the housing shortages and the scarcity of skilled construction labor, resulting from World War II, European countries turned to industrialized housing. European housing systems have been turning out 4 to 20 units per day, showing cuts in production costs by 20 per cent and in time by 50 per cent as against conventional construction. Of new European homes built in the last fifteen years, industrialized housing has accounted for 60 per cent of those in France; 42 per cent of those in the United Kingdom; and 85 per cent of those in the Soviet Union.

The impetus for modulars in Canada was Habitat '67, part of Expo '67 in Montreal — brilliant architecturally, but clumsy, technologically, with an average cost of $103 per square foot. The lesson learned was that structural modules, made of a heavy slow-setting wet material like concrete, and requiring huge cranes to be hoisted into place to form a twelve-story building, could not as yet be mechanized and speeded up to the point where unit costs could be competitive with conventional.

Industrialized housing in the United States goes back to the emergency housing of World War I and to prototypes at the Chicago Exposition of 1933. During World War II prefabricated housing was used at defense installations. In the late '40's and early '50's, the Lustron Corporation set itself up to produce industrialized housing, but went bankrupt. In the mid-1950's, Monsanto built its home of the future by industrialized techniques, but it proved prohibitively expensive. These approaches encountered the barriers interposed by local building codes and the restrictive work practices of construction unions.

OPERATION BREAKTHROUGH

It became evident in the late 1960's that the United States was producing housing at less that 60 per cent of its stated needs, that it was losing housing at a rate faster than it was being replaced, and that housing was the biggest underdeveloped market in the country. The President's Committee on Urban Housing reported that there was a need for 26,000,000 new housing units to be produced between 1968 and 1978, but that only 1,400,000 units per year had been produced so far in the 1960's. It further became evident that there was a serious shortage of construction workers, and that ways must be found to reduce the cost of housing.

The Department of Housing and Urban Development therefore inaugurated Operation Breakthrough in the summer of 1969 to try to satisfy these needs. The Department sent out requests for proposals to more than 4,000 construction organizations, asking them to submit suggestions to double housing production and reduce housing costs. The proposals received were divided into housing systems ready for production, and advanced components requiring further research. In early 1970, the Department of Housing and Urban Development named the twenty-two winners. They all employed industrialized techniques, ranging from complete production of modules in a factory, to on-site assembly of completed panels, to on-site poured concrete systems. Seven of the proposals used concrete; six, wood; five, metal as structural framing; two, plastic foam-core panels or modules; and two, plastic fiberglass.

THE WINNERS

For the most part, the winners were consortiums of sponsors, that had agreed on components, materials, and equipment. The objective of all was to develop high-volume housing production systems and to aim these at large markets. The majority of the systems selected stressed single-family, low-rise, or row houses in the familiar American suburban life style.

All the systems selected showed efficient technological advance over traditional building processes. For these systems, the Department of Housing and Urban Development provided the eight sites on which their prototypes were to reside; the use of Section 235 and Section 236 funds to enable people of low- and moderate-income groups to buy or rent the prototype housing to be produced; and its help to try to remove the major constraints of varying building codes and the opposition of the construction unions. The winners were to produce 2,796 units, and the difference between their Fair Market Value and their cost was to be absorbed by the Federal Government. The prototype units so far produced average $22,410 per unit, and range in costs from $8,825 to $50,000.

Operation Breakthrough took the most fragmentized industry in the United States, and made it think big. It developed performance criteria for evaluation. It enlisted almost every big name in construction in its program. It made the public aware that manufactured housing is something more than World War II pre-fabrication. It stimulated an interest among home-builders in cost-savings systems.

It has not, however, produced a true industrialized housing industry. There is no consensus on production goals, on the proper materials to employ, and on the marketing mechanisms to use. There is no public relations counsel. Instead of manufacture, there is an assembly operation of parts and elements made elsewhere.

CONSTRUCTION WORKERS

In times past construction unions have not reacted favorably to industrialized housing. They have seen in it a threat to the jobs of their members and to the strength of their bargaining power. But there has now occurred a breakthrough against their opposition. Among the unions with contracts with modular plants are the Brotherhood of Carpenters and Joiners, the Sheet Metal Workers Union, the International Laborers Union, and the United Auto Workers Union. They have come to realize that industrialized housing is inevitable, that it will not put their skilled craftsmen out of work, and that it will provide in-plant work for their members, in season and out, with no interruptions for bad weather. They also welcome the increase in dues-paying members that it will provide.

Women workers do extraordinarily well in industrialized housing, becoming home makers in the literal sense, and showing themselves in many applications to be more adept than their masculine counterparts. In major plants they constitute 25 to 30 per cent of the work force. They do wall panelling application and finishing; cabinet piece work assembly; roof trusses; and countertops.

MATERIALS

Although the primary structural material continues to be wood, steel and other materials are making inroads. The use of steel lends itself well to on-line operations, with semi-skilled workers; steel travels better and stacks better than wood; and the price structure and supplies of steel are more stable than those of wood. Steel can be precision-fabricated. Three-dimensional steel framing has shown that it can withstand the most severe earthquakes.

The big thrust now in research and development is in concrete systems. Concrete is inexpensive, a good insulator, and fire resistant. Aluminum also is making new inroads, primarily in framing and in wall systems. Plastics, likewise, are increasingly being used for structural components. The National Aeronautics and Space Administration has commissioned a study to determine what materials and equipment may be transferable from its field into industrialized housing.

ASSEMBLY

This consists of a central assembly line with bays or "work stations" arranged alongside. The floor is commonly built at the first station, and walls, ceiling, roofs, plumbing, wiring, kitchen systems, doors, trim, tile, or carpet are added at successive sub-stations. Ninety to 95 per cent of the finishing work is done inside the factory.

A system by which a floor a day can go up in a high-rise has been developed. After the foundation is poured and the hydraulic and mechanical jacks are in place, then the top floor and the roof are installed. This floor is jacked up, and then the next floor's modules are installed and connected. Proceeding in this fashion, a fifteen story building can be installed. The vertical building loads are transmitted to the foundation through the integrated supporting post and beam design. The fast installation saves time, and provides a quick return on the investment.

Rather than assemble the components inside the factory, they may be shipped to the site, and assembled there. This saves on transportation costs, for the components can be shipped flat. Nor are the components subject to the limitations of highway widths. They are, however, exposed on site to inclement weather, which can result in longer erection time.

Assembly problems arise both off-site and on-site. Components and sub-assemblies from suppliers may not be complete. Exposed materials may not be pre-finished. Delivery may not be on time, and production lines may therefore be held up. Lumber may not come pre-cut to the proper width and length. Plumbing fixtures may not be pre-plumbed. Kitchen cabinets may not arrive in complete assemblies.

BUILDING CODES

Building codes are designed to complement and administer conventional building methods. They are not designed for industrialized housing. They do not provide for performance criteria. They vary widely from one locality to another. They may be so dated or so curiously written that they discourage innovation.

There are hundreds of differing local building codes in the larger states. Local building inspectors may be neither qualified or funded to evaluate new methods and materials. The local building code scene is one of localism, provincialism, and home-rule gone wild. This may make it necessary to change design for each new production run. Every unit may have to be inspected individually.

To progress, the modular industry requires state building codes, pre-empting the contrariety of local ones. The modular industry also needs reciprocity between state building codes. As of February 1, 1973 over thirty states had set up and passed building codes, which evaluated and certified industrialized housing techniques. Once so certified, the individual producer is in general freed from the restrictions of local codes.

It is one thing to adopt a state building code. It is something else to make it meaningful and enforceable. It should not be necessary for every differing floor plan layout to be re-submitted for approval, so long as the same system is utilized. If a production system has been used for a reasonable period of time, it should receive approval from plans alone, without the necessity for further testing.

For federally sponsored housing programs, performance criteria have been established by the National Bureau of Standards. Legislation being proposed in Congress would provide that no local code, ordinance, or labor agreement may restrict the use of new technology or pre-assembled products on federally assisted projects. Congress is also giving consideration to the establishment of a federal corporation to set both performance and specification standards for building technologies.

TRANSPORTATION PROBLEMS

Factory-assembled homes are usually delivered to the site by truck and placed by crane on a foundation already in place, and then bolted together. Unfortunately, because of trucking requirements, the size and shape of modules are limited, thereby imposing restrictions on designs. Most states limit modular widths to 12 feet, and height, to 13 feet, 6 inches.

Highway regulations may also prohibit the transportation of over-size loads and widths after dark, and this limits the geographical radius within which modules may be transported. As truck transportation is thereby restricted to 300 or so miles from the plant, this makes necessary a number of plants, serving limited marketing areas, rather than one large plant. This in turn limits the extent to which economies of scale in manufacture can be enjoyed.

Secretary Romney has estimated that 10 to 25 per cent is added to transportation costs by requiring state-to-state highway permits and by prohibiting the shipment of two modules on a single trailer. Other transportation costs may consist of the weather proofing required to protect the exposed surface of the modules during transit; the damage from vibration in the course of transit; and in meeting federal standards on safety, lights, brakes, braking systems, and coupling devices.

Because of trucking problems, consideration has been given to rail transportation, but there are mixed reactions with regard to it. One school of thought brings out that there are also width limitations on flat bed cars on the railroads; that special scheduling, with attendant delays, may be required; that mass produced modules may have to be redesigned to meet varying width and height requirements of the different railroads used; that additional unloading, transportation and site erection equipment will be needed; and that modules will suffer damage from the extra handling to get them on to the flat cars, and then off again to the trailer.

The other school of thought points out that modules have been transported without damage over 1,000 miles by rail; that the railroads can

readily handle loads wider than ten feet; that the product does not have
to be redesigned to meet the railroad requirements; that no vandalism
problems have been encountered; and that no additional unloading or site
erection equipment is necessary. This school says that the problem in
shipment by rail is one of excessively high rates, being based on what
the traffic will bear, rather than having any relationship to costs and to
a fair profit.

Modular assemblers near navigable waters have used barge transportation. This is inexpensive, and presents no width or clearance
problems. Helicopters have also been used to deliver modules to the
site and to place them on their foundations, but the cost of transportation
by helicopter is high and the downwash of air from the helicopter makes
it difficult for workers on site to place the module accurately on its
foundation.

ERECTION

The usual mode of erection is by crane, lifting the module from the
truck and hoisting it into position on a prepared foundation. If a crane
is not used, wheels may be attached to the floor of the module, and it
may then be rolled on over the foundation on accurately placed and
secured steel beams.

In an erection demonstration at Cape Cod sites in Massachusetts,
seven modular two-section, five-room vacation homes were erected on
site in just two hours.

TESTS FOR QUALITY

The first modular home tested by government engineers for durabil-
ity exceeded the criteria of the National Bureau of Standards. Its
strength was superior to anything obtainable in a conventionally built
home. Testing for the Federal Housing Administration, done by an
independent testing agency, showed that a steel frame modular home
was capable of withstanding the shaking of the most severe known earthquake as well as hurricane force winds.

APPEARANCE

Modular designs range from advanced technology in pseudo-Franco-
American colonial to the lowest common denominator ranch house.
They take in concrete boxes in staggered patterns of room-units and
open space. They show up as well-proportioned slab structures with
balconied facades. They embody life style concepts, including streets
and yards above ground, in a standardized lightweight building frame.

Although the low slope gable roof is most common in industrialized
housing, the mansard roof is growing in popularity. Its high slope
strikes a contemporary note, and adapts well to residential styling. A
breakthrough in roofing has also come about through a silicone and
chipped stone roof.

Painted dry walls are harmonized with the carpet in the living room
and dining room. There is an extensive use of rugged wood siding.
Shapes extend to hexagonal configurations. Exterior beauty may be

provided by dark stained cedar "barn shakes" and rustic "board and batten."

Design innovation may include sunken fire or conversation pits, step-down living rooms, step-up dens, and atrium-patio areas. Modules may have vaulted ceilings, and may be built with recessed foyers.

Modular assemblers are creating total living environments. They are masterplanning new communities based on architectural design. They have evolved environmental homes which are innovative, private, quiet, easy to maintain, expandable, flexible, and convenient.

FINANCING

Start-up financing may be secured from the sale of limited partnership participations, real estate investment trusts, syndicates, joint ventures, and extended terms from building material suppliers. A corporation, already established and with a credit rating of its own, may be able to take over an existing modular producer. There are also many examples of public acceptance for stock offerings of companies with a successful track record in the housing field.

Established mobile home producers, seeing in modulars a logical extension of their present sphere, have installed facilities for modular production. Giant and well financed corporations have gone into modular for profitable diversification, as captive markets for their products and showcases for their wares.

Federal Housing Administration insurance and Veterans Administration guarantees are available for modulars, just as are subsidies from the Section 235 and Section 236 programs under the National Housing Act. Some modular producers have set up their own acceptance subsidiaries to provide construction loans to builders and permanent mortgage financing for home purchasers.

MARKETING

Some modular producers wholesale their units to land developers, building contractors, and to retail home dealers. Some have set up their own dealer organizations. Others have established their own marketing subsidiaries. Modular stores have been marketed directly to merchandising chains.

The major marketing problem is to create an acceptable public image. The public regards modulars as standardized boxes; equates them with mobile homes; associates them with low-cost public housing; and feels that modulars are cheap and sterile, aesthetically displeasing, and of shoddy construction.

Modular producers have told their story to modular suppliers, and modular suppliers have told their story to modular producers. Innumerable speeches have been made by heads of modular companies to each other. Motion pictures on modulars have been made, and shown to the people employed in this field. The industry has been aggressive in making itself known to itself. But the forgotten entity in this mass of mutual education has been the public. The public wants to be told the most. The public has been told the least. When a modular home is opened up for the public to see, the public comes in droves. The proto-type units, now on display, are attracting crowds of people.

But even in the face of this public interest, some modular producers will not permit plant visitations. The writing they do on modulars is for professional journals, not for the general public. Perhaps the way in which modulars have been marketed is responsible. When modulars are sold for public housing projects, the marketing need is only to educate these agencies. When modulars are distributed through one's own marketing subsidiary, modular producers may feel that no mar-keting problem exists. So far as modular homes themselves are con-cerned, there is a discreet silence about the fact that they are modulars. The thought is expressed that they must not be distinguishable from conventionals, and the implication is that if they can be passed off as conventionals, then all is well and good.

But Operation Breakthrough demonstrated that the public can get interested, and even excited, about modulars. The current exhibition of modulars on site is now evoking a public response. But the momen-tum thus generated must be supported by a continuity of other education-al media to be sustained. Why not set up model homes of modulars, and call them what they are, and cite their quality superiority over conventionals? Why not write articles on modulars in "Reader's Digest" style, readable and understandable by the general public? Why can't companies like U. S. Steel, Westinghouse, General Electric, Alcoa, and St. Regis Paper — all with a stake in the modular field — turn their advertising and sales promotion talents to public education in modulars?

"A rose by any other name would smell as sweet." A modular, on the other hand, by any other name would sound a lot better. If modular producers had sought far and wide for a set of repelling nomenclature, they could not have been more successful than in their present grisly glossary. The word "module" suggests some technical animal, perhaps out of aerospace. "Modular" compounds this into collectivity. "Sec-tional" suggests a piece of uncovered furniture. "Industrialized housing" suggests the press and roar of a factory. Other technical jargon only makes confusion worse confounded. Why not use "precision engineered homes" in place of "industrialized housing?" "Rooms" in place of "modules?" "Homes" in place of "modulars?"

MOBILE HOMES

They are defined by the Mobile Home Manufacturers Association as "movable or portable dwellings, constructed to be towed on their own chassis, connected to utilities, and designed without a permanent founda-tion for year round living." They are differentiated from modulars, in that they are not built to conform to building codes, and are classified legally as personal property, rather than real property.

They account for the bulk of the sales of housing units priced under $15,000. The average retail price, in fact, ranges between $5,600 and $5,800. They offer the living conveniences of four- to six-room homes, but at a substantially lower cost. They come furnished with equipment and appliances. They depreciate faster than conventional homes, and their loan maturities are for shorter periods. This, in turn, means that monthly payments can be relatively substantial.

The income of the average mobile home owner is slightly below the national average. He owns a car, and has a family of three. Fourteen per cent of mobile home owners are skilled workers; 38 per cent are semi-skilled; 18 per cent are retirees; 11 per cent are military personnel; and the remainder are scattered over a wide range. The majority are under 35 years old.

Mobile homes are not to be confused with trailers. A trailer is usually acquired as an adjunct to recreation and to travel, and is not as large as a mobile home. It would not have sufficient living space to provide for comfortable living. A mobile home, on the other hand, is acquired for domestic living, for amenities, and for pleasant and comfortable decor and surroundings.

Federal Housing Administration insurance and Veterans Administration guarantees may now be secured on mortgage loans on mobile homes. Federal Savings and Loan Associations are now authorized to make mortgage loans on mobile homes.

Almost 600,000 mobile homes are now produced and sold each year. The leading manufacturers show above average earnings growth, and their shares sell at high multiples. Their growth prospects have been enhanced by diversification into other forms of manufactured housing and into land development.

Many of today's mobile home parks are paved; lawns are landscaped; maintenance standards are high; utilities and sanitary facilities are adequate; they are well lighted; and their density is no more than eight to ten units per acre. Mobile home parks may secure Federal Housing Administration insurance on their mortgage loans. Today, there are 23,000 parks in operation, and 52 per cent of mobile homes reside in these parks.

THE FUTURE

It is therefore evident that industrialized housing is taking over in an area long bereft of advancing technology. The end result should be a plateau as against the ever rising crescendo of construction costs. Not only will there be a substantial reduction in the labor costs in construction, but there will also be a lowering of interest costs on the construction money outstanding, achieved because of the shortening of the period of construction time. Automation, at long last, will come into its own in the construction industry, casting out the brick on brick and stick on stick methods of times past, enabling construction to enjoy the assembly line techniques, weather free production, standardization of operations, and quality controls, all part and parcel not only of the twentieth century, but also of the twenty-first century to come.

TRUE AND FALSE QUESTIONS

1. The modular is the completed structure, composed of the individual modules. T F

2. The sectional is formed by joining two modules at the home site. T F

3. Panels are two dimensional units, assembled on site. T F

4. Pre-fabs are structural parts, fabricated in advance, and assembled on site. T F

5. Mobile homes are required to satisfy local building codes. T F

6. Mobile homes are now regarded as real property. T F

7. There is as yet no industrialized housing industry. T F

8. Construction unions still forbid their members to engage in industrialized housing. T F

9. Women workers are efficient in industrialized housing. T F

10. The primary structural material in industrialized housing is steel. T F

11. Steel can be precision fabricated. T F

12. Local building codes are in general designed to accommodate the special characteristics of industrialized housing. T F

13. The National Bureau of Standards has established performance criteria for industrialized housing for federally sponsored programs. T F

14. Most states limit modular widths on the highways to fourteen feet. T F

15. States have reciprocity, one with another, in building codes. T F

16. There is general agreement that rail transportation is preferable to truck. T F

17. Barge transportation presents width and clearance problems.   T   F

18. The usual mode of modular erection is by crane.   T   F

19. Tests of modulars show they exceed the criteria of the   T   F
National Bureau of Standards.

20. The low slope gable roof is the most common in in-   T   F
dustrialized housing.

21. Modulars may not secure FHA insurance.   T   F

22. The major modular marketing problem is to create a   T   F
favorable public image.

23. Modular stores have not yet been marketed.   T   F

24. Modules are three-dimensional units.   T   F

25. Shell housing is composed of sufficient panels to form the   T   F
house shell.

26. Mobile modulars rest on transport wheels.   T   F

27. European countries have not as yet turned to industrialized   T   F
housing.

28. Habitat '67 demonstrated how inexpensive modulars could   T   F
be.

29. The United States engaged in no industrialized housing   T   F
until Operation Breakthrough.

30. Operation Breakthrough was started by the Department   T   F
of Commerce.

31. Most of the Operation Breakthrough winners stressed the   T   F
use of wood.

32. There is now a breakthrough against construction union   T   F
opposition.

33. Aluminum is used, primarily in framing and in wall systems.   T   F

34. Local building codes do not usually provide for performance   T   F
criteria.

35. There are as yet no state building codes.   T   F

36. Highway regulations may prohibit the transportation of over- T F
width loads after dark.

37. Helicopters have proven both economical and practicable T F
for transportation.

38. The mansard roof is growing in popularity with modulars. T F

39. Some mobile home producers have also taken on the pro- T F
duction of modulars.

40. VA-guaranteed loans are now available for modulars. T F

MULTIPLE CHOICE QUESTIONS

41. Of the European countries, the one which, since World War II, shows the largest percentage of industrialized housing is:
    ( ) England
    ( ) France
    ( ) The Soviet Union
    ( ) Sweden

42. Industrialized Housing in the United States goes back to:
    ( ) The emergency housing of World War II
    ( ) The emergency housing of World War I
    ( ) The Lustron housing of the late '40's
    ( ) The Monsanto housing of the mid-1950's

43. Women workers in major industrialized housing plants constitute:
    ( ) Between 25 per cent and 30 per cent of the work force
    ( ) Over 50 per cent of the work force
    ( ) A token percentage of the work force
    ( ) Cheap labor

44. A system has been developed for high-rise modulars by which:
    ( ) A floor a day can be erected
    ( ) A floor a week can be erected
    ( ) Helicopters drop the various floors in place
    ( ) Sky cranes do the entire erection process

45. In most instances, where state building codes have been adopted, they:
    ( ) Are subordinate to local building codes
    ( ) Provide for reciprocity with other states
    ( ) Provide for reciprocity with the federal government
    ( ) Pre-empt the contrariety of local building codes

46. Truck transportation of modulars is usually limited to:
    ( ) 300 to 350 miles from the plant
    ( ) 1,000 miles from the plant
    ( ) 50 miles from the plant
    ( ) 100 miles from the plant

47. Modules have been transported by rail without damages:
    ( ) Up to 100 miles
    ( ) Up to 1,000 miles

( )   At only minimal distances
( )   From Maine to California

48. Giant and well financed corporations have gone into modular production, not only for profitable diversification, but also:
( )   To do their part in the production of low- and moderate-income housing
( )   As captive markets for their products and showcases for their wares
( )   Because required to do so by the Department of Housing and Urban Development
( )   Because of the tremendous profits to be made in such production

49. Modular designs:
( )   Are in the shape of uninteresting boxes
( )   Are all scaled down for inexpensive public housing
( )   Range from advanced technology to the lowest common denominator ranch house
( )   Are usually like those of Habitat '67

50. A steel frame modular home has been made:
( )   Capable of withstanding the shaking of the most severe known earthquake
( )   At one-quarter the cost of wood
( )   Satisfying the requirements of all local building codes
( )   Satisfying the requirements of all state building codes

ESSAY QUESTIONS

1. What is the public image of modulars and how can this be corrected?

2. How is the assembly-line technique employed in modular assembly?

3. What problems do local building codes present?

MOBILE HOMES

CHAPTER SIXTEEN

WHAT ARE THEY?

A mobile home is "a movable or portable dwelling constructed to be towed on its own chassis, connected to utilities, and designed without a permanent foundation for year round living. It can consist of one or more units that can be telescoped when towed, or of two or more units separately towable but designed to be joined into one integral unit." So says the Mobile Home Manufacturers Association.

A mobile home is presently the only type of living unit under $15,000 that can provide a family with reasonable amenities and decent standards of living. Being mobile, it is responsive to the mobility of population so characteristic of our times. It can come in standard form or with options that make for increased livability.

It is becoming increasingly popular as a second home in resort and vacation areas. In the current period of acute housing shortage, it is doing yeoman's service in alleviation. Until the current experimentation with modular and sectional housing, it has seemed to be the only way to beat the high costs of construction. Being regarded still as personal property, it has not been subject to the financial restrictions imposed on real property. Its use is by no means limited to low income groups. It is a "natural" for retirees, desirous of travel during the free time now available, but wanting some place to which they can always return as home headquarters. It is to be distinguished from the unsightly trailer of times past and from the camper, serving merely as a vehicle for vacation trips.

HOW DID THEY COME ABOUT?

The prairie schooners of westward migration were among the progenitors of the mobile homes as we know them today. They were the covered wagons which crisscrossed the Old West. They moved their passengers from the towns into the backwoods and across the states. They were literally propelled by horsepower.

With the introduction of the automobile, a new era began. Older buses were converted to homes on wheels. They were used as mobile dwellings by itinerant workers, circuses, and by carnival people. Somewhat quiescent in their use and development for a number of years, mobile homes received a regeneration in interest during World War II. The priorities of the defense effort then took first place and the construction of conventional single-family dwellings had to take a backseat. The shortages in housing were keenly felt by individuals deployed in defense facilities and military installations. They therefore fell back on the resource provided by mobile homes. Masonite and other nonpriority materials were used to build transportable housing. The Federal Government bought hundreds of mobile home units for wartime workers.

Then came the end of World War II and the full consciousness of the vacuum in housing dawned. Virtually none had been constructed during the war period. Veterans returning from overseas, getting married, wanting homes of their own, found their desires unfulfillable. The demand for housing spilled over into the mobile home industry, at least as temporary shelter until permanent homes could subsequently be erected. They were viable as an emergency solution and the discomforts then attendant were tolerated for the necessary duration. It was during this post-war period that mobile homes developed their unsavory connotation as an unsightly mess, spawning out their boxes and littering up the landscape.

In the late 1940's, mobile homes moved out of the emergency housing field into the permanent low-cost residence field, and with improved quality. The size of mobile homes was enlarged. New entrepreneurs came into the business. Mobile home owners were no longer forced to acquire land on which their units could reside. Mobile home parks increased in size and number. Some of these provided a package which included maintenance, landscaping, playgrounds, man-made lakes, and open space. During the 1950's units with widths of ten feet and lengths ranging all the way from 34 feet to 60 feet were introduced. By 1960 these large size mobile homes comprised 98 per cent of the market. By 1962 twelve foot widths had been introduced and it was not long until they had taken over 60 per cent of the market.

As we begin the 1970's, mobile homes have come of age. They now offer us, as buyers, every living convenience that can be found in a four to six room house, but at much lower cost. They come completely furnished with all equipment and appliances. They show remarkable improvements in design. They are functionally laid out. Their economy appeals to families of modest means. They provide more value per dollar than any existing form of housing.

Over 90 per cent of all new single family homes under $15,000 are mobile homes. Instead of migratory workers being the principal inhabitants, 81 out of every 100 households intend to continue residing in their mobile homes. The majority of owners now fall into the category of less than 35 years of age. They are usually young married couples just starting out in life. But a substantial number are retired couples who no longer need their big old houses.

WHAT BENEFITS DO THEY PROVIDE?
They come fully equipped - appliances, stoves and refrigerators, draperies and furniture, lamps and carpeting. They are centrally heated by gas, oil, or electricity. For an extra charge, they will provide air conditioning, automatic dishwashers, and garbage disposals. They have a living room, kitchen, dinette, one or two bathrooms, two or more bedrooms, and custom designed cabinets. Their decor may be early

American, contemporary, Mediterranean, French provincial, Oriental, or traditional. They may come with wood parquet floors, prefabricated fireplaces, sliding glass doors, cedar closets, and built-in intercom and stereo systems.

Their exteriors have been enhanced with bay windows, raised roofs, cedar shingles, and aluminum siding. They are designed with every conceivable floor plan. They are now providing for a variation in lot placement. Their aesthetic appearance is also being varied to create a visually harmonious community, without repetitive monotony. Producers have made design changes to permit traditional styles to become more prevalent.

Their low cost provides the buyer with savings compared to the purchase of a conventional single family home. The buyer also saves in his decreased consumption of utilities. The smallest single family home available is larger than the largest mobile home. The mobile home buyer thereby saves the expense of this extra space. The marginal utility of the extra space does not justify the extra cost. The mobile home needs less heating, less electricity, less by way of housekeeping items, and less maintenance. There is no need to buy furniture. It comes with the home.

WHO LIVES IN THEM?

The average mobile home owner has an income slightly below the national average and owns a car. Fourteen per cent of mobile home owners are skilled workers; 38 per cent are semi-skilled; 18 per cent are retired; 11 per cent are military personnel; and the remaining 19 per cent are scattered over a wide range of categories.

The majority of mobile home owners are less than 35 years old and have only two persons in the household. They are people who may not be able to afford a conventional single-family home. Their financial position may be such that they could not meet the down payment and monthly installments required for such an investment. They find easier and more readily available financing better suited to their capacities. Their work may call for a transfer in the future to another location and they therefore like the flexibility of movement the mobile home provides.

A growing number of people are using mobile units as a second home, sometimes in a resort locale, to provide a vacation habitat. Or they may be retirees, seeking the smaller quarters and corresponding freedom from excessive household chores the mobile home provides. As retirees, they may wish to spend a large part of their time in travel, but still like a modest haven to which they can return from time to time.

AREN'T THEY THE SAME AS TRAILERS?

No, they are not.

You acquire a mobile home for domestic living, amenities, pleasant and comfortable decor and surroundings. You may not live in it all your life, but your residence is at least semi-permanent. You acquire a trailer, on the other hand, as an adjunct to recreational purposes and travel.

The mobile home and trailer likewise differentiate on the basis of size. If your original purpose in acquiring a 60 by 12 foot unit was for recreation, you found that moving it was not easy, and it therefore came to be a form of permanent housing. If, on the other hand, you bought a camper trailer with the intention of living in it, you soon found that you did not have enough living space and therefore switched over to the larger mobile home unit.

HOW DO YOU FINANCE MOBILE HOMES?

We have made remarkable progress in financing mobile homes. Some years ago credit was hard to get. Mobile home buyers were then considered as nomads, without roots or responsibility. As mobile homes were not stationary, lenders were apprehensive that the security for loans would drive away at will. But they experienced relatively few defaults, and less than one per cent repossessions. Their early fears proved groundless and they developed a welcome attitude toward mobile home loans.

As mobile homes in the eyes of the law are regarded as personal property, they can be financed without the restrictions, such as usury regulations, which may apply to real property loans. The interest charge is commonly around 13 per cent. The loan period usually ranges from seven to ten years. They may be financed just as you would a car, with a down payment of anywhere between ten and 25 per cent. The mobile home dealer originates the loan contract with the home buyer and cashes out by selling it to a financial institution. Interest computation may be the add-on type under which the installment payments are computed after the interest on the entire principal at the stated rate has been added.

Federal Housing Administration insurance and Veterans Administration guarantees may now be secured on mortgage loans on mobile homes. Federal savings and loan associations are now authorized to make mortgage loans on these units.

Because of the higher interest that may be paid on mobile home loans and because of their shorter pay-out period, they have not labored under the disadvantage of tight credit as have conventional single-family dwellings.

ADVANTAGES IN MOBILE HOME LIVING

In essence they are the same as those of single-family dwelling living. The mobile home payments build up an equity, just as the installment payments do on a single family home. In both instances there are the psychic rewards of home ownership, the security it affords, the pride of ownership, the privacy provided, and the forced savings required in the form of the monthly payments that must be met, come what may. The interest on mobile home loans is a tax deductible item. Favorable capital gains treatment is available on subsequent sale, assuming the property has been held over six months. Property taxes are lower. There is less housework to do. You can live better for less. You enjoy more leisure time.

DISADVANTAGES IN MOBILE HOME LIVING

You pay less than for a single family home. Therefore, you get less. You may find the amount of storage space inadequate. You may feel cramped because of the smaller living quarters. Living in a mobile home park, the density of other homes may be too much for you to bear. The physical, functional, and economic life of your unit will, other things being equal, be less.

You may be looked down upon by people who still associate mobile homes with the image of the squalid trailer parks of years ago. The snobs may cast a social stigma upon you. If you have to move your unit on the highway, you may be ham-strung by barriers, such as weight limitations, speed limits, and the hostility of other drivers who feel you are in their way. You may have all kinds of difficulties getting space in a mobile home park. If you have to leave your park, you may have to sell your unit at a sacrifice. Mobile home owners are also saddled with a variety of restrictions on their transportation, construction, and installation.

Some communities ban mobile homes altogether. They think their appearance is unsightly; their owners, undesirable; and their presence, a sin, a shame, and a subtraction from real estate values. They may set up building codes so exacting that it is impossible for mobile homes to comply therewith. In this, they may be aided and abetted by powerful construction unions who see in mobile home building by assembly line techniques a threat to their employment.

MOBILE HOME PARKS

The public image of mobile homes has been clouded by the unattractive trailer courts of times past. These were overcrowded, unpaved, strewn with debris, without trees and shrubbery, suffering from inadequate utilities and sanitary facilities, a mess of dreary monotony.

Today's mobile parks' roads are paved, lawns landscaped, maintenance standards high, utilities and sanitary facilities adequate, and units showing some variety of design. They are well lighted. The density is now six to eight units per acre contrasted with 16 per acre in the older parks. They may provide swimming pools, tennis courts, shuffleboard courts, and golf courses. Clothes washer and dryer services are made available. The parks are policed.

Some parks are university oriented in that they cater to married students and their families. In these instances the university itself has been unable to provide suitable quarters. The financial situation of the students is not such as to enable them to acquire a single family home. Many students prefer life off campus.

Other parks are military oriented and cater to the temporary shelter needs of military personnel. Subject to transfer after present tours of duty, these parks accommodate themselves to the transient quality of their population. The military installation itself may be of only short duration. The families concerned may be faced with the possibility of moving every year or two.

Still other parks are industry oriented. These serve the housing needs of construction workers and their families engaged in a large project requiring a year or two to complete. They likewise cater to the requirements of industrial technicians in plants nearby.

Many parks are service oriented. They emphasize recreational facilities and resort activities. They are particularly attractive to retirees. They are most often to be seen in California, Florida, and Arizona. Potluck dinners, square dancing, and swimming are among the communal activities. The spaces for mobile homes are larger than in other type parks. The space rentals are correspondingly higher.

Some parks require the mobile owner to buy his lot and own his property rather than pay rent therefore. They may be of the condominium type in which the resident would receive a deed to his lot and secure a joint interest in the common elements. Or they may be of the cooperative type in which the mobile home owner would secure stock in an overall corporation which would own the lots and the common elements and provide the individual residents with a proprietary lease.

Smaller parks may be operated by the owner and his wife. Larger parks usually require specialized management and maintenance personnel. The large resort and service type parks may have a full time social director. The most important factor in successful park operation is competent management.

Space rentals extend over a broad range, with $40 to $55 per month being the most common. But rentals can be found for as low as $12 a month and as high as $350. Other sources of revenue to park owners are sales of bottled gas, groceries, coin operated laundries and dry cleaning plants, and vending machines.

Inasmuch as mobile homes are in general regarded as personal property, they are not subject to real property taxes. They may, however, have to pay annual license fees and, of course, personal property taxes. Indirectly, in the rent for which they are liable will be the proportionate share of real property taxes assessable against the space they occupy. In California, however, mobile homes without wheels are taxed as homes. In Texas such homes enjoy the homestead tax exemption.

The current shortage in mobile home parks has led some park owners to require that applicants for space buy their mobile homes from the park operation before they may rent a site. Other park operators say that if an occupant sells his home, it must be removed from the park. The takedown charges and the costs to put the unit up in a new location run well over $100.00. The transportation charges to a new location range from fifty cents to $1.00 per mile.

It may cost as much as $250,000 to open up a typical park with 100 spaces. The trend is now toward larger parks and some operators estimate a minimum of 200 spaces for a profitable park operation. Many mobile home manufacturers are acquiring parks as an essential concomitant to the sale of their units.

A prospective park owner will make sure in advance that extensive grading and filling costs will not be encountered. He will also check on proper surface drainage. He will avoid locations affected by noise, smoke, odors, and rodent infestation. He will not locate his park on a main thoroughfare, but will make sure it has access to a principal traffic artery. He will assure himself that utilities will be made available.

The supply of park space has not kept pace with the supply of mobile homes. The Federal Housing Administration therefore currently insures loans up to 90 per cent of park value to encourage park developments. Large insurance companies and corporate conglomerates are moving into the mobile park field, along with their interests in the mobile homes per se. The rate of return on park investments has been running between 20 and 25 per cent. This in itself is a prime motivation for the new entrants into this field. They are bringing with them a high degree of sophistication in management and marketing techniques, together with the facilities and the funds for research and technology.

WHAT OF THE FUTURE?

The future for the mobile home industry forecasts continued gains in sales of individual units and in the marketing of park sites. The growth in sales for the homes themselves has been running between 20 and 25 per cent a year. As this growth is predicated on their relatively low cost; their appeal to the younger and the older segments of our population, both of which show the greatest proportionate growth; their adaptability to the population mobility of our times; the increase in the amenities they provide; and their suitability as second homes - and as all these attributes bode well to continue, the future looks even brighter than the past.

Will modular and sectional housing provide such competition as to make for severe inroads on the mobile home market? It would seem not. As yet, there is no assurance that these types can be constructed in a price range to compete with mobile homes. As yet, there is no volume production of these types.

With the enhancement of the public image of mobile homes, will there be a relaxation of zoning ordinances and building codes to permit their use in areas hitherto barred to them? Yes, there will, but this will take time. Old prejudices die hard. Frozen hostilities take time to thaw.

Will mobile homes anchored to the ground for permanent residence be regarded as real property? Yes, they will, but this will also take time. Laws will have to be changed. Previous court decisions and precedents must be over-ridden. When this time comes, mobile homes will not be open to the charge that they are not paying their fair share of the taxes.

Will the present box-like structures be changed to a more pleasing design? Yes, they will, and this event may signal some merger or meeting with modular and sectional housing.

The mobile home industry is not only a growth industry. It is also a dynamic industry, receptive to innovations and advancing technology, spurred on by these forces.

TRUE AND FALSE QUESTIONS

1. Mobile homes are becoming increasingly popular as second homes.   T   F

2. For the most part, mobile homes are regarded as personal property.   T   F

3. The use of mobile homes is limited to low income groups.   T   F

4. Mobile homes serve primarily as vehicles for vacation trips.   T   F

5. The standard width for mobile homes is now ten feet.   T   F

6. Mobile homes come completely furnished.   T   F

7. The majority of mobile home owners are under thirty-five.   T   F

8. The average mobile home owner has an income slightly below the national average.   T   F

9. Trailers are acquired for travel and recreation.   T   F

10. Lenders now regard mobile home owners as nomads.   T   F

11. A relatively large percentage of defaults is experienced on mobile home loans.   T   F

12. FHA insurance and VA guarantees may be secured on mobile homes.   T   F

13. The interest paid on mobile home loans is not tax deductible.   T   F

14. Most mobile home parks still look like the unsightly trailer courts of the late 1940's.   T   F

15. Service oriented mobile home parks are popular in California.   T   F

16. The most important factor in mobile home park operation is competent management.   T   F

17. The current trend is toward larger mobile home parks.   T   F

18. The supply of mobile home park space exceeds the demand.   T   F

19. It does not now seem that modular housing will compete   T   F
price-wise with mobile homes.

20. The mobile home industry is a growth industry.   T   F

21. Mobile homes are responsive to the mobility nerve in our   T   F
population.

22. Mobile homes come only in standardized form, and options   T   F
for extra amenities are not available.

23. Over 90 percent of new single family homes under $15,000   T   F
are mobile homes.

24. Mobile homes and trailers are now the same size.   T   F

25. The ceiling interest charge on mobile homes is seven per   T   F
cent.

26. The usual loan period on mobile homes ranges from seven   T   F
to ten years.

27. Interest computation on mobile home loans may be the add   T   F
on type.

28. In times of tight credit mobile homes have labored under   T   F
the same difficulties of financing as have conventional
homes.

29. Capital gains tax treatment is not available for mobile   T   F
homes.

30. Mobile homes depreciate at the same rate as con-   T   F
ventionals.

31. Military oriented mobile home parks cater to the temporary   T   F
shelter needs of military personnel.

32. Mobile home parks cannot be set up under the condominium   T   F
arrangement.

33. Mobile home manufacturers may acquire mobile home   T   F
parks as an essential concomitant to the sale of their units.

34. Mobile home parks should be located facing main thorough-   T   F
fare.

35. The rate of return on mobile home park investments has been relatively low.   T   F

36. Mobile homes are so constructed as to be towed on their own chassis.   T   F

37. The prairie schooners of westward migration were among the progenitors of mobile homes as we know them today.   T   F

38. Migratory workers constitute the principal inhabitants of mobile homes.   T   F

39. The floor plans of mobile homes are of uniform design.   T   F

40. Mobile home households commonly consist of two persons.   T   F

MULTIPLE CHOICE

41. Usury regulations on real property loans:
    ( )   May be waived in the case of mobile home loans
    ( )   Do not apply to mobile home loans
    ( )   Are more liberal in the case of mobile home loans
    ( )   May be disregarded if both seller and buyer agree

42. Federal savings and loan associations:
    ( )   Are now authorized to make loans on mobile homes
    ( )   May now make 100 per cent loans on mobile homes
    ( )   Are prohibited from making loans on mobile homes
    ( )   May make loans on mobile homes only to low- and moderate-income families

43. Favorable capital gains tax treatment is available on sale of mobile homes, if:
    ( )   The proceeds from the sale are reinvested in another home at a price the same or higher than that derived from the sale
    ( )   The mobile homes are held under Section 236 of the National Housing Act
    ( )   The mobile homes have been held over six months
    ( )   The installment method of reporting capital gains is employed

44. Mobile home parks serving the housing needs of construction workers are called:
    ( )   Service oriented
    ( )   Industry oriented
    ( )   Construction oriented
    ( )   Project oriented

45. If the resident in a mobile home park receives a deed for the space he occupies and a joint interest in the common elements, this arrangement is:
    ( )   The cooperative type
    ( )   The condominium type
    ( )   The joint tenancy type
    ( )   The tenancy in common type

46. FHA insurance on mobile home parks is now available up to:
    ( )   100 per cent of fair market value
    ( )   90 per cent of fair market value

( )   80 per cent of fair market value
( )   70 per cent of fair market value

47. The renewal of interest in mobile homes came about:
( )   During the depression days of the 1930's
( )   Because of the emergency housing needs of World War I
( )   Because of the lack of conventional housing production during World War II
( )   Because of Operation Breakthrough

48. The loan contract with the mobile home purchaser is commonly originated by:
( )   A second mortgage company
( )   The Federal Housing Administration
( )   The Federal Home Loan Bank System
( )   The mobile home dealer

49. Construction unions have not looked with favor on mobile homes because:
( )   They confuse them with modulars
( )   They see in them a threat to their employment
( )   They fear they will tear down the wage structure of construction unions
( )   Mobile home workers fall under the classification of industrial workers, rather than crafts workers.

50. Space costs in mobile home parks are highest for those that are:
( )   University oriented
( )   Service oriented
( )   Military oriented
( )   Government oriented

ESSAY QUESTIONS

1. What is the future of the mobile home industry?

2. In what respects can it be said that mobile homes have now come of age?

3. What are the specific cost savings in a mobile home?

4. What is the profile of the average mobile home owner?

COOPERATIVES AND CONDOMINIUMS

CHAPTER SEVENTEEN

WHAT IS A COOPERATIVE?

A cooperative is usually a corporation, whose shareholders are occupants of its building, paying monthly carrying charges covering their proportionate share of taxes, mortgage payments, and maintenance on the property. The cooperative corporation may stipulate that its shareholders may sell and assign their stock only to a buyer approved by the cooperative corporation.

Stock ownership entitles the occupants to proprietary leases. These are between the cooperative corporation as landlord and the purchasers of blocks of stock allocated to given units. All the leases expire at the same time. The will of the majority of the tenant-shareholders determines the policy to be pursued thereafter. If the majority so decided, the property could be sold and the proceeds distributed to the tenant-shareholders in proportion to the amount of stock each holds.

Cooperative shareholders customarily pay all cash for their stock. The rent they pay under their proprietary lease is comprised of their proportionate share of mortgage amortization of the cooperative corporation, as well as their share of expenses on the property, such as taxes, insurance, interest on the mortgage loan, labor, fuel, and repairs and maintenance on the parts of the structure used in common with the other tenant-shareholders. As stockholders, the tenants participate in management to the extent of voting for the directors.

It may be that title to the land and building will be taken by a trustee under a trust indenture, rather than by a corporation. The trustee then issues certificates of beneficial interest which entitle the holders to proprietary leases on specific units. Or it may be that the tenant participants belong to a club which owns the land and the building and gives them rights of occupancy to a specific unit by virtue of their membership. If a tenant shareholder fails to pay the assessment against him and it is not possible by legal action to obtain the amount owed, a default arises that must be cured by the other tenant shareholders.

Each tenant shareholder's proportionate obligation is based on the amount and terms of the over-all financing arranged by the cooperative corporation. Even if he should so desire, the tenant shareholder cannot pay cash beyond the down payment required, nor may he avail himself of individual sources of financing providing him with a better financial deal than that secured by the corporation. As a tenant shareholder, he is only a lessee. His property rights are restricted to those of a lessee. His interest is subject to a right of entry reserved to his lessor corporation. He may make use of storage space, laundry facilities, and parking areas only subject to a revocable license.

The cooperative corporation's long term mortgage loan entails no personal obligation on individual tenant shareholders. They are in the same position as shareholders in any corporation. They cannot be reached out of their personal assets for the debts of the corporation. They assume no personal liability for deficiencies in mortgage payments by the cooperative corporation.

"Rental" Charges

The Board of Directors of the cooperative determines operational policies and directs their execution through the manager of their appointment. The manager prepares a budget showing what is required to pay for operational expenses, such as real estate taxes, interest and amortization, insurance, labor and supplies, and a reserve for contingencies. This in turn is divided by the shares allocated to the units and an assessment per share is determined. This is multiplied by the number of shares representing each individual unit, and gives the charge per unit. This is billed as proprietary rent.

Suppose the tenant is unable to pay these charges. He may then resell or sublet in accordance with the terms of his lease. If he continues in defau.., however, he is subject to dispossession and termination of his lease.

The tenant shareholder is responsible for decoration and repairs to his unit. The cooperative corporation is responsible for the public portions of the building, the grounds, and repairs to steam, plumbing, and electrical lines.

As a portion of the "rental" charge is applied towards reduction of the mortgage indebtedness of the cooperative corporation, each payment thus increases the equity of the tenant shareholders. There is no profit to a landlord. There are no problems of periodic lease renewals. The standards of management and operation are maintained through the real estate manager. This prevents curtailment of services, deterioration of the property, and detrimental changes in the property. These "rental" charges may well be less than rent for a comparable unit in a privately owned rental building. The board of directors may increase "rental" charges if necessary to meet increased maintenance expenses.

Cooperative Advantages?

Each tenant shareholder may deduct his proportionate share of the real estate taxes and mortgage interest paid by the cooperative corporation so long as 80 per cent or more of its gross income is derived from tenant-shareholders. If a cooperative unit is employed for the production of income, as in the case of a professional occupant the tenant is permitted to depreciate his equity against his income tax liability.

Cooperative housing requires that the tenant shareholders work together for their joint interests. Hopefully, this should engender a spirit of neighborliness and develop a pride in their surroundings.

By its very definition, the cooperative eliminates the landlord's profit, and should thereby lead to lower occupancy charges.

Federal programs assist low and moderate income families to purchase the shares of stock necessary to qualify them for cooperative tenancy.

Although cooperative leases may have a definite expiration date, they may be automatically renewable or extendable at the will of the proprietary leaseholders.

If the governing board of the cooperative corporation approves, an individual proprietary leaseholder may sell his unit at a profit and retain his capital gain. With the continuance of inflation, the owner of a conventional cooperative could thereby look forward to a potential profit from his holdings.

As a corporate borrower with high credit capacity, the cooperative corporation is in a strategic position to negotiate a favorable interest rate with financial institutions.

WHAT ARE CONDOMINIUMS?

They are unit ownerships usually in multi-unit structures. They are undivided ownerships in the land and parts of the structures used in common with the other occupants. They are both horizontal and vertical divisions of real estate. They may be in the form of high-rise apartments, garden type apartments, town houses, detached single family homes, office buildings, industrial plants, lofts, industrial parks, ski resorts, golf courses, marinas, and beach clubs. The buyer purchases space outright and gets a recordable deed to show for it. He pays taxes on his unit and his interest in the common elements. Most tax assessors evaluate each condominium unit separately.

They are particularly popular in congested areas where land costs make it economical to provide for horizontal ownership at space levels, rather than to build individual units next to each other on a plot of ground. Instead of homes being alongside one another, condominium homes can be placed, one on top the other. They have long been popular in Europe and in South America.

The economics of each owner's liability to maintain the property is established when the condominium is formed. The prospective condominium owners at that time agree on how to manage the building and share in the costs of maintenance. An instrument is drawn up, subjecting the entire property to condominium use, by-laws are framed to govern the building and ground operations, and deeds are made out for the individual units. This governing instrument may be called a "declaration" or a "master deed."

The governing instrument may provide that if a condominium owner wishes to sell, he must first offer his unit to the other co-owners, who have a period of time within which to act. This right of first refusal is often used. If an owner should sell without complying with the right of first refusal, the co-owners would have the right within a limited period to redeem the property at the purchase price. As the governing instrument is made a matter of public record, each prospective buyer is put on constructive notice as to its contents.

The governing instrument describes the land, the common elements, and, likewise, each individual unit. It states the percentage interest of each unit in the common elements. It provides a number or number-letter identification for every unit. It may employ a floor-plan method of dividing the air space among the units. It also provides for a lien on each unit and the interest in the common elements to secure its share of operating costs. It makes provision for rebuilding in the event of destruction or for distribution of the insurance proceeds.

Each condominium deed incorporates the governing instrument by reference and describes space location by the reference numbers and letters set forth in the instrument. It incorporates the percentage of ownership in the common elements of land, basement, heating units, elevators, stairways, parking areas, private roads, recreational facilities, and swimming pools.

Federal Housing Administration insurance on condominium loans is authorized by Section 234 of the National Housing Act. As this applied on a nationwide basis, it provided the impetus for individual states to pass enabling legislation for condominiums in their jurisdictions. All states now have condominium laws.

CONDOMINIUMS VS. RENTING

The condominium owner by virtue of his monthly payments on the principal of his loan is building up an equity in his unit. The renter's monthly payments yield him merely a stack of rent receipts.

The condominium owner may deduct from his income tax liability the real property taxes on his unit together with the portion attributable to him of the taxes on the common elements. The renter has no corresponding recourse. The condominium owner may likewise deduct the interest he pays on his mortgage loan and his share of the interest on the mortgage loan covering the common elements. The renter has no such opportunity.

As opposed to the tenant, the condominium owner can appropriately call the space he occupies his home or office. If it is a retail condo-minium on the street level of a large building, its owner can avoid the rent escalation chargeable against him in proportion to the increase in the amount of his business.

The condominium owner can sell his unit in a rising real estate market and enjoy the capital gain. The renter cannot. Condominiums can be bought now as a hedge against higher prices later on.

Besides carrying with them the satisfactions of ownership, the cost of their ownership will normally be less than the amount of rent that would have to be paid for a corresponding unit. A condominium owner transforms his unit into income property when he rents it out, and, during this period, he may deduct depreciation. A renter has no such opportunity.

By virtue of his undivided interest in the common elements, the condominium owner also enjoys a voice in the management policy applicable the these areas. Such a right is not open to the renter.

CONDOMINIUMS VS. CONVENTIONAL OWNERSHIP

As a condominium owner, you save free time otherwise spent sweating over a lawn mover, rake, or snow shovel. You have no outside maintenance problems. You are no longer burdened physically and psychologically by the exterior chores associated with home ownership. You enjoy all the amenities of a home without having to shoulder the responsibilities for the exterior chores.

In a high rise condominium and a town house condominium, you conserve on land space as compared to a single family home. In a high rise condominium, you make much more use of air space than you would in a single family dwelling.

Because of the wholesale character of its construction, building costs room for room, unit for unit, are less in a condominium than they would be for single family homes.

The condominium's common element can provide for swimming pools, sauna baths, and tennis courts which might be beyond the budget of a single family home owner. By virtue of common use, these facilities are available to condominium owners at much lower individual cost. Recreation rooms can double as meeting rooms or gathering places for parties.

A large condominium can be self-contained and enjoy within its confines such service facilities as a restaurant and cocktail lounge, a grocery and drug store, a beauty parlor and barber shop, and a cleaning and pressing shop. Such conveniences would not be available to a conventional home owner.

CONDOMINIUMS VS. COOPERATIVES

A proprietary lease on a cooperative does not provide ownership. It is the cooperative corporation which owns the land and the buildings. A condominium, on the other hand, gives ownership in the occupied structure, whether it be a town house on the ground or a cube of space in the sky. In a cooperative, a tenant cannot sell his lease without the approval of the governing board. In a condominium, the owner may sell his unit to whom he will, subject to the right of first refusal in the case of the co-owners.

In contradistinction to the cooperative tenant, the condominium owner can properly call his unit his home. He owns it. He negotiates his mortgage on it. He picks the bank or the savings and loan to provide his financing. He pays real property taxes on his unit. He enjoys the same tax advantages as a home owner.

In both the cooperative and the condominium, the cost of maintaining common elements is shared by the occupants. If anyone reneges on his share of these common costs, the others have to assume his obligations. In a cooperative the common costs include real estate taxes and mortgage charges on the entire property. If a tenant cannot meet his share, the remaining members have to assume his obligations. In a condominium, on the other hand, the owner is responsible only for his taxes and mortgage payments, and his alone, just like any other home owner. He is not his brother's keeper, as he would be in a cooperative. If any condominium mortgagor defaults on his indebtedness, it is his mortgagee-creditor that must bear the risk, not the other condominium owners.

As a rule, maintenance and common element costs are more reasonable in a condominium than they are in a cooperative. There is more flexibility in financing the original acquisition in a condominium. There is also more flexibility in re-sales, for the condominium can be refinanced, but the cooperative unit cannot.

RESORT CONDOMINIUMS

The resort condominium enjoys design flexibility and adaptability to almost any location with minimum risk to the developer. For example, the investor appeal of an Aspen, Colorado, condominium project is aptly described as follows: "The apartments gross between $5,000 and $6,000 rental income each year and even more on larger units. Cash outlay for expenses of $2,000 to $2,500 leaves a $3,000 to $4,000 return on the investment. This can be leveraged through borrowing much of the purchase price."

There are resort condominiums, ranging from one room studios to four bedroom villas. Sales price ranges are from $15,000 to $50,000, including furnishings, whose value may be from $3,500 to $10,000.

It is advantageous to plan design so that there is flexibility in rental use. This can be carried out by providing a foyer and equipping each bedroom with its own private bath. A three bedroom apartment with a living room wall bed or convertible sofa can then rent to as many as four separate parties.

If a resort condominium is available for rental over a predominating portion of the year, it will qualify for taking depreciation as against the owner's income tax liability. In such a case, business expenses are also deductible. These will take in maintenance, repairs, insurance, and management fees.

As opposed to single-home resorts, condominium multiples use relatively little land and optimum locations can be enjoyed by a larger number of buyers spreading the cost. Condominium owners can get better mortgage terms because lenders find them a better value at less risk than single family homes.

Resort condominiums enjoy quick sales campaigns per construction segment, thus permitting a developer to move quickly into a large-scale project. If professional management is assured, this proves attractive to potential mortgagee-creditors.

CONDOMINIUM PROVISIONS

A subdivision plat is drawn, dividing the unit spaces into air lots, in a high rise condominium and thereby permitting the conveyance of a particular unit by air lot number. As the plat will not be drawn until the building is erected, this insures that as actually built the units fit into their respective air lots. If the building were destroyed, the sky would still remain subdivided into these separately owned cubes.

The percentage of each condominium's ownership in the common elements is determined on the value this unit bears to the value of the project as a whole. If the unit were valued at $20,000 against a project value of $300,000, the per cent of the undivided interest would be $20,000, divided by $300,000, or 6.666 per cent. Each unit owner would then pay his proportionate share in the common expenses on this basis.

In order to insure that each co-owner pays his proportionate share of the overall charges on the common elements, a lien is reserved on each owner's interest to secure this obligation. This lien gives the right to foreclose on the defaulting party's interest. A power of sale may be attached to this lien and, under this power, a private sale, in many jurisdictions, may be held, thus eliminating court costs and attorney's fees.

The right of first refusal, spelled out in the governing instrument, is inapplicable to any sale under a power or pursuant to foreclosure. It is inapplicable when the owner makes a gift or a devise.

Under the New York Model Statute, followed in many jurisdictions, it may be provided in the governing instrument that if the premises are damaged or destroyed and if a timely decision to rebuild is not made, the individual units shall be deemed to be owned in common by the unit owners. This metamorphosis makes it possible to convey marketable title. The net proceeds from such a sale, together with the insurance received, would constitute a single fund to be divided among the condominium owners, on the basis of their fractional interests. The New York Model Statute goes on to require prompt repair of the damaged premises unless three quarters or more of the building is destroyed and fewer than 75 per cent of the unit owners agree to reconstruct.

By setting up a corporation to control the common elements, the unit owners avoid unlimited personal liability for damages to persons or property on the common elements. The governing instrument will also make public liability insurance mandatory on this corporation.

THE FUTURE OF CONDOMINIUMS

The reasons for buying condominiums in the present apply equally in the future. People like the idea of part ownership of a building but without the outside responsibilities associated with conventional home ownership. People buy condominiums in order to enjoy more free time. Condominiums mean less yard work, limited upkeep, and more time for travel. People buy condominiums because of their desirable locations. They buy them because of the luxuries associated therewith.

People will continue to purchase multiple units in a condominium to rent them out and realize a return on their investment. They are, however, subject to restrictions. FHA-insured condominiums limit ownership to three additional units for any resident owner of a single unit. By-laws may require that units be essentially occupied by their owners.

Condominiums will increasingly provide home ownership for low- and moderate-income groups. Section 235 of the Housing and Urban

Development Act of 1968 provides for mortgage assistance payments to low- and moderate-income purchasers of condominium units. Experience shows that such condominiums will require resident management.

Condominiums are bought and sold through real estate brokers, just as conventional units are. There is competition on this score, however, from the managing agents of the condominium as a whole, possessing the advantage of close contact with would-be sellers and the greater knowledgeability that comes from their management experience and access to condominium records.

To business and professional people, condominium ownership will provide assurance of location and constancy of payments and thereby motivate increasing establishment of commercial condominiums. Industrial parks will find the condominium form well-adapted to their objectives.

But the big market will be in housing. As population expands and housing shortages grow ever more critical, the economy of the condominium and the convenience it affords will enable it to enjoy an increasing share of the housing market.

TRUE AND FALSE QUESTIONS

1. The condominium owner owns his unit and a share in the   T   F
   common elements.

2. Condominiums are vertical, but not horizontal divisions of   T   F
   ownership.

3. A condominium buyer purchases space outright and gets a   T   F
   recordable deed to show for it.

4. A condominium owner is not chargeable for the real   T   F
   property taxes on his interest in the common elements.

5. The governing instrument of a condominium is not made a   T   F
   matter of public record.

6. The deed to the condominium contains the usual warranties   T   F
   as to title.

7. Title insurance may be secured on condominiums.   T   F

8. Although a condominium owner may get Federal Housing   T   F
   Administration insurance, he may not as yet get a Veterans
   Administration guarantee.

9. Condominium owners enjoy a voice in the overall manage-   T   F
   ment of the condominium.

10. If a condominium owner chooses to sell his unit, he may do   T   F
    so only to an overall condominium corporation.

11. Retirement communities have not yet been set up in the   T   F
    form of condominiums.

12. In a high-rise condominium, a subdivision plat is drawn up,   T   F
    dividing the unit spaces into air lots.

13. If a condominium owner defaults on the payment of his   T   F
    share of common charges, a lien may be foreclosed on his
    interest.

14. A condominium owner is usually liable for the personal damages incurred when a third party suffers injury on the common elements.　　T　F

15. The opportunity to defer capital gains tax on the sale of a condominium used as one's personal residence is not available.　　T　F

16. Condominiums as homes are limited to high-rise residential units.　　T　F

17. Condominiums are not being used for office buildings.　　T　F

18. Occupants of a cooperative own a share or shares of stock in a cooperative corporation.　　T　F

19. The ownership of stock in a cooperative corporation entitles the holder to a proprietary lease.　　T　F

20. The cooperative corporation pays the taxes and the interest on the mortgage loan.　　T　F

21. The occupants of a cooperative use the common elements under a revocable license.　　T　F

22. The occupants of a cooperative are subject to the problems inherent in periodic renewals of their leases.　　T　F

23. The occupants of a cooperative have no real property taxes or interest they can deduct from their income tax liability.　　T　F

24. There is no opportunity for the occupants of a cooperative to build up their equity in the property.　　T　F

25. Monthly charges in a cooperative may be increased in the course of a year when necessary to meet increased expenses.　　T　F

26. The lessee in a cooperative does not have to contribute to the profit of a landlord.　　T　F

27. As stockholders, the tenants in a cooperative participate in management to the extent of voting for the directors.　　T　F

28. The economics of each condominium owner's liability to maintain the property is established when the condominium is formed.　　T　F

29. Each condominium owner negotiates his own financing for his own unit.　　T　F

30. If there is a board of directors for the condominium, each   T   F
condominium owner may vote for the nominees of his choice.

31. The mortgage lender to condominium unit owners cannot   T   F
spread his mortgage risks, for these are concentrated in
the corporation.

32. If a condominium high-rise is destroyed, it will be possible   T   F
to identify the cubes of space in the sky belonging to each
unit.

33. Most tax assessors evaluate each condominium unit   T   F
separately.

34. The percentage of each condominium's ownership in the   T   F
common elements is determined usually by the value his
unit bears to the totality of the value of all the units.

35. If a mortgage lender becomes the involuntary owner of a   T   F
condominium unit, he is not chargeable for a share in the
expenses of the common elements.

36. Cooperative shareholders customarily pay cash for their   T   F
stock.

37. The cooperative corporation's long term mortgage loan   T   F
entails no personal obligation on individual tenant shareholders.

38. Cooperative shareholders cannot be reached out of their   T   F
personal assets for the debts of the cooperative corporation.

39. A portion of the "rental" charge in a cooperative is applied   T   F
toward the reduction of the mortgage principal of the
cooperative corporation.

40. Condominiums can be bought as a hedge against inflation.   T   F

MULTIPLE CHOICE

41. The greatest conservation of land space is attained by:
    ( ) Shopping center condominiums
    ( ) High-rise condominiums
    ( ) Townhouse condominiums
    ( ) Garden-type condominiums

42. The lease for cooperative shareholders is:
    ( ) A straight lease
    ( ) A percentage lease
    ( ) A proprietary lease
    ( ) A net lease

43. If a lessee in a cooperative fails to make good on his obligation, his default must be made good by:
    ( ) The other lessees
    ( ) The cooperative corporation
    ( ) His mortgagee-creditor
    ( ) The Federal Housing Administration

44. The lessee in a cooperative may assign or sublet:
    ( ) To anyone he chooses
    ( ) With the approval of the cooperative corporation
    ( ) On the posting of a surety bond
    ( ) With the individual approvals of the other lessees

45. The lessees in a cooperative usually control the standards of management by:
    ( ) Their individual floor committees
    ( ) A cooperative association
    ( ) A separate corporation
    ( ) A real property manager

46. If the overall cooperative corporation defaults on its obligations, the individual tenant-shareholders are:
    ( ) Subject to the attachment of their personal assets
    ( ) Immune from personal liability
    ( ) Subject to personal bankruptcy proceedings
    ( ) Subject to an assessment on their stock

47. For decoration and repairs to the unit he occupies, the tenant-shareholder in a cooperative is:

( ) Personally responsible
( ) Able to look to the cooperative corporation for these charges
( ) Subject to a 50 per cent assessment
( ) Responsible for decoration, but not for repairs

48. The governing instrument for a condominium subjects:
( ) Part of the property for cooperative use and part for con-
dominium use
( ) The entire property for condominium use
( ) The ground floor for conventional use, and the upper floors,
for condominium use
( ) The property to an easement for a condominium

49. The opportunity for other condominium owners to buy the unit of
an owner who chooses to sell is called:
( ) An option
( ) A pre-emptive right
( ) The right of first refusal
( ) A purchase agreement

50. A condominium owner may get FHA insurance on his unit up to a
percentage of its:
( ) Cost
( ) Book value
( ) Liquidation value
( ) Appraised value

ESSAY QUESTIONS

1. What are the basic advantages of the cooperative?

2. What are the advantages of condominium ownership as against renting?

3. What are the advantages of condominium ownership as against conventional?

RESORT AND RETIREMENT REAL ESTATE

CHAPTER EIGHTEEN

RESORT REAL ESTATE

In all the fields of real estate, there is none showing more growth than resort and retirement real estate. The reason they are linked together is because resort areas are so often chosen as places for retirement.

Sparking the growth of resort real estate is the affluence of America, putting resort pleasures within the economic reach of the average family.

The market for resort real estate has likewise expanded with the increase in life expectancies and the desire of older people for a resort locale in their retirement years.

The increase in vacation time, from two weeks to three, and now even four and five, brings about a corresponding increase in the demand for resort facilities. Many of us now take both a summer and a winter vacation and may thereby enjoy, for example, both Maine and Florida alike. And as time goes on our vacations will lengthen even more.

The provision of fast interstate highways and other improved arterial facilities makes it so much easier now to get to the resorts of our desire. In fact, we no longer think of the distance in mileage to our favorite resort, but rather in terms of the driving time required. All this makes resorts seem so much closer. Or we may fly to our destination and rent a car at journey's end.

We Americans like to travel. Getting to resorts is half the fun. "Go now, pay later" plans have been established, enabling us to arrange our financing on easy terms. In fact, travel clubs are currently soliciting our memberships on this basis. We can make periodic payments in advance to them, just as we would do in a Christmas Club, and when the time comes, our transportation expenses have already been provided. Besides financing our transportation, travel clubs will arrange our itineraries and book our reservations. Where travel groups are assembled, travel clubs will try to provide for an even male and female mix, participant sports, and music and entertainment.

Also, more and more of us are acquiring a second home on the beach or in the mountains for resort purposes. Such seasonal homes now enjoy the financial advantage of Federal Housing Administration loan insurance. We may fashion their decor and facilities to suit the tastes and desires of ourselves and our families. We may rent the home and secure an attractive income from it during the "season" and we and our families may use it during the "off season". And, during the period it is in rental status, it is, of course, income property and subject to the tax advantage of depreciation.

We will find that we can effect substantial savings to ourselves by reason of our resort second homes. They save us the travel expense to resorts far afield. They save us the lodging expense we would incur elsewhere. And we are happy in the status symbol they provide.

We also enjoy recreational advantages in our resort second homes. They establish the base for father and son combinations on hunting trips. They can be used for executive retreats in a sports paradise. Where hunting lodges and sports safaris are established in connection with them and when these are used to win and keep customers, and, providing we can get approval from the Internal Revenue Service, these second homes may constitute a tax deductible benefit for us.

Resort Real Estate Promotions

Many and varied are the appeals to promote resort real estate. There are the "See America first" campaigns. These have a patriotic ring and keep our money at home, rather than sending it abroad.

Many of us have taken up photography as a hobby, in some cases even doing the development work ourselves. As camera fans, we become responsive to the photographic allurements of scenic resorts.

Or we may take up boating for all the delights it affords. What could be more natural, therefore, than for us to be sold on the delights of having our own boats at the shore resorts of our choice!

Business conferences always seem to be more fun when held at resort retreats. We can mix recreation and relaxation with the seriousness of the thought provoking sessions.

Or, as members of conservation organizations, like the Audubon Society or the Sierra Club, we may hold our get-togethers at resort facilities adjacent to wildlife sanctuaries and scenes of bird migrations. We will enjoy the thrill of photographing and recording the birds and wildlife we have seen. We will be reclaiming our outdoor heritage.

Some resort promotions identify resorts with culture as well as with sport, like the highly successful promotion of Aspen, Colorado, where skiing and studying meet. A session with Goethe in the morning may precede the ski slopes in the afternoon.

Taking a leaf out of Florida's success book, more and more resorts are converting from seasonal to year-round. Florida at one time was just a winter resort, but it was successfully promoted by reason of lower rates and the maintenance of high resort standards into "sun and fun" the year round. Just three quarters of a century ago Florida was the winter retreat of a handful of rich and famous persons. Today, on a year round basis, it is the destination of more than 20 million in all income brackets.

Some resort promotions publicize special events, such as New Orleans' Mardi Gras and Carnival - marathons of social whirls, tableau balls, and spectacular street parades. Washington, D. C., has long been a tourist mecca at its cherry blossom time. Holland, Michigan's tulip festival attracts thousands of visitors every year. The world fairs in New York, Seattle, San Antonio and Montreal have established new highs in tourist promotions.

Skiing

When an area becomes popular for skiing, real estate values soar. Sales of residential lots take off and boom. Real estate values double and triple their original projections.

Time was when the skier had to count the pennies and brought along his lunch in a paper bag. Time was when he bunked in a dormitory. Now his profile is changing. Now the typical skier spends $40 a day at a plush resort, $7.50 of which goes for his lift ticket and at least $20.00 for his room. The ski area, rather than the skier's pocketbook, dictates how much he spends.

Making a success out of a ski resort comes about by attracting the fast-spending jet set by becoming known as a total resort. The resort is so planned as to have within it everything the skier wants - the lift, the attractive hotel, and the glamorous cocktail lounge and restaurant. First class surroundings enable you to unwind after a vigorous day on the slopes. Servicing airlines are promoting "package deals", including in them both transportation and accomodations.

Life is casual at ski resorts. There is lots of socializing as well as skiing. Camaraderie reaches its peak in the game room, the living room with its huge log-burning fireplace, or at the convivial bar. Local art festivals, carnivals, and shows abound. You can have it as exciting as you want - boisterous beer gardens, apres-ski pubs, intimate gourmet restaurants, and candlelight dinner dancing.

Snowmobiling

This new sport will likewise promote the outdoor life and resort facilities. It combines the thrills of skiing and bob-sledding. Towns, hotels, and resort areas that went into hibernation during the winter are now stirring out of their sleep with the snowmobile and the tourism it attracts with "snowfaris", "snodeos", and "sno-mo-cades".

There are now over a quarter million snowmobiles in use in North America, and over 200,000 additional units are currently being produced. There are 1,000 snowmobile clubs in the United States and about double that number in Canada. Anyone, from eight to 80, can handle a snowmobile. It is the fastest growing winter sport in North America.

Resorts catering to winter trade are acquiring snowmobiles for rental to their patrons and are likewise developing nearby areas for snowmobile use. Ski areas also have snowmobiles for rent and have developed trails where they can be used.

Tracts of land are being converted into "snow ranches", where fans pay $5.00 for a half hour of snowmobiling. Snowmobile marathons are bringing additional business to the resorts which promote them. Many golf courses are enjoying additional revenue by opening their fairways and roughs to snowmobilers.

Boating and Fishing

Boating is so popular in resort areas that the demand for cottages and resort facilities along the boating shore has soared. Developers are also combining subdivisions of luxury vacation homes with expanding hotel operations along scenic shorelines of lake and sea. More and more people now crave the good life afloat, and the demand for houseboats is outrunning the supply. Aquahomes are being rented out to vacationers by resort operators.

Gambling and Resort Real Estate

How can we explain Las Vegas, Nevada? It can't be its climate. It is located in parched and windswept country. It can't be its accessibility. Even in the jet age, it is hours away from the eastern seaboard. It can be explained only in terms of something in human nature - the desire to take a chance, the wish to make a "fast buck", the exhilaration that come with "the big kill", and the "kicks" from the jackpot. "Free nylons with jackpot", "bingo for the discriminating player", "the ultimate sin machine" - these are among the signs providing the backdrop for this exciting city, jammed with people looking intently at the tables and slot machines.

And the races at Hialeah and Tropical Park play their magnetic role in bringing tourists to Miami. They have their counterparts elsewhere in other horse, dog, and trotting races. Resort real estate is in demand, not only for the racing provided, but also for the hotels and the motor inns, the bars and the nightclubs, and the gourmet restaurants and smart shops that service those in attendance.

With state laws becoming more liberal and permitting betting on the races, more race tracks will spring up near resort areas, and provide an added allurement. Ever more tourists will be coming in and the facilities to accommodate them will be built. As gambling is the prime profit motive, the entertainment, the room charges, and the meals may, as in the case of Las Vegas, be modestly priced.

Motor Inns

This is a growth industry for fair. It will increase in numbers in the United States by 30 per cent by 1976. It belongs under resort real estate, for vacationists, business confereees, and week-enders all converge on it facilities.

Motor inns are increasingly catering to conferences and conventions, meetings and seminars. Over and above providing relaxation for the off-moments, they have rooms large enough for assemblies, audio-visual aids, projectors for opaque representations, screens and blackboards, and facilities for demonstrations.

Motor inns with their putting greens, swimming pools, shuffle board courts, sauna baths, dancing and entertainment, likewise cater to family groups. They make reservations for their guests at other motor inns. Their covered areas for entrance into their public rooms give the shelter required. They are conveniently located, often near the access or egress road to an interstate highway. Their outdoor signs give directions on how to reach them. They give their guests booklets, showing the locations of other inns in their chain, together with the rates charged. Their guest rooms frequently contain magazines with interesting articles and stories on the scenic and other attractions of the areas they serve. Their standards of service, decor, food, and rooms correspond throughout their chain. This gives the traveler the assurance of knowing just what he is to get wherever he stops.

Franchising plays a leading role in motor inns. Franchises authorize motor inns to operate under the name of the franchisor, such as Holiday Inn. Franchises give the franchisor's management techniques and specialized staff services to the franchise for a fee. Franchises benefit through increased occupancy by reservation referrals from the franchisor's electronic computer, guest cards, purchasing power, and marketing programs.

The franchised properties must be located where there is a need for motor inn facilities. They must be financed on a conservative basis. They should be sponsored by individuals or investing groups of established reputation. Actually, most motor inn franchise chains are networks of individually owned units.

In addition to the income the motor inn chain derives from the sale of its franchise, it also enjoys fees from the units serviced and sales of its subsidiaries, such as sales of food, linens, supplies, and equipment.

Certain of the chains own outright some of the units in their network. It is interesting that Howard Johnson seems to have recently changed its policy from one of franchising to one of outright ownership, thinking thereby to secure closer control over its operations. Sixty per cent of their motor inns are now company owned as against 47 per cent in 1960.

Some motor inns in resort areas are alleged to be owned and controlled by the Mafia, but this allegation has not cut down on their patronage. Guests seem to be far more concerned about the state of their suntan than whether the bellhop is a hood. Travel agents seem unconcerned, selling the motor inn on its service, not on who owns it.

Motor inn chains are now bent on their largest expansion programs ever, making their guest rooms not only more generous in size, but better arranged for maximum comfort and usefulness.

Resorts — A Summing Up

The past, present, and future of resort real estate may be best appreciated by an analysis of changes in the American way of life. Increasingly, Americans are taking to the out of doors. The big factor at work is rising income. Preference, rather than necessity, dictates how it is spent. What was done in necessity years ago is now being done for pleasure and recreation. The outdoor heritage of America is being reclaimed.

Many American families believe that the ultimate in affluent good living is not just a second car in the garage, but a second home in the driveway. This second home is a recreational vehicle, ranging from the camper type to the travel trailer and the motor home. Two million recreational vehicles are now on the highways.

A four-day week for all workers is now the top bargaining and legislative objective of organized labor. It believes that this new objective can be won within the next four years and without a reduction in earnings.

Congress has already voted many three-day holiday weekends and longer vacations have shrunk the standard work year of 2,080 hours substantially. The unions are even now driving in Congress to get the Fair Labor Standards Act amended to make the 32-hour workweek universal. The added leisure time will in large part be spent in vacationing in resort areas.

Affluent Americans have boomed leisure into an 83-billion-dollar business. This tops the annual outlays for national defense. Much of this goes into travel and motor inns, into summer homes and vacation retreats. Self-powered motor homes now rate as the mansions of the highways.

The Forestry Service is studying the trend of second homes so as to better estimate demands on natural resources. The data they collect will be of great import in forecasting second home demand.

Vacation condominiums are in increasing demand. They are a booming part of the real estate business and are selling fast. They provide built-in recreation facilities, domestic services, and property maintenance. They afford the opportunity to profit from management-supervised rental of property when you are not there. They offer a vast variety of locations and prices. If you rent them out part time, you can deduct, for that period, for insurance, repairs and maintenance, and depreciation. Your opportunity for a sizable capital gain in the event of sale is good. Many condominiums have jumped in value 25 per cent to 40 per cent inside of two years.

America is looking for a place to go. Although Florida still holds first place in tourism, seven other states are hotly competing for an increasing share. Tourism is among the top three revenue producers in each of the 50 states and is, by all odds, the nation's fastest growing industry. Population growth, a rise in automobile travel, more leisure time, the jumbo jets, and higher incomes all contribute to this rise.

And let's not forget the black travel market. There are 22,600,000 black Americans. A large proportion in times past have been denied the freedom of travel and resort opportunities. Now these privileges are theirs. They want an excursion into another environment where they can be flattered into being someone else. They like to travel in groups - and for psychological reasons. They can lean on each other for courage and companionship on journeys into new areas. Travel to resort areas enables them to get away from the frustrating daily reminder of what they have been, to the welcome glare of what they would like to be. Their payment of their travel bills is outstanding.

RESORT RETIREMENT COMMUNITIES

Their growth is remarkable. And there are many reasons. One is earlier retirements. Many organizations now have provisions for retirement at 55 or younger. Life expectancy is increasing and, therefore, proportionately more people are of retirement age. There is a natural desire for independence in one's later years and the financial ability to gratify this desire. There is a satisfaction that comes from consort with one's peers. The facilities are available in resort retirement communities for the gratification of hobbies and sports inclinations.

Over and above the retirement pay from their employers, older people now get retirement annuities from their insurance carriers, investment income from their real estate and blue chip stock portfolios, and the financial assistance of both Medicare and Medicaid.

Older people now have a wide variety of resort retirement communities from which to pick. They have variety in the choice of climate. They have variety in the choice of individually owned conventional homes, cooperatives, or condominiums. They have variety in the type of operation - commercially or charitably operated. They may choose communities set up as separate legal entities devoid of school age children, and, therefore, the serious tax burdens of school districts.

Resort retirement communities can provide mild climate, mild recreation, and a mild life under the sun. They can make available comfortable, but not demanding homes. These can be large enough for spacious living, but small enough for effortless living. They can be located close to houses of worship, shopping centers, bowling greens, golf courses, shuffleboard courts, and public transportation. Their location can provide all the amenities of country living and still keep the excitement of the big city within easy reach.

Resort retirement communities try to provide the activities the residents enjoyed back home. So there are meetings and luncheons of service clubs, the camaraderie of fraternal and sorority organizations, the interests of hobby societies, the get-togethers of veterans associations, and panels and discussion groups on topics of both general and specialized interest.

They make it a point to be equipped with the features required for comfort and convenience. And so you find handholds at the end and at the side of the bathtub. You see shower rods that will support a person's weight. You walk over nonskid strips in the bathtub. The doors are wide enough to admit a wheelchair, and ramps and grab rails are present.

Contrary to popular notion, retirement communities are increasing in the north. A northern location permits many residents to keep their roots in the areas where they have spent most of their lives. The northern location may be closer to children and grandchildren, as well as friends of long standing. And a northern location may be nearer the attractions of metropolitan areas.

The Developers of Resort Retirement Communities
Some have been a stigma to the real estate profession. Some have sold tracts in desert wasteland, representing them as attractive resorts. Some have stated that all utilities were available, only to have a complete absence of water, telephones, and electricity. Some have sold land under water, lots without roads, homes without sewage disposal - all completely contrary to the lavish pronouncements in their brochures.

Some have sold swamps, lake bottoms, muck pockets, and jungles as investment acreage. Others have used high pressure tactics, befuddling entertainment, and "free trips" to the site to get retirees to "sign on the dotted line". Others have glossed over taxes, development costs, "add-on fees", and understated "carrying charges".

The foregoing have been distinctly in the minority, but the tactics in which they engaged have been so publicized as to create in the minds of many people an unfavorable public image of resort retirement community developments. So - for the record - let it be said: Most developers have been conscientious and have striven to do a good job. Many developers have built self-contained communities from scratch. They have provided not only the roads and public utilities, but also the churches, shopping centers, and public buildings.

To protect retirees, state laws may now require that the developer file with public authorities an offering statement on the sponsor, property, terrain, utilities, sewage, and financial status and responsibility of the developer. They may also stipulate that the developer give every customer a sworn report detailing all the bad features of the property and that he post bond guaranteeing that roads and utilities will be in place at the time retirees are ready to move in. State laws may also regulate the developer by checking up on his financial resources, by prohibiting false and misleading advertising, and by revoking the license of any developer who fails to make full disclosure regarding the location of the property and character of its drainage. Some states require that state officials go to the out of state site of the development and see for themselves whether it lives up to its representations before any state real estate broker may offer it for sale.

The Federal Housing Act of 1968 also provides protection from the Federal level. Under this Act, it is unlawful for a developer to sell or lease through the mails or otherwise in interstate commerce any lot in any subdivision of 50 or more lots offered as part of a common promotional plan, unless:

1. The subdivision is registered with the Department of Housing and Urban Development.
2. A printed property report is furnished to the buyer in advance of the signing of an agreement for sale or lease.

Comments

Resort retirement communities qualify potential residents by ascertaining whether their health is such as to enable them to fit in. Their health histories are scrutinized and they are made subject to medical examination.

They also qualify potential residents on the basis of their ability to carry the financial load. They determine whether the applicant has sufficient financial resources to cover the purchase of his unit. They find out whether he can carry the monthly maintenance charges imposed. They ascertain whether the applicant has a financial reserve sufficient to cover any financial contingencies that may arise.

Resort retirement communities further qualify potential residents on the basis of their compatibility in educational and cultural background, in service, in hobbies and recreational pursuits, in respect and tolerance for those of other religious faiths, and in consideration for the rights of others.

Resort retirement communities are hard put to find a name that will not stamp their occupants old, put on the shelf, and being turned out to pasture, but will nevertheless indicate their true character. Among the names that have been acceptable are "Leisure World", "Holiday City", and "Sun City", but the search still goes on.

The growth of resort retirement communities is assured, due to increased life expectancies, earlier retirements, and increased retirement incomes. The majority will cater to the middle income class. The higher income class can afford to tailor facilities to suit individualized taste and preferences. The lower income class will not afford resort retirement communities as presently constituted.

Nursing homes, likewise are also a growth industry. They presently have more beds than do all the hospitals combined. They have shown a remarkable increase in number since Medicare and Medicaid. They have proven quite profitable. They provide more intensive medical care than resort retirement communities; they are usually staffed with a doctor and nurses; and their guests may range from the bed-ridden to the reasonably healthy. Some of their patients may be senile, but the majority have full use of all their faculties.

TRUE AND FALSE QUESTIONS

1. Resort pleasures are now within the economic reach of the average family.   T   F

2. The increase in vacation time brings about a corresponding increase in the demand for resort facilities.   T   F

3. Seasonal homes do not qualify for FHA insurance.   T   F

4. Snowmobiling is the fastest growing winter sport in North America.   T   F

5. Motor inns do not cater to family groups.   T   F

6. Franchising plays a minor role in motor inns.   T   F

7. Most motor inns are individually owned.   T   F

8. Motor inns have decidedly curtailed their expansion programs.   T   F

9. The outlays for leisure are now second only to the outlays for defense.   T   F

10. Vacation cooperatives are now more in demand than vacation condominiums.   T   F

11. Tourism is now the nation's fastest growing industry.   T   F

12. Florida still holds first place in tourism.   T   F

13. The black travel market is of sizable potential.   T   F

14. The increase in the birth rate has been offset by the decrease in life expectancy.   T   F

15. Retirement communities have not taken hold in the north.   T   F

16. Developers are now regulated both by state and Federal laws.   T   F

17. The majority of retirement communities will cater to the   T   F
    middle class.

18. Nursing homes are a growth industry.   T   F

19. Nursing homes now have more beds than do all the hospitals T   F
    combined.

20. Nursing homes take in only the bed-ridden as their guests. T   F

21. The majority of the patients in nursing homes are senile.   T   F

22. Financial assistance to those in nursing homes is available T   F
    from Medicare, but not from Medicaid.

23. The lower income class cannot afford resort retirement   T   F
    communities as they are presently constituted.

24. Resort retirement communities usually bear this name.   T   F

25. If a development must be registered under the Federal   T   F
    Housing Act, this registration must be with the Department
    of Housing and Urban Development.

26. Resort retirement communities qualify potential residents   T   F
    in part on the basis of their ability to carry the financial load.

27. Retirement communities are only charitably operated.   T   F

28. Aqua-homes are located along the shoreland.   T   F

29. Only younger persons are able to handle snowmobiles.   T   F

30. A total ski resort is one which has within it everything the T F
    skier wants.

31. Tourists now think in terms of driving time to their favorite T F
    resorts, rather than in terms of the mileage required.

32. The spending profile of the skier has changed in recent   T   F
    years.

33. Snowmobile marathons are now being promoted.   T   F

34. Increasingly, Americans are taking to the out of doors for T   F
    their vacations.

35. The majority of new labor union contracts now provide   T   F
    for the four-day week.

36. Vacation condominiums now afford the opportunity to profit from management-supervised rentals when the owners are not there. T F

37. Many large employers now have provisions for retirements at 55 or even younger. T F

38. Retirement communities may be set up as separate legal entities devoid of school age children, and their tax burdens. T F

39. Resort retirement communities try to provide the activities their residents enjoyed back home. T F

40. Many developers have provided the roads, public utilities, the schools, the public buildings, and the shopping centers for their developments. T F

MULTIPLE CHOICE

41. It is unlawful for a developer to sell or lease through the mails or otherwise in interstate commerce any lot in any subdivision of 50 or more lots offered as part of a common promotional plan, unless the subdivisions:
    ( ) Is registered with the State Real Estate Commission
    ( ) Is registered with the National Association of Real Estate Boards
    ( ) Provides a printed property report to be furnished to the buyer
    ( ) Is registered with the Securities and Exchange Commission

42. Motor inn franchises:
    ( ) Usually provide limited partnership participations for the franchisee
    ( ) Authorize the franchisee to operate under the franchisor's name
    ( ) Operate on the basis of percentage leases
    ( ) Usually provide for equity participations on the part of the franchisee

43. Unions are now driving in Congress to get the Fair Labor Standards Act amended:
    ( ) To make the closed shop mandatory
    ( ) To make the 32-hour week universal
    ( ) To make the 25-hour week the standard
    ( ) To require double time for hours worked beyond 32 in any one week

44. The black population in the United States has now reached:
    ( ) 22,600,000
    ( ) 22,000,000
    ( ) 32,000,000
    ( ) 32,600,000

45. Checking up on potential residents of retirement communities to make sure they meet the standards specified is called:
    ( ) Registering
    ( ) Qualifying
    ( ) Classifying
    ( ) Investigating

46. Among the names found acceptable for retirement communities is:
    ( ) 60 plus
    ( ) Senior citizens
    ( ) Sun City
    ( ) Sunset years

47. The chief criticism leveled at developers of retirement communities is that they:
    ( ) Have not agreed to limited dividend status
    ( ) Have been guilty of discrimination
    ( ) Have engaged in high pressure sales tactics
    ( ) Have not been sufficiently discriminating in their selection members

48. Among the advantages of a northern location to most residents of retirement communities is:
    ( ) That they can continue to enjoy the stimulating winters
    ( ) Can continue to engage in all the usual winter sports
    ( ) Can keep their roots in areas where they have spent most of their lives
    ( ) Can thereby maintain their memberships in the Audubon Club and the Sierra Society

49. Among the reasons for the growth in vacation or second homes is:
    ( ) The financial assistance for them made possible by the Farmers Home Administration
    ( ) The insurance provided by the Farm Credit Administration
    ( ) The increasing number of mini-weekends made possible by the transplantation of most legal holidays to Monday
    ( ) Credit life insurance

50. "Go Now, Pay Later Plans" for vacations are now being promoted by:
    ( ) Life insurance companies
    ( ) Travel clubs
    ( ) Savings and loan associations
    ( ) Mutual savings banks

ESSAY QUESTIONS

1. How do you account for the success of the total ski resort?

2. What is the attraction of snowmobiling?

3. What is the role of franchising in motor inns?

PART VII
FARM, COMMERCIAL,
AND INDUSTRIAL
REAL ESTATE

FARM
REAL ESTATE

CHAPTER NINETEEN

NOSTALGIA AND REALITY

Time was when we were a rural nation. Most of our productivity sprang from the soil and we worked sun-up to sun-down and at farm chores before and after. Time was when the farmer was the backbone of the country.

That time was, but it has gone forever. Values, it nurtured; people, it built; virtues, it instilled. But now a different scene unfolds. Where crops once grew, "estate developments" rear their ugly heads. Farm land gives way to "hen coop housing" and "trailer tenants". The backroads of yesteryear become the demon speed highways of today. The pastoral quiet of rural retreat becomes the horrendous shrieking of horror films at the drive-in movie. The hot rod takes over where the horse and buggy left off. The shrill cry of writhing brakes replaces the calm and serenity of countryside solitude.

THE DYNAMICS OF CHANGE

Farms are consolidating to spread costs over a broader area. Farms of years ago are becoming the suburbia and exurbia of today. Farms are being taken over as the sites for new industrial plants, shopping centers, and housing developments.

The small farmer is having a hard time making a go of it. A wheat farmer can no longer survive on an 80 or a 160 acre tract. Hedged in by crop restrictions, cramped by low prices for farm products, he can no longer keep pace with advancing costs. He can use his mechanical equipment - his combines, seeders, plows, tractors, and cultivators - only for a short time each crop year. If he is to stay in farming, he has to increase his yeild by acquiring other farms or by acting as a tenant for absentee landlords. If he cannot do this, he must sell out to others. His farm becomes merged into larger ones, and a more practicable economic unit emerges. The individual farmer bows out and the corporate farmer moves in.

FARM LISTINGS

Exclusive right to sell listings are always important, but especially so in the case of farms. The agent must have full control over the sale. He cannot run the risk of having the farm sold out from under him at the time he is negotiating with a prospective purchaser.

As in the case of all properties, the best way to secure farm listings is by having a reputation for honest, efficient and effective service. Here, above all, word of mouth advertising from satisfied customers is supremely important. Such referrals bring to you the majority of your farm listings.

You will be helped in securing listings through the contacts you develop by virtue of membership in and association with farm organizations. You will find centers of influence among local farm machinery representatives, who may be the first to hear of intentions to sell a farm. Your friendship with them will be worth its weight in gold. Your contacts with local attorneys will pay off in the form of knowledge as to when farms presently held in an estate will be put up for sale. Your "Sold" signs on farms will recommend you to prospective listers.

You can get listings from farmers who start out by trying to sell their farms themselves. You must be able to show them that you can do more for them than they could do for themselves and that this is more than worth the commission you will derive. You will speak more persuasively if you yourself have had farming experience. You can then talk the farmer's language. You will have an insight into farm problems. You will gain the farmer's respect.

FARM PROSPECTS

You find them through your contacts with farm machinery organizations and farm associations. You develop lists of farm property investors. You check the neighbors of your listed farm. They may want to add to their present acreage. You talk with farm tenants. They may desire to own farms themselves. You find out who the farmers are who desire to expand. A grain farmer may want to round out his operation with a stock farm. A stock farmer may desire to round out his operation with a grain farm.

You find prospects among land speculators. You may interest them in the possibilities of your listing becoming the site of a residential development, shopping center, or industrial plant. You develop prospects among food processing businesses. They may want farm land as a feeder to their operation. A canner may want to acquire a vegetable farm. A frozen food company may want to acquire an orchard. And, in these inflationary times, you find prospects who desire land ownership as a hedge against inflation and who enjoy the thrill of complete control and possession of a piece of mother earth.

Developing your prospects is one thing. Qualifying them is another. The guiding principle here is to get the prospect to do what is best for him. You therefore find out what his experience and record show he is best qualified to do in farming, and you steer him to the type of listing that will match. You find out what his financial position is to determine whether he can make the down payment and sustain the mortgage indebtedness. You find out his family situation so as to determine whether his wife and children will help with the operation.

FARM SHOWINGS

By knowing your prospect, you, in turn, will know what features to stress at the time of the showing. By knowing the reason your prospect wants to buy, you can concentrate on what your listing has that ties in with this reason. If there are detracting features, point them out before the prospect himself becomes aware of them.   Otherwise, he will suspect you of concealment.

If there are tenants on the farm, they will usually not be cooperative, for they will see their own ouster as a result of the sale. You will therefore avoid them, if you can.

You will point out the possibilities of higher yields through better management and land use. You yourself must know what the land is best suited for. Its present low yield may be due to planting corn where wheat should grow. Or the land may have been "wheated" to death and its exhaustion spelled out in its declining production. You will point out that it needs rest and recuperation through the life giving forces of soil enrichment, rather than soil depletion.

FARM CLOSINGS

It is never too early to close, so long as you sense the prospect is ripe and ready. It is always a mistake to try to close when the prospect is not ready. If negotiations have reached a stalemate, don't become impatient. Get the prospect to understand you want him to have plenty of time to make the decision that will best serve his interest. You will take care to avoid the use of any terms - financial, or otherwise - that the prospect does not thoroughly understand.

Your sales presentation will encompass the yield as determined by authenticated records over a reasonable period of time, the taxes, improvements, acreage, the topography, access to transportation arteries, soil conservation measures and their results, farm subsidy payments, tax advantage of deduction of conservation expenses, analyses made of soil content, the sales prices on comparables, and potential of land development.

It helps to frame your questions to the prospect to elicit agreement. This puts him in the proper psychological mood for the sale. If you sense the prospect is ready but will not offer the price listed, it will help to get his name on the purchase agreement, anyway. It is easier to negotiate later if he has already put down his signature.

Once the purchase agreement has been signed by both parties, crucial steps remain to be taken. You must estimate closing costs as accurately as you can and the reason for the inclusion of each and get the buyer to understand their why and wherefore. The terms of the sale must be fully spelled out in the closing agreement and made clear to both parties.

FARM KNOWLEDGE

The farm salesman must know farm buildings and machinery. He must know feeding operations, stock breeds, and crops. He must be familiar with the new varieties of grains and their potential. Government farm programs, farm bookkeeping, irrigation, and land use must be part of his everyday knowledge.

You as an effective farm salesman should know what comparable land has been selling for. This is the most persuasive evidence you can furnish both lister and prospect. But you will have problems.

There may have been no recent sales. Farm commodities may have gone up or down in price since the last sale. Government controls, parity price support plans, diversion programs and payments by the Federal government for compliance change periodically, and in themselves make for differences in income from one time to another.

Basically, your prospect wants to know whether the farm can make money for him. This depends on its price, its size, its crop yields and its livestock production, the productivity of the soil, and the utility value of its improvements.

Your knowledge should enable you to prepare a brochure for each of your farm listings. This should contain location, description, price, soil types, capital improvements, water supply, timber, taxes, and inventories of livestock and machinery. You should supplement this with a map showing field layouts with acreage, building set-ups, and productivity history.

Your brochure should be complete, to give cooperating brokers all the data they require. It should be persuasive, to get potential buyers to make inspections. You will follow it up with phone calls and personal contacts.

FARM FINANCING

Farm financing is long term. You should find out the practices and policies of your local lenders for such long term financing secured by farm land. They may finance on the basis of mortgages or land contracts. Land contracts may be preferred in jurisdictions where, in the event of default by the borrower, action to regain possession is shorter and less expensive than mortgage foreclosure proceedings.

You will find out from lending institutions the type of farm property acceptable for loan, the term of the loan, the maximum percentage of property value loaned, the maximum amount loaned, the amortization requirements, and the prepayment privileges available. You will also find out the terms on which your prospects can secure the equipment they require.

Before institutional lenders will advance their money on farms as security, they will require that an appraisal of the farm be made. They will also ask for a survey to make sure that the actual dimensions accord with those as stated in the mortgage.

FARM DESCRIPTIONS

Farm descriptions often begin near the center of the state. From this point the state is laid out in townships. A line running east and west from this point is called the base, and another line running north and south is named the meridian. The base line is broken down into ranges and each range covers one township. A township is six miles square. Each township contains 36 sections. A section is one mile square, and contains 640 acres.

Land may also be described by metes and bounds. Metes mean measures. Bounds mean distances. They are appropriately called a walk-around description. You start from a certain point, preferably a readily identifiable one, such as the nearest corner of a quarter section. You then state the distance to the point of your parcel and the direction you follow to get to it. From here, depending on the size of the parcel, you would state, for example, that you would go 100 acres to the north, 100 acres to the east, 100 acres to the south, and, from here, back to the point of origin.

FARM SOILS

A horizon is a horizontal layer of soil, parallel to the surface, a particular soil being made up of several horizons of different textures. A profile is a vertical cross-section of a soil, showing the several horizons of which it is constituted.

A series is a group of soils having similar horizons. An example would be a group of dark grayish, brown-surface soils.

A soil map is an indication of the soil types that will be found on a particular farm. If the soil is acid, for example, it should be limed for best results with legumes.

The soil map may show that erosion has removed most of the surface. The land may have been cropped too heavily, and its productive possibilities thereby weakened.

FARM TAX FACTORS

Farms are income properties and depreciation may therefore be taken on farm buildings and equipment used for the production of income. Depreciation is a deduction against ordinary income. It represents tax-free cash.

Farm sales enjoy favorable capital gains treatment, the benefits of "tax-free exchanges", installment sale reporting and deferred payment options. If a large capital gain tax would apply when a farm is sold, the owner should be told of the opportunity of tax deferral by resort to an exchange. If the farmer is about to retire, he might be amenable to an exchange of his farm property for city income property.

Under the tax reform laws effective in 1970, there are provisions intended to defeat the chances of a high-bracket taxpayer being able to convert ordinary income into capital gain through the use of farm losses and later sale of the farm property at capital gain rates. The gain from a sale will be taxed as ordinary income to the extent of the farmer's losses that have been used to reduce nonfarm income. But an individual farmer will be subject to these recapture rules only if his nonfarm adjusted gross income exceeds $50,000 and his farm net loss is over $25,000.

FROM FARM TO SUBDIVISION

A great deal of farm land is rapidly being converted to urban use. As the city spreads out toward the farm, its highest and best use undergoes a change which results in an increase in value. The change may be from farm to commercial or industrial use. Or the change may be from farm to residential subdivision.

You must plan for the subdivision and you must do so intelligently and thoroughly. Will you, as subdivider, have to pay for sewers, storm drainage, utilities, and road construction? Will you have to dedicate to the municipality the land required for streets, parks, schools, and easements?

You will find out from the Federal Housing Administration the rating it gives the area. You will supplement this by a corresponding inquiry to local lending institutions. You will learn from them what the drawbacks are to the subdivision and how these drawbacks may be corrected. You will ask them what is needed to make the subdivision a profitable venture.

You will ascertain what the costs will be for interest, payrolls, taxes, and custodianship to hold the land for subsequent development. You will try to find out what the market will be for the houses and lots when the development is complete.

FARMS AS INVESTMENTS

You may be more interested in the amenity returns than in the monetary. The farm may serve you as an interesting sideline, perhaps a hobby, to engage your spare time. Or it may be that you just like the out of doors and look on the farm as a recreational facility. You like to see things grow. You enjoy a reasonable amount of physical activity in seeding, cultivating, and harvesting.

Perhaps your experience has soured you on farms as investments. The fluctuations in farm income, the seven years of drought and the seven years of wet, the hail storm ruining your wheat crop overnight, the dust storms carrying your top soil away, the unpredictability of it all - these become too much of a burden for you to bear. You conclude reluctantly that the only certainty about farming is its uncertainty.

More and better commodities will be produced with less and less human effort. The application of chemurgy, the science of crop rotation, the employment of mechanical equipment doing several jobs concurrently, such as the combine, the analysis of soil content, contour farming, terracing, sod waterways, long range weather forecasting, irrigation - all these will contribute to this objective. Their effect will be to make farm land more valuable and therefore more desirable as an investment. The use of mechanical equipment will require a broader expanse over which to spread its investment. This will make for large scale farming investments, the extinction of the marginal farmer, and the amalgamation of smaller tracts into large investments.

FARMING'S FUTURE

Food is basic. Outdoor relaxation is essential. Open space is invaluable. Farm land provides for these. It will therefore always be with us. The market will always be there.

The decline of the farm population will bring about a decline in political pressures for farm relief, farm subsidies, high parity-price supports, and farm handouts. Farming will have to stand on its own, rather than lean on the government. A political crusade for help for the big farmer will meet with no more political response than one for big industry.

Farming as a way of life, the farmer as the backbone of the nation, the sun-up to sun-down hours, the never-ending uncertainties of the weather - these will lose their attractions, if actually they ever had any. Farming will become corporate, impersonalized, objective, the profit motive uppermost. Farm properties will be recognized for what they are, namely, investment properties, and their sales presentations will be tailored accordingly.

New uses will be developed for old products. Ways will be found for making effective use of farm surpluses and waste. Bagasse used to be a drug on the market. Now it is used in plastics. Soybeans used to be only a food. Now they are employed in industrial applications.

More and more farm land will be converted to urban use - residential, commercial, and industrial - as the pressures of population move against a fixed supply of land. This will make for increases in land value as it responds to these new directions for highest and best use.

GLOSSARY

CENTER OF INFLUENCE - one, who, by the nature of his occupation, is in a position to hear first of business potentials and opportunities.

CHEMURGY - the application of chemistry to farm products

COMPLIANCE PAYMENTS - payments for complying with farm programs

CONTOUR FARMING - farming following the natural contours of the land

CROP ROTATION - varying the kinds of crops planted on a certain piece of land from season to season

DEFERRED PAYMENT OPTIONS - taking advantage for tax purposes of the privilege of deferring income payments

DIVERSION PROGRAMS - programs of the Department of Agriculture for diverting farm acreage into other usages

INSTALLMENT REPORTING - a method of reporting capital gains by installments for successive tax years and thus escaping the impact of the totality of the capital gain tax in the year of sale

PARITY PRICE SUPPORT PLANS - plans of the Department of Agriculture to try to get farmers paid the prices for their products which will keep them in reasonable relationship with the higher prices they have to pay for their equipment

RECAPTURE RULES - rules under which part of the money saved by taking advantage of tax shelter may subsequently be recaptured by the government

SOD WATERWAYS - conservation measures to hold flood and run-off waters

STOCK FARMING - farming in livestock

TAX-FREE EXCHANGES - tax devices under which income property, when exchanged on an even basis for other income property, does not at the time have to pay a capital gain tax. Rather, this is deferred until such time as the property acquired in exchange may subsequently be sold

TERRACING - providing hillocks on the surface so as to hold flood and run-off waters, and thereby prevent erosion.

"WHEATED TO DEATH" - an expression referring to the depletion of the soil experienced when wheat is planted on it year after year after year.

TRUE AND FALSE QUESTIONS

1. Farms are consolidating to spread costs over a broader area.   T   F

2. The real estate farm broker must have full control over the sale.   T   F

3. The most effective way to secure farm listings is by advertising.   T   F

4. Having had farm experience recommends the farm salesman to the farm owner.   T   F

5. Food processors may desire farm land as a feeder to their operations.   T   F

6. Land speculators should be avoided as prospects for farm sales.   T   F

7. Farms may be purchased as a hedge against inflation.   T   F

8. Farm tenants will usually be happy to cooperate in farm showings to farm prospects.   T   F

9. It is never too early to close, so long as you sense the prospect is ripe and ready.   T   F

10. If negotiations reach a stalemate, then is the time to press the prospect into closing the sale.   T   F

11. Farm subsidy payments should not be mentioned to the prospect.   T   F

12. Prospects are not interested in analyses of soil content.   T   F

13. The reason for each of the closing costs must be spelled out to the purchaser.   T   F

14. Government farm programs change so rapidly that it is pointless for the farm broker to gain a knowledge of current ones.   T   F

15. Parity price support plans change periodically.   T   F

16. Farm financing is usually short-term.   T   F

17. Mortgages are always to be preferred to land contracts. T   F

18. The farm must be appraised before a lending institution will   T   F
grant the loan.

19. Principal payments on farm loans are almost always made   T   F
monthly.

20. Each range covers one township.   T   F

21. A township is six miles square.   T   F

22. Each township contains six sections.   T   F

23. A section is one mile square.   T   F

24. A section contains 160 acres.   T   F

25. A horizontal is a vertical layer of soil.   T   F

26. A profile is a vertical cross-section of a soil.   T   F

27. A series is a group of soils having similar horizons.   T   F

28. A soil map is an indication of the soil types that will be   T   F
found on a particular farm.

29. Farms do not provide amenity returns.   T   F

30. Farm income is relatively stable.   T   F

31. The trend is now toward large-scale farming.   T   F

32. The decline in farm populations will bring about a decline   T   F
in political pressures for farm relief.

33. A political crusade for help for the big farmer will not meet   T   F
with a favorable political response.

34. Farm properties are basically investment properties.   T   F

35. Political pressures will keep the marginal farmer in a   T   F
relatively profitable business situation.

36. An individual farmer will be subject to the new recapture   T   F
    tax rules on capital gains only if his nonfarm adjusted
    gross income exceeds $50,000.

37. Farm sales do not enjoy the benefit of the installment   T   F
    method of capital gain reporting.

38. Depreciation is a deduction only as against capital gain in-   T   F
    come.

39. Depreciation may be taken both on farm land and buildings.   T   F

40. If the soil is acid, it should be lined for best results with   T   F
    legumes.

MULTIPLE CHOICE

41. A horizontal layer of soil, parallel to the surface, is called:
    ( ) A top level
    ( ) Top soil
    ( ) A horizon
    ( ) A cross section

42. A vertical cross-section of a soil, showing the several layers of which it is constituted, is called:
    ( ) A profile
    ( ) A delineation
    ( ) A grid
    ( ) An area

43. Metes and bounds descriptions are approximately called:
    ( ) Parallels and meridians
    ( ) Ranges and base lines
    ( ) Walk-arounds
    ( ) Gridirons

44. Lines running north and south from the base are called:
    ( ) Parallels
    ( ) Meridians
    ( ) Ranges
    ( ) Base lines

45. The guiding principle in qualifying a farm prospect is:
    ( ) To get him to pay the top price
    ( ) To show him how inconsequential his objections are
    ( ) To get him to do what is best for him
    ( ) To get him to make the highest possible down payment

46. The type of financing in which the seller retains title until all the payments have been made is called:
    ( ) Purchase money mortgage
    ( ) Land contract
    ( ) Sale and leaseback
    ( ) Sale and buy back

47. Bounds mean:
    ( ) Measures
    ( ) Directions

( ) Limits
( ) Environs

48. That erosion has removed most of the soil surface may be shown by:
( ) Seismic equipment
( ) Bore and augur
( ) A soil map
( ) Bit and drill

49. The subdivider can find out from the Federal Housing Administration:
( ) What rating it gives the area
( ) How much it will loan him on the farms he acquires
( ) The extent to which it will guarantee his debentures
( ) The type of blanket mortgage it will approve for his purposes

50. Soybeans are used:
( ) Only as food
( ) As food and in industrial applications
( ) As health foods and in medicinal preparations
( ) Only in salt-free diets

ESSAY QUESTIONS

1. Please comment on farming's future:

2. What are the encouraging features about farm investments?

3. How is the small farmer being affected by the dynamics of change in farming?

APARTMENT HOUSES

CHAPTER TWENTY

THEIR POPULARITY

Apartment house residents? Cliff dwellers, you may derisively call them. They don't care. This is their way of life and they like it. They are freed from the burdens of exterior household chores. They are not tied down to any one place of residence. Executive transferees need not concern themselves with securing funds for a down payment on another home every time they are moved. There is a club like atmosphere in many apartment houses - swimming pools, pitch and putt golf courses, sauna baths, recreation rooms, even tennis courts. There is an impersonality about apartment house living which meets the desire for privacy and detachment.

Apartment house investors? They may be life insurance companies, real estate investment trusts, pension and annuity funds, and occasionally private individuals. They like the relatively high rate of return, the opportunities for depreciation on the buildings, the capital gain potential, the cash flow and tax shelter. They enjoy the "tax-free exchange" possibilities and the resultant privilege of tax deferrals.

Their special appeal to the older and younger segments of the population? The younger segment likes them because no down payment is required for their acquisition. The older segment likes them, because the apartment superintendent and his staff take over the burdens of providing care and maintenance.

THE APARTMENT HOUSE BOOM

As our population becomes increasingly mobile - and right now one family out of every five moves every year - apartment house living becomes increasingly attractive. It is attuned to the transiency of our times. It makes things so much easier when you have to move and pull up stakes. You don't have to look around for a buyer for your home. You don't have to look around for another home in the place to which you are being transferred. You can get the exact size you require for any stage in life - for a young couple just starting out, for a growing family, or for the father and mother who have raised their children and now see these same children as adults in homes of their own.

When you live in an apartment house, you enjoy more spare time. You do not have to take the time to mow the lawn, tend to the garden, repair the leaking roof, fix the plumbing, shore up the sagging gutters, and do something about the basement seepage. This time is your own for gratification of your hobbies or for other gainful occupation to supplement your income. If your wife works, she does not have to be

351

doubly burdened by the exterior household chores that would be her lot in a single family dwelling.

Widows and widowers and divorcees find apartment house units well-adapted to their limited space requirements. Families now tend to have fewer children and therefore do not need as much space as formerly.

The high incidence of crime in our larger cities has made for a high degree of security protection in apartment houses. This holds a marked appeal to prospective clientele.

The economics of the apartment house boom is readily apparent. Apartment house investments yield a relatively high rate of return. They provide a hedge against inflation. They afford a high ratio of building to land value and the resultant tax savings from more depreciation. They conserve on scarce land. This attribute is especially important in densely populated sectors. They incur less cost to the community, for the proportion of school-age children is less, fire protection and police protection can be concentrated into a smaller area, and less by way of streets and sidewalks is required.

The construction of apartment house units is less costly than the construction of comparable single family dwellings. It does not take as many man-hours to build one apartment as it takes to build a corresponding single family home. The amount of land per unit is less than in the case of a single family dwelling. The economies of scale apply in the operation of an apartment house. Supplies may be purchased in bulk. Full time carpenters, plumbers, and painters may be employed in larger apartment houses, thus cutting down on costs and spreading their compensation over a wide area. The principle of reciprocity may be applied to advantage with suppliers to apartment houses.

Financing can be more readily secured. An apartment house corporation need not be subject to the limitations of the usury laws. A corporate conglomerate promoting an apartment house may have high credit stature, thereby making it easier for it to secure financing than would be the case of an individual seeking financing for a single family home. A special attraction to institutional financiers is the equity participation privilege they may enjoy in an apartment house investment.

The signs of the apartment house boom are readily evident. Almost as many new apartment house units are now being built as are single family homes. In many of our large cities the vacancy rates in apartment houses are running as low as from one per cent to three per cent. The tide is now running stronger than ever before for the construction of apartment houses in suburban areas.

The expertise of apartment house management feeds the fires of the boom by producing greater profits. It is reducing tenant turnover and bad debt losses. It is increasing rents. It is automating wherever possible. It is securing fees and revenues from concessionaires. It is making the tenant pay for more services.

The apartment house boom plays no favorites. It extends to high rise as well as to low rise, and to the garden type as well.

APARTMENT HOUSE MOVEMENTS

Although apartment house rentals have risen, their rates of increase have not been as high as those for the construction of single family homes. In fact, their increases, the country over, have been slightly less than the increase in the cost of living.

Most of the new apartment houses being built today are out in the suburbs, rather than in the central city. Families want to spread out and get the benefit of open space and be relieved of crowds and congestion. They dislike the population density in the larger city, the high incidence of crime, the deterioration in the public school system, and the onerous tax burden.

The increase in the proportion of our population in the 20-34 age group is reflected by a corresponding increase in demand for apartment house living. This is the age group most likely to rent. It has, on the whole, acquired relatively little by way of savings, and therefore is not in a position to buy a home. The increase in the proportion of our population in the 65 and over age group reflects a similar increase in the demand for apartments. As these families retire, they may no longer desire to keep up their homes. One person households have likewise increased in their proportion of our total population, and they, too, are naturals for apartment house living.

There has been a shift away from single family homes to be used for rental purposes. The vacuum this shift created has been filled by apartment house units. Single family homes available for rent have become, in many cases, the run down, marginal dwellings.

Part of the shift to apartment house living comes about through a change in popular psychology. People have changed their aspirations. Rather than desiring homes of their own, they are now in many instances satisfied with living in a new apartment house on a permanent basis. The sanctity of individual single family home ownership has lost some of its appeal. Being renters gives people more mobility. When they move, they do not have to liquidate their equity in a dwelling.

APARTMENT HOUSE FINANCING

The apartment house developer contracts for the construction with his own "front money" and a short term construction loan. He arranges with an institutional lender for a long term loan to materialize on building completion. The proceeds of this he uses to pay off his short term construction loan. Life insurance companies are common sources for the long-term loans. Over and above the rate of return as interest on their loan, they derive yields from the equity participations they require in the apartment house projects.

The equity participation may come about by the lender taking a certain percentage of the developer's return from the apartment venture. The apartment house may be sold to the life insurance company on condition that it lease the property back to the developer for a period of time measured by the building's anticipated functional life expectancy. The investor in some cases puts up part of the equity and thereby becomes a partner with the developer.

If the lender requires an equity participation in the form of the earnings from the apartment house, it may be an outright percentage of the structure's income. Or it may be a percentage of higher rentals that may subsequently be set. Or it may be a percentage of the net profit from the apartment development. Sometimes the participation is without limitation of any ceiling amount. Sometimes the participation is a percentage after a fixed return to the developer has been reached.

In the sale and leaseback, the buyer-lessor's return is the rent he derives and the depreciation he takes. In the sale and buy back, the developer, by reason of his re-purchase, is entitled to the depreciation deduction. The seller secures a higher yield from the developer to compensate for his not enjoying depreciation.

Where the lender also takes an outright equity participation in the apartment house, he enjoys the appreciation the property may show. He shares in the rewards of the enterprise and also shares in the risks of the undertaking. If the developer is a corporation, the lender's equity may consist of part of the stock. In some instances, the lender insists on warrants or options as a basis for making the mortgage loan.

APARTMENT HOUSE TYPES

The high rise is not only high, but also large. It enjoys a convenient location. It tries to build up an aura of prestige. It aims to provide all the amenities and services and conveniences the tenants could possibly want. It, of course, has high speed elevators. It may boast a view for every apartment. As it is so large, a miniature post office and mail delivery may be lodged within the structure itself. There will usually be a nice dining room and cocktail lounge. Recreational facilities may include a swimming pool and sauna baths. Ample storage will be afforded the tenants. In most areas, air conditioning will be provided. Steps will be taken to minimize the repellant factor of cooking odors.

The low rise apartment house is usually located in peripheral and suburban areas. It may consist of a series of town houses. The garden type apartment house will often be three stories high and have ample garden space in the form of a court out in front. The extra space and recreation facilities of this type make it especially attractive to families with children.

Increasing in popularity is the environmental apartment. This makes use of lakes and landscaping to enhance and beautify the view. It may have a putting green or a golf course. Rents are higher, but so are the occupancy rates. Many of the tenants are frustrated home owners. They want space, escape, and privacy. They like the glorified gardens. They enjoy the waterfalls. They build up their health and physique with the therapeutic baths, massage rooms, sun rooms, and gymnasiums. They are based on the principle that people are buying more than just living space - they are buying a community and a way of life.

APARTMENT HOUSE TENANTS

It is not enough to say that apartment houses hold the greatest appeal for the 20-34 age groups and for the 65 and over age groups. What are the people like within these age ranges?

These people want the amenities and the good things of life. They want to be relieved of the onerous work and care involved in running a house. They have become disenchanted with suburban home ownership. Their wives are tired of painting and weeding, cajoling maids, replacing light bulbs, feeding cats and shaking out dog mattresses.

They are willing to pay for more luxuries than they now enjoy. Surveys show they will pay increased rentals for air conditioning, wall to wall carpeting, self-defrosting refrigerators, self-cleaning ovens, washer-dryer combinations, a fireplace, draperies, for larger storage areas. They are more concerned about noise than any other problem.

They are quality conscious. They have the financial capacity to pay the higher rent associated with the modern apartment house building. The younger apartment house dwellers seem to be economically secure, but emotionally insecure; confident of tomorrow, but scared of today. They are reassured by burglar alarms and security guards. They like to be able to make moves without emotional outbursts and tugs at the heartstrings which might be their fate with single family dwellings. They are usually well educated and quite often both husband and wife are working.

Among the young couples in apartment houses are many who plan eventually to buy, but seek apartment shelter until they can choose their neighborhood.

APARTMENT HOUSE EXPENSES

It is safe to say that a new apartment house will generate higher rents and lower operating expenses than an old apartment house. Typically, the vacancy and collection loss will be about five per cent of gross income based on 100 per cent occupancy.

Fire and hazard insurance, real and personal property taxes constitute the fixed expenses. The depreciation write-off is, in part, an accounting concept based on an anticipated functional life for the building. If the apartment house is furnished, there must also be a depreciation expense for the furniture. Although depreciation is a fixed expense, it is not a cash money item.

Maintenance, management, janitorial services, heating and air conditioning, utilities and building supplies constitute operating expenses. The salaries of building employees, including fringe benefits; contract services, such as elevator maintenance, gardening, trash removal, pest control, and equipment services must be paid for. Apartment decoration, painting, and floor refinishing are also part of the expense of operation.

The apartment house must set up a reserve for replacement of heating systems, air conditioners, stoves, plumbing, electrical fixtures, and refrigerators.

APARTMENT HOUSE PROBLEMS

There are problems galore - picking tenants and keeping them; knowing how to put the apartment house to its highest and best use; how to hire and fire; how to maintain the property, physically and functionally from within and how to protect it from adversity without.

There are all the problems of management - problems of help, automation that won't automate, plumbing that regurgitates. There are problems of tenants - the slow pay, the psychiatric cases, the drunks and degenerates and perverts and the chronic complainers.

And then there are the problems of soot and incinerators, suicides, peddlers, beggars, and solicitors - of doormen who walk the dog, but don't watch the door - problems of treading heavily on toes in the lightest way imaginable, of being a diplomat, keeping your temper, and trying to avoid the aches and pains of ulceritis - running the gauntlet, leaving both parties smiling - the tenant, placated, and the owner assured of his return.

How can you prevent the apartment houses of today from becoming the slums and the shanty towns of tomorrow? How can you keep the glass type windows in apartment houses today from leaking wind-driven rain water, soot, dust and cold air? Promotors try to sell the apartment house building after completion. Tenants who suffer the consequences of bad windows may have an uninformed manager who promises correction by window caulking, until it is learned that nothing short of replacement of windows can effect a permanent cure.

What problems lie in the wake of the formation of tenants' unions? Does this mean withholding of rents? Does this mean tenants' strikes? Does this mean tenant militancy, formation of picket lines, activist banners and parades? Does this mean mass meetings and demonstrations before municipal housing boards? Are the headaches resulting more than the property is worth by way of yield?

Is it possible to meet the demands for low income apartment housing and still make a profit? Can adequate relief be derived from the new finance plan aimed at stimulating construction of low income apartments? This plan involves tandem financing by the Government National Mortgage Association, a government-financed corporation, and the Federal National Mortgage Association, a government-sponsored, but privately owned corporation. The Federal government has earmarked vast sums to cover GNMA commitments to provide financing or assistance for low- and middle-income multifamily units.

How can apartment houses fight back against the discriminations to which they are subject? The best areas in municipalities are zoned for single-family dwellings, not for apartment houses. Apartment houses are assessed at higher proportion to values than are single-family homes. Apartment houses enjoy no tax immunities, such as the homestead tax exemptions available for single family. There are no VA loan guarantees on apartment houses. Only about ten percent of the FHA loans are on apartment houses. In some areas of our country, apartment houses are still subject to rent controls.

Can the parking areas around apartment houses be used both for tenants and also for the visitors to the business apartments during the office hours on the regular business day? This is possible. In apartment houses for tenants, the peak use hours for elevators in the morning are from seven to eight thirty. For the offices in the apartment houses, the peak use hours in the morning are between 8:45 and 9:15. The same patterns hold for the evening hours, with the office callers leaving before the tenants come back in. Since office parking space is used only during the working day, the evening and weekend periods can be used by visitors.

Although most large apartments have their own maintenance crews, quick service in an emergency often proves to be a problem. This is because the skilled help required is in such short supply. This, in turn, means that the repairs that should be made with dispatch are often made with exasperating slowness.

APARTMENT HOUSES - THEIR FUTURE

The environmental apartment is now spreading across the United States, winning new converts to high density living and support from lenders and local planning boards. Because of population pressures and the high costs of building and owning a home, two out of three housing starts in the years ahead will be in apartments.

Most new apartments are now rented within nine months after completion. Increasing construction costs influence the trend toward multiple dwelling units. More and more people will find it financially impossible to own their own homes. Occupational and educational shifts will be accompanied by shifts in favor of apartment house units. This is mainly because the population will be more mobile and too busy to take the time necessary to maintain a home. The new luxury apartments are enticing to both young and old families. The housing package the new apartments offer, which includes maintenance, swimming pools, a club house and modern facilities, is enough to entice many people to sell their homes and move into one of these luxury apartments.

As costs continue to rise, moderate income families see their chances of buying a home as increasingly dim. And they may actually prefer apartment house living. Many of them like the new high-rise complexes or the clusters of garden apartments. As population density tightens, the economic pressure is toward stacking family units upwards rather than pushing them farther away from job centers.

A major reason for the switch to apartment building is the relative availability of mortgage money. Apartments will be more attractive to lenders because mortgage rates can be highest and lenders can participate directly in the profits generated by the apartment project.

Even the smaller and medium-sized towns, once considered poor apartment markets, will find apartments to be sound financial investments.

It will become axiomatic that the higher the population density, the lower will be the average vacancy rate in apartment houses. Likewise, the higher the population density, the lower will be the home ownership factor.

Trends in the future social and demographic picture all make for increasing apartment house attraction - trends as shown by the increase in marriages, the increase in the proportion of our population of young adults, the increase in the proportion of our population of individual households like those for widows and widowers, the trend toward smaller families, the increasing proportion of working wives, and the increasing sector of professional people.

The round ahead will be the round of the renters, not the owners of single family dwellings. The apartment house boom will be a different ball game for the vendors of grass seed and patio furniture, for makers of garden tools and lawn mowers. Apartment houses will use more steel, and less glass. It is going to be uneconomic for the average family to reserve a plot of land for its exclusive residential use. Apartment house construction will increase both numerically and as a percentage of private housing starts. The new financing trends will permit apartment house builders to defer payment of their principal until their apartment units begin to fill up. And the demolition of existing dilapidated apartment buildings will be accompanied by the construction of new apartment houses. Dilapidated units cannot now be removed unless other housing provisions for the occupants are available.

The mounting appeal of apartment houses will attract important capital. Much of this will come from abroad, attracted by the relatively high yields here.

TRUE AND FALSE QUESTIONS

1. Apartment house living provides freedom from exterior household chores.   T F

2. Real estate investment trusts are not permitted to invest in apartment houses.   T F

3. Pension and annuity funds may now invest in apartment houses.   T F

4. Being income properties, apartment houses lend themselves to the advantages of "tax-free exchanges".   T F

5. Apartment house living appeals to the older, but not the younger segment of the population.   T F

6. Apartment house living lends itself to the mobility of our population.   T F

7. Apartment houses can provide the exact amount of space required for any stage of life.   T F

8. Apartment house living provides for more spare time for the tenants.   T F

9. Apartment house living has no appeal for working wives.   T F

10. Apartment houses cannot provide the degree of security pro-protection required in these days of lawlessness and disorder.   T F

11. Widows, widowers, and divorcees find apartment house units adapted to their limited space requirements.   T F

12. Apartment houses provide a relatively high ratio of building land value.   T F

13. Apartment houses do not conserve on scarce land.   T F

14. The economies of scale apply in apartment house operation.   T F

15. Apartment house corporations are subject to the restrictions of the usury statutes.   T F

16. Almost as many new apartment units are now being built   T   F
    as single family homes.

17. Most of the new apartment houses being built today are   T   F
    in the central city.

18. The 20-34 age group is the one most likely to rent.   T   F

19. Life insurance companies are common sources for apartment   T   F
    house long term loans.

20. The low rise apartment house is usually located in peripheral   T   F
    and suburban areas.

21. Environmental apartments are not attractive.   T   F

22. Typically, vacancy and collection losses will be about five   T   F
    per cent of gross income, based on 100 per cent occupancy.

23. Apartment house operations do not require a reserve for   T   F
    replacements.

24. Apartment unit occupiers enjoy homestead tax exemptions.   T   F

25. VA-loan guarantees are now available on apartment houses.   T   F

26. As population density tightens, the economic pressure is   T   F
    toward stacking living units, one on top the other.

27. The environmental apartment is now spreading across the   T   F
    United States.

28. It is predicted that in the years ahead two out of three   T   F
    housing starts will be in apartment house units.

29. The parking areas of apartment houses cannot be used both   T   F
    for tenants and for visitors to the business apartments.

30. The majority of FHA insured loans are on apartment houses.   T   F

31. The depreciation writeoff on apartment houses is in part   T   F
    an accounting concept.

32. Depreciation is a fixed expense.   T   F

33. Apartment house living does not appeal to the age group   T   F
    65 or over.

34. The low rise apartment house can consist of a series of   T   F
    townhouses.

35. Equity participations lend themselves to enjoyment in part   T   F
    of the appreciation the property may develop.

36. In the sale and buy back, the developer enjoys depreciation   T   F
    deduction.

37. In the sale and leaseback, the seller lessee enjoys the   T   F
    depreciation deduction.

38. Equity participations may not be in the form of a portion   T   F
    of the net profit from the apartment house development.

39. There has been a shift away from single family homes for   T   F
    rental purposes.

40. Good apartment house management automates wherever   T   F
    possible.

MULTIPLE CHOICE

41. Compared with single family conventional homes, apartment houses:
    ( )   Incur less cost to the community
    ( )   Require a higher per capita police and fire protection
    ( )   Require a higher per capita public school expenditure
    ( )   Are assessed a smaller percentage of their fair market value

42. The mobility of our population is now such that:
    ( )   One family out of every ten moves every year
    ( )   One family out of every seven moves every year
    ( )   One family out of every five moves every year
    ( )   One family out of every three moves every year

43. With regard to suppliers to an apartment house:
    ( )   The principle of reciprocity may be applied
    ( )   They afford the opportunity for taking rebates by the manager
    ( )   They usually give the apartment house owner equity participations
    ( )   They usually furnish the financing for the apartment house

44. The long term loan from the institutional lender:
    ( )   Will usually bear a usurious rate of interest
    ( )   Cannot provide for a hedge against inflation
    ( )   Cannot carry a prepayment penalty
    ( )   Will be used in large part to pay off the construction loan lender

45. The team plan of FNMA and GNMA for financing apartment houses is called:
    ( )   Cooperative financing
    ( )   Tandem financing
    ( )   Primary market mortgaging
    ( )   Secondary market mortgaging

46. Apartment houses are subject to:
    ( )   Rent controls
    ( )   Government ceilings on points
    ( )   MGIC financing
    ( )   Opportunity allowance programs

47. The trend toward multiple dwelling units has been accelerated by:
    ( )   Increasing construction costs

( )   More favorable property tax treatment for multiple than singles
( )   The investment tax credit
( )   The pressure of construction unions

48. A greater amount of open space is provided tenants in:
( )   High-rise apartments
( )   In garden type apartments
( )   In apartment houses in central business districts
( )   Multi-story condominiums

49. In the sale and leaseback, the investor's return is derived from:
( )   His purchase money mortgage
( )   His blanket mortgage
( )   His rent and the depreciation he takes
( )   His land contract

50. The Federal National Mortgage Association is:
( )   Government owned
( )   Privately owned
( )   Part owned by the government and part owned by private stockholders
( )   Part of the Federal Reserve System

ESSAY QUESTIONS

1. What social and demographic trends make for an increasing popularity of apartment house living?

2. What are the economic factors back of the apartment house boom?

3. How are apartment house constructions financed?

SHOPPING CENTERS

CHAPTER TWENTY-ONE

HOW THEY HAVE GROWN!

It is hard to realize that in 1950 in our entire country there were only 100 planned shopping centers. As of 1972, there are over 12,000 planned shopping centers. And these bare figures do not tell the whole story. As time has gone on, the planned shopping centers have become larger. Time was when the neighborhood shopping center was predominant. That time is past. We now have plenty of community shopping centers and a growing number of regional ones. The newest arrival is the super-regional. One of these large shopping centers could incorporate within its confines several of the centers from time past.

As of 1972, the proportion of the retail market for which shopping centers account is well over 40 per cent, as against a miniscule proportion in 1950. Department stores have more than doubled their outlets during this period and almost all of this has been in new shopping centers. Full-line discount stores in shopping centers were a rarity in 1950. Now they are commonplace.

Along with their growth in retail facilities has come about a growth in community services. Shopping centers have, in fact, grown to be a focal point of community life - fairs, exhibits, art shows, the theater, post offices and municipal administration, church services, and town meetings. The visual attractions of shopping centers have grown apace - landscaped malls, sculpture and statuary, trees and gardens.

THE APPEAL OF THE SHOPPING CENTER

There's a reason for all this growth and this lies in the appeal of one-stop shopping. We can drive to the center, park our car, and do all our shopping at one time, frequently under one roof, deposit our purchases in our car, and be on our way home. We save ourselves the time otherwise required to go from one store in one section to another store in another section. We save ourselves the tedium and frustrations of trying to find a place to park in various areas. We can engage in comparison shopping in the variety of stores available. We can satisfy all our wants - from groceries to drugs to ladies' dresses - in one shopping area. We can enjoy the amenities afforded by nice restaurants and glamorous cocktail lounges.

Shopping centers enable retail chains to increase their market penetration by going into new marketing areas. People have been moving in increasing numbers out to the suburbs. The greater amount of space there available provides a welcome response to the demand for more room. Over and above this, it is axiomatic for trade to follow the customer.

Shopping centers set themselves up for the greatest possible convenience of their market clientele - plenty of parking, adjacency to new subdivisions and developments, and evening and Sunday openings. Wherever there is new industry and new employment, the economic base for a new shopping center is provided.

THE ECONOMICS OF THE SHOPPING CENTER

The shopping center affords a relatively high ratio of building to land value and therefore an opportunity to enjoy the benefits of depreciation.

The rents the shopping center stores pay are deductible against their income tax liability. The sale and leaseback device may be employed, thereby enabling the seller-lessee to deduct through his rent both the charges against the land and the building.

Where they have been in the path of directional growth, they have enjoyed the increment of capital appreciation. This capital gain potential provides an extra bonus to the investor, over and above the relatively high rate of return from the investment itself.

The lender financing the shopping center is able to secure a hedge against inflation by reason of "equity participations" in the rentals derived. Or he may secure this hedge by means of an escalation clause in the lending agreement.

The owners of the shopping center capitalize on the principle of leverage through securing their loans on a high ratio to value. This enables them to keep their equity low and return high. As shopping centers attain value enhancement, this may pave the way for a second mortgage loan with resultant additional liquidity.

THE SWAN SONG OF DOWNTOWN RETAIL?

Does the growth of shopping centers spell the swan song of downtown retail? Certainly the vast majority of new shopping centers are opening up out in the suburbs. On the other hand, will urban redevelopment programs in the inner city bring downtown retail back to life? Will the promotions to bring the shoppers back be successful? Will the provision of rapid transit persuade suburbanites to get on the train and do their shopping "in town"? Will the growth in office buildings downtown spawn the shoppers at lunch hour for downtown shopping?

It would seem that lunch hour shoppers would be a slender reed on which to lean. It would seem that, no matter how nice rapid transit became, lady shoppers from the suburbs would still dislike carrying their shopping bags on the train. The trip into "town" takes time. If the shoppers from out of town prefer to drive, it would seem that the shortage of parking and the problems of traffic congestion would become too onerous. Even if these difficulties could be surmounted, the high incidence of urban crime would still stand in the way.

This would seem to leave downtown retail with urban residents as the bulk of their market. On the whole, their incomes would not be such as to support high class shopping centers. In New York City alone, one out of every seven residents is on relief. It is said, in effect, that only the very rich and the very poor can afford to reside in the city. And of these two groups, the very poor are predominant.

FINANCING THE SHOPPING CENTERS

Institutional lenders will not commit themselves until assured of drawing cards like department stores and supermarkets. The rental commitments from such AAA tenants must be sufficient in amount to make the interest and principal payments on the mortgage loan, together with fixed charges on the property. But these drawing card tenants are conscious of their own desirability and trade on the advantage they offer. They may be able to negotiate relatively low rental levels. They may drive a hard bargain in the form of a donation to them of the land on which their buildings will reside.

This means in turn that the satellite tenancies will pay the freight. This raises the question whether they can do so in the face of the relatively high rents correspondingly demanded and still make a go of it. It would not raise the public image of the shopping center for these businesses to fall by the wayside and their stores to be vacant.

Of the financing techniques employed, the sale and leaseback has become a favorite. The shopping center store likes it because it can keep its capital in its merchandise, enjoy rent deductibility, and present a clean working capital position on its balance sheet. The sale and buy back with long term installment payments accomplishes these objectives, plus enabling the shopping center store to deduct depreciation. Or resort may be had to a long term ground lease under which the store would put up its own building. Joint ventures and equity participations are also popular.

KINDS OF SHOPPING CENTERS

Many shopping centers just "grew". They had no planning. They enjoyed no market research. They were based on no feasibility studies. A car dealer, for example, "happened" to locate in a certain spot. Other car dealers joined him. Service stations, as next of kin, sprang up in conjunction. And the area became known as automobile row. Or a small drug store would locate on a corner adjacent to a residential development. Then a delicatessen moved in. It was followed by a cleaning and pressing shop. These were a natural progeny for the residential neighborhood they served. They formed an unplanned shopping area.

These shopping areas, in one form or another, have always been with us. Useful as are the purposes they serve, our real estate study does not focus on them, but rather on the relatively new planned shopping center developments. The one closest to us is our neighborhood shopping center. It will be within five minutes driving time of its marketing clientele. It will have about ten stores - a supermarket, a drug store, a variety store, a cleaning and pressing shop, often a combination delicatessen and luncheonette, perhaps a bakery, maybe a hardware store, stationery supplies and greeting cards, nowadays a laundromat, and often a beauty parlor.

Next on the scene is the community shopping center. It will be within 15 minutes driving time from its customers. The variety of its offerings will be displayed in 30 or more stores. Chief among these will be supermarkets, department stores, drug stores, variety stores, shoe and apparel stores, together with the others comprising the neighborhood center. It will offer, on a larger scale, all the convenience goods of the neighborhood center, plus many of the shopping goods found in the regional center.

Within 30 minutes driving time of its customers will be the large regional shopping centers, with 40 or more stores, shopping and convenience goods galore, and community service facilities for its entire trading area. Its supermarket or supermarkets will be in sections distinct from the rest of the stores. It will enjoy convenience of access to principal traffic arteries round about. It will have nice restaurants and cocktail lounges. It will go in for lovely landscaping. Its concourse will be the scene of art shows, junior achievement exhibits, antique collections, Easter bunnies, Santa Claus and Christmas decorations - whatever is fitting for the particular season of the year. In it may be incorporated a police department, a postoffice, municipal offices, and even facilities for the conduct of church services. It is taking the place of the village square in times past and becoming, in its twentieth century way, the focal point of regional civic life.

Some planned shopping centers are dominated by one merchandiser - the king pin in all the stores and service facilities - like the K-Marts in the middle west and Korvette and Two Guys in the East.

The newest entrant on the planned shopping center field is the super-regional. It is hard to describe in exact terms. Suffice to say, it is one-third to one-half bigger in every way than the present regionals. It caters to an even wider trading area. It stands out with three to four large department stores. For the convenience of its customers, it may employ so-called zone parking, breaking up its large parking areas into several smaller ones. Each business has the number of parking spaces it needs right in front of its own building. This makes it unnecessary for shoppers to walk several hundred feet to get what they want. It goes in for climate controlled, enclosed malls.

Another new type is the agri-business planned shopping center. It is so set up as to enable farmers to buy everything they require from lumber to tractors, credit to veterinary care, groceries to cars - and all this in an enclosed all-season mall for a modern atmosphere in a rural setting. It also has separate odor-proof livestock facilities.

Business has come to the core and ghetto areas of our cities in the form of shopping centers catering to minority ethnic and language groups. For example, a shopping center for Spanish speaking Puerto-Ricans has opened up in Newark, New Jersey's central city. An all black shopping center, in both ownership and management, financed by the Equitable Assurance Society and the Small Business Administration, has come to Memphis.

An interesting development on some university campuses has been the non-parking shopping center. It is located in the heart of student pedestrian flow between class buildings and dormitories. It provides its customers with bicycle parking racks.

EVENING AND SUNDAY OPENINGS

The "in thing" is now evening and Sunday openings, unless restricted by blue laws. The reason is there for all to see: More business. You see more family groups, particularly on Sundays. People enjoy coming out on shopping expeditions as a family group. Sundays may be the only time the family as a whole can get together. They can plan an outing to a shopping center many miles away and don't have to hire a baby sitter. Sunday shopping with them is becoming an accepted way of life. It's an opportunity for Mother to stick Dad with the kids for a few hours. It's a substitute for a trip to the zoo or park.

With 40 to 50 per cent of the business done evenings and Sundays, the economic pull toward such hours becomes irresistible. It overcomes the forces in opposition - religious scruples, reluctance of employees to work during these times, the outraged feelings of the small independent who gets virtually no time for himself. The bowling alley or other recreational facilities nearby brings more shoppers out at night.

There is considerable controversy as to whether evening and Sunday openings actually increase the overall volume of sales. Many retailers contend that such business is merely taking it out of your right pocket and putting it in your left pocket, that without such openings the same volume would still be there. Others assert that by reason of such openings they are getting people into their centers who have never shopped there before. Most stores report no problem with employees about such openings. Perhaps the reason for this is the premium pay that they may thereby earn.

SHOPPING CENTERS ABROAD

Yes, their impact is being increasingly felt in foreign countries. Fourteen Russian supermarkets are scheduled, equipped with everything from mechanical shoe cleaners to refrigerators and food packaging machinery. They will be in operation in Moscow, Leningrad, and elsewhere. Russian shoppers in these cities will no longer have to repeatedly stand in line in retail stores - first to order their goods, secondly to pay for them, and thirdly, to pick them up. Russian planners can now determine what foodstuffs to produce by checking on what was moving and what was not moving at check-out counters.

Sales at supermarkets recently opened near Zurich, Switzerland; Paris, and in the Tokyo area exceed the original forecasts. The boom in supermarkets in West Germany is already (1972) in its fifth year. Sweden has set up "residence oriented" shopping centers within walking distance of apartments and family homes and is now about to establish "traffic oriented" centers as well. The larger shopping centers abroad, just like those in the United States, are made up of department stores, supermarkets, and specialty shops.

As would be expected, Swiss insurance firms are backing the shopping center promotions in Switzerland, and Ruhr coal companies are investing in shopping centers in West Germany the compensation they have received for closing down marginal mines.

As yet, planned shopping centers abroad have not cut down on retail sales in the central city as they have at home. The attractions of quaint shops and open air markets there may account for the maintenance of their position.

SHOPPING CENTER PROBLEMS

In some areas the market is saturated. There are as yet just not enough customers to sustain the stores that have been set up. These centers are premature, so to speak. To get the revenues required, they have gone in for more satellite tenancies than the market can absorb. Part and parcel of this problem is the building of too many competitive centers. Some of these have intercepted the trade that would otherwise have gone to the established center.

Because of the large proportion of land area that must go for parking, heavy expenses are encountered for maintenance, traffic facilities, and security protection for space that in itself is not productive of sales.

A new shopping center may have to undergo a long period of seasoning and promotion before it becomes accepted and enjoys the patronage it requires. It may go "broke" during this breaking-in period.

No one gainsays the attractions of the malls with their fountains, aviaries, gardens, and landscaping. What is perplexing, however, is whether these provide the necessary yield in the form of increased sales and profits.

Despite shopping center efforts to provide activities to interest the children, some of them are bound to get out of hand and engage in vandalism and malicious mischief.

So long as money continues to be tight, shopping centers will have to continue to pay high interest rates and grant increasing equity participations to their mortgage lenders. And this will dampen their profits.

THE WAVE OF THE FUTURE

Never before in all history will there be so many stores pushing so hard to expand their operations. Shopping centers will continue to grow throughout the 1970's and the 1980's. Projections of population and family formations and the rise of smaller metropolitan areas support this thesis. Major department stores are planning a 75 per cent increase in the next five years in their shopping center branches. Shopping centers as a whole now account for over 40 per cent of the retail market and will rise to 50 per cent by 1975. By 1980 it is estimated that new shopping center space will eclipse all present retail space in New York, Chicago, and Los Angeles, combined. Huge new shopping centers will tie in with the development of housing and office complexes.

The shift to the far-out suburbs will accelerate this momentum. Trade follows the customer. The chains will increase their penetration by going into these new markets. Population will continue to enjoy its greatest growth in suburbia.

Supermarkets will be relegated to a separate wing away from the main line of the big, general stores. The reason for this is that the shopper who comes in for food does not usually go into adjacent stores to buy clothing and home furnishings. These supermarkets will go for much more automation to speed customer service and streamline warehousing and bookkeeping. This will not only cut down on their costs; it will also be a defensive measure in neighborhood shopping centers against the inroads of mini-markets offering small selections, but fast service.

Shopping center design will see change. It may be based on a central pedestrian mall with branches leading into a series of satellite plazas, each planned and landscaped to give an individual character to its own set of shops. Pedestrian avenues may be clustered with trees. Some centers will be built vertically, rather than horizontally and with wrap around ramps and parking.

Sizable additions will be built to present shopping centers, amounting to new, contiguous centers. Shuttle buses will operate between the far corners of the new super-regionals. Moving sidewalks will save on walking. Central package pick-ups will be provided. Cocktail lounges will enjoy a lively tea-time trade from bored housewives and weary teachers. Women's and church groups will sponsor shoppers' outings. Merchandising classes will use the shopping centers as their indoor and outdoor laboratories. There will be an increase in service station facilities.

The successful shopping center sponsors will be those who will devise ways of overcoming the wave of increasing costs - cost of loans, building, taxes, maintenance, and operation. The successful shopping center promoters will be those who acquire their sites ahead of time of their developments. Otherwise, houses and subdivisions would have spread all over the available land.

The new super regionals will draw on markets beyond the borders of the metropolitan areas in which they will be located. Over 50 per cent of their gross leaseable area will be in department store space. Banks and office buildings will be part of their building mix.

Shop by phone supermarket facilities will be established. They will endow the home-delivery concept with a variety of supermarket products and utilize computerization for selection and delivery. The computer system will be programmed to act on grocery list items available, quoting to the customer updated prices, specials and volume discounts. After the customer confirms the final total, the computer will instruct personnel which items to pick out and how to route them through automated conveyor systems to the delivery truck depot and inform the dispatcher of delivery scheduling.

The drawback with this home delivery concept is that it would not lend itself to impulse buying, such a large factor in supermarket sales. On the other hand, specialty shops in the neighborhood might spring up to provide the "pickup" items people forget at the supermarket, as well as fancy cuts of meat that the shopper might prefer to purchase individually.

TRUE AND FALSE QUESTIONS

1. One of the larger shopping centers being built today could   T   F
   incorporate within its confines several of the smaller centers
   built in times past.

2. Department stores have more than doubled their outlets   T   F
   since 1950.

3. Full-time discount stores in shopping centers are common-   T   F
   place today.

4. The larger planned shopping centers have become focal   T   F
   points in community life.

5. The basic appeal of the shopping center is one-stop shopping.   T   F

6. Because of the limited number of types of stores in shopping   T   F
   centers, it is not possible to engage in comparison shopping.

7. Trade follows the customer.   T   F

8. Evening and Sunday openings provide for a relatively small   T   F
   percentage of a shopping center's business.

9. Because of the vast parking areas, the shopping center shows   T   F
   a relatively high percentage of land value to building value.

10. The rents the shopping center stores pay are not deductible   T   F
    as against their income tax liability.

11. The investor financing the shopping center may secure a   T   F
    hedge against inflation by virtue of "equity participations".

12. There is now a swing back to shopping centers in downtown   T   F
    areas.

13. In New York City, one out of every seven residents is on   T   F
    relief.

14. Institutional lenders on shopping centers will not commit   T   F
    their funds until assured of drawing cards like department
    stores and supermarkets.

15. Satellite tenancies in shopping centers "pay the freight"   T   F
for the relatively lower rentals charged the drawing cards.

16. Long term ground leases are not employed in shopping   T   F
centers.

17. Joint ventures are not used in shopping center developments.   T   F

18. Unplanned shopping areas are counted in among the census   T   F
of shopping centers.

19. Neighborhood shopping centers are usually about 5 minutes   T   F
in driving time from their market clientele.

20. The community shopping center is usually about 30 minutes   T   F
driving time from its market clientele.

21. The supermarkets in the regional shopping centers are   T   F
usually in sections distinct from the other stores.

22. There are no non-parking shopping centers.   T   F

23. Shopping centers have not as yet been established abroad.   T   F

24. Major department stores do not plan an increase in their   T   F
shopping center branches.

25. Future shopping center design may be based on a central   T   F
pedestrian mall.

26. Shopping centers will not incorporate service station   T   F
facilities.

27. Over 50 per cent of the gross leaseable area in the new super   T   F
regionals will be in department store space.

28. Banks and office buildings will be part of the building mix   T   F
in the new super-regionals.

29. It is expected that shop by phone supermart facilities will be   T   F
established.

30. Shop by phone will lend itself to impulse buying.   T   F

31. New shopping centers will not tie in with the development   T   F
of new housing and office complexes.

32. The agri-business shopping center caters to the farm market.   T   F

33. Shopping areas have always been part of the merchandising scene. T F

34. The sale and leaseback financing device has been used in shopping centers. T F

35. The relatively low per capita incomes of downtown residents will not support high class shopping centers. T F

36. There is general agreement that urban redevelopment programs will bring shopping centers back on a large scale to downtown. T F

37. Wherever there is new industry and new employment, the economic base for a new shopping center is provided. T F

38. The capital gain potential of the shopping center provides an extra bonus to the investor. T F

39. Second mortgage loans are not used in shopping centers. T F

40. The development of rapid transit into the city will cause a substantial revival of downtown shopping. T F

MULTIPLE CHOICE

41. Shopping centers that just "grew" without planning or market research are called:
    ( ) Shopping sprawls
    ( ) Shopping areas
    ( ) Random developments
    ( ) By guess and by golly developments

42. The planned shopping center, within five minutes driving time of its market clientele, is called:
    ( ) The neighborhood shopping center
    ( ) The community shopping center
    ( ) The four block shopping center
    ( ) The convenience shopping center

43. The planned shopping center, within 15 minutes driving time of its clientele, is called:
    ( ) The community shopping center
    ( ) The regional shopping center
    ( ) The peripheral shopping center
    ( ) The metropolitan shopping center

44. The new super-regional shopping centers are:
    ( ) Twice as large as present regionals
    ( ) One-third to one-half as large as present regionals
    ( ) Cater to a market clientele within 30 minutes driving time
    ( ) Tending to eliminate supermarkets

45. Family groups tend to shop together:
    ( ) Particularly during evening and Sunday openings
    ( ) Particularly during Saturday openings
    ( ) Particularly on holidays
    ( ) Particularly during school vacations

46. Shopping centers within walking distance of apartments and homes are called:
    ( ) Pedestrian oriented
    ( ) Residence oriented
    ( ) Traffic oriented
    ( ) Family oriented

47. It is estimated that new shopping center space will eclipse all present retail space in New York, Chicago, and Los Angeles, combined by the year:
( ) 2,000
( ) 1980
( ) 1990
( ) 1975

48. The K-Marts, the Korvettes, and Two Guys are examples of shopping centers:
( ) Concentrating on supermarkets
( ) Concentrating on junior variety stores
( ) Dominated by one merchandiser
( ) Where satellite tenancies have been eliminated

49. The neighborhood shopping center usually has:
( ) About five stores
( ) About ten stores
( ) About 20 stores
( ) About two or three supermarkets

50. Downtown retail counts in part for its survival on:
( ) The lunch hour shopper
( ) A swing back to downtown shopping from suburban shopping
( ) Minority group spending
( ) The popularity of food stamps given at downtown stores

ESSAY QUESTIONS

1. What are the measures being taken to revive downtown retail?

2. Describe the regional shopping center.

3. What are the principal problems encountered by shopping centers?

INDUSTRIAL PROPERTIES

CHAPTER TWENTY-TWO

WHAT IS IT?

It is property used for purposes of manufacture. It ranges from a giant steel mill to the shed in your own back yard for plastics fabrication. It includes research and development facilities forming the basis for new products and design. It takes in the warehousing of raw materials awaiting subsequent processing.

WHAT ARE ITS CHARACTERISTICS?

An industrial plant requires a heavy investment. It is not the structure alone. It is also the machinery and the equipment that must be installed. It is the sprinkler system to be put in. It is the protective and security devices that must be incorporated.

Industrial properties are subject to a high non-liquidity factor. They are unique unto themselves. They are not readily adapted to other forms of manufacture. They are anything but standardized. A search for comparables may well prove unavailing. They are not commonly bought and sold in the market place. They cannot therefore be quickly liquidated to advantage.

Hand in hand with the characteristic of non-liquidity goes the fact that industrial properties are customized. They are built to suit the industrial needs of a particular user. They are structured around his specific methods of production. They fit in with his processing flow and directional scheduling. They are built to his plans and specifications.

Industrial properties are subject to a high degree of functional obsolescence. The multi-story plant has given way to the one-story. The ramps and elevators have been succeeded by a production line flow on the ground floor. The computer may now do the production scheduling formerly the lot of middle management. The pace of engineering advance leaves the models of yesteryear far behind. The pressure is on for lower and lower production costs and these are achieved by the new look in innovation and technology.

WHAT ARE THE LOCATIONAL FACTORS?

If the products made lose weight in the manufacturing process, you will try to locate your plant in proximity to your raw materials. You will, so to speak, be raw materials oriented. This would apply, for example, in the cases of ore which must be smelted and cotton which must be ginned. If, on the other hand, the products you make gain weight in the manufacturing process, you will locate your plant in proximity to your market. You will be customer oriented. This would apply, for example, to beverage bottling plants, which add water to the syrup.

You will try to avoid locating your plant on uneven or sloping land. Topography, such as this, can add heavily to your site development costs. Reasonably level land, capable of being graded without undue expense, will be advantageous as an industrial site.

You will make sure that the location provides surface and sub-surface drainage; that the soil has sufficient load bearing capacity; and at the same time has adequate permeability for waste disposal.

You will make sure that you have access to the type of transportation required - highway, rail, water, or air. You will likewise check on the water, sewer, and electrical power facilities provided.

The location desired must be zoned for the particular use required. The setback and sideline restrictions must not be such as to cramp you in floor area you need. The increasing air and water pollution controls must not be of such a nature as to make unprofitable your particular type of manufacture. Industrial water must be available for your protection.

Steel mills tend to locate at the most economical meeting point for coal and iron ore. Provo, Utah was therefore ideal for the U. S. Steel mill because of the conjuction there of these basic materials.

The labor supply at the particular location must be adequate. It is a big help if it is also cooperative and tractable. One of the reasons industry moved south was because of the difficulties in coping with labor problems in northern cities.

Suburban and rural areas are becoming increasingly attractive to industry. Here it finds room for the wide stretch one-story plant, where, ideally, raw materials could come in at one end of the plant and, by virtue of assembly-line processing, emerge as finished products at the other end. In the one-story plant no space is wasted for elevators and ramps; the machinery can rest on bedrock; overhead cranes can freely move about; conveyor belts can operate in continuous movement; and there is less congestion in the manufacturing process.

It used to be that industrial plants located in the city to have access to rail transportation. This is no longer necessary. Belt-line railroads now go around the urban peripheries. It used to be that the labor supply was available only in the city. Now factory workers live in the suburbs. They are not dependent on urban transportation to get to their place of employment, for most of them have their own cars.

It is so essential that the people in the area extend a welcoming hand to industry. If they do, their governments will. This receptiveness to industry can take many forms. It may be in the form of tax concessions. It may be in the form of donation of industrial land and financial assistance in the construction of the plant itself. It may be in the form of zoning variances to make a particular type of manufacturing feasible and legal. The south has in large part become industrialized through these aids to industry. Operation Bootstrap in Puerto Rico has magnetized industry to come down there and enjoy the tax forgiveness on the large scale provided. On the other hand, the possibility of expropriation in various South American countries has deterred industry from locating in this market.

LOCATION BOOSTERS

Industry has been wooed and won for particular locations thanks to the attractions delineated above. Acting as marriage brokers in the process have been railroads, public utilities, and state industrial commissions.

Each of these naturally acts in its own self-interest. Railroads try to persuade industry to locate in the areas they serve because of the additional traffic it will provide.

The power and light and the gas companies have been even more aggressive than the railroads in persuading industry to come to the areas they serve. Not a day goes by but one sees the advertisements of these public utilities pointing out the advantages to industry of locating in its situs. They work hand in hand with industry in preparing marketing and industrial surveys of the areas to be tapped. They point up the attractive utility rates available to large-scale industrial users.

What utilities are doing in their sphere of operations finds its counterpart in what state industrial commissions are doing for the state as a whole. Whether it be an advertisement featuring the grinning face of Governor Rockefeller warming up to industry locating in New York State or a lavender and old rose ad - with magnolias thrown in for free - offering industry the hospitality of Ole Miss, it is evident to one and all that the particular state is hungry for industry and is putting its best foot forward to "trip it in".

What state industrial commissions do at their level, city industrial commissions do at the local level. *Nota bene* the enticing ads for industry on the part of Atlanta, Houston, and Los Angeles. They, like the state, are hungry for the tax ratables, the employment, the primary and secondary economic bases for which incoming industry will be responsible.

Industrial development organizations are also aggressive in the hunt for light industry to locate in the area of their new airports. And not only industry per se has been responsive. Added thereto have been research and development laboratories and industrial parks.

The gravitational pull of large universities, with extensive technical and scientific facilities and their attendant individual expertise, has made itself felt in the location within their purview of industrial research and development organizations. Princeton, New Jersey consequently seeks to make itself known as the research center of the northeast and Ann Arbor, Michigan, as the research center of the midwest.

INDUSTRIAL PROPERTY TRENDS

Our industrial population, just like our residential and commercial population, has become increasingly mobile. The trend toward decentralization has long been evident. Instead of adding large capacities to existing plants at the headquarters location, these industrial properties have been set up in other geographic locations. This avoids the risks of concentration - of having all of one's eggs in one basket.

It also helps to penetrate new markets for the products made.

The migration of industry south has been going on for the last forty years. The textile industry of New England has lost out to the new textile industry in the South. The provision of cheap power from the Tennessee Valley Authority has made decentralization into the southeast especially attractive. The tremendous population surge in the great southwest had made it attractive for industry to locate near these growing markets.

Most of us did not realize the scope of the growth on the Pacific Coast until it was announced a few years ago that California is now the leading state in population. The many new branch plants in the Los Angeles area, as well as in the Richmond-Berkeley section have been in part responsible.

The migration of industry to the Pacific Northwest has been encouraged by the provision of cheap power in this area, by the growth of the aircraft industry here, by the increasing trade emanating from Seattle and other port cities with Japan and other Asiatic countries.

Along with the migration of industry has come the suburbanization of industry. It is no longer necessary to locate in the city itself for nearness to labor supply and transportation. Both are available in the quantities desired out in the suburbs. Most of our industrial growth is now in suburbia. The amount of land desired can be obtained there. The amount of traffic congestion is less. Highway arteries are near at hand. Industrial workers prefer suburban locations. They drive to work and ample parking is provided for their cars.

Time was when the bulk of manufactured goods moved by rail. Now a large part moves by truck. And an increasing amount of light manufactured products is going by air. These alternate forms of transportation give industry greater flexibility of movement. They have had the net effect of reducing the amount of inventory that must be carried. Shipments can move faster and more frequently.

The trend toward the one-story plant has been brought out in another connection. It has made for lower production costs. It has made for greater ease in production flow. The larger space acquired has made it possible to attractively landscape the factory grounds. They are still a far cry from a thing of beauty, but they are a godsend as contrasted with the dreary multi-story industrial boxes of times past.

A Rip van Winkle, waking up after a 20 year sleep, would not recognize today the factory of 20 years ago. In the here and now he would see automation on every hand. He would note a reduction in the amount of human labor required to produce a given quota of goods. He would observe a far greater efficiency in the use of floor area. He would be astounded by the increased land requirements of industry.

INVESTMENT CHARACTERISTICS OF INDUSTRIAL PROPERTY

Most large manufacturing corporations own their own plants. Most have enjoyed high value increments in the land they own. Most have benefited by depreciation write-offs of the structures they built or acquired. These investment characteristics have constituted a distinct plus in their profit position.

Some industrial properties have been financed by the sale-and-lease-back and the sale-and-buy-back techniques. Some have been built on land under long-term net ground lease. Capital appreciation and tax-free cash flows have been enjoyed by the industries themselves and by the institutional investors responsible for the financing. Other industrial properties have been financed out of the retained earnings of the individual companies. The profit productivity of such properties has furnished an attractive investment yield on the money disbursed.

Industrial properties lend themselves to the principle of leverage, for they furnish attractive security for mortgage loans. The lenders are by no means confined to institutional investors, like life insurance companies. The lenders are also pension funds, real estate investment trusts, and financial syndications.

Attractive investment yields have been made on loft-type buildings. In many instances, these are old-time multi-story industrial plants, which have been converted into individual small light manufacturing units and rented out to their occupants. This makes use of an old structure, which otherwise would have seen its day. It is frequently located in a low rent district and therefore provides inexpensive occupancy space to its tenants.

INDUSTRIAL PARKS

The industrial park developer subdivides his tract into usable sites and sells or leases these to prospective users. He puts in the facilities and the utilities required. He creates a controlled environment. He improves his tract on a wholesale basis, and markets it on a retail basis.

The developer sees to it in advance that his area will be zoned for the uses his customers require. If his property is not zoned at the time, he incorporates restrictive covenants on use in his deeds or leases. He makes the shape and size of his lots to fit the requirements of the industries he would like to attract.

His tract is strictly for industry. Therefore, residential uses and structures are banned from the confines of the park. He sets up the standards and controls by which the occupants of his park are guided. Among these will be the prohibition of unreasonable noises, smells, smoke, waste, heat, and vibration.

His is a planned environment. He plans for compatible uses. He plans for light industry, warehousing, and the office facilities in conjunction therewith. He plans for the ingress roads, egress roads, and the arteries within.

Why locate in an industrial park? The building you require is there. The servicing for the area has been pre-arranged. The necessary zoning has been provided. Protection is yours against adverse land uses. The water supply, the sewer, and the power facilities are already in. The park management takes care of the landscaping, street cleaning, and security protection. The costs are distributed over you and the many other occupants and, thereby, the economy is provided of a lower per unit cost than would be yours in a single site. You have the assurance of a continuity of management.

Who are the industrial park developers? They may be professional land developers and real estate brokers. Railroads and public utilities may be the sponsors, looking forward to the patronage they will enjoy from the occupants. They may be joint ventures on the part of the community and its government as a whole. They may be sponsors of New Towns, such as Reston, Virginia, or Columbia, Maryland, desirous of providing industrial employment for the residents.

What are the costs? They are great, and, seemingly, never-ending. There is the basic cost of land acquisition. There is the cost of providing the facilities and the utilities. There is the cost of land preparation. There is the cost of streets and rights of way. There are any number of indirect costs, such as the costs for engineering services and the preparation of plans and surveys. There are the costs of construction - for materials, labor, and supervision.

How are the costs financed? It may be possible to acquire the land under a purchase money mortgage, with a subordination clause, under which the mortgagee agrees to subordinate his claim to a first mortgage subsequently to be obtained from a lending institution. It may be possible to obtain a construction loan through a mortgage banker from a commercial bank. Permanent financing may be secured from a life insurance company, from a real estate investment trust, from a pension fund, or from a financial syndicate.

How is the park marketed? The market is defined and the sights are aimed. The market will usually be confined to a limited range of users. The prospects will be more oriented toward markets than to labor or raw materials. They will be offered the advantages of quick and easy access to the transportation they require. They will be assured of the availability of power and water supply, sprinkler systems, and a sewage treatment plant and pumping stations.

Some industrial parks are university oriented, thereby offering access to academic facilities, scientific and technical installations, and the talent and expertise of members of the faculty. These parks may be set aside for research and development, computer centers, and related administrative functions. Other parks may be airport oriented, a natural for lightweight, high added value goods, with the availability of fast and frequent delivery to customers. Still others may be devoted to light manufacturing, service, and distribution businesses. They may be within easy driving distance of massive industrial complexes, business and commercial centers.

Parks may be set up for occupants who will be servicing a defense or aerospace center nearby. A special training institute for new employees may be established, offering beginning and advanced training in electronics and data processing, thereby serving industry with on-premise instruction.

Mindful of the exodus of industry to the suburbs, both New York and Chicago plan on developing parklike settings where companies can place facilities on reasonable terms. Developers may lease the land from the city at a fixed price, with taxes, improvements, and debt service included therein. Developers are taxed only on the factories they build. They thereby tie up little of their capital in non-depreciable improvements.

In conjunction with the new town industrial parks, but outside their confines, are residential subdivisions for the industrial park employees. The homes are priced in a range from low and moderate income to high. Cultural, entertainment, and recreational facilities are provided for the residents.

Industrial park experience shows that tenancies are relatively stable and compatible, that there is a high ratio of the value of the improvements to the overall property price and consequently substantial tax benefits from depreciation.

Urban renewal has in some instances taken the form of industrial parks. The developer here has been advantaged by the provision of Federal Housing Administration insurance, by the local urban renewal authority having arranged for the necessary zoning and for the ingress and egress arteries, and by the opportunity to conserve on his funds by reason of a minimal down payment. Urban renewal industrial parks are often ancillary to a large industry in the urban environment. Urban renewal locations have been well-suited to customer oriented and land intensive operations.

TRUE AND FALSE QUESTIONS

1. Industrial property is property used for the purpose of manu- T F
   facture.

2. An industrial plant requires a heavy investment. T F

3. Industrial properties are subject to a high liquidity factor. T F

4. Industrial properties are standardized. T F

5. Industrial properties are subject to a high degree of fuctional T F
   obsolescence.

6. The one-story plant has now given way to the multi-story. T F

7. If products lose weight in manufacture, the plant should be T F
   located in proximity to raw materials.

8. If products gain weight in manufacture, the plant should be T F
   located in proximity to the market.

9. The soil for the industrial plant must have adequate permea- T F
   bility for waste disposal.

10. Steel mills tend to locate at the most economical meeting T F
    point for coal and iron ore.

11. In the one-story plant there is waste space for ramps and T F
    elevators.

12. Overhead cranes can move about freely in the one-story T F
    plant.

13. Conveyor belts can operate in continuous movement in a T F
    multi-story plant.

14. It is necessary to locate industrial plants in the city to secure T F
    access to rail transportation.

15. Factory workers are usually dependent on urban transporta- T F
    tion to get to their places of employment.

16. Railroads try to persuade industry to move into the areas   T   F
    they serve so as to derive for themselves the additional
    freight.

17. Light industry may find it to its advantage to locate in airport   T   F
    areas.

18. The gravitational pull of large universities results in the   T   F
    location of many research and development industries in their
    areas.

19. The trend toward decentralization in industry has long been   T   F
    evident.

20. The migration of industry south has now come to an end.   T   F

21. The migration of industry has not been accompanied by the   T   F
    suburbanization of industry.

22. Most industrial growth is now taking place in suburbia.   T   F

23. Industrial workers prefer in city locations for the plants in   T   F
    which they work.

24. The one-story plant has made for lower production costs.   T   F

25. Most large manufacturing corporations lease their plants.   T   F

26. The construction of new industrial plants is not financed out   T   F
    of retained earnings.

27. Loft-type buildings are often old-time multi-story plants.   T   F

28. The industrial park developer provides a controlled environ-   T   F
    ment.

29. The industrial park may combine industry with residences   T   F
    therein.

30. The industrial park caters both to light and heavy industry.   T   F

31. The servicing for the industrial park has been pre-arranged.   T   F

32. There is assurance of continuity of management in an indus-   T   F
    trial park.

33. The market for the industrial park will usually be confined   T   F
    to a limited range of users.

34. Industrial parks cannot be university oriented.   T   F

35. Industrial parks may be airport oriented.   T   F

36. Federal assistance will not be provided for new towns which   T   F
    incorporate industrial parks.

37. Tenancies in industrial parks are relatively unstable.   T   F

38. Urban renewal may take the form of industrial parks.   T   F

39. Urban renewal industrial parks may enjoy the advantage of   T   F
    FHA-insurance.

40. In industrial parks, there is a high ratio of building value to   T   F
    land value.

MULTIPLE CHOICE

41. Research and development industrial parks are usually:
    ( ) Airport oriented
    ( ) Urban renewal oriented
    ( ) Urban rehabilitation oriented
    ( ) University oriented

42. The lending institution on an industrial park may be:
    ( ) A life insurance company
    ( ) A real estate investment trust
    ( ) A pension fund
    ( ) Any of the above

43. If the lending institution on an industrial park is to be persuaded to make the loan, then the purchase money mortgage on the basis of which the land was acquired must contain:
    ( ) A lease and release
    ( ) A take-out letter
    ( ) An advance commitment
    ( ) A subordination clause

44. The industrial park provides protection against:
    ( ) The entry of minority groups
    ( ) Adverse land uses
    ( ) Inflation
    ( ) Stepped-up rentals

45. Loft-type buildings are frequently located:
    ( ) In a low rent district
    ( ) In a high rent district
    ( ) In new suburban areas
    ( ) In exurbia

46. The textile industry of New England has lost out to:
    ( ) The new textile industry in the south
    ( ) The textile industry on the Pacific Coast
    ( ) The textile industry of the middle west
    ( ) The textile industry of the northwest

47. The campaign, providing tax concessions, to persuade industry to locate in Puerto Rico is called:
    ( ) Operation Breakthrough

( ) Operation Bootstrap
( ) Everything for Industry
( ) Decentralization for industry

48. A plant losing weight in the manufacturing process is said to be:
( ) A shrinking industry
( ) Depleting
( ) Raw materials oriented
( ) Semi-finished goods oriented

49. A plant gaining weight in the manufacturing process is said to be:
( ) An expanding industry
( ) An accretion industry
( ) Value oriented
( ) Market oriented

50. Industrial plants no longer need city locations for access to rail transportation, because now there is provided on the urban peripheries:
( ) Supplemental truck transportation
( ) Belt-line railroads
( ) Light cargo air transportation
( ) Helicopter and short take off and landing air transportation.

ESSAY QUESTIONS

1. What are the characteristics of industrial properties?

2. What are the locational factors for industrial properties?

3. What are the investment characteristics of industrial property?

PART VIII
REAL ESTATE
AND URBAN
DEVELOPMENT

URBAN RENEWAL AND REHABILITATION

CHAPTER TWENTY-THREE

URBAN RENEWAL

Urban renewal is doing whatever is necessary to end blight and clear slums, to repair and renovate, to restore progress and end decay.

City areas may fester and go to seed. Physical deterioration and functional and economic obsolescence take their toll. The downhill road to degradation follows the line of least resistance. What was once an area of fine homes is now a district of disreputable slums. What was once a high class business district has become cheap and "honky-tonk". Urban renewal tries to "x-ray" out these cancerous growths and, in the process, make for a city reborn.

In most cities of the United States, the need for urban renewal is obvious. Obsolete office buildings meet the eye. Residential properties are now dismal tenements. Neighborhoods are in a state of degeneration. Blight is begetting blight. Downtown is frayed, shabby, and down at the heel. Watermains are breaking. Buildings have been torn down and rubble left in their place. There are acres of abandoned buildings. Traffic congestion is a sin and a shame - bumper to bumper, with attendant frustrations. Building facades are frowzy and forlorn. Archaic buildings, uncollected garbage, overturned ash cans, holes in the streets and pitfalls in the sidewalks, torn paper and debris, broken beer bottles and empty cans - all this, an apalling panorama making a plaintive plea for diagnosis of ills and prescription to cure.

What has happened? The more affluent residents - those who care about their properties - have moved away, first to the suburbs and then beyond, to exurbia. They work in the city, but they live in the country. Trying to find a place to park downtown, the crime in the streets, the traffic congestion on downtown traffic arteries have caused a stampede to the suburbs. Stores have moved out of downtown. So have banks. Industries have expanded in urban peripheries and abandoned downtown locations.

What comes about as the result? As higher income groups have moved out, lower income groups have moved in. As the economic base has shrunk, so has the tax base. As the city has tried to keep its services viable, it has raised taxes to do so and these higher taxes in turn have deterred new tax ratables from moving in. Payrolls have declined. Population has gone down. Sluggish transportation has led to the slough of despond of further stagnation. The lead in the air has brought about mental and physical lethargy and an accompaniment of sporadic hostility. Air pollution is four times as bad in the city as it is in the country. The water the inmates drink becomes a mess of polluted pottage, embalmed in chlorine. The effluents on the city beaches make them unsafe to use.

So you muse and ponder on what can be done. What is the cure? How can you get higher income groups to move back to the city? How can you persuade high class stores to stay in the city? What additional space can you find for off-street parking? How can you bring industry back to the central core? How can you provide mass transit that is fast, economical, and free from hoods? How can you get the money for city beautification, cultural and recreational areas, shopping malls, and social amenities.

Who is to start urban renewal? It can start from individuals and organizations sincere in their desire for betterment and dedicated to the consummation of this objective. It can start from civic neighborhood associations, service clubs, chambers of commerce, church groups, fraternal organizations, and educational societies. Local real estate boards can be, and are, a viable force in the promotion of such civic betterments.

The greater the degree of interested participation at the local level, the greater the chances are for the success of urban renewal. The groups may overlap. Their functions may duplicate. But they realize that they can accomplish more as a team pulling together than they can by pulling apart.

The Government and Urban Renewal

If these individuals and organizations acted on their own in urban renewal, they would be beset by the problems interposed by property owners who would balk at their properties being taken over. Either they would just not permit it, or they would exploit their monopoly position by charging exorbitant prices. Speculators would also get into the act and buy up all the properties they could, anticipating a handsome windfall in the form of the higher prices that urban renewal takings would bring about.

Interested and worthwhile as these urban renewal entrepreneurs are, they must be armed with an official weapon under which they can take over the property required from recalcitrant property owners. Consequently, it is necessary for stable enabling legislation to be enacted authorizing the local urban renewal authority to exercise the power of eminent domain and the use of condemnation proceedings where necessary.

The Federal Government assists financially by subsidizing the costs for making urban renewal projects ready for development. The local urban renewal authority submits to the Federal Government a workable plan. This shows the need for renewal, presents a master plan for the community's development, assures the execution of the project in accordance with health and safety requirements, and provides evidence of the local organization responsible for implementation.

If the workable plan is approved, the Federal Government will pay two-thirds of the net cost of renewal and the local government must pay one-third. The net cost of renewal means the difference between what it costs to acquire and clear the properties, and what is secured for them from the urban renewal developer.

Private developers on urban renewal may apply to the Federal Housing Administration for insurance on the loans they require to carry out their developments.   The FHA will evaluate the properties on the assumption that the improvements set forth will be carried out.   It thereby becomes possible for a developer to secure control of a large property with the advancement of a small equity of his own.   Over and above this, he is relieved of the headaches of securing zoning ordinance variances and building code exceptions, for these have all been provided for by the local urban renewal authority.   It has likewise taken the measures to provide ingress roads to and egress roads from the area set up for development.

The local urban renewal authority must now provide displaced families with housing within their financial means.   Federal grants are provided for moving and relocation expenses. Such relocation payments are not taxable income.   The Federal Government provides funds for public housing for those displaced.

The Realtor and Urban Renewal

Where does the Realtor fit in this scheme of things?   His real estate experience and knowledge of the area qualify him for preparing the background studies to establish the workable program.

He is well equipped to serve on the local urban renewal authority. He knows values. He knows what is needed. He knows what areas are blighted. He knows whether it is feasible to try to effect a cure. But he may have problems. The local urban renewal authority does get embroiled in controversial issues as to where urban renewal should take place and what particular forms it should assume. Serving on the authority, the Realtor will have to take sides. This may make for opposition and this in turn may alienate customer potential.

The Realtor is well qualified by virtue of his experience and the taking of courses to acquire his professional designations to evaluate the properties to be taken for urban renewal.   He is equally well qualified to hypothetically evaluate their worth on the basis of the improvements that urban renewal will effectuate.

It is only natural that those displaced from their residence or place of business by urban renewal should look to the Realtor to find them their new locations.   The Realtor may look to the payments they have received from their old properties as qualifying them for the down payment at least for the homes and places of business they would now like to have.

The Realtor may himself be the developer in urban renewal. If not, he may sell or rent the improvements the developer has put up.   He may likewise be of assistance to the developer in negotiating the financing required.   He knows the sources of mortgage money and the likely attitude of lending officials.

What Has Urban Renewal Accomplished?

It has converted downtown shopping districts into giant shopping plazas.   It has cleared streets for pedestrian traffic.   It has established office building complexes in places of slums and civic blight. It has developed thriving industrial parks. In downtown Philadelphia, Penn Center has taken the place of the old Chinese Wall. Society Hill has replaced a slough of slums. The area around Independence Hall has been modernized and renovated. In Pittsburgh an industrial slum in a smoke-laden area has been transformed into an urban show place. In Indianapolis, the James Whitcomb Riley Center, a city within a city, has taken the place of decayed buildings and sub-standard housing.

In city after city urban renewal has developed new transportation systems and traffic has been expedited; new parking areas have been made, both overhead and underground; smog has been eliminated; new street lighting has turned night into day; the Lincoln Center in New York has set the pace for other new cultural centers giving mental and aesthetic enrichment; and new recreational areas have been opened up where strong bodies can be built and maintained.

Urban renewal has introduced new and attractive architectural styles; has made its new buildings reasonably consistent in appearance with one another, and yet refreshingly varied; has used the latest in air conditioning and temperature controls, and in sound and weather insulation. It has made for beautification and landscaping in commercial downtown.

Urban renewal has worked best where the responsible public has been behind it, participated in it, contributed to it, and regarded it not as an expense, but an investment.

URBAN REHABILITATION

This has the same objective as urban renewal, namely, to stop blight and urban decay. Urban rehabilitation does whatever is necessary to bring a basically sound, but run down or presently unsuitable property into condition for constructive use.

Unlike urban renewal, it does not engage in slum clearance, bulldozing, and demolition. Unlike urban renewal, it confines itself to repairs, renovation, modernizing, renovating, and refurbishing. Like urban renewal, it receives both Federal and state financial assistance.

Unlike urban renewal, urban rehabilitation does not present the problems of relocation of displaced families and places of business. Unlike urban renewal, it does not uproot and break up existing neighborhoods. Urban rehabilitation does preserve what is sound, improves on it, and makes it more useful and up to date.

Under urban rehabilitation, buildings to be spared must meet standards set up. This means that housing inspectors check these buildings and determine what must be done to bring them up to scratch. This has stirred housewives to anger with comments such as these:

> "It's like having another cook in our kitchen or having our mother-in-law visit."
> "It's mostly a woman's war. This is our domain. Our husbands don't like it either, but they're not livid because they're not around when the inspectors come."

Those opposed to urban rehabilitation allege that building inspectors violate the Fourth Amendment which guarantees the security of houses, papers, and effects. They claim that they are forced into debt to pay for improvements they neither want or need and that the inspectors assume the role both of judge and interior decorator.

Nevertheless, the tide is ebbing away from urban renewal and toward urban rehabilitation. The recent tax reform bill, for example, now permits five year accelerated depreciation on urban rehabilitation for low and moderate income housing. Realtors are finding that structures, when improved by urban rehabilitation, develop into attractive listings for them.

URBAN DEVELOPMENT PROGRAMS

There are so many. They try to fit every category of need. Most of them at the Federal level are under the jurisdiction of the Department of Housing and Urban Development.

Of the many divisions of this Department, the one most concerned with urban renewal is the Renewal Assistance Administration. This administers Federal loans and grants aids to communities to plan and complete urban renewal projects. It establishes procedures for urban renewal specialists to follow.

Neighborhood development programs have been established, not to provide aid for an entire community, but, rather, for specific blighted neighborhoods which may be widely removed from one another. The loan or the grant will be in amount to cover the cost of the activities planned for a 12 month period. If funds still continue available and the neighborhood still needs aid, it can secure this in subsequent years for acceptable programs.

Some cities under urban renewal, instead of selling the land to developers, have been leasing it to them. The lease is for a term of years at least as long as the anticipated functional life expectancy of the buildings. Cities find it more advantageous to lease their property when they can carry the land at less cost than the rent received from the developer. The developers find leasing advantageous in that it enables them to secure the land without the disbursement of any capital on their part.

THE FEDERAL HOUSING ADMINISTRATION
AND URBAN RENEWAL

FHA insurance can be had for certified urban renewal plans for rehabilitation and new construction loans, as well as for home improvement loans.

The push is now on for low-cost relocation housing. In response thereto, loans may now be insured for 100 per cent of FHA-appraised value to mortgagors who become occupants. Loans may be insured up to 85 per cent of appraised value to mortgagors who do not become occupants. Loans may be insured for relocation housing, even though the displacement occurs for reasons other than urban renewal. This could come about, for example, where families were displaced by eminent domain or as a result of the building they occupy not complying with the building code.

FHA insurance is provided now for co-operative housing, housing for the elderly, and home improvement loans outside of urban renewal areas.

A secondary market for these mortgage loans is assured through the Federal National Mortgage Association and the Government National Mortgage Association.

Where Has Urban Renewal Failed?

It has not lived up to its rosy predictions. Instead of housing costs becoming less expensive, they have become higher after urban renewal than they were before. Displaced families, to get any place in which to stay, have been forced to move into sub-standard housing. It has bull-dozed poor people out of their homes and increased population congestion in the central cities.

In the city of Cleveland, urban renewal diminished the housing available for the poor and decreased the tax base. Although a plan was formulated to provide new housing units for those displaced, no developer would bid on this and the land was sold for schools and other civic projects. There, urban renewal meant Negro removal, and the only place to which to go was the Hough district, the scene of riots.

In the city of Detroit, urban renewal also bulldozed the poor out of their dwelling space. This resulted in congestion in the riot scarred Twelfth Street are, the number of people there rising from 16,000 in 1957 to 34,000 in 1967.

In the city of Philadelphia political corruption in urban renewal has reared its ugly head. Forty-seven firms and individuals, officials, and civic leaders were indicted. The chairmen of the Housing and Redevelopment Authorities had to resign under pressure. Ties have been shown between organized crime and urban renewal. Payoffs have been made to building inspectors in Philadelphia urban renewal to persuade them to look the other way. Unqualified urban renewal developers have been approved for the job. Although 12,605 new units have been provided in the last ten years, 18,105 have been demolished. Instead of going for urban renewal housing for the poor, 20 per cent of the urban renewal dollar has gone for middle and upper income housing and 50 per cent has gone for commercial, industrial, and institutional units. In the leased housing program under urban renewal, owners of substandard housing have unloaded their headaches on the local urban renewal authority and secured guaranteed rent.

The administration of urban renewal has been lax. Many projects have been running one to four years behind schedule. Records have not been kept of where those displaced have been re-located.

Families with the least resources for mobility and coping with changes in location have been the most adversely affected by displacement. Existing patterns of segregation have been perpetuated. Psychological disturbances in individuals have arisen because of the uprooting experience caused by displacement. Small businessmen have been disadvantaged by the demolition of their properties and the pooling of cleared land for sale to corporate chains. The natural neighborhoods and the cultures which they engendered have been broken up. People, linked by custom, tradition, national backgrounds, and social affinities have been split up and transplanted and the natural ties, so sentimentally sealed, have been broken. Displacement has brought with it a weakening of the ties of church, kinship, and schools which have long linked neighborhoods together.

No one can deny that urban renewal has been oversold. It cannot construct moderate cost housing and still provide the architectural beauty desired. It cannot guarantee that the same people as before will live in the same areas and with the same shelter costs. It cannot guarantee the business life of small shopkeepers in the face of chain competition.

Listen to the poignant wail of Mrs. Mattie Dorsey of Ypsilanti, Michigan, about to be uprooted by urban renewal: "We human beings are being treated like cattle. We've been trying to pull ourselves up by the bootstraps. We wanted to continue living where we are. Urban renewal is not for us. If it was for us, we wouldn't be objecting. You have the fist of the municipal government to pound down upon us. We are the helpless victims."

Or hear the objections of Mrs. Pearl Myers at the same urban renewal hearing: "Please, please, people go away, and leave us alone, just please. I'm asking God to move you all. Please leave us alone, and let us live. I'm 74 years old, and what can a body do when it gets too old to work, and I've worked so hard till my heart almost give way. Now you all try to make slaves of us. Go someplace else, and leave us poor colored folks alone."

And in the same vein the testimony of Mrs. Erma Mashatt: "I'm trying my best to pay my taxes. I've had two heart attacks, and I've still paid my taxes, but I'm living on Social Security. I've tried to buy a home, but when I go to see it, the owner says it has been sold. Now I'm getting gray worrying about what tomorrow will bring. I'm satisfied with my end of town. What do you want me to do, live in a tent, like you forced the Indians to do?"

Sentiments such as these have altered urban renewal policy. In urban renewal projects now, prime consideration must be given to low-and moderate-income housing projects. Still troubling urban renewal, however, are the long periods of time required to get projects started, the many official approvals necessary, and the paper work and the red tape involved in procuring Federal funds.

FEDERAL FINANCIAL ASSISTANCE

Grants will be made to cover the cost of planning for the future for an entire area. Grants will likewise be made to determine the boundaries of a specific approved renewal project, the terms of eligibility for entrance therein, the costs of site clearance, and the expense of making improvements.

Demonstration project grants are now being made. They will defray two-thirds of the cost of pilot projects set up to determine feasibility.

Grants will be made to assist in urban planning for municipalities of less than 5,000 population. They will also be provided for areas confronted with the prospect of rapid urbanization, due, for example, to a new Federal installation.

A community has to make preparations for an urban renewal program. It has to identify deteriorated and declining areas. It has to check into what resources are available in the community for financing the project, relocating displaced families and businesses, and utilizing the land to be cleared. Grants will therefore be made to defray the costs of these preparations.

Many communities are far behind in their building code enforcement. To enable them to catch up, grants will be given them to cover two-thirds of the enforcement cost.

If a building is found to be structurally unsound or unfit for human habitation, grants for up to two-thirds of the cost will be made for its demolition. However, as a condition precedent thereto, those to be displaced must be assured of relocation assistance.

Reflecting the push toward rehabilitation, loans at low interest rates will be made to finance the rehabilitation necessary to enable structures to meet requirements. If property becomes uninsurable because of physical hazards, loans for its rehabilitation will be made either to tenants or owners. A low-income occupant of housing in need of rehabilitation may be given a grant of up to $3,000 for this purpose.

A particular neighborhood may find it necessary to set up facilities for job training and employment referrals, for family counseling, for the dissemination of information to citizens on their civil rights and legal aid, for adult and remedial education, for day care, and for physical and mental health consultation. If so, grants for these purposes will be provided.

Reflecting the increased interest in the environment and its beautification, the Department of Housing and Urban Development will pay up to 50 per cent of the cost for the acquisition, preservation, and development of land for recreation and conservation. If no urban space is presently available, these grants may be employed for the acquisition of land with structures thereon, which will be demolished and the land cleared. Relocation assistance will be provided for those displaced.

National housing partnerships have now been formed between the Federal government and private corporations. Their purpose is to engage in joint ventures for the development of low and moderate income housing.

SPECIAL HOUSING ASSISTANCE

For the construction of low rent public housing, the Federal government will guarantee the payment of principal and interest on the bonds issued by local housing authorities to provide the funds. It will also make loans to finance the preliminary developments. It will make annual contributions to permit operations at rents within the means of low-income families. The housing project, however, must be exempt from local taxes. But it may contribute, in lieu of taxes, up to ten per cent of shelter rent. This is gross rent minus utilities.

This public housing may be new construction or existing housing may be acquired. Since existing housing may be made immediately available, it is called "instant housing" or "turnkey housing", since all you have to do to get in is to turn the key.

The Department of Housing and Urban Development also makes loans at low interest rates and for long periods for the construction of college housing or the acquisition of existing housing which can be used for this purpose.

For the benefit of senior citizens, low-interest, long-term loans are also made.

TRUE AND FALSE QUESTIONS

1. The law requires that neighborhood development programs   T   F
   be in close proximity, one to another.

2. The law does not permit a city to deed urban renewal land   T   F
   to a developer.

3. FHA insurance is now available for home improvement loans   T   F
   under urban renewal.

4. For low-cost relocation housing, FHA will now insure loans   T   F
   up to 100 per cent of FHA-appraised value, regardless of
   whether the mortgagors do or do not become occupiers.

5. FHA will insure loans for relocation housing, only if dis-   T   F
   placement occurs because of urban renewal.

6. Demonstration project grants are available from the Depart-   T   F
   ment of Housing and Urban Development to pay for part
   of the cost of pilot projects.

7. Grants are available for smaller communities for urban   T   F
   planning to prepare for rapid urbanization expected.

8. A community drawing up a workable program for com-   T   F
   munity renewal is obligated to pay the entire cost itself.

9. Federal grants are not available for building code enforce-   T   F
   ment programs.

10. Before a Federal grant for demolition will be made, the   T   F
    community must provide relocation housing for those to
    be displaced.

11. Federal rehabilitation loans will be made only to owners -   T   F
    not to tenants.

12. Relocation assistance is not provided for those displaced by   T   F
    beautification programs.

13. National Housing Partnerships are limited to relocation   T   F
    housing.

14. The Federal Government will not guarantee interest on T   F
    bonds of local housing authorities for low-rent public
    housing.

15. Local public housing projects are required to pay local T   F
    taxes.

16. Public housing must be new construction.   T   F

17. Occupancy of senior citizen housing where Federal assist- T   F
    ance applies is restricted to low and middle income.

18. The Federal Government will guarantee the debentures of T   F
    accredited developers for approved planned communities.

19. Urban renewal low-income housing may not employ the T   F
    condominium form.

20. Both the tax base and the economic base of cities have T   F
    shrunk.

21. Urban renewal can start only with public agencies.   T   F

22. For effective urban renewal, state enabling legislation must T   F
    be enacted authorizing the local authority to exercise eminent
    domain.

23. The local authority must submit a workable plan to HUD. T   F

24. If the workable plan is approved, the Federal Government T   F
    will pay two-thirds of the net cost of renewal.

25. Private developers on urban renewal cannot secure FHA T   F
    insurance.

26. The local authority must provide displaced families with T   F
    housing within their financial means.

27. Federal grants are now provided for moving and relocation T   F
    expenses in connection with urban renewal.

28. The Federal Government does not provide public housing T   F
    for those displaced by urban renewal.

29. The Realtor may himself be the developer in urban renewal. T   F

30. Housing costs in general have become higher after urban T   F
    renewal than they were before.

31. Urban renewal has cured existing patterns of segregation.   T   F

32. Urban renewal in general has been oversold.   T   F

33. Urban rehabilitation has a different objective from urban   T   F
renewal.

34. Urban rehabilitation presents problems of relocation.   T   F

35. The new tax reform bill permits five-year accelerated de-   T   F
preciation on urban rehabilitation.

36. FHA insurance may be secured on loans for relocation   T   F
housing, only if the displacement occurs because of urban
renewal.

37. Federal grants are available only for planning within a   T   F
limited neighborhood area.

38. HUD will provide financial assistance for the acquisition   T   F
of scenic easements.

39. National Housing Partnerships are joint ventures.   T   F

40. "Instant housing" means the same thing as "turnkey   T   F
housing".

MULTIPLE CHOICE

41. When a city rents out its land for urban renewal to a developer, the period of the lease is usually based on:
    ( ) The physical life expectancy of the buildings
    ( ) The functional life expectancy of the buildings
    ( ) The period of the covering FHA loan
    ( ) The period required to recover amortization charges

42. The national housing partnerships of the Department of Housing and Urban Development are between:
    ( ) The government and private corporations
    ( ) Private corporations
    ( ) Low income groups
    ( ) Low and middle income groups

43. Shelter rent is:
    ( ) The gross rent for shelter
    ( ) The net rent after payment of taxes
    ( ) The gross rent minus utilities
    ( ) The rent allocable for shelter after deducting charges for open space

44. To facilitate financing for planned communities, the Federal government will:
    ( ) Make grants directly to the developer concerned
    ( ) Make loans directly to private accredited developers
    ( ) Guarantee the debentures of accredited private developers
    ( ) Guarantee the industrial revenue bonds of the municipality concerned

45. Urban rehabilitation receives:
    ( ) Only Federal financial assistance
    ( ) Only State financial assistance
    ( ) Both state and federal financial assistance
    ( ) Only FHA insurance and VA guarantees

46. Neighborhood development programs have been established:
    ( ) To provide aid for an entire community
    ( ) To provide aid for specific blighted areas
    ( ) By the Department of Health, Welfare, and Education
    ( ) To render aid only to those on welfare and relief

47. A secondary mortgage market for low-cost relocation housing loans is provided by:
( ) FHA
( ) VA
( ) FNMA
( ) The open market committee of the Federal Reserve System

48. For special housing assistance from HUD for low rent public housing, the project:
( ) Must be limited to welfare tenants
( ) Must be limited to those displaced by urban renewal
( ) Must qualify for Section 236 treatment
( ) Must be free from local taxes

49. FHA will evaluate urban renewal projects on the assumption:
( ) They will be limited to low income groups
( ) They will include minority groups
( ) They will be carried out
( ) That the properties will be subject only to physical deterioration

50. If the workable plan is approved, the Federal Government:
( ) Will pay the entire cost of urban renewal
( ) Will pay two-thirds of the net cost for urban renewal
( ) Will condemn the property
( ) Will submit the plan to a vote of the citizenry

ESSAY QUESTIONS

1. Where does the Realtor fit in urban renewal?

2. What has urban renewal accomplished?

3. Where has urban renewal failed?

TRANSPORTATION AND REAL ESTATE VALUES

CHAPTER TWENTY-FOUR

THE PROBLEM

Transportation in metropolitan areas has come to a critical state. Traffic congestion results in an appalling waste in manpower, time, and energy every working day. A special complication is the twice-daily peak of traffic at the rush hour. Our streets and highways then become strangled with cars trying to reach center-city locations or new industrial concentrations. The influx of workers into many cities doubles the population during the daylight hours. Delays in downtown traffic absorb 18 to 20 per cent of total vehicle running time.

Cities are no longer able to handle their transportation problems by themselves. Highways and motor vehicles have erased political boundaries and demand inter-city, state, and regional approaches for the solution of their problems. Those who move to the suburbs continue to contribute to central city traffic as they return each day as commuters. Taxes paid by the central districts of our large cities carry a large burden of compensating for public deficits. These in turn mean higher taxes on real estate and motivate business and industry to leave the city for the country.

If we continue on present course, people coming to work by car will spend almost as much time in commuting as they spend at work. More and more tax ratables will be transformed into more and more asphalt and concrete for driving and parking lots. Downtown will become less and less desirable as a place in which to shop. Open space will disappear.

Within the next 30 years our population will increase by substantial proportions. Where will these people live? Certainly not in the cities, if they can help it. They will spread out more and more into the suburbs. As they do so, more and more roads will be built to accommodate the cars they will drive to work, the shopping centers, schools, and recreational areas. The trips they make by car will be longer and slower.

If suburban communities continue to try to solve their population problems by zoning requiring larger lots on which to build, they will of necessity lose ground for recreational areas. The few stretches of woods and fields we still have will then become a thing of the past.

Traffic congestion on streets and highways is not the whole transportation problem. What are we going to do about the many new airports required? The situation at many present airports is becoming intolerable, not only with air traffic congestion, but also with congestion on the arteries leading to and from these terminals. Where should our new airports be located? What should we be doing about other new airports to supply feeder services to the big metropolitan air terminals?

Are we presently making full use of the port and harbor facilities we have? What new dredging should be done on our rivers to make them more attractive for cargo-carrying vessels? Are we fully exploiting the commercial opportunities we have for improved waterway transportation? What new bridges should be built? What old bridges should be improved and modernized?

How can we make transportation accessible to the disadvantaged groups in our society? How can they find employment if the bus does not go where the jobs are? Can mass transportation be so developed that the social purposes of transportation can be realized with greater economy and efficiency?

HOW IS THIS PROBLEM RELATED TO REAL ESTATE?

Real estate is concerned with any problem that affects the attractiveness and therefore the value of real estate. As civic-minded and constructive people, those in real estate are concerned with any problem that affects the future of their area.

As traffic congestion makes cities less attractive in which to work, shop, and live, urban real estate values decline. As highway congestion makes it more and more difficult and frustrating to get to resort and recreational areas, they lose their appeal for the market to which they cater.

As new shopping centers, industrial parks, and industrial developments are put up farther and farther out in the country, the transportation arteries to get to them must be provided. There must be convenient ingress and egress.

The provision of transportation is not only for the movement of people, it is also for the movement of goods and commodities. The raw materials and semi-finished shapes for industry must be transported to the factory and the finished products must move from factory to market. The economic base of an area cannot survive a blood clot in its transportation arteries.

We in real estate are concerned that land be put to its highest and best use. We therefore question whether the constant construction of more and more streets and highways will bring this about. In such construction we see the removal of tax ratables that could be devoted to economic productivity.

Instead of more and more streets and highways, we ask whether alternate means of transportation could be used instead - like the rail rights of way, present subway systems and the creation of new ones, and the monorail.

We are concerned with the economics of transportation. Convenient and flexible as the passenger car may be, is its use as economic as rail transit? Is the construction of new highways as economic as the preservation of present rail rights of way and the provision of new ones?

We in real estate are well aware of the financial plight of the commuter railroads. We know that most of them would like to give up their commuter service altogether. At the same time, we know that commuter operations have been successful, as in the Chicago metropolitan area, and it is difficult for us to see why a corresponding success could not be achieved in our own locale.

We become perplexed by what seem contrary and inconsistent trends in transportation. On the one hand, we see a rise in real estate values as more real estate developments spring up after new streets and highways have been built. On the other hand, we see a decline in real estate values when these transportation arteries reach the saturation point. Where is the breaking point? When is it reached? What should be done about it when it occurs?

We are seriously concerned about the displacements of families and businesses that come about through highway developments. How can we measure in monetary terms the uprooting experience from the neighborhood where one has lived, being torn apart from the friends one has made? How can we find a corresponding neighborhood for one so displaced? What about the business that is bulldozed out and has to transpose itself to a new and strange environment and try to rebuild a market anew in alien surroundings? Suppose the new highway has an adverse effect on the flora and fauna of an area? Suppose it eradicates a recreational or historical site?

HOW HAS IMPROVED TRANSPORTATION ENHANCED REAL ESTATE VALUES?

Improved transportation makes real estate more accessible. The more accessible real estate is, the more valuable it becomes. The evidence of this is there for all to see.

Improved transportation results in the setting up of shopping centers, factories, parks, recreational areas, and new residential communities. Highway routes exercise a decisive role as to where new plants will locate. Surveys show our interstate highway system has increased land values, such as motor inns, restaurants, service stations, and industrial plants have clustered near the interchanges. The improvement in economic activity has coincided with the improvement in transportation. Land values have increased with increases in economic productivity.

The 15 mile rapid transit line from downtown Philadelphia and Camden to the South Jersey countryside brought about the erection of over 100 new apartment houses. Property across from the terminal rose ten times in value. Surveys have been taken to determine why people chose to live in certain suburbs in northern New Jersey. About one-quarter of the questionees said it was because of the convenient commuter service of the Erie-Lackawanna Railroad.

A major factor in the move of industry and research and development facilities to particular locations has been the provision of rapid transit service. The companies concerned have known that their chances of getting the personnel they want are better when their people are assured of adequate rail transit.

In Houston, during a five-year period, land values along the Gulf Freeway increased 65 per cent more in dollar value than land distant from this facility. Also, the Houston Channel has been a major factor in making for Houston's phenomenal growth and rise in real estate values.

The Central Expressway in Dallas brought about an increase in valuation of abutting properties amounting to 544 per cent. Communities along Boston's circumferential freeway enjoyed an increase in property values of 700 per cent. In Atlanta undeveloped land rose from $100 an acre to $1400 per acre after its freeway was built. After Cleveland inaugurated its rapid transit line, over 30 commercial and apartment buildings were constructed along its route.

IS BUILDING MORE HIGHWAYS
THE ANSWER TO TRAFFIC CONGESTION?

Los Angeles thought this was the answer. Los Angeles built more and more highways and added to the lanes of existing ones. Los Angeles tried to meet its traffic needs by widening its streets and by building additional parking areas.

Los Angeles did these things, but this did not solve its traffic congestion problems. It did find out that construction costs were staggering and that the loss in tax ratables was tremendous. No one has figured out how to lay a tax on a city street. The more miles of freeways Los Angeles built, the more automobiles it put on them. The more automobiles it put on them, the more freeways it had to build. Aerospace engineers are even suggesting triple-decking the Los Angeles freeways to handle the rush-hour traffic, but this will not solve the problem of where to park the cars when they reach their destination.

Just think of it! 25 per cent of Los Angeles land area is taken up by streets, expressways, and parking facilities. Two-thirds of Los Angeles downtown district is so pre-empted. Holding congestion in Los Angeles to present levels will require 32 additional freeway lanes and 38 arterial street lanes by 1980.

Not only Los Angeles, but all urban centers have found that freeways take valuable land off the tax rolls and thereby increase the tax burden on the remainder. They have further found that freeways displace families and businesses. They have discovered that freeways cut suburbs in half and amputate neighborhoods from main commuities.

Visualize yourself in any American city in rush-hour traffic! Think of the excessive time it takes you to get into or out of a parking garage, to weave through congested streets to a freeway entrance, to get into line at the entrance, and then crawl up the ramp and try to push your way into the moving stream of traffic.

We have tried to accommodate commuter traffic by the construction of more highways. And we have met with many problems. So many of our people wish to commute and live in suburbia and exurbia. They are so scattered. We cannot devise a form of mass transportation to service these people where they live. Consequently, most of them try to do the whole commuting job by private car. But we cannot seem to build enough highways to keep up with this type of transportation. Soon these very highways become blocked out of the destinations they try to reach, for the cities into which they feed are unable to handle the increase of traffic on their streets.

By tearing down more houses to build more highways to accommodate increased traffic, we are compounding our problem by driving our residents farther and farther out into the country. And, by suburbanizing our countryside, we are destroying the very values people seek there.

Land in metropolitan areas is now at a premium. Rights of way are becoming more and more difficult to acquire. The alignment of every one of our new highways becomes a controversy as residents and businessmen fight displacement. Although every municipality wants good transportation, none wants to give up tax ratables thereby lost.

HIGHWAY CONSTRUCTION COSTS?

As our highway needs mount in geometrical proportions, the building of new ones becomes more and more expensive. They key portions of urban expressways now average out to a cost of about $25 million per mile. Individual portions are likewise exorbitant. A 1¼ mile downtown stretch of Boston's Central Artery cost more than $45 million a mile. It will cost $46 million a mile to build the proposed crosstown expressway in Manhattan.

Highway building has become a $7 billion a year industry, providing markets for cement, asphalt, and steel, and employing 850,000 construction workers and state highway department employees. At the Federal level alone, motorists and truckers pay $4 billion annually in highway taxes.

Are highway users paying their way with the taxes they have to bear? A study on this subject was made with regard to the 15-mile Northwest Expressway onto downtown Chicago.. This was built at a total cost of $238 million. If placed on a financing basis equal to that typical for public transportation improvements, capital charges would amount to $11.0 million a year. On the other hand, fuel and other related taxes paid by vehicles operating over the Expressway amounted to $3.8 million a year. Therefore, it would seem that user taxes cover only one-third of the capital cost. Nothing is left over to cover the expressway maintenance costs, the operating costs, the cost of traffic control, and annual charges. Where does the extra money required come from? From taxes on fuel consumed by vehicles operating over roads and streets *already* completed, some for decades.

If a freeway built to handle peak-hour urban commuting would cost $2,000,000 per lane mile, the tax on gasoline burned on the freeway at peak hours would have to be increased by 75¢ a gallon to cover the cost. The subsidy to rush-hour motorists on typical urban expressways and streets is about 10 cents a mile per automobile. A person driving 25 miles to work and 25 miles from work during rush hours in a metropolitan area is subsidized about $5.00 a day, or perhaps 50¢ or $1. less if he passes toll gates.

In addition to the construction costs of the highways themselves, there is the time lost because of congestion in travel itself and in the functions related to travel, such as deliveries.

HOW ARE HIGHWAY CONSTRUCTION COSTS FINANCED?

State highways almost totally, and local roads and streets to a considerable extent, are financed from highway-user taxes, principally motorfuel taxes and vehicle registration fees.

The Federal government has a continuing grant in aid program to assist the states in highway improvement. But the entire burden of maintenance, administration, and regulation falls on the states and the localities. The states choose the routes for development, select and plan the projects to be built each year, acquire the necessary rights of way, and award and supervise the construction contracts. The states pay for the work that is done and then get reimbursement from the Federal Government for its share of the cost.

Interstate highway authorizations are apportioned proportionally among the states on the basis of estimates of the cost of work remaining to be done. The Federal share of Interstate projects is 90 per cent and the state's share ten per cent. The primary and secondary systems are called the ABC programs. The Federal share of ABC projects is 50 per cent and the state's share is 50 per cent.

There is Federal aid for the construction of new roads and bridges; for the betterment of existing roads and bridges by widening and strengthening their surfaces; for the elimination of steep grades and sharp curves; for the replacement of narrow bridges; and for engineering surveys and design; and the acquisition of the necessary rights of way.

Highway construction costs are also financed by systems of toll roads, such as the New Jersey and Pennsylvania Turnpike Authorities, the New York State Thruway, and the Garden State Parkway. Bonds are issued to provide funds for construction. Tolls are earmarked for bond amortization and the payment of interest.

CAN RAIL COMMUTER LINES
ALLEVIATE HIGHWAY CONGESTION?

Yes, they can. Rail rapid transit is safe. It can be made convenient. It can be made comfortable. Overall, it is less expensive than travel on the highways. It frees the expressways, to the extent that these commuters get off them. If more people ride the commuter trains, those who still have to use their cars enjoy a proportionate benefit. If more suburbanites use the trains to come downtown to shop, downtown retail establishments benefit. If more persons use the trains, it will not be so necessary constantly to enlarge existing highways and to build new ones.

Railroads use less land than the highways. They are faster, point to point. They do not suffer to the same degree from fog, rain, and snow. Their rights of way are already in place. This obviates new construction. But their service must be re-equipped with high-performance, self-powered cars. Stations must be modernized with car-floor-level platforms and automated fare collection.

Rail transit can absorb home to work travel peaks. It can complement and supplement private transportation whenever the density of urban development and concentration of urban travel dictate. It can not only alleviate weekday needs, it can also provide for social and recreational travel requirements on weekends and holidays.

WHY DON'T MORE COMMUTERS USE THE RAILS?

Why have commuters been deserting the railroads for competing forms of transportation on the highways? The railroads may not schedule their trains to coincide with commuter patterns. Many railroads do not want commuter business and do everything they can to discourage it. It may be necessary for commuters to make changes en route which are inconvenient for them. Commuters object to the dirty cars and the unsanitary toilet facilities. They say they get their sleeves dirty every time they lean on the window sill. Window shades may not work properly. The trains are frequently late, resulting in commuters being late for work. Many commuter trains do not have air conditioning. Engine failures are all too common.

Women commuters are particularly vehement in their denunciations of the commuter railroad stations. These stations have become a haven for derelicts and degenerates, "scruffy" characters rifling the garbage cans and trash containers, bicycle riders and teen-age vandals. The stations themselves are not kept clean and tidy.

Service on commuter trains has deteriorated and the railroads have failed to keep pace with technological change. Rising costs and declining patronage have led to a succession of fare increases, only to be succeeded by further reductions in service. All this has made rail commutation less and less attractive.

Many train cars, purchased between 1914 and 1934, are older than the passengers themselves. The trains are musty and lack proper ventilation. What commuters want is speed, on time schedules, convenience, frequency of service, accessibility of service, proper seating, lighting, air conditioning, freedom from noise, and smooth riding qualities.

You have to offer commuters transportation attractive enough to get them out of their automobiles. Presently, 90 per cent prefer to drive. You have to give commuters swift, unobtrusive, and dependable service, more comfortable than their own cars, and less expensive. You have to engage in aggressive advertising and sales promotion, show the commuters the extras you have to offer, and persuade them that it is to their advantage to commute by rail.

You have to transform the attitudes of railroad trainmen from surly indifference to personal interest in the commuters and replace the frown and sour look with friendly smiles and courtesy.

IS RAIL COMMUTATION A LOST CAUSE?

No, it is not. Look what the Chicago & Northwestern Railroad has done! It was confronted with conditions comparable to those faced by the railroads serving the New York metropolitan areas. Equipment was old and in need of repair. The commuter fleet was obsolete.

Delays were frequent. Power was a mixture of steam and diesels.
The new management eliminated steam engines. It realized that its
job was not one of repairs on coaches, but complete replacement for
the highly specialized type of commuter service. It found that it not
only had a commuter market, but that it was a growing one. It made
the most out of its opportunities by building a completely new type of
commuter service.

The suburbs it served were growing by leaps and bounds. It knew
that it had to modernize and prepare for greater patronage if it hoped
to compete with the modern expressways then under construction.

It replaced 417 old cars with 200 modern double-deckers having a
greater total seating capacity. Its new cars do not require costly
maintenance. Its air conditioning units are inside the cars over the
ceiling in the vestibule and they have no individual generators. All
power comes from the locomotive. The units require no fueling, as do
cars with conventional air conditioning equipment.

Its cars are attractive, comfortable, and roomy, cleaned by hosing
down the interior. They seat 160. Windows are large and made of
tinted glass, which makes costly window shades unnecessary. There
are no painted surfaces inside the cars. Such surfaces as walls and
ceiling are of textured vinyl permanently bonded on metal. Exposed
metal surfaces are stainless steel or aluminum. Seats have foam-
rubber cushions upholstered in attractive, but durable vinyls. Cars
with three or four years of service still look like new.

Under the usual type of operation, locomotives coming into its Chicago terminal had to be backed out and turned for movements outbound.
The same was true at the other end of each suburban run. The management therefore developed push-pull equipment which now works at both
ends of the run. This means that the locomotive always stays at one end
of the train, pulling on the trip out and pushing on the trip in. When the
train gets to the station, it is ready to go again in ten minutes and the
relaying requires no switch engine or extra crew. The same number of
trains are now able to make extra runs during the peak hours.

The management expanded parking areas at the suburban stations. At
least half their customers drive or are driven to the station and 25
per cent park.

The Northwestern found that 85 per cent of its riders walk from its
downtown station in Chicago to their work locations. For the other
15 per cent the management arranged with the Chicago Transit Authority for a new and improved shuttle service to and from the downtown
location. Buses now pull up directly to the station doors. The buses
are empty on arrival, so that the riders get seats.

The Northwestern spends one per cent of its gross commuter revenue
on promoting its commuter service. In its suburbs there are 275
Realtors. The Northwestern cooperates with them. As Realtors find
residences for the people moving into its area, the Northwestern contacts these brand-new potential commuters and familiarizes them with
its service. Its rationale is that if these new residents know about its

service, they will not try to drive into Chicago. It advertises its services in the classified real estate sections of the Chicago newspapers. It points out to home buyers that the trip between home and work is an important consideration in the selection of a particular home site in a particular suburb.

In other areas, pilot studies have been conducted to find out whether the commuter public will accept mass transit in preference to individual driving. The conclusions drawn are that they will if the quality of service is improved. This means vehicle comfort, schedule reliability, speed, amount and frequency of service, improvements of stations, and ease of transfer.

The average commuter lives within two and a half miles from his station. When he gets to the city, he often needs to ride a bus or a subway to get to his place of employment. He needs a transportation system that interlocks. He should have feeder buses, taxi stands, and parking lots at his suburban station. Ideally, there would be a transfer system so that a single fare would take him from his home to his office.

SUPPOSE THE COMMUTER TRAINS STOPPED RUNNING?

Abandonment of commuter service would have catastrophic effects on the commuties served. Real estate values would be drastically deflated and traffic problems be drastically inflated. Large numbers of residents would move, causing an adverse effect on real estate values, which, in turn, would affect tax ratables both locally and on the country level. Local businesses would suffer loss of markets as their customers moved away.

There would be a need for more policemen to handle the increase in automobile traffic if rail service were abandoned. Potential real estate purchasers would be relunctant to buy in the absence of commuter service. With the decline in residential values, home owners would suffer a decline in the value of the equities their payments have built up. It would be necessary to raise taxes on the properties remaining to make good the lack of revenues on the properties given up or in a state of decline. It would take much longer to get to and from work if individual car driving or bus service were the alternatives.

When requests are made by the railroads for the complete abandonment of service, we are not inclined to take them seriously. We think that the Federal government will find a way to bail us out. But such abandonment has been happening. And it can happen even more.

CAN RAIL COMMUTER SERVICE BE MAINTAINED?

Can we expect the railroads to subsidize their commuter service? Most of them are not in a financial position to be able to do so. Nor does it seem fair to impose such a requirement upon them. We subsidize highway transportation. We subsidize air transportation. We do so because of public convenience and necessity. This works both ways. The need for public subsidy extends with equal effect to our commuter railroads.

Subsidy programs are presently embodied in legislation both at the

State and at the Federal level. Some provide for long-range solutions to chronic problems that have been characterized by cliff-hanging emergencies. They recognize that an adequate rail commuter system is a vital link in the economic life of our society. They acknowledge that capital improvements are the keystone for success in the attainment of objectives. They are not programs to aid private railroads which have become unprofitable. Rather, they are programs to discharge the obligations of government to its citizen commuters. This, they do by providing sufficient funds to enable the railroads to acquire new rolling stock, make essential capital improvements, and offset operating deficits.

The rapid transit trains of the future are most promising. The cars will be light weight. They will run over welded rails, and thus reduce noise. Starting, stopping, and opening of doors will be automatic. The trains will have acceleration capability over a wide range.

The monorail can be built over congested areas. With monorail we answer the question: Do we go underground at huge expense or go overhead with the monorail with no extra taxes and the fare box paying the way?

UP IN THE AIR

It is becoming more difficult to preserve existing and establish new airports. The land is often pre-empted by more profitable forms of development. Highways encroach on suitable sites. Residents in the vicinity of proposed airports tend to oppose them. The forces of conservation set up a hue and a cry over what these airports may do to plants and wildlife. There is already so much building on runway approaches that plane operation becomes difficult. A minimum of one-half mile of relatively clear area should be available beyond each dominant runway.

Why so much local opposition to the expansion of existing and to the establishment of new airports? They say that too much noise would result. They allege that the air would be polluted by the emission of jet fumes. A community must therefore weigh the adverse effects from these sources against the economic advantages that result from the airport - industrial parks, commercial developments, parks, highways, and golf courses. Modern construction techniques do permit sound-proofing on outer walls in larger buildings, making building construction near air facilities more feasible. The Port of New York Authority's studies show that land values in the vicinity of major airports increased 30 to 40 per cent after construction.

Surface transportation to and from most airports is woefully inadequate and time consuming. The movement of people and goods to and from air terminals is the critical factor. Planning for airport facilities must therefore include mass transportation for their service.

TRUE AND FALSE QUESTIONS

1. The influx of workers into many cities doubles the population during daylight hours. T F

2. Cities are no longer able to handle their transportation problems by themselves. T F

3. Those who move to the suburbs continue to contribute to central city traffic as they return each day as commuters. T F

4. Traffic congestion on streets and highways constitutes the transportation problem. T F

5. As traffic congestion makes cities less attractive in which to work, shop, and live, urban real estate values decline. T F

6. Constructing more and more streets and highways removes tax ratables that could be devoted to economic productivity. T F

7. Railroads are desirous of preserving for themselves their commuter traffic. T F

8. Highway developments result in the displacement of people and of families. T F

9. Improved transportation makes real estate more accessible. T F

10. The more accessible real estate is, the more valuable it becomes. T F

11. Highway routes exercise a decisive role as to where new plants will locate. T F

12. The Houston channel has been a retarding factor in Houston's growth. T F

13. Los Angeles solved its traffic congestion problems by building more highways. T F

14. Freeways take valuable land off the tax rolls. T F

15. The alignment of new highways becomes a controversy as residents and businessmen fight displacement.   T   F

16. Highway needs mount in geometrical proportions.   T   F

17. Highway users pay their way by virtue of the taxes they bear.   T   F

18. State highways are almost totally financed from highway-user taxes.   T   F

19. The Federal government shares in the tax burden of maintenance, administration, and regulation of highways.   T   F

20. The Federal share of interstate projects is 90 per cent.   T   F

21. The cost of ABC projects is divided equally between the Federal and the state governments.   T   F

22. Tolls on the New Jersey Turnpike and the Pennsylvania Turnpike are earmarked for bond amortization and payment of interest.   T   F

23. Rail rapid transit is unsafe.   T   F

24. Overall, rail rapid transit is more expensive than travel on the highways.   T   F

25. Rail rapid transit frees the expressways, to the extent that commuters get off the expressways.   T   F

26. Railroads are faster, point to point, than the highways.   T   F

27. Railroads use less land than the highways.   T   F

28. Rail transit cannot absorb home to work travel peaks.   T   F

29. The railroads, by and large, have kept pace with technological change.   T   F

30. On the Chicago & Northwestern commuter cars, all the power comes from the locomotive.   T   F

31. The trip between home and work is an important consideration in the selection of a particular home site in a particular suburb.   T   F

32. Abandonment of commuter service would have no serious effect on the communities served.   T   F

33. The railroads can be expected to subsidize their commuter   T F
service.

34. The monorail cannot be built over congested areas.   T F

35. Residents in the vicinity of proposed airports tend to   T F
oppose them.

36. Sound proofing techniques can be employed on outer walls   T F
in buildings near airports.

37. Surface transportation to and from most airports is adequate.   T F

38. Planning for new airport facilities must include mass   T F
transportation.

39. Air and highway transportation have been subsidized.   T F

40. There has as yet been no abandonment of commuter rail   T F
service.

MULTIPLE CHOICE

41. Surveys show the public will accept mass transit in preference to individual driving, if:
    ( )   The fares are drastically reduced
    ( )   The quality of the service is improved
    ( )   Parking is provided at commuter stations
    ( )   The railroads will provide shuttle buses at downtown terminals

42. A study of the 15-mile expressway into downtown Chicago showed that user taxes paid:
    ( )   The costs
    ( )   One-third the capital costs
    ( )   One-half the capital costs
    ( )   One-quarter the capital costs

43. The subsidy to rush-hour motorists on typical urban expressways and streets is about:
    ( )   10¢ a mile per automobile
    ( )   2¢ a mile per automobile
    ( )   5¢ a mile per automobile
    ( )   7¢ a mile per automobile

44. The primary and secondary systems in interstate highway programs are called:
    ( )   Top priority
    ( )   ABC systems
    ( )   XYZ systems
    ( )   Federal State systems

45. The most outstanding commuter railroad in the Chicago area in its contribution to make commuter travel more attractive is:
    ( )   The Burlington
    ( )   The Rock Island
    ( )   The Chicago & Northwestern
    ( )   The Illinois Central

46. In the rapid transit trains of the future, the cars will be:
    ( )   All aluminum
    ( )   Aluminum and steel
    ( )   Lightweight
    ( )   Completely automated

47. The hue and cry over what airports may do to plant and wildlife comes primarily from:
( ) The Department of the Interior
( ) The Department of Natural Resources
( ) Conservation forces
( ) The Department of Agriculture

48. The average commuter by rail lives within:
( ) Five miles of his commuter station
( ) Two and a half miles of his commuter station
( ) Ten miles of his commuter station
( ) Eight miles of his commuter station

49. The commuter rail system under which the locomotive always stays at one end of the train is called:
( ) The constant motorman
( ) The push-pull system
( ) Reverse gears
( ) The stationary system

50. Highway-user taxes are now limited to:
( ) Motorfuel taxes and vehicle registration fees
( ) Motorfuel taxes
( ) State and Federal taxes
( ) State taxes

ESSAY QUESTIONS

1. What is the size of highway construction costs?

2. How are highway construction costs financed?

3. How has improved transportation enhanced real estate values?

NEW TOWNS AND MODEL CITIES

CHAPTER TWENTY-FIVE

NEW TOWNS

The name is new, but the concept is old. Way back in ancient times, it was fostered in Athens as a means for population dispersal and a frontier guard against attack from a hostile foe. In our own colonial days, the Act for Building a Towne dealt with the planning requirements for Jamestown, Virginia. In the latter part of the 17th and the early part of the 18th centuries, some 20 sites in Virginia were set aside for the development of New Towns. Later in the 18th century some 57 sites in Maryland were so designated. Mobile, Alabama and New Orleans, Louisiana were both planned new towns. So were Savannah, Georgia and Pensacola, Florida. The French designer, L'Enfant, planned Washington, D.C.; Brigham Young, Salt Lake City; and William Penn, Philadelphia.

The Australian capital of Canberra was a planned new town, almost dreary in the regularity of its design. The magnificent modernistic architecture of Brasilia, the new capital of Brazil, was spurred on by the desire to open up its interior. Within the past 25 years a tremendous impetus for new towns has taken place in England. In order to remedy the crowding and decay of cities like London, it was deemed desirable to siphon off people and industry into self-sufficient new towns in semi-rural areas. These became the models to be followed in Scandinavia, France, Germany, and Holland.

One of the best and most beautiful of modern new towns is Tapiola, a garden city on 670 acres of Finland's forestland, just 20 minutes from downtown Helsinki. It was privately planned and financed. It is planned for people - benches scattered round about, landscaping, ramps for baby carriages, pedestrian shopping malls, no neon or other signs, no screaming billboards and auto graveyards, no dreary tract housing. It is symmetrical, yet varied; commercial, yet aesthetic; functional, yet beautiful.

Unlike the United States, western European governments are moving aggressively to channel population and industry into planned new towns. They regard them as investments, rather than outright expenditures. In heavily populated areas, they are turning to high-density new communities. Some are out and out high-rise projects. Some are tied in with their central cities in opposition to the notion that the new town must be in itself self-sufficient. In most instances, public authorities do the planning and then call on private enterprise to do the building.

Realizing that the residents must have jobs, western European countries try to attract business and industry by offering an appealing environment. In some cases they exert pressure on commerce to locate in these new towns by withholding approval from expansion within the big cities. Unlike the United States, they employ industrialized building techniques. Their new towns conserve on land and save on construction costs.

Unlike western Europe, in the United States so far, governmental intervention for new towns has been relatively minor. Oh, it is true that during the depression years, our Federal government, through its Resettlement Administration, did build new towns in Greenbelt, Maryland; Greenhills, Ohio; and Greendale, Wisconsin. Their very names suggest the stress that was laid on open space. These developments were, however, subsequently sold to private enterprise.

Some of our governmental new towns have sprung up in conjunction with large-scale governmental projects. We erected Boulder City, Nevada, as a necessary residential and commercial adjunct to the Hoover Dam in 1932; Norris, Tennessee, as a concomitant to the Tennessee Valley Authority, in 1935; and, in connection with the necessity for security and labor force needs for the Atomic Energy Commission - Los Alamos, New Mexico; Oak Ridge, Tennessee; and Hanford, Washington.

The first new town to receive aid under the Federal program to stimulate development of new cities is Jonathan, Minnesota, near Minneapolis-St. Paul. The purpose of this new town is to provide a more harmonious setting for the lives of modern Americans. It is to be innovative. It will combine natural beauty with modern technology. The objective is to build five villages, each with some 7,000 persons living in homes. Another 10,000 will live in apartments and townhouses and 5,000 in an educational center. There will be small shopping centers and one hub with all the specialty stores and businesses normally found downtown in a city of 50,000. There will be sites for schools and churches and land for industry.

Johnathan, Minnesota, is just the beginning of massive transfusions of Federal assistance for the creation of new towns in our country. Here are the reasons why: our cities and suburbs in 1970 had a population of 140 million people. By the year 2000 this will grow by substantial proportions. The crowding, pollution, crime, physical decay, and snarled traffic have become unbearable. The National Committee on Urban Growth Policy has therefore recommended that the Federal Government help build at least 100 new towns of 100,000 population and ten larger cities within the next 30 years.

It is one thing to put this down as a recommendation on paper. It is another thing to see it transformed into actuality. Regardless of the Federal government's initial financial assistance, these new towns must become autonomous and self-supporting. They must have economic drawing power. They must be endowed with an economic base to provide employment for their residents and a tax ratable for their communities. As the jobs to be made available will have varying wage and salary scales, the people making up these new towns will necessarily be of different income levels and, consequently, the housing and other facilities must be planned in accordance.

The costs of these new towns will be enormous. It is not only the cost of land planning and development, land acquisition, and subsequent construction. It is also the tremendous carrying costs of the projects for several years before they will reach full fruition and be economically productive in the form of sales and rentals.

Aside from the problem of surmounting the costs to be incurred, there is also the problem of opposition from the existing municipalities which see in the new towns a competitive threat to themselves. They see themselves losing population and taxpayers, industries and tax ratables to the new towns. What is the new town's gain will be the old city's loss.

It had been thought that land near the peripheries of present cities could be made available for new towns, but this has not been the case. It had been anticipated that there was much surplus government land to which resort could be had for the new towns, but in most instances this has not been the case.

Some of the planning for new towns on the part of governmental agencies looks more utopian than practical. In certain instances, percentages have been laid down for ethnic mix, age mix, and income mix, which would be most difficult to achieve.

Aside from the foregoing problems, there is also the duplication of utilities service, police and fire protection service, and education service which the new town would represent, over and above these same services now provided for by the cities from which are expected to come much of the new town population.

Rather than locate new towns far from the main stream of economic activity in present cities, it would seem reasonable to establish them relatively close by. Otherwise, it will be most difficult to attract to them the population desired. But to locate them close to present cities will also serve to accentuate the competitive and duplicative features they will represent.

New Towns in the Private Sector

As our industrial history shows, industry has developed new towns in conjunction with and relatively adjacent to the plants it has established. These have come to be known as company towns. Their purpose has been functional, rather than aesthetic. Many of them have not emphasized the residential amenities or gracious living concepts. They have served an economic rather than a social purpose. They are now, relatively speaking, a thing of the past. With our economy geared to the automobile and with practically every workman having his own car, the element of adjacency to the industrial plant has lost its significance. They were an echo of a paternalistic society, a benevolent aristocracy, which has passed from the American industrial scene.

One of the most highly publicized of our private new towns has been Reston, Virginia. It is located some 18 miles west of Washington, D.C.

Concentrating, as it did to start with, on the sale of homes in the $35,000 and up class, it failed to find the buyers. Its difficulties were compounded by lack of access to the nearby freeway. It was a financial failure. It was subsequently bailed out by additional financing from the Gulf Oil Corporation and John Hancock Life Insurance Company and a more practical plan of operation was established with homes more within the financial means of the market being erected.

Also highly publicized has been the new town of Columbia, Maryland, located between Washington, D.C. and Baltimore, Maryland. It was developed by the planning firm of Rouse Associates and financed by Connecticut General Life Insurance Company, Teachers Insurance and Annuity Association, and Chase Manhattan Bank.

In order to keep down the price of land acquisition, more than 15,000 acres were purchased privately, without disclosure of the backers, over a period of 15 months. In making his request for new town zoning from the county, Rouse stated the central philosophy of his concept for this planned community - a design to meet the real needs of the people - the provision of opportunities and activities through which the people can feel important and uplifted - a scene for creating growth in human personality, character, and operativity. He won his point and allocated the land resources to residential plots, multi-family use plots, industrial plots, open space, and for commercial, public, and quasi-public activities. It will take until 1980 to see the full consummation of his objectives.

It was decided at the outset to start with low-density housing. It was determined to set up a system of neighborhoods, villages, and towns. A mass transit system was to be provided, within a three minute walk of a substantial percentage of the population. Works of art are distributed at strategic vantage points. Community facilities and community activities are emphasized throughout. Open space, cluster subdivisions, and curvilinear streets are part of the grand design.

Among other well known new towns in the private sector is Irvine Ranch, California, four times the size of Manhattan, whose master plan is projected over a 20 year period. It is being developed in phases, permitting large areas to be reserved for farm land and, thus, during the transition period, enjoying a lower tax rate.

Lake Havasu City, Arizona, is a unique new town in that it was created without any pre-existing economic base. This will be supplied, however, by its developer, McCulloch Oil Company, which will undertake its future expansion in this location. The new towns of Clear Lake City and Bayport, Texas, are combinations of government, heavy industry, and residential developments. Litchfield Park, Arizona, is a product of the Goodyear Tire & Rubber Co. Westinghouse has developed Coral Springs, Florida, and is planning to set up a large plant of its own at this location. Del Webb's new town of Sun City, Arizona, is a most successful resort and retirement community.

These are but a few of the new towns being developed by corporate conglomerates. They reflect an appreciation of the long-term gains in such real estate projects.   In some instances they represent an opportunity in the structures to incorporate their products and consequently have a ready made captive market.   They also provide an opportunity to diversify.   This is one of the reasons why railroads, such as Santa Fe Industries and the Union Pacific system, have been so prominent in these endeavors.   In other instances, as in the case of Standard Oil Company of California, they enable the developer to pre-empt for marketing purposes the most desirable service station locations.

New Towns and Greenbelts

Faced with the dreary prospect of a megalopolis all the way from Boston to Miami, from Detroit to Chicago, to mention just two examples, we look for relief not only to the new town concept, but also to the provision of greenbelts.   Hopefully, they will prevent our encirclement by the urban maze.   Hopefully, they will solve the problems of urban sprawl and waste.   Hopefully, they will relieve racial, social, and population pressures on existing cities by means of the creation of new communities in outlying areas.

We cannot acquiesce to the cities swallowing up the countryside at the present horrendous rate.   We cannot consent to the constant withdrawal of agricultural land from the production of food to the production of helter-skelter subdivisions.   We cannot agree to more freeways and expressways accelerating the process of destroying our countrysides.

It is a sorry spectacle just to look out on unrelieved configurations of houses and shops, freeways and airports, garish neon signs and auto graveyards.   How much more inviting it is to see stretches of greenbelt, offering play and recreational space to the city's inhabitants, right in their own backyard.

We are fortunate in having vast land areas.   We are unfortunate in that we have not yet learned to use them wisely.   We have crowded 90 per cent of our population into 15 per cent of our available land. We do not propose, however, by the creation of new towns to dismantle our present cities.   We propose, rather, to link new towns to an urban strategy in the spectrum of society's problems.

MODEL CITIES

Like new towns, the Model Cities program aims to relieve the racial, social, and population pressures in urban life.   Unlike the new towns program, however, it aims to do so in the here and now, in specific neighborhoods, rather than in a dispersal to peripheral areas.

Fed up with the many faults of the urban renewal program, President Johnson in 1966 asked Congress for the enactment of a new plan that would concentrate on the human and physical needs of people living in specific blighted areas, rather than rushing the bulldozer in as was done with urban renewal, and wiping the slate clean.

The objective of the Model Cities program that resulted was to rebuild entire slum neighborhoods.   These areas would not be told what to do by directive from on high. But they would be persuaded to understand their problems and solve them on the basis of guidelines as suggested by the Department of Housing and Urban Development.

Under the Model Cities program, the cities themselves make the plans to improve specific slum neighborhoods. The residents therein must participate at all stages of the planning process. Existing social programs are employed in connection with the planning. All the neighborhood problems become proper subject matter for concern, attention, and solution. These problems include the incidence of crime, the deterioration of health standards, the lack of adequate transportation, and inefficient educational systems. The neighborhood must be primarily residential. The project should result in the provision of increased low and moderate income housing.

If the initial plans developed comply with the guidelines of the Department of Housing and Urban Development and are superior to competing plans for funds from other cities, the Department will allocate 80 per cent of the costs of making detailed plans and final proposals. The cities then evolve and submit their final plans. The Department, in turn, reviews these and picks the cities with the best plans and authorizes them to get started on their programs.

Approved programs receive from the Department a refund of 80 per cent of the matching funds the cities normally put up in connection with a Federal program. Additional funds are available for the cities whose plans conform with a metropolitan-wide plan.

Among the projects for which funds were granted was one for the establishment in Newark, New Jersey, of a guaranteed minimum income; one in Philadelphia for aiding small business and using it for job training; and in St. Louis a complex to train poor people for greater economic productivity. Seattle received a generous grant to set up a non-profit corporation that would build 7,000 housing units within a five year period.

Model Cities Problems

As with so many programs, progress has been retarded for lack of funds. Congress simply has not appropriated money in the amounts required for the consummation of projects planned.

Under the Model Cities program, there must be maximum employment of residents in Model Cities areas for its execution. This ran into opposition from the construction unions. As a compromise, the guidelines were modified to call for the hiring of local residents under special payment arrangements by contractors at the level of journeymen, (skilled), if qualified, or at a lower level if not qualified. In Boston, consequently, unions have agreed to accept area residents as apprentices, trainees, or journeymen, depending on their previous training.

It has been difficult for the residents of an area to agree on just what should be done to relieve its blight. In some instances, they have decided on neighborhood amenities - more adequate lighting fixtures, bus stop shelters, tree plantings, street furniture, litter receptacles, and telephone booths. In other instances, they have gotten together on child care services, neighborhood health centers, recreational areas, improved legal services for local residents, and the construction of low rent housing.

Some neighborhoods have resisted the Model Cities program for fear that it was urban renewal under just another name. They have, therefore, been told that urban renewal concentrates on the physical aspects of an area and attempts to right what was wrong in these respects, and that Model Cities, on the other hand, concentrates on the human aspects, projects therefore resulting in the attainment of goals in the areas of employment, health, transportation, and education.

Other neighborhoods seem to have an ingrained hostility to the inclusion of business people on their boards. They thereby fail to make use of the talents, services, and experience these individuals would be able to provide.

TRUE AND FALSE QUESTIONS

1. New towns are a new concept.   T F

2. In order to remedy the crowding and decay of cities like   T F
London, it was deemed desirable to siphon off people and
industry into self-sufficient new towns in semi-rural areas.

3. Tapiola was publicly planned and publicly financed.   T F

4. In heavily populated areas in western Europe, the trend is   T F
toward high-density new communities.

5. Western European new towns have not employed in-   T F
dustrialized building techniques.

6. Western European new towns contain mostly single-family   T F
detached homes.

7. In the United States, governmental intervention for new   T F
towns has been relatively substantial.

8. The costs of new towns are limited to land planning and   T F
development.

9. Some existing municipalities see in new towns a competi-   T F
tive threat to themselves.

10. The purpose of company new towns was aesthetic, rather than   T F
functional.

11. Columbia, Maryland started with high-density housing.   T F

12. Lake Havasu City was created with a pre-existing economic   T F
base.

13. We have crowded 90 per cent of our population onto 15   T F
per cent of our available land.

14. Under the Model Cities program, the residents of the   T F
neighborhood selected must participate at all stages of the
planning process.

15. Existing social programs are employed in connection with   T   F
    planning the Model Cities programs.

16. The neighborhood for a Model Cities program must be   T   F
    primarily residential.

17. HUD will allocate, upon approval of the initial plans for   T   F
    Model Cities, 80 per cent of the costs of making detailed
    plans and final programs.

18. Approved programs in Model Cities receive from HUD a   T   F
    refund of 80 per cent of the cost of the matching funds
    the cities put up.

19. Progress in Model Cities has been retarded for lack of funds.   T   F

20. Residents of Model Cities neighborhoods have usually shown   T   F
    ready agreement on plans to remove blight.

21. Some cities have resisted Model Cities programs for fear   T   F
    they were just urban renewal under another name.

22. Urban renewal concentrates on the physical aspects of an   T   F
    area.

23. Model Cities concentrates on the human aspects of an area.   T   F

24. Under Model Cities there must be maximum employment   T   F
    of residents in Model Cities areas for the execution of the
    programs.

25. Only a limited number of neighborhood problems become   T   F
    the proper subject for concern and attention under the
    Model Cities program.

26. A Model Cities program should result in the provision of   T   F
    increased low- and moderate-income housing.

27. Model Cities programs are told by directive from HUD   T   F
    how to carry out their proposals.

28. It is proposed by the creation of new towns to dismantle   T   F
    present cities.

29. It will take until 1980 to see the full consummation of the   T   F
    objectives of Mr. Rouse for Columbia, Maryland.

30. Reston, Virginia was a financial success from the very start.   T   F

31. Boulder City, Nevada was set up as a concomitant to the   T F
    Tennessee Valley Authority.

32. Some western European countries have exerted pressure   T F
    on commerce to locate in new towns.

33. Western European countries have regarded new towns   T F
    as investments, rather than outright expenditures.

34. Tapiola was planned for people.   T F

35. Brasilia was spurred on by the desire to open up Brazil's   T F
    interior.

36. Canberra was unplanned.   T F

37. Jonathan is near Minneapolis-St. Paul.   T F

38. New towns must have economic drawing power.   T F

39. Land near the peripheries of present cities has been readily   T F
    available for new towns.

40. Company new towns are now, relatively speaking, a thing   T F
    of the past.

MULTIPLE CHOICE

41. Industry in the United States in times past has developed new towns in conjunction with and relatively adjacent to:
    ( )   The cities in which it operated
    ( )   The plants it established
    ( )   Its headquarter offices
    ( )   Its marketing and warehousing sectors

42. Litchfield Park, Arizona is a product of:
    ( )   Westinghouse
    ( )   Goodyear
    ( )   Del Webb
    ( )   McCulloch

43. The initial objective of the Model Cities program was:
    ( )   Urban rehabilitation
    ( )   Urban renewal
    ( )   To rebuild entire slum neighborhoods
    ( )   Planned Community Development

44. Among the railroads prominent in new town developments has been:
    ( )   The Penn-Central
    ( )   The Rock Island
    ( )   The Union Pacific
    ( )   The Chesapeake & Ohio

45. The new town of Coral Springs, Florida was established by:
    ( )   General Electric
    ( )   Westinghouse
    ( )   Reynolds Metal
    ( )   Kaiser Aluminum

46. The Teachers Insurance and Annuity Association has figured prominently in the financing of the new town of:
    ( )   Lake Havasu City
    ( )   Reston, Virginia
    ( )   Columbia, Maryland
    ( )   Whittier, California

47. A new town set up to serve the needs of the Atomic Energy Commission was:
( )   Norris, Tennessee
( )   Boulder City, Nevada
( )   Jonathan, Minnesota
( )   Los Alamos, New Mexico

48. The government agency which built the new town of Greenbelt, Md. was:
( )   The WPA
( )   The PWA
( )   The National Industrial Recovery Association
( )   The Resettlement Administration

49. The first new town to receive aid under the Federal program to stimulate development of new towns is:
( )   Lake Havasu City, Arizona
( )   Sun City, Arizona
( )   Greenbelt, Maryland
( )   Jonathan, Minnesota

50. The organization recommending the creation of 100 new towns of 100,000 population and ten of 1,000,000 population was:
( )   The Department of Housing and Urban Development
( )   The National Committee on Urban Growth Policy
( )   The Urban Land Institute
( )   The Urban Planning Division of the Department of the Interior

ESSAY QUESTIONS

1. How does the Model Cities program operate in practice?

2. What are the characteristics of the new town programs of western European governments?

3. Please comment on the importance of economic viability for new towns?

POLLUTION —
AIR, NOISE
AND WATER

What an odd subject for a book on real estate! Does it really belong? Why should real estate people be interested in ecology, balance in nature, decibel counts, electrostatic precipitators, and emphysema? Why should real estate people promote interest in a subject which may result in measures depriving them of marsh land for land fill, bay land for tract development, and swamp land for airports?

So - let's figure this out by going back to basic things. What is it that over the long run most promotes real estate values - an ugly or an attractive environment. What is it that makes an area desirable for homes, work, and play - an atmosphere conducive to health or sickness. Wouldn't we rather enjoy our natural heritage in wildlife and water-fowl, in wood and stream, than have it fade away through lack of nurture and protection? Asking questions in this simplistic way will elicit a conservationist's response. But our personal problems come in our day to day operations when a decision here and a decision there, seemingly minor in themselves - cutting down a tree or dumping our garbage in the stream nearby - set up a chain reaction of erosive forces.

HOW BAD IS THE POLLUTION PROBLEM?

We see the headlines about pollution every day in our local paper. We hear references to it over the radio. We note that "hippies" and campus militant groups, waxing tired of the Vietnam war issue, are now parading and carrying banners about pollution. And we ask ourselves whether this is just another passing cause, or is it the real thing?

So - let's look about us. Suppose in our middle age we go back to Lake Erie where we had so much fun swimming and fishing when we were young. What do we see today? We see the most polluted of our great lakes, slowly becoming America's dead sea, clogged with municipal wastes and industrial effluence, with pesticides and fertilizer runoff from farm operations. We see monstrous growths of algae, using enormous amounts of oxygen, and fish requiring high oxygen content, like pike, being replaced by those needing less, like suckers and carp. We see the effects of five states pouring 1.5 billion gallons of sewage and 9.6 billion gallons of industrial wastes daily into this once fine lake. We note that bathing beaches along Lake Erie are being closed as health hazards.

Some of us remember the lilting music of the "Beautiful Ohio." But the tune is no longer appropriate for the Ohio River, for it has become a cesspool. Those of us who have lived around Akron and Cleveland think back to the time the Cuyahoga River was nice and clean. But that was long ago. The Cuyahoga is now slicked over by oil. It catches fire periodically. It has earned for itself the dubious distinction of being the only body of water ever to be classified as a fire hazard. Its bacteria count matches that of raw sewage and its stench reeks to high heaven.

But it has a close rival for foul smell in the historic Potomac River, stinking as it does from the sewage of Virginia, Maryland, and the District of Columbia. And, impressed as we are with the oil refineries lining the banks of the Houston Channel, we must acknowledge that it is one of the filthiest of bodies of water. The shellfish and crabs we used to enjoy from Biscayne Bay are no more. The dumping of generator-heated water has killed them off. Proud as we are of the Garden State of New Jersey, we have to admit that the oily, murky Passaic River is a disgrace. Over the past 30 years we have polluted it and every water shed east of the Mississippi and are now embarked on a similar drive against those west of the Mississippi.

Although polluted water is a health problem for those of us who swim and boat, although it kills off fish we depend on for food and sport, water treatment plants in most of our cities can still produce perfectly pure water for domestic use. The problem it presents is not nearly as bad as that of air pollution. We breathe the pollution by which the air is infected. If we have asthma or emphysema, we suffer seriously from air pollution. It burns our eyes and blackens our lung tissues. It is a major factor in lung cancer. It is a silent killer hovering over every city in our land. In the form of smog, it has become a permanent part of Los Angeles.

The pollution in the air attacks not only man - it attacks nature as well. Millions of trees are dead or dying from polluted air. Where the smog level is acute, it is no longer profitable to grow vegetables, such as lettuce and spinach. Air pollution has cut citrus yields in half and, in many areas, has diminished the growth of lovely flowers. It has made for ecological imbalance.

Air pollution has become so bad that it is even altering the weather. Dirty air screens off sunlight, and makes for fog, hail, and thunderstorms. And, by the reverse token, it can so overseed the clouds that no rain falls at all.

Air pollution is not only coloring the skies - it is darkening our homes, dissolving our nylon hosiery, corroding our metal, and hardening our rubber. The Department of Health, Education, and Welfare estimates the cost to us of air pollution at 13 billion dollars per year.

And who could even venture a guess as to the cost of noise pollution? The noise of the riveter, the welder, the wrecker's ball, the bulldozer, the air compressors, the jackhammer, the honking of horns, the roar of the mufflers, the decibel crescendo as the jet takes off - all these take their toll. Our blood vessels constrict, our skin pales, our muscles tense, and adrenal hormones are injected into our blood stream. If the noise in our cities continues at its present rate of increase, we shall be on our way to being stone deaf by the year 2000. In fact, one bank in New York City suffered such employee turnover in its noisy check tabulating room that it has now resorted to hiring only deaf people for this operation.

With cities constantly getting noisier, those who want to be heard shout all the louder. They do so at work and at home, where they suffer from the noise competition in the kitchen of the dishwasher, the garbage disposal, and the blender. If they live near airports, they are subject to the deafening roar of the jets unceasingly both day and night, shattering their nerves and shaking their windows.

Today, the cacophony of city noise is destroying the quality of urban life. It comes from operations essential to the life of the municipality - from transportation, manufacture, construction, heating and air conditioning systems, and the activities of the police, firemen, and sanitation departments. It is a major factor in the flight from the city.

WHO IS RESPONSIBLE?

We all are. We are a nation of litterbugs. We drive cars spewing deadly exhaust fumes into smog. We are responsible for five pounds, each of us, of solid wastes per day, not including sewage or industrial waste. We burn leaves and garbage in our backyards. We double the noise level in our homes every ten years by reason of our new mechanical installations. We threaten our lakes and landscapes with our unwanted bottles and cans. Some of us, unfortunately, turn camping grounds of our national parks into virtual slums.

If we have an incincration plant we may burn our garbage in it or we may bury it in landfill, and what we get is poisonous methane gas in the one case and poor foundations in the other. The fly ash from the incinerators is now called summer snow and covers our cars, patios, and swimming pools. We have invented a way to reach the moon, but our last real invention in garbage disposal was the garbage can.

We do not know what to do with the garbage that litters our countryside. Much of what is mixed in with our garbage is "non-biodegradable". The soil bacteria which may feast on ordinary garbage cannot stomach nylon and plastics, the aluminum can or the non-returnable bottle. By dumping solid wastes into streams and rivers we cause water pollution, by burning them we cause air pollution. Our worn out septic tanks from our cottages along a lake cause nutrients to enter the water and promote the growth of algae.

We have so much garbage to dispose of, particularly with all the convenience packaging toward which we are predisposed, that we are running out of places to put it. And wherever we do put it, we spread scenic blight.

We love our cars, but they are the chief offender. They give off carbon monoxide and other pollutants. No other gaseous air pollutant is found at such high concentrations in the urban atmosphere. Our cars are not only major polluters of the air, but also spur our urban sprawl into irreplaceable farm land. We race up and down our freeways and leave in our wake 76 per cent of the carbon monoxide in the air, more than half the hydrocarbons, and most of the lead and nitrogen oxides.

We dam our waterways, re-channel them, dredge them, and fill them in. We thereby create more power, flood control, and cheaper transportation. But we pay a price in making our rivers black with mud, killing off the fish, wreaking environmental havoc, and disrupting nature's cycle. We discharge oil wastes at sea, and kill off thousands of seabirds. We wash out the cargo tanks of our tankers with salt water after each load and dump the washings into the ocean, with consequent contamination. We threaten our Great Lakes with death from the sewage from our communities, commercial vessels, and pleasure craft, and the seepage from our stockyards and mining wastes. We discharge large amounts of hot water from our atomic plants into our lakes, rivers, and bays, and thereby kill off aquatic life and upset the balance of nature.

We discharge untreated chemical wastes into a river. Our smelters discharge toxic fluorine gas and dust into the atmosphere and create more air pollution problems. The race is on between the rising production of our industrial waste products and our ability to develop the technology to dispose of them so as to cause the least possible pollution.

WHAT CAN BE DONE ABOUT IT?

We could issue governmental directives forbidding air, noise, and water pollution. And, assuming they were complied with, what would be the result? Our economy would grind to a stop. Our cars and trucks, our planes and trains, would no longer operate. Our power plants would be paralyzed. Our industrial plants would shut down. Our farms would no longer be cultivated.

So - we do have to live with some degree of pollution. How much of it can we stand? How can we employ technological advance and at the same time live in a comfortable and enjoyable environment? Can we remove the pollutants from the wastes of our industrial plants before they are discharged into our rivers, streams, and lakes? Can fresh water fish and forests survive in our industrial civilization?

As cars and trucks are the chief offenders, why don't we sound the death knell of the internal combustion engine and switch over to the electric car? We can't. We do not know how to store up enough energy in the ordinary size car for the high speed, long distance driving of today. We would need transmission lines and a power supply at every service station to re-charge the batteries. To produce the electricity, we would have to have power plants burning oil or gas and themselves thereby polluting the atmosphere.

Can we install equipment on our present cars and trucks to reduce the rate of pollutant emissions? Yes, we can. The unanswered question is whether we can reduce this rate faster than the rate of increase in the numbers of cars and trucks. The other unanswered question is whether the driving public will use them. It is easier to coerce an industry than it is to coerce the public. Where blow by devices have been installed on cars, reducing the exhaust emissions, they have cut down on the power of the vehicle and the drivers have taken them off. Although Federal law even now requires auto manufacturers to provide cars with fume control equipment, enforcement has been left up to individual states and they are doing little or nothing to assure the effectiveness of these controls.

We are even now requiring airlines to install equipment by 1975 to reduce jet-smoke emission from short distance planes, responsible for the greatest amounts of pollutants, because they take off and land more often. We are even now experimenting with soundproof homes in the vicinity of airports to determine whether this is economically feasible. Although it is true that the new jumbo jets are quieter, this does nothing to tone down the noise levels of the thousands of commercial and corporate jets that are presently flying. Adding sound-suppressing materials to planes now in operation would create an impossible penalty in payload.

Can't we find a better way to dispose of our garbage? We now build community incinerators on the outskirts of our cities, not only resulting in pollution, but also creating a traffic problem that results in still more pollution. Why can't we compress our garbage into bricks to be used for land fill or as a building material? Why is it not feasible to transport urban trash to rural areas to fill abandoned mine cavities or build ski slopes? The Germans have developed a garbage crusher that handles even household appliances and furniture. It looks like a concrete mixer, but operates silently. Why can't we go and do likewise?

There seem to be so many ways by which we could improve our garbage disposal. What's wrong with using it to fill in the land along highway rights of way so as to build up their shoulders and thereby reduce traffic accidents? Why can't we get the railroads to haul away trash pressed into cubes wrapped in polyethylene for burial in out of the way places? Can't we develop processes for separating the paper, rags, glass, and metals in the garbage for resale to industry? Could we not manufacture the residue into compost for farm use?

Why not take a leaf out of the experience of cities that have been successful in reducing pollution? Killer smogs in London caused thousands of deaths and London banned the burning of soft coal. The result is that air pollution on bronchial patients is diminishing. Plants and wildlife are reviving. Laundry bills are down. And paintwork lasts longer.

This remedy, however, will not be easy to apply. The city of St. Louis has found it no easy matter to cut down on soft coal consumption. And, caught between the firing lines are the big coal using manufacturing plants in St. Louis, ordered by the city to reduce the sulfur dioxide for which they are responsible, but unable to buy low sulfur coal to comply with the directive.

Pittsburgh is even now considering a code that would prohibit open fires, require the steel industry to find ways of eliminating pollution from its furnaces, and outlaw the use of water to quench slag, a process resulting in hydrogen sulfide gas. Steel companies are even now installing pollution control treatment equipment on their present facilities. They are equipping their new facilities with control systems that equal or exceed government regulations.

Some electric utility companies are committed to building no more fossil-fueled (coal, oil, or gas) power plants within the big cities themselves. Electrostatic precipitators, designed to remove 99 per cent of the fly ash from power plant's stack gases, are in increasing use. These same precipitators are being used by modern refineries to filter out dust particles from the atmosphere.

There are plenty of laws on the books against air, noise, and water pollution. But they are not adequately enforced. New York City's ordinances require the upgrading of incinerators. But New York City itself in its own operations is the worst violator. The Metropolitan Sanitary District of Greater Chicago is the chief polluter of the Illinois River. The penalties for air pollution in many states and localities are no more than a wrist slap, with fines as low as $10. It is cheaper to pay the fines than it is to comply with the laws. And four states - Nebraska, South Dakota, Alabama, and Maine - have no air pollution control laws at all.

This suggests that legislative control should be at the Federal level. Air, water, and wildlife do not observe state lines. They are of an interstate character. So should be their control. What North Carolina does about its estuaries affects the fishing off the coast of New England. It would therefore seem appropriate for the Federal government to outlaw or limit the use of air, water, and noise pollutants.

It has even been suggested that industries should be charged on a per-pound basis for the waste they dump into our lakes and rivers. The proceeds of these charges would be divided between Federal aid to municipalities to build waste treatment plants and to regional water management associations.

President Nixon has declared that the price tag for clean air, clean water, and open spaces is high, but must be paid, and paid low. He has therefore proposed a $10 billion water program that would put modern municipal waste treatment plants every place in America where they are needed. His remarks indicate that environment has now become a major political issue. Fighting pollution has become a popular crusade.

WHAT WILL HAPPEN IF WE DO NOTHING?

Our sickness and mortality rate will increase at an accelerating rate as we breathe more poisons in the air. Our hearing will be weakened. Our fish and wildlife will be in large part destroyed. Our water sports will be a thing of the past. Scenic beauty will be replaced by scenic blight. Our flirtation with upsetting the balance of nature will result in man-made deserts.

DDT and other chlorinated hydrocarbon insecticides will pollute our soil and kill off beneficial insects. We ourselves may be threatened by DDT, as it appears to be linked with cancer and liver disorders.

We are even now on collision course. On the one hand there are the advancing forces of technology, making for more and more production, and on the other hand, its wastes and by-products are despoiling our natural resources. On the one hand there is the increasing use of the automobile, and on the other hand, the exhaust fumes by which it poisons the air, and the depressing health standards which result.   On the one hand there is the increasing use of air transportation, and on the other hand, the sonic booms and the interference with bird and wildlife which result.

Can we have our cake and eat it too?   Can we constantly grow more wealthy by reason of the advances in our scientific and technological skills, and at the same time constantly grow poorer in the availability of our natural heritage?

A balance must be struck.   We want the best of both worlds, but we do not want them to be mutually destructive.   Spending vast sums of money on anti-pollution measures will not be enough.   Before we can get back on even course, we must ourselves be persuaded that there is a worthwhileness to ourselves in the open sky above, in the exhilaration of drawing a long breath of pure air, in undefiled water from the mountain stream, in the preservation of the bald eagle and even the alligator, and in the holy science that lives in nature's realm.

GLOSSARY

ALGAE - aquatic plants
DECIBEL COUNTS - units for measuring the loudness of sounds
ECOLOGY - the relationship between organisms and their environment
EMPHYSEMA - distention of the lungs
HORMONES - products of living cells

TRUE AND FALSE QUESTIONS

1. Lake Erie is the most polluted of our Great Lakes.   T   F

2. Bathing beaches along Lake Erie are being closed as health hazards.   T   F

3. The historic Potomac River has been kept relatively free from pollution.   T   F

4. The state of Texas has taken effective measures to stop pollution in the Houston Channel.   T   F

5. The state of New Jersey lives up to its reputation as the Garden State in the high standards of prevention of water pollution it has exercised.   T   F

6. Polluted water is a health problem for those who swim and boat.   T   F

7. Polluted water kills off fish we depend on for food and sport.   T   F

8. Water treatment plants in most of our cities can no longer produce pure water for domestic use.   T   F

9. Air pollution is not as yet a major factor in lung cancer.   T   F

10. Smog has become a permanent part of Los Angeles.   T   F

11. Air pollution has not as yet made for ecological imbalance.   T   F

12. Air pollution is altering the weather.   T   F

13. Nylon hosiery is the only kind which is resistant to air pollution.   T   F

14. City noise is destroying the quality of urban life.   T   F

15. We double the noise level in our homes every ten years by reason of our new mechanical installations.   T   F

16. Soil bacteria feast on nylon and plastics.   T   F

17. Convenience packaging eliminates problems of garbage disposal.　　T　F

18. Cars give off carbon monoxide.　　T　F

19. Governmental directives can forbid pollution, without putting brakes on our economy.　　T　F

20. The solution to the problem of pollution caused by automobiles is to switch from the internal combustion engine to the electric car.　　T　F

21. We can now store up enough energy in the ordinary size car for the high speed, long distance driving of today.　　T　F

22. By 1975 jet-smoke emissions from short distance planes will be reduced.　　T　F

23. The Germans have developed a garbage crusher handling household appliances.　　T　F

24. The City of London has banned the burning of soft coal.　　T　F

25. Using water to quench slag results in Hydrogen sulfide gas.　　T　F

26. Electrostatic precipitators are designed to remove fly ash from power plant's stack gases.　　T　F

27. Electrostatic precipitators are used by refineries to filter out dust particles from the atmosphere.　　T　F

28. Four states in our country have no air pollution control laws.　　T　F

29. The environment is a minor political issue.　　T　F

30. DDT appears to be linked with cancer and liver disorders.　　T　F

31. Spending large amounts of money on anti-pollution measures should be able to effectuate the cure.　　T　F

32. It is suggested that industries should be charged on a per pound basis for the waste they dump into lakes and rivers.　　T　F

33. Air, water, and wildlife tend to observe state lines.　　T　F

34. The penalties for air pollution in many states and localities are presently no more than a wrist slap.　　T　F

35. The discharge of oil wastes at sea does not do any damage.   T   F

36. Air pollution can so overseed the clouds that no rain falls   T   F
at all.

37. As of the present time, about one-half the water sheds east   T   F
of the Mississippi River are polluted.

38. The problem of water pollution is far worse than the prob-   T   F
lem of air pollution.

39. The patrons of our national parks have taken great pride in   T   F
their preservation, and have maintained the highest standards
of cleanliness and orderliness.

40. The record shows that the car driving public will cooperate   T   F
in the use of blow by devices on cars, to reduce the exhaust
emissions.

MULTIPLE CHOICE

41. The chief polluter of the Illinois River:
    ( ) Is made up of the people of Chicago
    ( ) Is the Metropolitan Sanitary District of Greater Chicago
    ( ) Is the Chicago stockyards
    ( ) Is the discharge of effluents from Chicago industries.

42. Legislative control over pollution should be at:
    ( ) The state level
    ( ) The local level
    ( ) The regional level
    ( ) The Federal level

43. President Nixon has proposed a $10 billion program for:
    ( ) The elimination of carbon monoxide from cars
    ( ) The elimination of current practices by industries of dumping
         effluents into rivers and lakes
    ( ) Modern municipal waste treatment plants
    ( ) Educating America in the problems of pollution

44. Incinceration plants:
    ( ) Are the cure for air pollution
    ( ) May put poisonous methane gas in the air
    ( ) Reduce smoke in the air
    ( ) Provide for industrial land fill

45. Worn out septic tanks from cottages alongside a lake:
    ( ) Constitute scenic blight
    ( ) Are subject to condemnation proceedings
    ( ) Can be readily rehabilitated
    ( ) Promote the growth of algae

46. The discharge of large amounts of water from atomic plants:
    ( ) Can solve the problem of water shortages
    ( ) Can be used for irrigation
    ( ) Can be used for industry
    ( ) Can kill off aquatic life

47. The chief volunteer in incinerator pollution in New York City is:
    ( ) Industry
    ( ) New York City itself
    ( ) Commerce
    ( ) Schools

48. The Ohio River:
    ( ) Is still safe to bathe in
    ( ) Is still safe to fish in
    ( ) Has become a cesspool
    ( ) Has become an example of what can be done by anti-pollution measures

49. Where the smog level is acute:
    ( ) It can be reduced by blow by devices
    ( ) It can be brought down by solar heat
    ( ) It is no longer profitable to grow vegetables
    ( ) It can be blown away by appropriate technology

50. The cost to us of air pollution has been estimated at 13 billion dollars per year by:
    ( ) The Department of Housing and Urban Development
    ( ) The Department of Health, Education, and Welfare
    ( ) The Department of the Interior
    ( ) The Department of Agriculture

ESSAY QUESTIONS

1. Who is responsible for pollution?

2. What can be done to cut down on pollution?

3. What are the results of air pollution?

INDEX

ADVERTISING, 231
  Classified & Display, 233
  Direct Mail, 236
  Novelties, 237
  The Plan, 231
  Preparing Newspaper Ads, 232
  Signs, 235
  What to Feature, 232
  Why, 231
AGENCY, 91
APARTMENT HOUSES, 351
  The Boom, 351
  Expenses, 355
  Financing, 353
  Movements, 353
  Popularity, 351
  Problems, 356
  Tenants, 355
  Types, 354
APPRAISING, 131
  Application of Value Approaches, 140
  Background Data, 132
  Contents of Appraisal, 132
  Cost Approach, 134
  Economics, 133
  Evaluating Lease Interests, 140
  Formulae & Techniques, 136
  Income Approach to Value, 135
  Market Data Approach to Value, 138
  Nature, 131
  Problem, 131
  Special Techniques, 139
  Value Approaches, 133
CLOSINGS, 102, 111
  Costs, 116
  The Date, 112
  Documents, 114
  Examinations, 116
  Statements, 118
CODE OF ETHICS, 25, 33
COMPUTERIZED REAL ESTATE, 191
  Effect of Computer, 197

How Computer Does It, 191
How You Join Up, 193
Use in Investment Property Analysis, 195
Use in Residential Selling, 194
What Computer Does, 191
CONDOMINIUMS, 309
  Provisions, 312
  Resort Condominiums, 312
  Versus Conventional Ownership, 311
  Vs. Cooperatives, 312
  Vs. Renting, 310
COOPERATIVES, 307
  Advantages, 308
  "Rental" Charges, 308
DEED, 52
EASEMENTS, 50
EVALUATING INVESTMENT PROPERTIES, 139
EVALUATING LEASE INTERESTS, 140
FARM REAL ESTATE, 337
  As Investments, 342
  Closings, 339
  Financing, 340
  From Farm to Subdivision, 341
  Descriptions, 340
  Knowledge, 339
  Listings, 337
  Prospects, 338
  Showings, 338
  Soils, 341
  Tax Factors, 341
FEDERAL HOUSING ADMINISTRATION, 397
FEDERAL NATIONAL MORTGAGE ASSOCIATION, 178
FINANCING, 167
  Farm, 174, 340
  GNMA, 177
  Governmental Agencies, 175
  Housing Opportunity Allowance Program, 179
  Land Contracts, 55, 172, 254

New VA Entitlements (FNMA), 178
90-100% Financing, 180
Sale & Leasebacks, 173
Term Mortgage, 167
Vacation, or 2nd Home, 179
Variable-Rate Mortgages, 179
GOVERNMENT NATIONAL MORTGAGE ASSOCIATION, 177
INDUSTRIALIZED HOUSING, 277
Appearance, 282
Assembly, 280
Building Codes, 280
Construction Workers, 279
Erection, 282
Financing, 283
Marketing, 283
Materials, 279
Mobile Homes, 284
Modules, 277
Tests for Quality, 282
Transportation Problems, 281
INDUSTRIALIZED PROPERTIES, 379
Characteristics, 379
Industrial Parks, 383
Investment Characteristics, 382
Location Boosters, 381
Locations Factors, 379
Trends, 381
INVESTING IN REAL ESTATE, 247
Computerized Analysis, 255
Corporate, 254
For Growth, 248
For Small Investor, 249
Hedge Against Inflation, 248
Housing, 250
  APARTMENT HOUSE, 250
  OFFICE BUILDING, 251
Land Contracts, 55, 172, 254
Leverage & Tax Shelter, 249
Mortgages & Equity Participation, 253
Raw Land & Industrial, 253
Resort, 252
Shopping Centers, 252

INVESTMENT TRUSTS, 263
How Organized, 263
Nature of, 264
Their Yields, 265
What Money Market Thinks of, 266
JOINT VENTURES, 267
LAND CONTRACTS, 55, 172, 254
As Investments, 254
LAND USE, 1
Controls, 6
LEASES, 56
LICENSE LAWS, 21
Administration, 23
Care & Custody, 22
Exemptions, 23
Legal Authority, 21
Requirements for Licensure, 22
Suggested Pattern, 25
Suspension, Denial & Revocation, 23
LIENS, 56
LIMITED PARTNERSHIPS, 267
LISTINGS, 96
The Process, 98
Securing, 96
MARKET BEHAVIOR, 10
Determinants of, 10
Markets, 9
MOBILE HOMES, 284, 293
Advantages, 296
Benefits, 294
Disadvantages, 297
Financing, 296
Mobile Home Parks, 297
How Came About, 293
What Are They?, 293
Who Lives in Them?, 293
MODEL CITIES, 429
Problems, 430
MODULAR HOUSING, 277
MORTGAGES, 167
The Market, 175
Sources of, 170
Term, 167
Variable-Rate, 179
MULTIPLE LISTING SERVICE, 192, 194
NEW TOWNS, 425
& Greenbelts, 429

In the Private Sector, 427
OFFICE MANAGEMENT, 215
  Budgets, 220
  Controls, 223
  Interior & Furnishings, 216
  Location, 216
  Managing Salespeople, 215
  The Office Personality, 223
  Procedure, 219
  Terminating, 216
OPERATION BREAKTHROUGH, 278
  HUD, 278
PLANNING, 71
PLANNING COMMISSION, 72
POLLUTION — AIR, NOISE & WATER, 439
  How Bad is The Problem?, 439
  What Can Be Done?, 442
  What If We Do Nothing?, 444
  Who Is Responsible?, 441
PROPERTY MANAGEMENT, 151
  Attributes Required, 151
  Compensation For, 157
  Developing the Program, 153
  Development, 151
  Operation of Office, 156
  Operation of Program, 155
  Securing Management Business, 157
PROPERTY RIGHTS & INSTRU-
    MENTS, 43
PROSPECTS, 100
  Closings, 102
  Qualifying, 100
PUBLICITY, 238
  News Releases, 239
REAL ESTATE, 1
  Business of, 1
  Investing In, 247
  Significance of, 7
    As economic indicator, 8
    As mirror of sociological change, 7
REAL PROPERTY, 43
  Bundle of Rights Concept, 44
  Contract for Sale of, 51
  Contractual Rights, 44
  Deed, 52
  Easements, 50

Estates in, 45
Fixtures, 43
Land Contract, 55, 172, 254
Leases, 56
Liens, 56
Mortgage, 53, 167
  KINDS OF, 54
Nature of, 43
Ownership, 46
Rights & The Government, 48
Title Evidence, 58
Title To, 44
Transferring Rights, 49
The Will, 60
REALTOR, 25
  Code of Ethics, 25, 33
  Obligation to Client, 29
  Obligation to Fellow-Realtors, 29
  Obligation to Public, 25
RESORT REAL ESTATE, 321
  Boating & Fishing, 323
  Gambling & Resort, 323
  Motor Inns, 324
  Promotions, 322
  Skiing, 323
  Snowmobiling, 323
RESORT RETIREMENT COM-
    MUNITIES, 326
  Developers of, 327
SALE & LEASEBACKS, 173
SALES, 207
  Compensating, 214
  Interviewing for, 209
  Selecting Salespeople, 207
  Training in, 209
SECTION 235 PROGRAM, 175
SECTION 236 PROGRAM, 176
SHOPPING CENTERS, 365
  Appeal, 365
  Economics, 366
  Evening & Sunday Openings, 369
  Financing, 367
  Problems, 370
  Shopping Centers Abroad, 369
  Swan Song of Downtown Retail?, 366
  Types, 367
SIGNAGE, 235
STANDARDS, PROFESSIONAL, 21

SYNDICATIONS, 268
TITLE, 58
  Evidence of, 58
TRANSPORTATION & REAL
  ESTATE VALUES, 409
  Commuters Deserting Rails?, 415
  Commuter Rails a Lost Cause?,
    415
  Highway Construction Costs, 413
  How Financed, 414
  How Improved Transportation
    Enhances Values, 411
  How Relates, 410
  If Commuter Trains Stopped
    Running?, 417
  More Highways the Answer?, 412
  The Problem, 409
  Rail Commuter Lines?, 414
  Rail Commuter Service Be Main-
    tained?, 413
  Up in the Air, 418
URBAN RENEWAL, 393
  Accomplishments, 395
  Development Programs, 397
  FHA, 397
  Federal Financial Assistance, 399
  Government, 394
  Realtor, 395
  Rehabilitation, 396
  Special Housing Assistance, 400
  Where Has Urban Renewal
    Failed?, 398
ZONING, 74
  Board, 81
  Districts, 77
  Language of, 76
  Techniques, 78